CONRAD UNDER FAMILIAL EYES

CONRAD
under familial eyes

texts selected and edited by
ZDZISŁAW NAJDER
translated by
HALINA CARROLL-NAJDER

CAMBRIDGE UNIVERSITY PRESS

Cambridge
London   New York   New Rochelle
Melbourne   Sydney

Published by the Press Syndicate of the University of Cambridge
The Pitt Building, Trumpington Street, Cambridge CB2 1RP
32 East 57th Street, New York, NY 10022, USA
296 Beaconsfield Parade, Middle Park, Melbourne 3206, Australia

First published 1983

Printed in Great Britain at
the University Press, Cambridge

Library of Congress catalogue card number: 83-5187

British Library Cataloguing in Publication Data
Conrad under familial eyes
1. Conrad, Joseph – Biography
2. Novelists, English – 20th century – Biography
I. Najder, Zdzisław
823.'912   PR6005.04Z/
ISBN 0 521 25082 X

CONTENTS

ACKNOWLEDGEMENTS

The general shape of this book was worked out during my stay at the Villa Serbelloni in Bellagio; I am grateful to the Rockefeller Foundation for enabling my wife and me to spend several weeks in exceptionally congenial surroundings, enjoying lavish hospitality and stimulating company.

Both my wife and I thank most cordially Mrs Catherine Mannings for her advice and help with the translations.

This volume is dedicated to the memory of Dr Ugo Mursia, a distinguished Conradian and good friend, whose encouragement and patient interest made the realization of this project possible.

INTRODUCTION

In the last twenty years interest in Joseph Conrad's cultural roots has grown considerably, and with it the awareness of the importance of the Polish aspects of his biography. The present volume supplies English-speaking students and admirers of Conrad with a collection of texts which not only supplements the contents of *Conrad's Polish Background*, published in 1964 and of *Joseph Conrad: A Chronicle* (1983), but also considerably broadens and amplifies the picture of the great English writer's Polish connections. Very few of these texts so far have been available in English; several have never been published even in their original Polish.

To lend the collection an internal continuity of presentation, the texts are printed not in the order of their dating but rather according to the sequence of events and subjects they refer to. It has not been possible to do so always with strict consistency or to achieve a completeness of design. To attain that it would have been necessary to reprint many texts published in *Conrad's Polish Background*. And although the present book and this preface can be read separately and treated as self-contained pieces of scholarship, the reader, if he wants to get a fuller picture of Conrad's Polish links, is advised to become acquainted with both *Conrad's Polish Background* and *Conrad Under Familial Eyes*.

The texts included here fall, roughly speaking, into eight categories: (1) documents related to Conrad's parents; (2) documents related to his uncle and guardian, Tadeusz Bobrowski; (3) early documents of Józef Teodor Konrad Korzeniowski (Joseph Conrad); (4) letters to Konrad Korzeniowski; (5) Conrad's letters to Polish addressees, not included in *Conrad's Polish Background*; (6) reminiscences of Conrad, written by his Polish relatives and friends; (7) the interview Conrad gave to a Polish journalist in 1914; (8) two samples of the reaction to his work in his native country.

All these, I believe, are of much importance to everybody interested in Conrad's life and the cultural background of his work, but the first category is likely to have the greatest impact on what is being written about Conrad's family relationships and their psychological importance. It is not the object of this introduction to analyse various (and often wondrous) theories concerning Conrad's early experiences and

his attitude towards his parents and their memory. The present collection is intended as a documentary basis for future speculations on these
subjects. But one cannot refrain from expressing surprise and regret that
so many critics have ventured in this field unhampered by even a
rudimentary knowledge of facts. None of the psychoanalytic interpreters
of Conrad's attitude towards his father has acquainted himself with
Apollo Korzeniowski's writings and letters; all assertions and hypo-
theses have been based on a few, by no means unambiguous, statements
of Conrad and on a few out-of-context opinions of Tadeusz Bobrowski's
about his brother-in-law. To formulate a biographical theory plausible
within the framework of psychoanalysis, one ought to study the pertinent
facts no less carefully than one has studied Freud. Even if what Conrad
wrote about his parents were liable to only one interpretation, still we
could not know what his relations with them might have been if we did
not know what kind of people they were. It is not a matter of indifference
whether Conrad's father was really a brooding, humourless fanatic, and
his mother a 'cold' and 'austere' person (as some biographers imagine),
or not. Making their letters available should at least put a stop to such
irresponsibly fantastic statements.

Let it be clear, however, that this volume does not contain all
documents, nor all the evidence which ought to be taken into consideration by Conrad's (and his parents') biographer. It is not intended to
supplant research into Conrad's family background; that would have
been an impossible undertaking. It is a collection of the most basic and
typical texts, meant to serve as an assemblage beacon, illuminating and
warning at the same time. For instance, Tadeusz Bobrowski's claim that
Conrad's father Apollo Korzeniowski was a man of unclear principles
and general mediocrity is easy to quote and remember. To verify this
assessment, and ultimately to refute the charges, is a thing which cannot
be done by quoting a counter-claim, by using another simple judgement.
One has to ascertain Bobrowski's attitude and evaluate his veracity; to
compare his sentiments with those of other contemporaries; and, above
all, to study all relevant facts. Therefore, the opinions expressed in this
preface are based not only on the evidence contained in the present
volume. And lest I be suspected of the chauvinistic belief that only a Pole
can understand another Pole, I shall point to a most interesting essay by
Czesław Miłosz, 'Apollo N. Korzeniowski: Joseph Conrad's Father'
(translated by Reuel K. Wilson, *Mosaic*, vi, 4, 1971/2), which, due
simply to the fact that its author had no access to unpublished material
(and, writing abroad, only limited access to the published), is marred
not only by some factual errors, but by an evident slant in its presentation of Apollo Korzeniowski's personality.

Conrad's parents both came from Polish *szlachta*[1] families, who for many generations had owned estates in the central Ukraine. This part of the country had belonged to the Polish kingdom since the fourteenth century; it was annexed by Russia in the second partition of Poland (1793). The educated classes were almost entirely Polish, the administration predominantly Russian; most peasants spoke Ukrainian, but the latter began to exhibit marked feelings of a separate national identity only in the second half of the nineteenth century. Poles considered the country occupied by a foreign and tyrannical power. Although private Polish schools, theatres and publications were tolerated (while strictly censored) and often flourished, only people who professed themselves Russian and belonged to the Orthodox church had any chance of a public career. All mention of autonomous Polish social and political organizations was forbidden and contacts with ethnic Polish territories, even those also occupied by Russians, were carefully watched. By comparison, Poles in the two other 'zones' of partition, Austrian and Prussian, enjoyed considerably more freedom. Also, under the tzars Poles felt oppressed by a state completely alien to the Western civilization of which Poland had been a part since the tenth century, barbaric and hostile to all social and political reforms.

The lives of Conrad's parents and of his entire family were inexorably linked with the political events of the time, events determined on the one hand by the Russian official policy of suppressing Polish national sentiment, and on the other by the enduring power of Polish aspirations to independence.

Conrad's mother, Ewa, née Bobrowska (1831–65), was by all accounts everybody's favourite in the family. Daughter of a fairly well-off landowner, she was renowned for her beauty and also for her intelligence. Educated at home, she wanted to become a teacher – an unheard-of thing at that time for a girl with substantial dowry – which in itself shows her as an exceptional person. Calmly emotional, intensely loyal, deeply patriotic and religious, she commanded both respect and affection. For several years unable to obtain her father's permission to marry Apollo Korzeniowski, she resolutely stuck to her choice. Later she became a faithful companion of Apollo's conspiratorial enterprises; suggestions that she was only a passive accomplice

---

[1] The term has no precise equivalent in English. It encompasses both the nobility and the gentry; there were no legal distinctions within the *szlachta*, which in pre-partition Poland formed about 8–10% of the population and was the only politically and culturally active class. Any member of it could be elected to the Sejm (parliament) or, in theory at least, elected king.

are completely unfounded: on the contrary, all evidence shows her as a spontaneous and enthusiastic ally. There is every reason to consider her marriage a very happy one; all misfortunes came from outside.

The personality of Apollo Korzeniowski (1820–69) was not so well balanced. He was both proud – and painfully conscious of his inadequacies; ready for sacrifice – but with a touch of self-centredness; a born enthusiast – but sometimes opinionated. He had his fair share of enemies; most of them, however, seem to have been politically motivated, because nobody ever questioned his integrity, good intentions, and kindness of heart. Quite well educated, sociable, witty and emotional, he had two passions in life: literature and politics. As a poet he was mediocre, and he knew that; a late follower of the Romantic school, original neither in his imagery nor in his thought, he would express lofty visions and ideas in verse often banal and strained. I suspect that under the whole layer of pretentious verbiage he was hiding a concrete and empirical mind, obsessed and befuddled by conventions on which he had been nourished and which he was unable to shake off. He did better as a satirical comedy writer, and also as a translator from French (Vigny, Hugo) and English (Shakespeare, Dickens). His two plays, *Komedia* ('A Comedy', 1855 – based partly on Aleksandr Griboedov's *Gore ot uma*, though he refused to admit this and *Dla miłego grosza* ('For the Love of Money', 1859), are often staged even today and testify to the mordancy of his wit and expressiveness of his language.

Many of his poems remain unpublished and most of them deservedly so; however, several fragments are worthy of attention. There is among them an unfinished drama *Ojciec* ('The Father'), centred around the choice between fidelity and death versus betrayal and life, and presenting all the basic aspects of this choice: honour and happiness, shame and fear, reputation and care for others.

Although he was apt to put his poetic efforts to religious and political uses, he was by no means contemptuous of art which did not serve any practical purpose: witness his keen enjoyment and high praise of Shakespeare's comedies. Korzeniowski's criticism of Art for Art's sake was not (like Tolstoy's) general, but only occasional: he believed that there are circumstances in which 'the questions of art must give way to those of life', mainly social and national life. Ruefully, he realized that such an attitude resulted in 'sins against the indifferent heavens of Aesthetics'.

In politics he was an outspoken democrat and a fiery patriot,[1] a

---

[1] The term 'nationalist', though commonly used, is misleading, as it suggests exclusive preoccupation with Polish national interests. Apollo Korzeniowski, like most Polish political leaders of his time, wanted to liberate all nationalities of the old Polish Commonwealth: Poles, Ukrainians, Lithuanians, etc., and did not consider that this precluded their future autonomy.

believer in social and national justice; often naive in his optimistic assessments of the possibilities for radical social change coupled with a restoration of pre-partition Poland; obviously simpleminded in his socioeconomic agrarianism. His political ideas, if not too well organized logically, were emotionally consistent and adhered to unswervingly. Korzeniowski was for the liberation of peasants and against capitalism, industrialism and the rule of money. While not a revolutionary in the sense of advocating violence, he was one in the sense of believing in equality and brotherhood of all men. But again, this was supposed to have been not a brotherhood of some proletarians without history, but one grounded in the traditional ideals of fidelity, honour, patriotism and piety; and equality not of privilege but of human dignity, conceived in the Christian sense.

If his political moralism sometimes seems pathetic to our jaded sensibilities, his organizational talents and energy have to be fully acknowledged. The stereotype of Apollo Korzeniowski as an impractical and indolent day-dreamer, which we owe to his brother-in-law, does not stand up to scrutiny. He did not, it is true, prosper as administrator of the estates he leased; but he was immensely bored by that job. There may also be some truth in Tadeusz Bobrowski's accusations that he badly mismanaged his personal finances – but only some: Korzeniowski saved enough money to join a publishing enterprise, and later to launch his planned periodical *Dwutygodnik*. He was certainly not a squanderer, nor was he devoid of practical capabilities in the sphere that interested him more than money-making: stirring up and organizing underground patriotic activities. Here he displayed both zest and skill.

Impatient and moody as he was, he showed perseverance in what he considered most important. In his secret and semi-secret political activities he seems to have been fairly prudent and took care to cover his tracks. That much we may gather from the fact that his most serious 'transgressions' remained unknown to the authorities. If he was 'foolhardy', as it is claimed, then he was no more so than anybody who rebels against an oppressive might.

Arrested in October 1861 in Warsaw and sentenced, together with his wife, to an unspecified period of exile in Russia under constant (and secret) police surveillance, Korzeniowski would impress not only other Polish and Ukrainian political exiles but also Russians with his uncompromising moral posture and aura of authority.

When today one reads his 'Song for the Day of Christening' written for 'my son born in the 85th year of Muscovite oppression' (one of several patriotic poems), one may perhaps wonder if the exalted phraseology is not a sign of affectation, or of some pathological strain in their author's mind. Such suspicions serve to underpin some interpretations of Apollo's personality, but to me they seem entirely unjustified, resulting from lack of intuition and of a proper historical perspective. Apart from the banal truth that to sacrifice one's health and life for one's country is no more pathological than to drive oneself to breaking point by toiling to earn more money for the newest generation of gadgets, Apollo Korzeniowski's attitude was not at all exceptional; that is to say, the pattern of his behaviour was similar to that of tens if not hundreds of thousands of his contemporaries. Such names as Garibaldi or Petöfi epitomize the fact that in nineteenth-century Europe many people considered service to the national cause the lynchpin of the meaning of their lives. This surely did not make them 'death-oriented': they wanted to live, and very much so, but not on their knees. Poland, the biggest and most severely oppressed of the countries deprived of national independence, perhaps had a particularly large proportion of them, especially among the *szlachta* and the newly developing intelligentsia.[1] The fate of thousands of them was even more tragic than the fate of the Korzeniowskis.

Likewise, the fact that Apollo Korzeniowski broke down and despaired after the death of his beloved wife cannot be considered abnormal. And although he passed through periods of despondency, he managed to work quite hard: in spite of his own progressing illness (tuberculosis and heart disease) within the last four years of his life, he translated several books and wrote a number of essays. When reading his own descriptions of his morbid moods, half-mystical broodings, and days of total passivity, we also have to remember that they were written in a late Romantic convention which emphasized the unusual, emotional and sombre. If we ask whether he became philosophically despondent, whether he professed despondency, then the answer must be in the negative. In March 1867, two years after the death of his beloved wife, Korzeniowski wrote in his essay on Shakespeare: 'By the innate power of his spirit and his will, man often, if only momentarily, masters the events, and then he notices how they become even more sluggish and stubborn by the way he has compelled them to proceed. And in this struggle, finally, when his life is smashed to pieces, man perishes – but with that quality, with which God has endowed him for all time in the act of creation, still *intact*.' He saw the duty of a dramatist as giving 'the audience the feeling of man's moral greatness ... which rises above man's struggle against fate'. These are words of heroic defiance, not of despondency.

---

[1] This term first came to be used in its modern sense in Poland in the 1820s; later it was adopted into Russian.

Tadeusz Bobrowski (1829–94), his brother-in-law, was a man of a completely different stripe. He prided himself on being a level-headed rationalist and openly disapproved of all anti-government activities. He was conscious of an urgent need for socioeconomic reforms and in the 1850s spent much time and energy taking part in debates on the best ways of implementing the long-overdue liberation of the serfs – not because he was particularly compassionate, but because such a position accorded with his principles, which stemmed from the traditions of the Enlightenment. Later, in his memoirs, he recorded these discussions, held in numerous committees convened by thousands of Polish landowners in the Ukraine; but although the fact that the immense effort of these committees was totally ignored by the tzarist authorities disenchanted him, it did not change his general attitude of political appeaser. Endowed with a sharp, critical mind and a caustic wit, self-righteous and not without a touch of malice, he would sometimes adjust facts so as to make them fit his theories and assessments better. In his private life he was not a happy man: he lost his wife very early and his only daughter died at the age of twelve after a protracted illness. Following the death of his father he must have felt isolated within his own family, since all its other members represented opposite political and emotional attitudes. This would at least partly account for his reputation of coldness in his personal relations. He was greatly prized as an adviser in financial, administrative and legal matters. Undoubtedly, his warmest and most attractive side was revealed in his relationship with the son of his beloved sister. On him he bestowed his money and advice, trying to steady him both physically and morally; to him he preached his gospel of perseverance and duty – which Joseph Conrad adopted, while converting Bobrowski's idea of duty as accepted in passive resignation into his own concept of duty as consciously and actively chosen.

Józef Teodor Konrad Korzeniowski, son of Apollo and Ewa, was born on 3 December 1857 in Berdyczów. Eleven and half years later, when his father died in Cracow on 9 May 1869, he became an orphan. A son of political martyrs, he could be sure of some assistance financial and otherwise, even if members of his own family were not able to support him. He was, however, a Russian subject, and to return to Russia, where his parents had been political criminals, would mean risking a long military service. This was the reason for early, and unsuccessful, attempts to secure Austrian citizenship for him. The fact that for sixty-one of Joseph Conrad's almost sixty-seven years of life there was no Polish state and that all Poles were subjects of foreign powers has to be remembered when one attempts to answer the outwardly simple question: why did Konrad Korzeniowski leave Poland? Hundreds of thousands did the same for many reasons, of various kinds but usually connected with the political situation of their country.

Not many letters to Joseph Conrad have been preserved; of the early ones the most valuable are undoubtedly those of Tadeusz Bobrowski, published in *Conrad's Polish Background*, a veritable mine of information about his nephew's formative years of wandering. The sole surviving letter from Adam Pulman, short and inconspicuous, contains in fact valuable biographical data. Young Korzeniowski's difficulties with his school studies, his poor health, and his depressive tendencies are here unequivocally confirmed; we also learn that he was supposed to have left Poland a year later than he actually did. Reminiscences of a few ladies who knew him at that time do not have such a solid documentary value, but, with the help of a brief remembrance by his youthful friend Konstanty Buszczyński, let us form a general idea of what Conrad the teenager was like.

Konrad Korzeniowski left Poland in September 1874, going to Marseilles. After nearly four years in France and on French ships he decided to try his luck in the British merchant marine and for the next fifteen years served under the Red Ensign, with intermittent long periods ashore in London (and an abortive attempt to work in the Upper – later Belgian – Congo). His main contact with Poland was his uncle Tadeusz Bobrowski, who supported him generously till he reached the age of thirty. (Conrad's letters to Bobrowski perished during the Revolution of 1917.) Conrad exchanged letters with several other members of his family and also with some friends, but only a few scattered relics of that correspondence have been preserved, and even fewer reminiscences.

All in all, available documents concerning Conrad's relations with his compatriots during the first twenty-five years after he left Poland present a very inadequate record of his Polish contacts: the most important and most intriguing items have been lost. They fare much better as a record of misunderstandings. Three factors made it gradually more difficult for his compatriots to understand Conrad: first, his wanderings which provided him with experiences hard even to imagine for landlubbers and finally made him a citizen of the most powerful and prosperous country in the world; second, his loss – under the influence of his uncle Bobrowski – of faith in the possibility of a restoration of Poland; third, his passionate rejection of an instrumental approach to art in general and novelistic fiction in particular.

A long article by Jan Perłowski, one of Tadeusz Bobrowski's many wards, recounting Conrad's visit to his homeland in 1890 (pp. 150–70), shows the two first factors at work. Perłowski was not a sympathetic witness – he evidently did not care much for Conrad and his comments on 'Amy Foster' sound strangely peevish and obtuse – but his account of the lack of rapport between the local *szlachta* and Bobrowski's sea-going nephew has a ring of truth. Forgetting that Conrad had spent half of his conscious life in foreign lands and was now coming to their backwaters from the teeming capitals of world trade and finance, they wished him to think like they did; he could not identify with them, and while trying to remain faithful to the memory of his parents and his country, he was exasperated by and resentful at attempts to dictate to him how that fidelity was to be attested. Any guilt he may have felt only exacerbated his anger and deepened his alienation.

Another confrontation took place a few years later in Cardiff, where well-intentioned Polish *émigrés*, the Kliszczewskis, exhorted Conrad to write about the 'unhappiness of his native land'. We do not have to follow Witold Chwalewik in taking Conrad's cynical retort (see below, p. 175) at face value. He did not care all that much about his public, as many of his letters and several of his books testify; but he would have been ashamed to appeal to their pity and would not condescend to use his work as a medium of any kind of propaganda.

The third and most momentous misunderstanding happened, in a different way and without Conrad's direct involvement, in 1899, while he was working on *Lord Jim*. Wincenty Lutosławski, a Polish philosopher and eccentric, who had visited Conrad some time earlier, published an article on 'The Emigration of Talent' which contained grossly misleading information about Conrad's literary career and opinions. Eliza Orzeszkowa, the *grande dame* of the Polish novel, who had unsparingly devoted her energy and considerable gifts to the service of a spiritually independent Polish culture, attacked Conrad–Korzeniowski fiercely for failing in his national duties. It is debatable whether she would have understood Conrad's artistic and philosophical attitude; it is, however, quite certain that she would not have lashed out at him had she known the facts as they were. And, whatever we may think of the merits of her general standpoint, we have to say that she was later unjustly vilified by some defendants of Conrad, who did not remember that she had been acting on false information.

Conrad certainly read Orzeszkowa's article and it made his attitude towards his motherland even more complex. Although he never repudiated his Polish national inheritance and professed fidelity to it (for instance, in his letters to Edward Garnett, Cunninghame Graham, Józef Korzeniowski and Kazimierz Waliszewski), he probably felt apprehensive lest other demands were made that he openly express his support for the Polish cause and officially declare his spiritual alle-

giance to Poland, while he considered that cause hopeless and wanted
to be an English writer.

It seems that his relations with Poland and Poles were at their loosest
during the decade 1904–14. Then, in 1914, a meeting with the young
Retinger couple turned the tide: for the first time in several years he
spoke Polish again, gave a revealing interview to a Polish journalist,
and decided to spend his first non-working holiday in twenty years in
Poland.

He never dreamt that the most important historical event of his
lifetime, the outbreak of the First World War, would find him in
Cracow. Although he had predicted that conflict in 1905 (in his 'Auto-
cracy and War'), he had looked at it without visualizing what it would
mean for his compatriots. In that summer of 1914, when talking politics
– and nobody talked anything else then – with his Polish friends and
acquaintances, he must have felt at the same time excited by their
hopes and grand designs and alarmed by their illusions. He knew only
too well (he had experienced it painfully, no doubt; it had been a major
source for his political pessimism and his reluctance to write about
Polish issues) that a rebirth of Poland did not interest any major power,
that it was a dream no responsible Western politician would take
seriously. This dichotomy of his reactions caused new misunderstandings; in the end, however, Conrad evidently let himself be carried away
by the buoyancy of his compatriots' spirits and even planned to do
some propaganda for the Polish cause when back in England.

It did not take him long to discover that he could do practically
nothing. During the war he tried to assist his friend Retinger in his –
not too successful – attempts to shore up the support of the British and
French governments for Polish national aspirations. His experiences in
dealing with British officials and watching H. M. Government's wary
and half-hearted acknowledgements of Polish efforts to re-establish an
independent state evoked much bitterness in him. Conrad had a complex attitude towards the restored Polish Republic: pride mixed with
incredulity, and probably a feeling of shame about his own former
excessive scepticism. And although after 1918 his contacts with Poland
became much closer, although his correspondence with Poles increased
remarkably and he even translated a play from his native tongue into
English, there remained on Conrad's side a distinct element of reserve
caused, I believe, by those mixed feelings of shyness based on shame
and cautiousness grounded in the memory of painful misunderstandings and disagreements. This reserve must have been strengthened by
the attitude taken by well-meaning but not too sensitive Poles like
Dyboski, who would almost ostentatiously address Conrad in English

– apparently to make it easier for him to converse, but at the same time underscoring his foreignness.

Knotty as his attitude towards Poland was, there can be no doubt that he greatly enjoyed the fact of his popularity there and was sincerely interested in the quality of the translations of his works into Polish. He did not live long enough to see that in his motherland he became not only one of the most popular authors of fiction translated from a foreign language but also a very influential writer, one of the most powerful and deeply felt voices in modern Polish literature.

He reached the epitome of his spiritual influence in the darkest hours of Polish twentieth-century history, in the years 1939–44, after Poland had been again invaded by her neighbours, while millions of her citizens were ruthlessly exterminated. He then became one of the chief moral authorities for the young members of the Polish resistance.

The two articles that close this collection offer but a sample of what Conrad has meant for Polish literature within the last fifty years. Gombrowicz – one of the most brilliant Polish prose writers of this century – illustrates Conrad's constant presence as a living writer; and Jan Józef Szczepański testifies to his moral and ideological stature, which has not diminished substantially within the last twenty-five years.

The source of the text is given above every item. Unless identified as English in the original, all texts have been translated from Polish. All references to Conrad's works are to the Dent Collected Edition, and to the volume *Congo Diary and Other Uncollected Pieces* (Doubleday, New York 1977). Where the original author supplies a footnote, this is indicated by an asterisk, and appears above the numbered footnotes supplied by the editor.

The Bobrowski family

Tadeusz Bobrowski, *Pamiętnik mojego życia*, ed. Stefan Kieniewicz, Państwowy Instytut Wydawniczy (Warsaw, 1979), vol. 1, 48. (Subsequently referred to as Bobrowski, 'Memoirs'.)

My grandfather Stanisław Bobrowski, an ensign in the national cavalry, had two sons by Katarzyna Błażowska: Józef (1790), my father; and Mikołaj (1792), a captain in the 2nd regiment of horse-fusiliers, knight of the Legion of Honour and of the Military Cross,[1] a bachelor; and two daughters: Johanna (1794), married to Hiacynt Czosnowski, son of the *starosta*[2] of Secygniów, and Salomea (1796, born after her father's death), married to Adam Jabłoński, a deputy in the Volhynia[3] *szlachta* commission. After the partition of the country my grandfather settled down in Volhynia having previously married Katarzyna Błażowska from Galician Podolia.[4]

Trouble with a stepfather

Bobrowski, 'Memoirs', 1, 49–50

In 1796 he [Stanisław Bobrowski] died, still young, leaving behind a young and beautiful widow, and, for a *szlachcic* on the rise, quite a little fortune. It amounted to several hundred thousand zlotys, as it later transpired in the Probate Court. This seems probable, since he had the lease of the entire Miropol estate for 20,000 zlotys, which were paid him by the mills and distilleries alone.

After my grandfather's death, Dzieduszycki[5] had extended the contract, and out of sympathy for the children of his army friend, he ordered a new contract to be drawn out in the name of the widow and

---

[1] The highest Polish decoration for military valour, established in 1792 under the name *Virtuti Militari*, reinstituted in 1807 as Military Cross.

[2] A local official, nominated by the monarch, controlling the administration of royal estates within the given district.

[3] Lands on the Słucz and the upper Bug, with Krzemieniec, Łuck and Żytomierz as the most important towns.

[4] Lands in the south-eastern part of the Polish Commonwealth, in the estuaries of the Boh and the Dniestr. In the first partition of Poland (1772) the western part of Podolia was annexed by Austria and became part of Galicia.

[5] Walerian Dzieduszycki (1754–1832), owner of the Miropol estate.

her children, thereby enabling those children later to recover something of their paternal inheritance from the hands of their stepfather.
The stepfather, Leon Staniszewski, ensign in the national cavalry,
cousin of the Pułaskis,[1] an adherent of the Sapieha[2] family, *quasi*
jurist, and man of the world, indulged in elegant clothes and pleasures,
dissipating his wife's money, or rather her children's, since he himself,
apart from good presence, possessed nothing. Basically, he was not a
bad man, but irresponsible and obstinate – he never gave a thought to
the upbringing of his stepsons. He placed them in a Dominican boarding school in Lubar, run by Abbé Vilemain. After my father had
completed his schooling, he was sent off to the judiciary at Żytomierz,
and my uncle to Prince Józef Poniatowski's[3] *uhlan* regiment. All this
did not prevent Staniszewski from depositing his stepchildren's entire
inheritance with his various friends and in his own name. He held
Hrycki in Volhynia and Starosielec near Żytomierz on pledge; he
leased and pledged here and there and to cover up the traces of his
financial deals he made sure that he did not stay long anywhere.
Luckily there were no children from this marriage, and his design to
dispossess his stepchildren came to light only in 1816, when Czosnowski had proposed marriage to the elder stepdaughter, whom he
eventually married in 1817.

To the personal appeal made by my father and by various friends to
name the size of the dowry, Staniszewski declared formally that the
whole fortune was his own; and he drove his wife out of the house for
siding openly with her children. Thus a bitter lawsuit began. First a
roof had to be found for the family, then money and the evidence
required for the legal action. The first need was met thanks to kind
friends: Mrs Weronika Giżycka (née Sulatycka), the colonel's wife,
leased the hamlet Czeczelówka to my grandmother, the rent for it to be
paid at the end of the term; and Mrs Anna Pieńkowska (née Brzo-
zowska), wife of the sword-bearer[4], helped to set up the new house
when my grandmother had been driven out of her old one without any
means of subsistence. After the various events which followed and
which had begun with the previously mentioned second contract for the
lease of the Miropol estate; after meeting and questionings at Miropol
and other places where Staniszewski had lived; after various proceed-
ings in which the main brunt had been unselfishly borne chiefly by my

[1] Name of a noble family with estates in south-east Poland.
[2] Name of one of the most important aristocratic families in Poland, of Lithuanian
origin.
[3] Polish national leader and Marshal of France, died in the battle of Leipzig
(1763–1813).
[4] *Miecznik*, titular local official.

father's friends, Antoni Poradowski (later a relative of mine) and Ludwik Dobiecki – the first a prominent lawyer from Żytomierz, the second, deputy justice of the peace in Starokonstantynów – while other friends, Jan Giżycki, Kazimierz and Marceli Budzyński, more than one helped with money; after all that, and since Staniszewski had hidden and even burned some documents, including family papers, a compromise settlement was reached in 1820, making Staniszewski return to his stepsons 60,000 zlotys from the pledge on the hamlet Łyczów in the district of Starokonstantynów.

From that time neither he (Józef Bobrowski) nor their mother ever met Staniszewski, and my grandmother died of gall-stones in Karlsbad in 1828. In the division of assets one-third went to the sisters and one-third each to my father and my uncle. In time conscience moved Staniszewski, who after the agreement had been reached had no reason to fear about the rest of his money and established himself near Lubar, leading the life of a fairly rich gentleman. He sent for my father, whom he had always liked, asking him to be friends and promising to leave him his entire fortune, but my father refused and after Staniszewski's death everything passed to his relatives. The experience with his stepfather filled my father with such an abhorrence of second unions that when a certain good, beautiful and rich widow, with one son, offered him her heart – which was worth having – he refused to become a stepfather; his refusal did not impair their mutual friendship which lasted until the death of this worthy lady, who remained a widow, and whose personality and home I hold among the nicest recollections of my childhood.

Bobrowski's parents
Bobrowski, 'Memoirs', 1, 51

In 1825, when he was living for the first time at Markusze, my father married Teofila Pilchowska, my mother.

Bobrowski's birth
Bobrowski, 'Memoirs', 1, 52–3

And so I was born to Józef and Teofila née Pilchowska, as their second child, in the seventh month of my mother's pregnancy, on the 19th of March 1829, on the day of my father's patron saint, at Terechowa, in the house of my grandmother, Ewa Pilchowska née Poradowska. I was so feeble that an emergency baptism was ministered by a Uniate priest,[1] our family chaplain. At the time of my birth my father was reading the life of Washington, and as an expression of his admiration – as he later told me – he gave me the names of three defenders of freedom: Tadeusz – in memory of Kościuszko,[2] Wilhelm –in memory of Tell, and Jerzy (George) – in memory of Washington; the name Józef was added as the one I brought to the world. The years of infancy and childhood did not augur well for my life or health – it was even thought that I would be a deaf mute because for a long time nobody heard my voice. Then at the age of five I became ill with parotitis, from which I barely recovered; in my seventh and eighth years it was feared that I would develop into a hunchback. I was given tonics, woken up at night and made to hang by my arms to straighten my back. Yet things turned out contrary to human expectations! Among numerous and far stronger siblings I survived four brothers and two sisters and many other contemporaries, as well as my wife and daughter. In my family only one brother and one nephew are left. Thus, many of my hopes had to be prematurely buried, but having remained faithful to their memory, I submit with resignation to the first signs of approaching old age and its unavoidable loneliness!

Childhood recollections
Bobrowski, 'Memoirs', I, 54

My first childhood memories go back to 1833. I was just over four years old at the time and the first event which struck my childish memory and imagination was my uncle's (Mikołaj Bobrowski's) return from exile in Russia. During the 1831 insurrection[3] my uncle, responsible for remounting the 2nd regiment of horse-fusiliers of the Polish army, had been staying at Miłołówka (then Machnów district), the main rallying point of the Polish army remounts. There all the officers responsible for remounting had been arrested and deported first to Kozielec (Chernikhov province) and later to the depths of Russia; in my uncle's case it was first Vyatka and then Astrakhan. In 1833 he returned home, having been discharged with only half of the pension he was qualified for, because of his refusal to join the Russian army.

---

[1] A Greek Catholic priest, member of the part of the Greek Church which, since the Union of Brześć (1595), has acknowledged the Pope's supremacy while retaining its own liturgy. Most of the Uniates were Ruthenians.

[2] Tadeusz Kościuszko (1746–1817), Polish national hero and military leader, also took part in the American War of Independence.

[3] Polish insurrection against Russian rule, begun 29 November 1830.

'A lovely couple'

Bobrowski, 'Memoirs', I, 56

'Your parents made a lovely couple,' I was told by a contemporary, 'when they turned up after their wedding at Sofijówka and later at the jubilee celebrations at Kuna.' But my mother paid no heed to her beauty, forgetting it for the sake of other, more important duties.

Teofila Bobrowska

Bobrowski, 'Memoirs', I, 57

She mostly stayed at home, devoting her time to the upbringing of her children for whom no sacrifice, no annoyance, seemed too great to bear; she suffered the worst whims of tutors and governesses as long as her children profited. She was one of the politest of hostesses, without being officious – as contemporary hospitality demanded – towards every visitor without exception as long as he was a decent and honest man; she retained this affability and *savoir-faire* until her death.

She was bedridden for seven years because of palsy in one leg as the result of an affliction in the spinal column. She used to receive guests lying in bed, never complaining, always considerate to her visitors. She regained the use of her leg on the death of her younger daughter (Teofila), whose bed stood, throughout the long and severe illness, next to my mother's so as to enable her to do the nursing. But my mother did not instantly regain the use of her leg and the ability to walk; it took about three years before she was able to walk well; later, until the time of her death, she walked a lot, even uphill, and also up the stairs. When she reached fifty her health began to improve as if her strength was growing in proportion to the ordeals that were still in store for her! Apart from losing her husband and three young children, she survived the loss of two grown sons and one son-in-law. She was constantly present at the death-beds of her two daughters, her daughter-in-law (my wife) and her grand-daughter (my daughter), all of whom she nursed to the end. She was truly religious and ready to accept without a murmur the painful decrees of Providence, she had a warm heart and a brave soul – she unfailingly knew how to suffer and how to love! She knew how to extend the warmth of her affection, her advice and help, not only to those near her, but even to utter strangers who were attracted by her tolerance and in whom she inspired confidence. She was able to gain the love and respect of all those who knew her well, and this in spite of her strongly held personal views.

The Bobrowski children

Bobrowski, 'Memoirs', I, 58–9

There were then four of us children: my brother Stanisław, two years older than I, and my sisters: Ewa, almost four years younger, and Teofila, only a few months old.[1] There had been another brother, Michał, between myself and the sisters, but he died when my elder sister was born. I do not remember him at all, except that after his death his draped cot was carried out of my sick mother's room.

Uncle Mikołaj

Bobrowski, 'Memoirs', I, 60–1

As I have already mentioned, my first childhood impression concerns my uncle's (Mikołaj Bobrowski's) return from exile in Russia. After staying for a few years in my parents' house he sub-leased the hamlet Bajkówka from Kalikst Gołrzewski, a county marshal[2] living on the estate of Father Jan, Count Chołoniewski. Disgusted by a disagreement with the original lease-holder, which ended in a compromise, my uncle again returned to live with my parents as soon as the lease had run out. By temperament he was a melancholic and a recluse, and although outwardly phlegmatic he was easily roused; his education was average, like the kind acquired in the military service which he entered at the age of sixteen after joining the Polish Army in 1811. Throughout his life he silently and unreservedly worshipped Napoleon, but he did not like to talk about this; also, unlike other Napoleonic soldiers he never spoke about his own exploits, although he had been decorated with the Legion of Honour and the military cross. Temporarily an *officier d'or-donnance* to Marshal Marmont, he was the last to ride across a bridge in Leipzig before it was blown up, as he himself carried the specific order. He was wounded only once, in the heel like the G[reat] Napoleon himself, a fact he would occasionally mention in moments of good humour. He never wore his decorations, saying that to have them was enough. Yet I saw him twice wearing medals: in 1837 at the wedding of a friend, Konstanty Bernatowicz, and twenty years later at my own wedding. He laughed when Napoleon III was distributing Napoleonic

---

[1] The fragment refers to the author's earliest memories and so apparently to the year 1833. It tallies with another (see p. 25) which also indicates that Teofila Bobrowska was born in 1833. If so, however, Ewa could not have been 'four years younger' than Tadeusz, but only three. As she was nineteen in early 1851 ('Memoirs', II, 8) she must have been born in early 1832.

[2] The elected head of a county's *szlachta* self-government.

medals, calling this 'Lilliputian coxcombry', and never applied for the one due to him in accordance with the decree. Although a soldier, he was most indecisive and easily submitted to his brother's advice. He was a man of great integrity as well as great egoism – or perhaps only great timidity; he was not an endearing person, and did not sympathize with others; he loved hardly anyone, perhaps only his brother and elder sister.

The Pilchowskis
Bobrowski, 'Memoirs', I, 63

Our relatives, Captain and Mrs Pilchowski, were frequent visitors in my parents' house. Piotr de Biberstein Pilchowski,[1] who sometimes used his title of count and sometimes was called count by others, was my grandfather's uncle twice removed; he was married to Józefa Kumanowska, his first cousin and a one time favourite of my grandfather.

Piotr Pilchowski
Bobrowski, 'Memoirs', I, 64

Mr Piotr, first cousin of the Major,[2] and a born Galician, felt that he had a right to use his title of count – which was even more to his wife's taste than to his own. He was a typical 'Galician' with a touch of an Austrian officer about him: he was lively, agile, physically nimble, pleasant in conversation and very cheerful. We, as children, used to adore him because he played with us, always inventing new tricks and new physical exercises; as he was himself extremely dexterous, we were filled with admiration at his performances. His only idol – as he used to say so himself – was honour, and indeed he was very sensitive on this point. He was also very brave. He proudly recalled that his discharge papers, which he received with the rank of a captain after the battle of Austerlitz, pronounced him 'unschreckbar' (fearless) in the face of the enemy.

Russian oppression
Bobrowski, 'Memoirs', I, 78

Wealthier landlords were perhaps in a relatively worse situation because, first, their estates tempted confiscation, and second, their

---

[1] Lived 1771–1862; the name Biberstein, used sometimes by the Pilchowski family, harks back to their ancestors' Silesian connections.

[2] Major Pilchowski, of unknown Christian name, brother of Ignacy.

names and their faces were known to Tzar Nicholas, who had a good memory and used personally to confirm the decrees concerning the *szlachta*. For instance, after he had signed the banishment of Prince Roman Sanguszko to Siberia,[1] the Tzar remembered that Sanguszko's parents could extract from the authorities a permission that their son be driven rather than made to walk on foot, and dispatched a special messenger with an order written in his own hand to prevent any possible act of leniency. And so Sanguszko walked for over a year to his destination, chained to one wooden bar along with common criminals.

A story of the 1831 insurrection

Bobrowski, 'Memoirs', i, 185

Their only son Florian (Rzewuski) lived under the terrible accusation that he had revealed the real name of Prince Roman Sanguszko, his childhood friend, taken prisoner during the 1831 insurrection. Florian served in the army, then married Miss Zawisza in Lithuania, was left a widower and died as a police superintendent in Wilno. Prince Roman returned to Poland only after 1842, when Rzewuski was already living in Lithuania, and most categorically denied the story of his betrayal (he told me this himself in 1869) explaining the incident in very simple terms. When he (Prince Roman) was brought with other prisoners to the headquarters of the unit whose *aide-de-camp* was Rzewuski, the latter was so flustered on seeing the Prince that he called out: 'Roman, you here!' This could not have been a betrayal because Prince Roman's companions had been captured together with him and knew who he was. Nevertheless, Florian Rzewuski lived all his life under the burden of this terrible accusation, and it is possible that his later life was ruined by the incident. Let what I have written here bring comfort to his memory.

Prince Roman Sanguszko

Bobrowski, 'Memoirs', ii, 386–8

I had not met him before and this was my first opportunity to be introduced to that highly respected, worthy and generally revered man of unrivalled integrity, noble-mindedness and strength of character;*

---

[1] For taking part in the 1830–1 insurrection. Roman Sanguszko (1800–81) is the hero of Conrad's *Prince Roman*.

[2] A high military commander, nominated by the king; in the Polish commonwealth there were two 'grand *hetmans*', one for the Crown, one for Lithuania, and two deputies.

* Prince Roman Sanguszko was the son of Prince Eustachy, deputy *hetman*[2] in 1811, and

a man who after the insurrection of 1831 spent a part of his life in the Siberian mines, then served as a private in the Caucasus wars, and finally, after having been promoted to the rank of officer, was allowed to return to his family and country about 1845. It was neither keen intellect nor education that made him stand out; on the contrary, he was a slow learner and there were many gaps in his education, which had been neglected in his youth. After he returned to his home country he tried to fill these gaps by extensive reading on diverse subjects; he devoted himself to this task with great enthusiasm, since complete deafness made him unable to take part in conversation. The only means of communicating with him was with paper and pencil which he always carried in the side pocket of his frock-coat; on greeting an interlocutor, Prince Roman immediately handed him his pencil and paper, read the notes made and invariably put all back into his pocket; at night he personally took care to burn the notes, never entrusting his valet or even his secretary with the task; he explained to me that once, when he had neglected this precaution, unpleasantness had resulted. With his fairly limited education and with his natural doggedness in abiding by his convictions – a doggedness no doubt intensified by his lordly position and upbringing, and which struck one as the dominating trait of his character – he was a man of sober intellect, intent on improving his knowledge, affable in company, full of traditional Polish courtesy, indefatigable in work and motivated by constant consideration for public weal. His work mainly, but not exclusively, pertained to economics and agricultural industry, and its aim was not self-enrichment. He concerned himself with all aspects of social life, with problems of keeping alive individual and national honesty and integrity. He never abstained from participation in the life of the *szlachta*, and verily loved the peasantry and was pleased with their emancipation. Those were the qualities which made him stand out from the rest of the

of a Princess Czartoryska. Prince Roman was married to a Potocka, the daughter of 'Staś' (Stanisław Potocki, 1752–1821), and the sister of August and Maurycy. Prince Roman's wife died in 1831, before the outbreak of the insurrection, leaving him a daughter Maria (later Countess Potocka, wife of Alfred). Prince Roman, serving in the Russian Guards but staying at the time on his parents' estate in Volhynia, joined the insurgent army and was later taken prisoner. At his trial a clerk of the military commission, who had been induced by Prince Roman's parents to take a soft line towards the prisoner, tried to bring to the Prince's mind the type of defence he wished him to take, namely that he had joined the rebels distracted by his wife's death and not aware of the consequences. Prince Roman answered in writing: 'I joined the insurrection from conviction.' I have heard that the Sanguszkos adopted the last words 'from conviction' for their device, but personally I have not seen them on Prince Roman's own seal.[1]

[1] The rumour is not confirmed by existing armorials.

contemporary aristocracy which, true to their past, showed always a strong tendency to rule arbitrarily or to lead their lives separated from and above other classes of society.

Mr Żmijowski

Bobrowski, 'Memoirs', II, 381–2

Mr Żmijowski, in addition to having a general education, was a specialist in mining; he did his training abroad, and then worked as the manager of a gold-mine in Siberia. He later published his memoirs of those days. After the death of Count Stanisław Potocki, and under the influence of Prince Roman Sanguszko and myself,* he became the administrator of paper-mills belonging to the Countess Potocka, wife of Count Alfred.[1] Later he worked on the board of the Warsaw–Vienna Railway Line, and died in the late sixties of this century.

Victims of the insurrection

Bobrowski, 'Memoirs', I, 79

My father did not believe at all in the success of the 1831 insurrection, nor in conspiracies, calling them 'noble madness'. He spoke of the victims with tears in his eyes, and tried to help the indirect victims, that is the bereaved families. One of the families he looked after was that of Karol Różycki,[2] his friend and the leader of the Volhynia insurrection.

A sickly child

Bobrowski, 'Memoirs', I, 141–2

My unsuccessful attempts at horsemanship discouraged me from all masculine exercises and I never managed to make up for this deficiency; I felt greatly humiliated at not being able to ride, drive carriages, shoot or swim. My poor health stood in the way of physical

---

* I write 'and myself' although this may appear ridiculous in a situation concerning father and daughter; yet it was the case that Prince Roman, determined to help Żmijowski, had asked me to recommend the latter to Count Alfred Potocki and to his plenipotentiary, Mr Romański, maintaining that my opinion would carry more weight: 'Because, you see, they don't believe me to be a good judge of men,' concluded the Prince.

[1] Alfred Potocki (1817–89), Prime Minister of Austria–Hungary 1870–1, after 1883 viceroy of Galicia; his wife Maria was the daughter of Prince Roman Sanguszko.

[2] Colonel Karol Różycki (1789–1870) commanded the Polish cavalry in Volhynia during the 1830–1 insurrection; later he went into exile.

exercise and my parents did not encourage me to participate in these activities. I was of weak constitution and my spinal column was at that time beginning to curve. I used to be woken up from my first sleep and made to hang by my arms to straighten my back; my diet was artificially supplemented and if it had not been for the directives of the kindly Doctor Stankiewicz and my mother's care, I would not have survived or else would have become a cripple. I did not develop into a hunchback but a slight curvature of the spine remained.

Physically weak, I was unable to take part in games natural to boys; I preferred to sit quietly on a small stool in the corner and to listen to adult conversation. Hence I remember hearing many things which my contemporaries could not have dreamt of; I sometimes expressed thoughts which would never have entered their heads.

Bobrowski's personality
Bobrowski, 'Memoirs', I, 167–8

On the whole, since childhood I have been fortunate in my relations with people, although this was not the case at home because my parents, my relatives and other members of the household loved my brother more; he had in fact a much easier character, and was also very kind-hearted, while I was rather unruly and short-tempered. But on the whole I have been 'lucky with people' throughout my life and this has often given me an exaggerated opinion of my gifts ... My schoolfellows also regarded me as intelligent, and at the high school as well as at the university I was respected for my prudence rather than liked as a nice fellow. It was the same when I grew up. From the time of my first public appearance I acquired the reputation of being gifted, educated and capable of discerning judgement; my opinion and advice inspired general acclaim, probably not entirely unfounded, but more than once I encountered people able to offer equally good or even better advice, who were by-passed on my account. In spite of this popularity which has remained unchanged, my feelings about it are the same as they were when I was at school: it is founded on respect rather than on love; for me, however, this has always been enough. Unable to secure both I would rather be esteemed than loved ... At school as well as in later life I have always been an influential person, someone to be reckoned with. Both then and now I have been accused of excessive conceit. I am not denying that I have always had a good dose of it, but I also used to know fools who were tolerated although they possessed and displayed it to a far greater degree than my own opinion of my worth would have justified! And to show that my conceit has not been excessive but only befitting our social conditions, let me say that I have always been capable of recognizing and respecting those whom I believed, for one reason or another, to be superior to me. This is in turn attested by the friendly relations I have had with the wisest and most respectable people in the province and even in the country as a whole. Moreover, I have never resented those people who were not prepared to accept my authority.

The Bobrowskis' social circle
Bobrowski, 'Memoirs', I, 220–3

The countryside around Oratów was beautiful and densely populated. Apart from the closest neighbours at Oratów itself – rather simple people who, but for Mr Stępkowski,[1] held no promise of pleasurable relations – there were about thirty country houses in the vicinity, some quite rich, some well off, others less so. And one could easily form a fairly large circle of reasonably well-mannered and pleasant people of different ages. At first my parents had planned to establish relations with the nearest country houses, but, as it is usual in the case of remarkable personalities, their circle of friends gradually expanded as people from further away sought their company; and often, disregarding social conventions, people who had lived in the neighbourhood longer or had known them earlier called on my parents without waiting for their visit.

Here, as in other places where my parents had lived, their home was a meeting ground for people from various social strata, separated by the then accepted notions about position, wealth and occupation. My parents' tact and hospitality, which did not try to emulate lordly grandeur or even the life style of the rich; their respect for wisdom and good breeding, even when those qualities were unconnected with wealth or social standing; their regard for attainments in social position, which they neither worshipped nor envied; their unvarying courtesy towards the meanest and the greatest – all of it contributed to making every visitor to our house feel at home. No one could complain of having been treated with disrespect and people from different social spheres enjoyed meeting there. Guests were often surprised at how pleasantly they could pass the time in a house that was neither rich nor in any way prominent according to the accepted standards. My father held no high office either in the province or in the district, nor had he a fortune to his name, and the title of Justice of the Peace given to him

---

[1] Correctly Antoni Stempkowski (d. 1858), a lawyer and local character.

derived from some obscure event that had occurred somewhere in the
Starokonstantynów district sometime in 1821 or 1822 when, against his
will, he had been elected by his friends to try cases of border disputes
between landlords. This office, as everyone knows, is honorary rather
than actual, since it operates only when the parties request recourse to
it. Thus visitors at my parents' house included people of noble stock
and great fortune, members of the rich *szlachta* who on account of their
money considered themselves equal to the aristocracy, and the *szlachta*
of average means, like my father, as well as quite insignificant *szlachta*,
neither wealthy nor high-born nor distinguished by their upbringing.
But there were also people with liberal professions, like physicians,
tutors, musicians – and all of them were equally welcomed and all
enjoyed visiting our house.

Among our closest friends were the Kozickis, our neighbours, who
lived at Oratówka. Mrs Celina Kozicka, born Rokicka, was a woman of
beauty and kindness. Her husband (Feliks) ... was a kind man and a
good neighbour, and an exceptionally loyal friend. Both young and
handsome, well-off and courteous, the Kozickis liked to entertain,
particularly as they had at home two marriageable nieces, nearly of the
same age as Mrs Kozicka herself. The Misses Maria and Karolina
Orlikowskis* were good-looking, well brought up and nice.

The former had a charming bearing, beautiful pensive eyes and more
education than her sister; the latter was warm-hearted, open and witty;
both were extremely attractive. Jan Zagórski, a rather emotional relative of ours, was in love with Miss Maria, and my brother Stanisław
with Miss Karolina. Both young men were cadets in the hussars, and I,
fifteen years old, in the sixth class at the time and without any young
maiden to adore, was desperately in love with the lady of the house,
who, of course, treated me like a child. This did not upset me as long as
I had a chance to be close enough to look into the beautiful eyes of the
lady beloved by my fifteen-year-old heart. I must have used up a great
deal of my heart's warmth and ardour then, as afterwards until the
time of my marriage, I never fell in love again. We all used to congre-
gate at my parents' house for the holidays, and my brother would
occasionally bring with him a few of his hussar friends. As there were
uhlans stationed at Oratów one could easily improvise evening dances
either at Oratówka, or at my parents' house, or at some other house in
the neighbourhood. A few years passed and the pleasant and merry

---

* Their father, a captain of the artillery in the Polish Army, married to Miss Rokicka,
 perished in 1831 in the battle of Majdanek, in the Lityń district. Having shot all his
 charges and with his eyes burnt out, he ordered the canon spiked and shot himself
 with it.

house at Oratówka became deserted. Miss Karolina was the first to die of typhoid fever, which she had caught visiting the village sick. Then Mr Kozicki himself died of the same illness and within a year the remaining children, a little boy and a girl, had died. The widow moved to her parents in Podolia and a few years later she married Mr Władysław Szczeniowski. I have not seen Mme Celina since those tragic events. The late Kozicki's father with his wife, the stepmother of the deceased owner, moved into the desolate Oratówka.

The fate and the love story of the charming Miss Maria were rather sad. She was in love with Vlasov, an officer of the *uhlans*, stationed at Oratów. He was a very pleasant, well-mannered and educated young man from a good family, but a Russian. Although convinced of his feelings for her, and herself in love, she considered their marriage an insult to her father's memory, and an altogether unthinkable act. After a long struggle, she personally confessed everything to Vlasov, destroying all his hopes; and not feeling too sure of her own resolve, she created an unsurmountable obstacle by marrying another suitor, Tadeusz Przygodzki, an honest but very commonplace man, without much breeding and quite unsuitable for her, with whom she had a miserable and short life; she died young, leaving a daughter. Maria's brother, Tytus Orlikowski, took care of his niece, who later married Aleksander Leśniewicz (son of Joachim, an officer of the Polish artillery, exiled to Siberia in 1838). Poor Vlasov, deprived of all hope, left our province and at the recommendation of my father joined a hussar regiment commanded by Mr Poradowski, a relative of ours. Vlasov was well received and made many good friends, as he fully deserved. In spite of that he shunned company and took to drink, which was hard to believe in a man of such refinement; only a few of his kind could be found in the army in those days. Unfortunately this was what happened, and the miserable Vlasov continued his unhappy existence until in Košice during the Hungarian campaign,[1] in the presence of our relative, Apolinary Zagórski, who knew the whole sad story, Vlasov – recalling his love and his friends – ended his life in an attack of *delirium tremens*.

A sad story indeed! And thinking about it I keep wondering about a phenomenon, concerning the Russian nation, which I have noticed more than once: why is it that in all classes in that society, despair usually takes the form of drunkenness?

---

[1] The intervention of the Russian army to suppress the Hungarian insurrection against Austrian rule, May–August 1849.

Stanisław Bobrowski

Bobrowski, 'Memoirs', I, 423–4

After completing my education I took a brief respite in my parents' home. At this time my elder brother Stanisław, a lieutenant in the hussars of the army, was being transferred to the Grodno hussar regiment of the guards. My father, disregarding considerable expense on uniforms and maintenance, planned and decided the transfer in the belief that such a step would bring a more spectacular career for my brother – who thoroughly approved of the idea. But our best of fathers, not having studied his son's character and disposition, misplaced his efforts. Apart from a most agreeable presence and equally endearing manners, both of which earned him the reputation of a handsome and pleasant man much loved by his friends, my brother was not cut out for a career. He never sought favour with his superiors and never thrust his services on them, even though he was always liked and respected as a good officer and an excellent horseman. He was so noble-minded and so set on good comradeship, or perhaps just unassertive, that he would never accept a post from his superiors if he knew that a colleague had been trying for the position. He was very popular among his peers, but all the prizes and promotions he could have received went to those friends of his who were interested in their own advancement. He was to be appointed the regimental *aide-de-camp*, but refused, because a German who had no other means of subsistence needed the post. Later, when the commander of the whole cavalry of guards, General Strandman, wanted him for his *aide-de-camp*, my brother again refused because one of his colleagues needed the position to enhance his prospects for an excellent marriage. This last incident caused a pointless altercation between my brother and myself.

Surrounded by the rich and having a weak character and a fondness for comforts, my brother was forced to live above his status and means; he ran into debt and forfeited his patrimony before he even took possession of it. Our father, who knew nothing about the conditions of life in a guard regiment located in an isolated territory (the regiment was stationed in the Nowogródek province in separate barracks), theorized that one could live modestly among the rich, and trusted that it would be so with my brother; a more mature man of firmer character and greater tact could have done so, but these qualities were not to be found in this twenty-two-year-old officer. So my brother led a difficult life, amidst constant worries and debts, drawing from his experiences the conclusion that 'human life is an unending battle with all kinds of creditors,' as he jokingly used to say.

Apollo Korzeniowski
Bobrowski, 'Memoirs', I, 425–8

The only young man in the neighbourhood whom I liked and found congenial was Apollo Nałęcz Korzeniowski (for he always signed himself in this rather affected manner), later my brother-in-law, with whom I renewed an old acquaintance dating back to my schooldays in Żytomierz. At the time of Żytomierz we had not been very close as there was a difference of eight years between us: while he was in the seventh class, I was in the third.[1] When I left for St Petersburg, he had just returned from there without having completed his university studies; I am not even certain what he had been reading. In our part of the country he had the reputation of being very ugly and sarcastic. In fact he was not beautiful, nor even handsome, but his eyes had a very kind expression and his sarcasm was only verbal, of the drawing-room type; for I have never detected any in his feeling or in his actions. Open-hearted and passionate, he had a sincere love of people. In his deeds he was impractical, often even helpless. Uncompromising in speech and writing, he was frequently over-tolerant in everyday life – evidently for the sake of balance, as I pointed out to him many a time; he also had two sets of measures: one for the weak and ignorant, the other for the mighty of this world. He was well read in French and Polish fiction of the lighter type, and although quite a gifted writer, he had no thorough knowledge of any particular branch of learning. He had a considerable talent for poetry and could be regarded as one of the more successful imitators of Krasiński[2] ('Seven Words from the Cross', known only in manuscript, very beautiful). As a translator of Victor Hugo and Heine he was unsurpassed and rendered to perfection the style and substance of the former and the bitterness of the latter. The choice of words used in his writings and in his translations is excellent. His own plays, 'Comedy' and 'For the Love of Money' (the last was even awarded a prize in Warsaw, at the same time as a play by Józef Korzeniowski)[3] won great popularity among the reading and thinking public, although to my mind both plays paint an exaggerated and false picture of some social groups. The latter play was successfully staged in Żytomierz and Kiev. At that

---

[1] Apollo had been much delayed in his studies by a repeated change of schools attended.

[2] Zygmunt Krasiński (1812–59), one of the most prominent Polish Romantic poets and thinkers, author of philosophical and religious dramas and verse.

[3] Józef Korzeniowski (1797–1863), a well-known novelist and author of comedies; see Eliza Orzeszkowa's article in this volume, p. 188.

time Apollo was paying court to my elder sister who was still very young; I could not then detect in her any inclination to accept him, and my parents did not want him for their son-in-law. My mother liked his company and manner, but did not think he had the makings of a good husband. Both she and my father were of the opinion that since Apollo was not working – for he lived with his father and had no practical occupation – and owned nothing, then, in spite of all his social qualities, he was undesirable as a suitor.

My father, also fond of Apollo, tried to hint to him that he was unwanted, and made plans to marry him off to someone else. He took Apollo almost by force to meet rich young ladies, but Apollo was always clever enough to evoke disapproval from either the girl or her parents. In the drawing-rooms, however, he was most pleasant, attracting women by his ugliness, originality and talent – it is well known that the fair sex is interested in everything unfamiliar – and men appreciated Apollo's traditional Polish courtesy towards the elderly and gentleness towards the young; as I said before, he was impetuous and mordant only with a pen in his hand, and his sarcasm in the presence of ladies was always contained within the limits of propriety. He reserved his (let me call it) public acrimony either for persons who offended him personally or for those who were inflated with a sense of their wealth and social position – and then he usually had the laughter on his side. Although he regarded himself as an avowed democrat, and others took him for an 'ultra' or a 'Red', he had in him – as I kept telling him – a hundred times as many *szlachta* traits as I, whom neither Apollo nor anyone else suspected of holding democratic views. Actually it was his tender heart and his sympathetic feeling towards the poor and oppressed which made some people, including himself, believe that he was a democrat. In reality this was nothing more than the case of a well-born Nałęcz being transported by his emotions and ideas, and not by any democratic principles.[1] I could never make out his political and social beliefs, except his vague leanings towards a republican form of government and towards something equally vague: *per modum* of [similar to] the rights guaranteed by the 3 May Constitution – which in our own day is already inadequate. Apollo was undecided on the subject of the enfranchisement of the peasants; he leaned towards my view of the problem (expressed as long ago as in 1854) but was non-committal and felt that it should be

---

[1] This is contradicted by evidence from all other known sources, including Apollo Korzeniowski's dramas and political pamphlets, where he expresses his democratic views quite unequivocally. Among his fellow-conspirators he indeed had the reputation of being one of the most radical 'Reds'; historians confirm this opinion.

left to the landowners to decide.[1] This does not surprise me at all, and all I wish is to state that poets and people of imagination and ideals are generally unable to state their life postulates clearly and that they would do better to leave this task to other less sublime and idealistic souls who are better aware of the struggles and needs of everyday existence.

The Korzeniowski family

Bobrowski, 'Memoirs', I, 428–30

Apollo Korzeniowski's parents were kind people respected by all their neighbours. The mother, born Dyakiewicz, was a good soul and a loving parent; dominated by her husband, she was a person of little consequence. The father, Teodor Korzeniowski, lieutenant in 1807 and captain in 1831, was a good soldier but a narrow-minded *szlachcic*,[2] convinced that he was the best warrior in Europe, the best estate manager, and the most worthy man in the whole country. In actual fact he was a utopian and a braggart of the kind that deceives himself, believes wholeheartedly in his own lies, tells those lies to others, and gets angry with people who refuse to believe him. It goes without saying that he regarded himself also as a great politician and patriot, because he was always ready to mount his horse and chase the enemy out of the country without consulting his head. People listened to his idle chatter and often believed in what he said, as it was common knowledge that at one time he had indeed been a good fighter, so hardly anyone asked whether he could also think well. Having forfeited an estate which formed a part of his wife's dowry (in the Winnica district), he took over, on behalf of the government, the administration of a large estate, Korytna, confiscated from Mr Jagiełłowicz. It was a fine estate, the lease was inexpensive, and Korzeniowski was quite an able and hard-working manager, but, pursuing irresponsible dreams all his life, he sank the rest of his money there. If he had a high opinion of himself, he had a real admiration for his adult sons, particularly when talking about them to other people – for when addressing them in private, and especially when he was in a bad temper, he would treat them like small boys, calling them fools and worse, which they bore with humility, kissing their father's hand.

---

[1] This again is contradicted both by Korzeniowski's poems, written in 1855, and by the reminiscences of his contemporaries. The underground National Government, the formation of which Korzeniowski helped to prepare and in which his brother-in-law, Stefan Bobrowski – brought by Korzeniowski to the 'Reds'' organization – played a prominent part, proclaimed the enfranchisement of the peasants in its first act of 17 January 1863.

[2] Member of the *szlachta* (see Introduction).

Of his three sons, who were indeed gifted, the eldest, Robert, was a gambler and drunkard, and having contributed considerably towards the family's downfall, he was killed in 1863, no longer a young man. The youngest, Hilary, was a utopian like his father and as sarcastic as Apollo, though he had none of the latter's geniality in his relations with other people. He spent all his life running estates, and quite efficiently at that, but laboured in vain, for the poor wretch built castles in the air, deluding himself and others – myself included – and hoping that it was possible to make something out of nothing. Finally, in 1863, before the outbreak of the insurrection, he was arrested and sentenced to enforced exile in Tomsk. There again he farmed, prospected for gold, and speculated until he died in 1873, heavily in debt. My brother-in-law was the only one without that streak of speculation which his father and his younger brother possessed. The good old Captain Korzeniowski reached old age immersed in personal, familiar, political illusions. He lingered out his days in poverty, and in 1863 he saw for himself where his beliefs had led to. In the spring of 1864 in Dubno, looking after his son Hilary's case, he ended his troubled days. It is interesting that a colonel stationed in Dubno, who had known Captain Korzeniowski, sent the regimental band to the funeral. Have we not regressed a long way nowadays from this kind of approach towards our respective affairs?[1]

Apollo Korzeniowski to Tadeusz Bobrowski

Biblioteka Narodowa, Warsaw, MS 2889

11 May 1849, from Popowice

Dear Mr Bobrowski,

On Sunday – i.e. 8th May, St Stanislas' day – I was at Oratów; on Monday, on my return to Popowice I found your letter: this is a profusion of pleasures I am not used to. With my mind filled with beauty and goodness by the conversation in your esteemed Mother's room, how can you imagine that I would laugh at your missive? Ask any indifferent man to read it and even he will experience that inner joy derived from the sight of anything good and sensible; think then of the impression it must have made on me, who intrude upon your friendship and for whom your kind words represent the nicest and most desirable form of flattery. This borders on selfishness – but I cannot help it.

---

[1] It is highly unlikely that Teodor Korzeniowski died in 1864. The presence of a regimental band at his funeral in spring 1864, at the height of the uprising, seems improbable. According to other sources he died in spring 1863.

If I were a believer in orderliness I would begin by answering your letter, or rather by writing an eulogy in praise of your system of social convention, which I found admirable; but to stay true to my nature I wish to reply to your last words.

Should a profound hope for the future blossom out in my soul I would much rather be indebted for it to you, dear Pan[1] Tadeusz, than to anyone else. Believe me, your letter made me sad and pleased at the same time; sad because I found there a sad truth, impossible for me to accomplish; pleased because I feel that all you wrote reflects your convictions, constitutes the norm of your life which will thus suffer but few disappointments; and those disappointments that may befall you, being not unexpected, will therefore be less painful. But what for some people is obvious truth, for others, on account of their inward disposition or complications of outer circumstances or moral enfeeblement, is unattainable excellence. Nevertheless, one ought to strive for it; and when perspiration breaks out on your temples, and you gasp for breath, when each step becomes more slow and painful for your injured foot, you must still listen to the voice that calls: 'Go! Go on!' You put forth all your strength – to come to a stop ... where? God alone knows.

All this may look like fantasy but believe me, it is true.

What should we call the essence of life? The endeavours, worries and petty troubles of our daily existence directed at the attainment of financial independence? Or the enjoyment of material pleasures which becomes an addiction and transforms nature, making the animal triumph over man? Or, as you say, honest life dedicated to spreading good all around you, as far as possible?

In the first I am submerged and slowly sinking – beyond all help! In self-justification I should only add: I do not do it for myself. The second course I used to follow in the past as a cure for dreams; but it did not prove omnipotent. Sometimes one word, one look of a superior person would suffice to render my life repugnant and I would fall back into that half-angelic, half-human state, so exasperating and, at the same time, as intoxicating as opium.

The third is to me the poetry of life, the most beautiful poetry for it is filled with beauty, truth and goodness, ennobling the soul which surrendered itself entirely to me.

It is like the eve of some great festivity: I know that on the morrow will come the holiday with all its delights and joys, but meanwhile all there is for me is fasting and mortification.

It is not my wont to complain about my fate. Some careless words in my previous letter provoked your noble response, which I feel and

[1] Polite form of address, like *monsieur, signor*.

understand. Thanking you for it, I had to make a partial confession. A full confession would require too much space and time; I shall spare you that. Although if you were acquainted with the details of my life, perhaps I could convince you that I am not to be blamed for what I am!

Let us talk about yourself. I do not believe very much in my future, but I am blindly confident about the future of those I love. Your present disappointments hurt me, but the pain is assuaged by a conviction of the infallibility of destiny which rewards the worthy. Thus I tried to console your excellent mother – there is a woman, of whom one can truly say *ecce mulier*! as it has been said of Christ *ecce homo*![1] Only the heart of a woman and mother can accommodate so much sorrow and so much wonderful faith! I always leave Oratów filled with momentary hopefulness and faith, a better and a more noble-minded man; but, pray, can you blame me for losing this faith the moment I return to my daily existence at Popowice?

You may already know, or perhaps you may not, that my father has taken on a lease from the Zielonkos, *les bien nommés*[2] who were supposed to leave for their estates in the Congress Kingdom of Poland;[3] but they are still here. Therefore I am fated to dabble in farming and my present existence resembles the history of the chosen nation who on their way to the promised land passed through a territory inhabited by heathens. The illustrious family is highly cultivated: all have woolly minds, all have roubles in their hearts, and all crack the same jokes; it seems they could all blow their noses into one handkerchief. Although you accuse me of lacking faith, you must not think me capable of kowtowing to golden, let alone silver, idols. Thus I give myself up to my duties, which set me temporarily free from the company where I cut a poor figure both physically and morally. Under the trivial pretext of wishing me good morning, the master of the manor pesters me with metaphysical talks. Then I fall into the clutches of his son, who reeks of the stable, for he is perpetually busy with his horse, harness and riding-whip. Had this last been used against him, he might have grown to be somebody. Wiszniewski's[4] fame as the author of 'Polish Literature' is dimmed by the education of that confident boor. There is a man for you with faith in the future – the faith of a clod. If I stay here a bit longer methinks I shall grow a mane and a tail, stand on all fours and

---

[1] Lat.: 'behold the woman', 'behold the man'.   [2] Fr.: 'the well named'.

[3] Formed by the Congress of Vienna in 1815, with the Tzar of Russia as its titular king and a separate administration and legal system guaranteed – theoretically – by constitution. It consisted of western provinces of the Russian part of divided Poland, with the rivers Niemen, Bierbrza, Narew and Bug as its eastern border.

[4] Michał Wiszniewski (1794–1865), philosopher and literary historian, author of *Historia literatury polskiej*, 10 vols, 1840–57.

buck like a well-fed jade. Then comes the worst moment of meeting the
fair sex. Imagine a blacksmith's bellows, puffing and blowing, and
absolutely convinced she looks like a woman. The insolence drives one
to distraction. There are also two maidens: one is the aunt who has
lived half a century in spinsterhood, the other is the daughter whose
fate would be the same if everybody shared my taste. If you know what
a spinster is, you may commiserate with me; if you do not, pray accept
my most sincere wishes to remain ignorant. It is impossible that God
created old maids.

And tell me now: is it worth going to Oratów where everyone is so
beautiful, pleasant, sensible and kind, in order to pass a short while
there and then return to this terrible world? Although I have not
written down the system of social conventions, here I must firmly
observe it. I am the object of ridicule and raillery for all those males
and females and I sometimes think that I have landed in the wild
forests of America where hordes of monkeys mock a stray human being.
But everything ends, and so this will end as well, and I am therefore not
despairing, but trying to act energetically to clear the way for their
departure abroad.

Since my arrival at Popowice, that is from Low Sunday (the Sunday
after Easter), I have only been once to Oratów, on the 8th of this
month. Your mother's health is as usual; the pity is that Bilski had to
leave to go to Hołowanieski, in whose house scurvy is rife, but there is
hope of his speedy return.

If openheartedness exists in the world, I can boast no mean pleasure
at being in the good graces of your worthy parents. During my visit to
Oratów your father had to leave to see Wysocki off, but I know he is in
good health. Miss Petronelka as kind as ever. Your sisters have not
changed – I cannot think of greater praise; pray believe my sincerity.
Thank you for remembering my parents and Hilary. My father is at
Kamieniec; my mother and sister are journeying from place to place
visiting relatives. Hilary is in love and courting, but his health is not too
good; he lives eleven miles away from here; I do not blame him for not
visiting me.

As to myself, I have written everything there is to say. I shall only
add that I entertain a strong affection and great respect for you; that I
wish to be worthy of your friendship, which I find most rewarding; that
I cherish blissful hopes that having read this letter you will place me
among dreamers and unrecognized geniuses and that you will laugh;
but if sincere feeling may evoke a reciprocity, then in spite of our
different characters you will remember that we share the same feelings
on human dignity, and you will not deny me your friendship.

But as the leopard cannot change his spots, so I will finish now my letter with a few rhymes I wrote after your departure and which seem to me even more true after I had read your letter; do not laugh or I shall feel embarrassed!

Your boat's ready; the sail is full
Of frolicsome breeze;
Life abounds in dangerous pitfalls,
But not all men are doomed to fail!
May cowards shrink at billowy waves,
To you they foretell fame:
You know the hidden reefs,
You fought in many a storm!
Your craft is swifter
Than falcon's wings;
Your rudder is Reason
Your sails will-power.
You steer towards the shores of fame!
And when you reach
Your journey's end,
The golden lands of bliss,
Please remember with a sigh
Those who perished in the storm!

Apollo Korzeniowski

My address is:

From 'A Little-Known Poet', by Stefan Buszczyński

Stefan Buszczyński, *Mało znany poeta* (Cracow, 1870), 4–6, 52, 53

Apollo Nałęcz Korzeniowski came from a family which in many respects deserved well of their country, particularly of (their native) Podolia. He was born on 9/21 February 1820 in the former Bracław province, in the hamlet of Honoratka, parish of Oratów. His mother, Julia, came from Lithuania, his father, Teodor, from the (Polish) Kingdom.[1] Teodor Korzeniowski joined the army in 1809 and fought his first battle at Raszyn.[2] He was wounded by an Austrian soldier, decorated, rose to officer, and remained in service throughout 1812. From 1825 until his death he was always extremely active in fulfilling his public duties with great devotion. Famous for his valour, he distinguished himself in 1831. Two military crosses, several wounds, the

---

[1] The Polish commonwealth had consisted since 1413 (Union of Horodło) of the lands of the Crown or Kingdom, and the Grand Duchy of Lithuania, the king of Poland being at the same time the Grand Duke of Lithuania.

[2] Between Polish and Austrian forces, near Warsaw.

farewell address from the soldiers of the unit under his command, with over two hundred names from Podolia and the Ukraine, represent to this day a glorious testimony of his life. He was almost eighty years old when, hurrying in 1863 to General Edmund Różycki's forces,[1] he died suddenly in Dubno.

Owing to adverse circumstances Teodor Korzeniowski lost the considerable estate inherited from his father, and, having generously paid off his debt to his native land, he entirely devoted himself to his family. He sent his son Apollo first to the high school at Kamieniec, later to Niemirów and Winnica. The young man's lively mind, warm heart and fearless character won him the love of his companions, but brought about several changes of school, as the Muscovite educational authorities kept accusing him of *independent thinking*. Apollo finished at the Żytomierz high school, and in 1840, unable to obtain a passport for Berlin, left for St Petersburg, where he remained until 1846, reading law and oriental languages.[2] From that time on, farming and quiet work in the country became his favourite occupations. Back in his native country, he regarded the cultivation of land as the most noble profession, for want of others, and a small circle of well-chosen friends as the most pleasant form of entertainment; however, accustomed to glamorous society in the metropolis, he liked to escape from his secluded spot now and again to resume his quiet work and meditation after a brief spell of hubbub and gaiety.

The most severe judge could not find anything reproachful in Apollo Korzeniowski's life. The only accusation one could perhaps bring against his writings was that *he never wanted to be consoled*. And such was the criticism raised against his poetry.

The suffering of his motherland was the inexhaustible source of his own suffering. He refused to be consoled because there was no consolation for his motherland. He yearned for an ideal, and for him Poland and nothing but Poland was the eternal ideal. He strove towards it through blood and tears and while his power lasted he fought with the 'strength of sacrifice'. He never lost hope; never gave up; until his last gasp he led others towards that promised land; his dying hand was still writing for Poland; his dying thought was about the motherland and God. He grieved and stormed in anger or despair at people of *ill-will* who

---

[1] Edmund Różycki (1827–93) commanded the Polish cavalry in Volhynia during the short-lived insurrection there (May 1863).

[2] These dates are uncertain; it is also not clear what exactly Korzeniowski studied and for how long. According to himself, he obtained a diploma in law.

delayed the *fulfilment* of his dream. He castigated the minority because all the while he had his eye on the majority, because he was concerned about all his countrymen, about the entire nation, about securing the independence of our Collective Mother through love and uprightness; and he himself served as an example of what he demanded from others.

Bobrowski's sisters

Bobrowski, 'Memoirs', II, 17–19

My sisters fulfilled their promise and took weekly turns to keep me company at Oratów. On one journey the sledge in which my younger sister Teofila was travelling got stuck and she was forced to get out into the snow; as a result she caught a slight cold and began to cough, but as her health was on the whole quite good, no one paid any special attention. However, once when I was away in Kiev, her condition suddenly deteriorated. She developed galloping consumption and died within six weeks. Her death occurred at the beginning of July [1851], in the eighteenth year of her life, to the great sorrow of us all. Teofila's outstanding qualities were not so much her education and beauty – in which my elder sister excelled, although Teofila had a pleasant appearance and an adequate education – but her common sense, sweet disposition, and an ability to adapt herself to people and situations. Her death was a great moral loss to us all, for it deprived us of that everyday assistance which can only be given by a woman convinced that in family life every occupation is worthwhile as long as it brings happiness to others. I am certain that if she had lived she would have brought a blessing to her home as a wife, mother, and mistress of the house; and that she would have always exuded an atmosphere of contentment, which she had the ability to create under all circumstances.

My elder sister possessed beauty and wordly deportment, and her education was above that of our contemporary women. She had a lively imagination and a warm heart. She was not as complaisant as Teofila, and at the time, her demands were more difficult to meet, as she needed more attention from other people than she was able and prepared to give herself. As she was rather weak in health, the conflict between her love for her future husband and the will of her father, whose memory and opinion she cherished, naturally upset her inner balance; dissatisfied with herself, she could not give others what she lacked herself. In later years, when she was united with the man she loved, her unusual qualities of intelligence, feeling, mind and heart blossomed out to the full. Amidst the greatest hardships of personal life, beset by all possible social and national misfortunes, she always chose, and with fortitude adhered to, her duties as wife, mother and citizen, winning the respect of friends and strangers, sharing her husband's exile and representing Polish womankind with dignity.

It happens sometimes in life that sorrows and solace come together. As my younger sister died – and her bed stood next to that of my mother, who although immobilized by palsy in one of her legs nursed and watched over her daughter – my despairing mother unaided sprang to her feet, regaining the use of her leg. Obviously the shock caused by my sister's death had been so violent that it revived my mother's entire nervous system. Another two or three years had to pass, however, before she could walk unaided and her paralysed leg, through gradual exercise, returned to its normal size. But it was not until 1855 that she completely regained the use of the limb, and in the next twenty years she walked a great deal and could even climb the stairs when living in town; only occasionally, when her leg became stiff, she would apply strips of medical adhesive tape along the sides of her spine to relieve the numbness.

Stefan Bobrowski

Bobrowski, 'Memoirs', ɪɪ, 21–2

My sister [Ewa] and I undertook to prepare our brother (Stefan) for school. My sister taught him religion and languages and I gave him lessons in classical subjects; he was a good pupil and his education progressed smoothly. My brother had an amazing memory and an even more amazing capacity for making shrewd assessments of people and historical events. History and geography were his favourite subjects. As there were no other children of his age in the family, my brother was precocious and of an easy disposition; he was liked, even loved, by everyone and his gift of observation was truly great. He always carried about with him a book which absorbed him at the time, and he used to open it and read whenever possible. He was extremely short-sighted, and in spite of our exhortations he insisted on reading with each eye in turn. My sister and I enjoyed teasing him by consciously making mistakes in history or geography which he immediately felt it his duty to rectify. He would run out of the room, snatch the appropriate compendium and produce the necessary 'documentation' to prove our error. He was most amusing when he caught a senior relative or guest making a mistake in one of his special subjects. My brother's good manners and his respect for his elders prevented him from contradicting, yet silence conflicted with his love of truth; but as he had a most expressive face and eyes, they reflected his inner struggle by grotesque contortions of features which at first were amusing but later proved impossible to eradicate. My brother retained his high sensitivity in later years, although he tried to control it; and the only thing that betrayed his vexation was the way he puffed at cigarettes, which he constantly smoked when in a state of excitement.

Stanisław Bobrowski in trouble

Bobrowski, 'Memoirs', II, 23–4

In the spring of 1852 my brother Stanisław unexpectedly came home, without any previous notice. He was then a lieutenant in the guard regiment of the Grodno hussars. On my return from a business trip, I found he had been at home for a few days. At the sight of his and my uncle's long faces and of my mother's troubled looks, I easily guessed that some explanation and confession had already taken place to bring about this gloomy atmosphere. Knowing my brother, I did not have to strain my imagination to conclude that his sudden return to the family nest, which was a long distance from where he was stationed, must have been caused by financial difficulty – that chronic illness of hussars all over the world, but in his case particularly acute. The sight of his slender baggage, whose only embellishment consisted of his precious hussar gala boots in their protective covering, confirmed my suspicion even before we had a confidential talk. I learned that his saddle-horses – he had two, and beautiful ones at that – had been sold, and his expensive uniforms and equipment pawned; his boots survived only because nobody wanted to accept them in pledge. It was necessary, therefore, to send three hundred roubles without delay to redeem from pawn the uniforms, which would cost three times as much to buy new, to buy two horses, and to pay three thousand roubles to settle all debts. These measures had to be taken in order for my brother to be able to remain in the army where he had a chance of reaching the rank of a commander of a cavalry regiment – a post much coveted by all the officers. My brother graciously addressed these requests to me as the head of the family.

Polish rural society

Bobrowski, 'Memoirs', II, 30–2

My sister [Ewa] and Mr Zagórski preached, without ever questioning their practicability, the most lofty ideals in regard to all aspects of intellectual endeavour, and in the context of individual and collective lives. Mr Sobotkiewicz, also an idealist, echoed their words, but his approach had a dash of humour and irony which betrayed a certain disillusionment stemming from experience. My brother [Stanisław], full of tolerance for real-life phenomena, professed calm scepticism with fatalism as its canvas on which various human foibles and passions formed an intricate pattern; he thought it would be futile to try to alter this state of affairs. In some respects, therefore, he was a 'determinist', just as my uncle [Adolf Pilchowski] was what is nowadays called an 'opportunist', although these terms were not used at the time. My uncle was always ready to change from lofty theoretical ideals to an almost absolute affirmation of the powerful influence caused by the interplay of passions in individual and collective lives; his frequently repeated maxim expressed his personal opportunistic credo: 'Say what you will, but he who does more than necessary is a rascal!' In other words, while my brother believed 'it is not worth it', my uncle thought 'there is no need to'; in the end both attitudes amounted to the same thing. And finally myself, a convinced doctrinaire, deeply confident of the inflexible and unchanging rights and duties of the mind, of critical judgement and free will which make man a master of his own fate and history; I reject all side influences issuing from emotions and passions and from other people; through clear thinking I have arrived at a ready formula to meet every problem in life. Sometimes, intentionally exaggerating my assertions, I used to enrage my uncle, stun Mr Zagórski and make my sister cry. Once when she was still smarting after an argument, she exclaimed that if I reasoned myself into killing her, I would take a knife and cut her throat! 'Quantum mutatus ab illo!'[1]... The few characteristics of a doctrine that I had in my youth have stayed with me until this day and people, quite justly, I must admit, reproach me for them. However, I have no intention of renouncing this trait, on which my character and my whole life have been based; I regard it as the source of that unity of opinion and consistency of purpose in life which have won me the esteem of others and have given me self-respect.

Such a small circle, limited almost entirely to relatives, provided the sole opportunity to enliven our minds through conversation and exchange of ideas, amidst the general inertia of people submerged in their petty, everyday affairs. For not only in our neighbourhood but throughout the whole of Ruthenia, widespread torpor prevailed among the rural *szlachta*. I shall refrain from mentioning other estates whose members were so absorbed in their professional duties that their lives often dragged on almost unnoticed. Intellectual activity was practically non-existent, and social life, although fairly animated, was meaning-

[1] Lat.: 'how changed from that [he was]!'

less. Intellectual activity encountered many difficulties because of the general situation in the country and more specifically the oppression by, and fear of, Tzar Nicholas's government, the orders of which were effectively implemented by Bibikov.[1] Bibikov regarded every periodical and new book from abroad as suspicious and compromising. But this state of torpor was aggravated by the laziness and sluggishness of the landowners, who regarded sending a messenger to the post office, even if only once a week, as a heroic enterprise. Judge Kozicki, for instance, a subscriber to the *Kurier Wileński*,[2] which he used to lend to his neighbours, was considered a statist and a benefactor of the area. Social life ostensibly existed: not to visit one's neighbours during holidays or on name-days would be taken as an affront. Thus there was a great deal of coming and going between country houses, although those visits entailed little food for thought and hard work for the ears, as one had to listen patiently to 'accurate' accounts of the same bits of gossip repeated countless times.

In that blissful state of inactive minds and untroubled consciences, and under the pressure of a patriarchal system of serfdom, 'God's gifts' were reaped and multiplied. All the activity, vigilance and providence of the landowning *szlachta* was directed to this end, and other estates too wished to reach the same 'privileged and blessed position'. In all fairness it must be said that peasants were not too badly off at this time; perhaps they were even less in debt than peasants are today. The inventories[3] introduced a certain general order into the system of enforced labour, which was, I think, on the whole observed. The peasants were respected and no one interfered in their personal relations beyond their working duties. This state of affairs resulted perhaps not so much from conviction as from our love of peace and our characteristic softness. At any rate, this is how matters stood; landowners who visibly oppressed their peasants were condemned by public opinion –to be sure this condemnation was silent, but it nevertheless existed. Thus on a purely factual basis, and in an atmosphere of general calm, minds were getting ready for momentous events to come.

Bobrowski falls in love

Bobrowski, 'Memoirs', II, 70

[In the spring of 1854] I found the [Lubowidzki] household exactly as my sister [Ewa] had described, and of the girls (even the younger ones,

---

[1] Dmitri Bibikov (1792–1870), known for his ultra-conservative views, Minister of Internal Affairs 1852–5.
[2] A Polish daily published in Wilno.
[3] Of tilled soil and the peasants' obligations.

Miss Cecylia Lubowidzka and Miss Maria Czarnecka, were already admitted to the company of adults) I liked best the eldest, Józefa; she was a beautiful young woman with dark hair and a complexion as fresh as a peach, with lovely eyes such as I have never seen before or since, and with a remarkably fine figure. She enjoyed playing the piano and was quite a proficient musician. Her mouth and teeth were not pretty, but her oval-shaped face was strikingly harmonious, her deportment serious and her look profound and full of expression. I left Odessa under a strong impression of my first encounter with her, and in spite of my natural inclination to be sober-minded about things and situations, I decided to overlook all possible obstacles and to try my luck.

The betrothal of Ewa Bobrowska to Apollo Korzeniowski
Bobrowski, 'Memoirs', II, 72

My sister [Ewa] was at the time [July 1855] preoccupied with her decision to accept her suitor of several years, Apollo Korzeniowski, for whose sake she had been discouraging all other suitors from the start.

Both my parents liked Korzeniowski and regarded him as a pleasant and well-mannered guest, but both of them, although for different reasons, looked upon him with disfavour as a prospective husband. My mother suspected Korzeniowski of being irresponsible and erratic in behaviour because of his sarcastic tongue. My father, on the other hand, thought him unpractical and lazy, because while supposed to help his father to run the estate, Apollo read, wrote and travelled around more than worked. My father made no secret of his views, and as my sister had a great respect for his judgement, both during his lifetime and after his death, she wrestled a long time with her affection before making the decisive step. Realizing that both her health and future were threatened, my mother and I believed that we should encourage rather than discourage her in taking a firm decision, as we knew that if she were not united with the man of her choice, she would remain single and not marry for the sake of getting married. Meanwhile Korzeniowski, having grown doubtful about the success of his endeavours, had moved away to the province of Podolia where for a few years he ran the estate of Mrs Melania Sobańska, born Uruska, mother of his friend Aleksander. When Korzeniowski learned of my sister's and mother's arrival at Terechowa, the estate of my uncle, Adolf Pil-chowski, who was wont to sympathize with all romantic adventures, he paid them a visit and my sister, prompted by her uncle, agreed to accept her suitor of many years. I was then summoned and the ceremony of betrothal took place, with the date of the marriage set for 26 April 1856.[1]

Conrad's certificate of baptism

Biblioteka Jagiellońska, Cracow, MS 6391

CERTIFICATE OF BAPTISM
In accordance with the ukase of His Majesty the Tzar:[2]

From the public register of baptisms of the parish church of Żytomierz, kept in the consistorial archives:

In the year one thousand eight hundred and sixty-two, in the Żytomierz Roman Catholic Parish Church, Father Eustachy Szczeniowski, professor at the Łuck and Żytomierz diocesan seminary, performed the rite of holy baptism, conferring the name Konrad upon the son of the lawfully wedded Ewelina born Bobrowska and Apollinary Korzeniowski, whose birth was in the year one thousand eight hundred and fifty-six on the twenty-first of November and who in the same year and month was christened at a private ceremony by Fra Jan Romański, member of the Carmelite order from the Berdyczów monastery. His godparents were Mr Adolf Pilchowski and Mrs Franciszka Dąbrowska. The official religious ceremony took place in the presence of: Mr Adolf Pilchowski with the chamberlain's wife Mrs Konstancja Pruszyńska, Mr Tadeusz Bobrowski with Mrs Gabriela Zagórska, and Mr Jan Zagórski with Mrs Maria Czarnecka. This extract from the book of the Parish Public Register was verified at the request of Mr Tadeusz Bobrowski at the Łuck and Żytomierz consistory, on the 31st day of May 1869.

Signed by: Judge Lateral, Prelate Ludkiewicz (in his own hand).
The Secretary P. Sikorski for and on behalf of the
Head of the Office, Woliński

N 3223 (L.S.)

I certify with my own signature and with my own seal that the translation from the Russian conforms to the original written on paper headed with the coat of arms and stamped with a duty of one silver rouble.

Cracow, 10 November 1872, Dr A. Nowicki, sworn translator for the Russian language at the I[mperial] and R[oyal] District Court at Cracow.

[1] In fact on 4 May 1856 (new style).
[2] The original text, in Russian, contains numerous mistakes in the spelling of names, and also an error in the year of Konrad Korzeniowski's birth. The Polish translation adds more mis-spellings.

Poem by Apollo Korzeniowski to his son

Biblioteka Jagiellońska, Cracow, MS 6794 (copy in Teofila Bobrowska's hand, with fragments missing)

To my son born in the 85th year of Muscovite oppression, a song for the day of his christening.

> Baby son, sleep without fear.
> Lullaby, the world is dark,
> You have no home, no country,
>   But sleep peacefully, for you're *poor*,
> The holy water flows upon you;
> The Holy Spirit descends upon you,
> You have a *soul* now and it has a *name*,
>   Hushaby my baby son!
> Baby son, sleep in peace.
> Alien spirits cast their shadows,
> Two hearts are all you have,
> And your only armour – *the cross*.
> But such treasures do not perish,
> The World's rust will not destroy the cross,
> The hearts are faithful. Close your eyes,
>   Hushaby, my baby son!
> Baby son, my thousand songs
> Will lull you to sleep,
> Wondrous and enchanted,
> Into stars, flowers, suns...
> *Beauty* and *goodness* will stream down on you,
> Rocked on their wings,
> Your world will be shining bright...
>   Hushaby, my baby son!
> Baby son, may this christening
> Give you strength to live,
> To look bravely into shadows
> ... although in mourning
> ... when God allows
> *Poland* to rise from the grave,
> Of captivity – *our only Mother*
>   Hushaby, my baby son!
> Baby son, sleep ... let Holy Water
> Flow on your soul, on your forehead;
> *Heaven* and *Godliness* surround you...
> Bless you, my little son:
> Be a *Pole*! Though foes
> May spread before you
> A web of happiness
> Renounce it all: love your poverty.
>   Hushaby, my baby son!

Baby son, when the *enemy* says
You're a Christian and Nobleman –
Tell yourself you're a pagan
And your nobility is depraved.
If I should be defiled
By the enemy's favours –
Renounce your renegade father...
     Hushaby, my baby son!
Baby son, tell yourself
You are without land, without love,
without country, without people,
while *Poland – your Mother* is in her grave.
For your only *Mother* is dead – and yet
She is your faith, your palm of martyrdom.
     Hushaby, my baby son!
Baby son, without ...
Without Her ...
Without Her ...
And no salvation without Her!
The time will come, the days will pass,
This thought will make your courage grow,
Give Her and yourself immortality.
     Hushaby, my baby son!
        23 November 1857
        Berdyczów

Bobrowski's courtship

Bobrowski, 'Memoirs', II, 85–6

While I courted my future wife [in 1856] I tried to maintain absolute independence of opinion, belief and action, allowing thereby the young maiden and her parents to get to know me thoroughly – as far as this is possible in the case of a suitor. And yet this is always possible, provided one sincerely wishes to shun all pretence and intentional concealment of one's faults and shortcomings. Unfortunately such practices are frequently, and without any qualms of conscience, performed by both sexes before marriage, bringing about irreparable damage to future family life. As a doctrinaire I was convinced that honest courtship and competition for the favours of a lady ought to be based on truth and sincerity, and that not to be chosen is a lesser evil than to be chosen under false pretences; I even carried the application of my principles too far by shunning the courtesies usually practised in the social intercourse with the family and neighbours of the lady whose favours I sought, and it was not until after the betrothal that I changed my manner without fear of being accused of self-interest and of trying to use indirect influences – which anyway more often than not tend to be ineffectual or harmful. I did not play the part of a 'pleasant and docile young man' in front of those who were to decide whether to accept or reject my proposal; I stood before them as a man of formed character, convictions and behaviour, and for people who take a serious view of life such qualities cannot but represent an ample guarantee. My method served me well. While my stand on serious matters was somewhat inflexible, I took care to display the intellectual and social qualities – such as they really were – which could make life with me pleasant.

The Korzeniowskis' first home

Bobrowski, 'Memoirs', II, 91

After our wedding [25 June 1857] my mother and brothers went straight to Derebczynka, the estate which Korzeniowski had leased from Teodor Sobański; the new owners, the Szymanowskis, had already taken up residence in Oratów, from where we all moved at the time of my wedding. Our mother, in order not to be separated from her daughter and wishing to keep a home for her unmarried sons where they could always come and stay, took upon herself one-third of the lease and of the housekeeping expenses. Three years later the lease came to an end, bringing a loss to all concerned. The Korzeniowskis had nothing left from it[1] and my mother very little, practically nothing.

Bobrowski's wife dies in childbirth

Bobrowski, 'Memoirs', II, 96–7

After Easter, which in 1858 fell early, in March, we left Morozówka to return to Nowofastów. The time of my wife's confinement was getting near and it was only fair to stay in our own home and not to inflict all the problems associated with the event upon her parents. On this occasion my wife, contrary to her disposition, was unusually emotional when leaving her parents' home. Was this a normal anxiety of a woman awaiting her ordeal, or did she have some premonition of the sad end? Her expressive eyes appeared to be bidding farewell to all the people and places so dear to her. It made a painful impression on me, but after a few days at home her mood improved; I took heart and for almost an entire month we lived peacefully and in good spirits. My mother came

---

[1] This was not quite true, as Korzeniowski had enough money left to enter into partnership, forming a publishing house in Żytomierz.

to stay with us; she had grown very fond of my wife and out of friendship for my wife's mother – who was anxious, but not always free to leave her home, and who also lacked the ability to nurse the sick – she promised to be with us during the critical period. Our family doctor, not to mention his female assistant, was constantly present, and if he went out it was only for a few hours; all the medicines likely to be needed were also ready. It so happened that on the eve of the confinement, which took place on the morning of 26 April, the daughter of my estate manager, Mr Głebski, was married to Dr Stefański; a friend of the latter, Dr Sałatko, was also present at the wedding. Half an hour after the delivery, which had been quite normal, Dr Tokarski deemed it necessary to let blood from the lying-in patient; this brought her obvious relief, but when after a short pause she suffered another heart and lung attack, Dr Tokarski decided to consult with the doctors present in Nowofastów at the time. The doctors ordered another blood-letting and I, meanwhile, sent for Dr Romański to Berdyczów and for Dr Placer, begging him to come and see my wife, for whom he always had a high regard. After he arrived a third blood-letting took place; as on previous occasions the relief was only temporary. The good Dr Placer wept bitterly looking at the slow suffocation of the patient; by the time Dr Romański arrived at about nine o'clock at night there was nothing left to be done. On 27 April[1] at four o'clock in the morning all was over! After ten months of married life I was left a widower and the father of an extremely frail little girl, who took the name of her dead mother.

The political situation in 1855

Bobrowski, 'Memoirs', II, 61

In view of such bitter disappointments and proofs of Europe's ill-will and indifference, there was, I thought, only one way open to us: to place all our hopes in the personal qualities of the new Tzar,[2] whose noble impulses justifiably raised our hopes[3] and those of the country as a whole. We met the new era of his reign under fairly favourable circumstances: we were politically not compromised, numerically not

---

[1] Old style, i.e. 9 May.
[2] Alexander II, born 1818, tzar 1855–81. This and the following fragments are most typical of Tadeusz Bobrowski's utopian ideology of appeasement. He apparently believed that the Russian authorities not only would tolerate Polish national identity, but were ready to strengthen it.
[3] And yet it was Alexander II who, during his visit to Warsaw in 1856, ended his speech with the words 'Point des rêveries, messieurs!' ('No more dreaming, sirs!').

decimated, financially not ruined, and we were governed by the same laws as all the other citizens. Moreover, possessing the most beautiful estates in the Empire and enjoying the most advanced and highest level of intellectual culture, we still had the power which, if used intelligently and with moderation, could, under the new reign free from prejudice and hatred, work towards the attainment of a fairly tolerable *modus vivendi* that would find its expression in a complete autonomy of the [Polish] Kingdom, a recognition of our basic needs and, in time, an acknowledgement of certain national rights of the old Polish settlers in Ruthenia. Such, I thought, were the only possible and realistic postulates in our situation, both past and present. In order to achieve these modest and yet realistic targets it would have been necessary to make a sober assessment of our position, to abandon our traditional dreams, to draw up a programme of national aims for many years to come, and above all, to work hard, to persevere, and to observe a strict social discipline. And this we could not do!

The irredentist movement

Bobrowski, 'Memoirs', II, 441–2

There was also no lack of internal reasons why the so-called 'movement' quickly became rampant throughout our country.[1] In the first place there was our inflammable national temperament, known for its gullibility, rashness and instability. The thirty-year oppression under Tzar Nicholas's reign, marked by the dates 1831, 1838 and 1848,[2] kept the entire Polish population in a state of constant emotional tension with thoughts of efforts aimed at raising the country from its deplorable condition. Finally, exaggerated hopes, lacking in sober criticism –hopes set on Tzar Alexander II's liberal inclinations, initially exemplified by the emancipation of the peasantry[3] – ought to have suggested, at least to the more sober minds, that the greater the scope of the first reforms, the slower would be the pace of subsequent reforms. However, arbitrary speculations were advanced in complete disregard

---

[1] The Polish irredentist movement, which had been spreading since 1859, and much more quickly after the bloody suppression of a patriotic demonstration in Warsaw on 27 February 1861.

[2] I.e. the uprising of 1830–1; Szymon Konarski's conspiracy, which addressed itself to the peasant question and was ruthlessly suppressed; the Russian intervention in Hungary in 1849.

[3] The decree partially abolishing serfdom and granting the peasantry in Russia limited civil rights was promulgated on 3 March 1861. In the Polish Kingdom an analogous decree, prompted by a proclamation of the underground Polish National Government and much more favourable to the peasants, was promulgated on 2 March 1864.

of the fact that even the most powerful ruler has to take heed of the times and of the environment in which he lives. Thus both the Poles and the liberal section of the Russian intelligentsia harboured, each on their own account, exaggerated hopes, which by the very nature of things had to be – at least for the time being – disappointed. In our case all came to an end with an ineffective revolution that deprived us, perhaps for ever, of the likelihood of a peaceful and legitimate national development – even if under Russian rule – that moderate Poles had expected, taking into consideration the general situation and the logic of facts ...

Ewa Korzeniowska to Apollo Korzeniowski
Kobieta Współczesna (Lwów), 1931, no. 17

(no date)

More than ever I wish you to stay where you are.[1] Who knows if it may not be our only chance to move. Who knows if after your return you might not find yourself somewhere else?[2]

For pity's sake find someone coming here and write through him openly what your definite plans are. I beseech you to beware of the post.[3] Guess, if there is something you cannot understand. I am writing in a terrible hubbub, hence this disorder. Lots of people here and I cannot delay, not to miss the opportunity.

The last letter received written on arrival at the Saski Hotel!

We are well.

Konradek, the dear boy, recalls you every hour, every minute. As good as can be. You will not get a letter from him.

I am waiting for something definite from you. You could telegraph if you have made up your mind. Sign the telegram A.N. Głąbski will forward it to me, to Nowofastów, where I shall be waiting for it; send it to Berdyczów.

Ewelina

---

[1] In Warsaw. The police in the Ukrainian provinces have evidently been alerted to Korzeniowski's 'subversive' activities in Żytomierz.

[2] Korzeniowska was afraid that her husband might be arrested if he returned home.

[3] Letters sent by post were opened by the police.

Ewa Korzeniowska to Apollo Korzeniowski

Kobieta Współczesna (Lwów), 1931, no. 16

10/22 May 1861, Nowofastów

This is my second letter to you. The first was written from Terechowa and addressed to The Main Dispatch Office of *Magazyn Mód.*[1] It seems I have made a mistake and that you wanted it to go direct to the Editor's Office. So now I right myself.

An hour ago I dispatched your letters to Berdyczów. I have reasons for sending this letter to Skwira.

We are in good health. We live or rather do not live at all – as in a grave. Mother, U[ncle] Józef, Tadeusz, I and our children[2] – that is our entire circle; no one else. All around us complete silence. Several books and all the Warsaw periodicals provide our sole distraction. Many of us were annoyed – and rightly so – by an ill-considered item in *Gazeta Codzienna*, no. 114, page 2.[3]

I know nothing about Mrs Zenona: I had no news either from her or from any other friends. But I heard said that the two Marzycki brothers from the Żytomierz district were taken away. The elder one returned several years ago from Tobolsk and now both are in Vyatka.[4] They say also that the fifth and sixth forms at the Żytomierz High School have been closed down and the admittance of the pupils by any other school forbidden. The last news is not as reliable as that about the Marzyckis.

Let me know if my last letter has reached you. And do not forget to change the address on your letters to me from 20 May, as I intend then to take my leave of Nowofastów and return home. What do you say to that?

Thank God I have no bad news to impart to you about the current agricultural reforms. True, in Nowofastów, Babin and Szepijówka, as you see, in the estates of the best landowners, distrust and disobedience take various forms; but generally speaking the methods of appeasement are the *kindest* possible. I do not know how it is elsewhere but in the Skwira district warm gratitude to the monarch has been awakened:

[1] *Pismo Tygodniowe Magazyn Mód i Nowości*, a Warsaw weekly.
[2] I.e., their son Konrad and Tadeusz Bobrowski's daughter Józefa.
[3] *Gazeta Codzienna*, a Warsaw daily, changed its name to *Gazeta Polska* on 3 April 1861. In an editorial commentary, reacting to a dispatch in *L'Indépendence belge* of 30 April (about the official ban on 'inciting the population in churches' imposed by the government in Warsaw), the paper wrote on 7 May: 'The houses of God are not a proper place for political incitements.' Ewa's annoyance was caused by the fact that the 'incitements' consisted of singing religious songs with patriotic overtones.
[4] In compulsory exile.

many communities have sent *proskurki*[1] offerings to St Petersburg; some others requested and received from Vasilchikov[2] portraits of the Emperor. In order to obtain those souvenirs of liberation most willing district collections were organized; but, of course, the authorities were sending them free.

Have you been to Częstochowa?[3] Is everyone there in good health? Are you all right? When do you think we shall see each other?

Do not forget to write in Eryk's Album. Think of me lovingly sometimes.

My regards to
Ćwierciakiewicz.[4]

Ewelina

Ewa Korzeniowska to Apollo Korzeniowski

Kobieta Współczesna (Lwów), 1931, no. 16

17/29 May 1861, Terechowa

Apolek, my beloved,

It so happens that I have a chance to write to you. I do not know when this letter will reach you but it suffices me to receive assurances that you will get it. Thankful for the opportunity as for some supreme grace I avail myself of it.

I sent four letters through the post, two of them addressed to Gregorowicz. I shall also be using Ćwierciakiewicz's address. I shall use your name on the envelopes as rarely as possible. Believe me, this is the way it must be.

After you had left I was asked at Żytomierz what had become of us. Radkiewicz said we were at Dziadkowicze. Next day the police superintendent arrived with two clerks, reproaching us violently for telling lies and warning us that the authorities always get to know the truth and that telling stories entails severe penalties. Telegrams were sent to Równe, to Berdyczów, and finally they found out about Terechowa. Thus spoke the police superintendent. It took place on the second and third days of the holiday.

On 15 May the superintendent returns and asks what we did with the servants. Having learned from Radkiewicz that we had left two of them in town, they demanded their names and addresses. That is all we know.

---

[1] Ukrainian: 'blessed bread'.
[2] Illarion Vasilchikov (1805–62), governor-general of the Kiev province.
[3] To the celebrated shrine of the Virgin Mary.
[4] Jan Ćwierciakiewicz (1822–69), a Warsaw journalist and Korzeniowski's fellow-conspirator, later a foreign emissary of the National Government.

My dear, please do something for my sake: write less frequently, write less. I correct myself: write a lot but keep it. Some day you will give it to me. Just let me know from time to time if you are well.

All your letters are obviously being unsealed at the post office, and the number of them, all addressed by the same hand, as well as the frequency of their arrival at Berdyczów, attracts people's attention at the local post office. Try to write to Skwira. Perhaps with God's help letters will arrive. Do not write to Żytomierz. I was going to leave for home but Hilary and Adolf[1] counsel me to return to Nowofastów. They say it is better to lock up the house and not be there. Anyway, do not worry about me. They know my whereabouts but do not bother me: evidently they are interested only in your return. But what would come of it? Vasilchikov has threatened that *restless* people will be exiled by hundreds.

Ewelina

Ewa Korzeniowska to Apollo Korzeniowski

Kobieta Współczesna (Lwów), 1931, no. 17

18/30 May 1861

Your last letter was of 7 May from the Saski Hotel and not a word since.

I have been here for two days. It was my plan to go home but Tadeusz sent a messenger after me to say that he was anxious about me and implored me to return and to stay with him until Mr Prusznic gets back. So I shall remain here till 23 inst. and then go for a couple of weeks to Nowofastów. Meanwhile the baths are being arranged.

Hilary is here. We telegraphed you today but as yet no reply. Let me know if you have received the letters? Four by post, one by hand. I am most concerned about the last one – consider it carefully, darling.

As usual staying here makes me feel better. It is more lively and, what is most important, it seems closer to you. My health is good and so is Konradek's.[2] I am sad but peaceful at heart: as it happens I have quite often the delight of meeting kind people.

I shall visit Hilary but not before the beginning of June. He is so kind! Such a dear!

Ed. Łozinski is here also. I've grown very fond of him indeed. I am sending you a letter from Kiev – for you or for Ćwierciakiewicz. I promised Idzikowski[3] to do so.

[1] Hilary Korzeniowski, Apollo's brother, and Adolf Pilchowski, Ewa's uncle.
[2] Diminutive of Konrad.
[3] Leon Idzikowski (1827–65), a bookseller and publisher in Kiev.

I beg you to write to Kazio. All I know about Stefek is that he will come to Nowofastów by mid-June.

Let me know if you have met Jackiewiczowa. Send me her and Żmichowska's[1] address. Let me know what you are doing and writing, and above all what are your feelings, thoughts and decisions.

Oh, Lord! If only that fifth letter reaches you! This one is the sixth.

Konradek is a good boy: it is amazing how God lets him win people's hearts. Everyone loves him. Even Adolf spoils him. He mentions you every day, asks that we should go to you. They are great friends now with Hilary.

I embrace you first on behalf of all those present here, then from Konradek and lastly from myself. Remember to keep this last embrace well secured in your heart until you get another one.

Ewelina.

Ewa Korzeniowska to Apollo Korzeniowski
Kobieta Współczesna (Lwów), 1931, no. 17

23 May/4 June 1861, Terechowa

Apoleczek.[2] I have sent you four letters by post, one by hand and then again one by post. This one, the seventh, by hand. I would be happy to know if all have reached you. The fifth was the most important. In it I told you that the Żytomierz authorities have been enquiring as to your whereabouts; that Radkiewicz lied in reply; that telegrams were sent to and fro to get to the truth; that Radkiewicz was reproached and threatened for lying; then questions about your servants; they searched for them all over town. That is all I know. But what worries me is that on about 15 May my presence in the district of Skwira was ascertained and yet no further enquiries followed. Evidently they do not want to cause alarm and would gladly see you return. Vasilchikov is getting more and more impatient and keeps repeating that he has been waiting *long enough for people to come to their senses and now, without the slightest scruple, he can deport fifty per day.* Everywhere commissions and investigations as to who promotes church services. They demand lists of hymns sung in churches and information about where those hymns came from. The fifth and the sixth forms were closed down in Żytomierz for singing on Easter Day. Pupils from both forms were sent off to districts where the marshals had received circulars instructing them to pacify the *indomitable* youth by threatening them with terrible repressions. Several older

---

[1] Narcyza Żmichowska (1819–76), a well-known intellectual, novelist and short-story writer, an advocate of the social emancipation of women.

[2] Diminutive of Apollo.

pupils were made to work in the army where they are subjected to questioning and ill-treatment. All this is certain.

For the last few days people have been saying that some more victims have been deported, but I am not giving their names as I am not certain that it is all true. In Żytomierz Father Szczeniowski[1] has been arrested. The town keeps tormenting the Bishop.[2] Otherwise mourning is still observed and all is quiet. Yesterday I received a letter from Pietkiewicz.[3]

In the Skwira district the homes of an extremely worthy man, Mr Wilga, and of the young Karnickis have been mercilessly searched. I do not know what happened to the people because I was just leaving to come here. Your mind can be at rest: the house is prepared for anything. Kind people have helped me to clear everything away, without my having to go home. I am returning to Nowofastów and there I shall await your instructions whether to go home or not. If you decide to stay where you are, as common sense advocates, it will be quite all right for me to remain here. If you decide to return, please write how I should behave until then. Where should I be? What line to adopt? How to answer possible questions at Tadzio's[4] or at home?

Yesterday I had the following experience. We were unsealing newly received newspapers when one of the guests noticed your name among those who had arrived in Warsaw, and exclaimed excitedly: 'If they have let Ap(ollo) Korz(eniowski) go, they will let me out too! I am applying for a passport straight away.'[5] He fairly danced for joy. Another guest (just back from Siberia) started arguing that it could not be so and said: 'It must be some Ap. Korz. from the Kingdom.' But having been convinced that it was Ap. Korz. from Podolia, and not knowing who I was, he became very excited and cried: 'How is it possible? Do you imagine they would give a passport to our Korz.? Do you not know he is the greatest enemy of the Muscovites? Would they not know it? He must have sneaked out illegally. But now that it has got into a newspaper, obviously he will not be coming back – there would be no point; he would soon find himself travelling elsewhere.' The man who spoke thus was Przewłocki, originally from the Kingdom, but now living here. We have become good friends since then. He is a colleague of Głuszecki and Czapski and knows your Jezierski

[1] The Rev. Eustachy Szczeniowski, a canon in Żytomierz, later chaplain of the insurgents.
[2] Apparently to secure the Rev. Szczeniowski's release.
[3] Antoni Pietkiewicz (1823–1903), poet and novelist writing under the pseudonym Adam Pług; editor, friend of the Korzeniowskis, imprisoned 1864–6.
[4] Diminutive of Tadeusz. Evidently, Tadeusz Bobrowski was not informed about Korzeniowski's plans in Warsaw.
[5] Passports were required in Russia for internal travel on longer distances.

from Lublin very well. Many people talk about the danger of your return.

Nothing has been heard of Kazimierz; it is as if the earth had swallowed him. T. Zaleski and other close friends do not seem to take him seriously; but I may be wrong.

As to the peasants – things are far worse here than in Kiev Province. True, large areas are calm but in the villages belonging to such scoundrels as, for example, the Giżyckis from Kutyszcze, the Kaczanowskis from Kordelewska and several villages of the Głębockis, people are being slashed to death. To this end Lobanov, the tzar's operational *aide-de-camp*, has arrived with unlimited power to use the knout. A dozen victims killed, others – barely alive. Poor wretches say, 'they gave us freedom to beat us all the harder'. One's heart bleeds to hear what goes on. Where a mere shadow of justice has been preserved things are calm; in several hamlets peasant communities have refused to accept any change or else just asked for no one else but the *landlord himself* to explain the law to them. Strange how in life good and bad things are woven together. Nowicki is not letting his wife join him, as he is hoping to get back soon. In Żytomierz all charitable institutions were closed down. Soon afterwards the old Bożydar died. His peasants got a merciless thrashing before the Governor, on the square which we know so well.

The University will remain closed for one year. Popowski committed suicide, apparently because of the over-democratic ideas of his sons.

The meeting of the Kiev Credit Society is to convene on 16 June. Vasilchikov has authorized Hołowiński to assemble fifty people from three provinces. That is including the marshals. Except for them, to date, no one is planning to go, not even Adolf and Tadeusz.[1]

None of your letters has been lost: with God's help may it be so in the future! Your return seems to me so dangerous that I do not very much want you to come. I prefer to pray to God for your protection, and to bestow love on you from afar. You do the same.

Ewelina

Daddy,

I am fine here, I run about the garden – but I don't like it much when the mosquitos bite. As soon as the rain stops I will come to you. Olutek has sent me a beautiful little whip. Please Daddy dear lend me a few pennies and buy something for Olutek in Warsaw.

Have you been to see this *Bozia*,[2] which Granny ...

Konrad.

---

[1] The 'not even' here is quite telling.

[2] Literally 'little God', the name used by Polish children for God and for the effigies of God (and sometimes of the Virgin Mary). The boy had probably in mind either the famous painting of the 'Black Madonna' at Częstochowa, or the celebrated crucifix in Warsaw cathedral.

Ewa Korzeniowska to Apollo Korzeniowski
Kobieta Współczesna (Lwów), 1931, no. 18

28 May/9 June 1861, Nowofastów
My beloved. I have just received your letter of 19 May, describing the Corpus Christi service. Thanks be to God that you could pray among them and thanks be to God that you are not suffering too much and that you are more or less all right.

This is my ninth letter to you; two of them were sent by hand. I cannot understand why they did not all reach you. How can I advise you, my dearest? The circumstances of your existence and personal situation *over there* are not known to me; *over here* I see nothing for us except insecurity. How is one to choose? I agree with all my heart with whatever you do. Just like you I trust least and rely least on newspapers. Just like you I wish you to enter into closer contact with the circles which are inaccessible to you on account of Kazimierz's[1] absence. Just like you I wish for an appointment in some theatre management. No less than you, I am prepared to renounce all the joys of life so as not to be defiled by *that* which throughout your life you have tried to shun and which until now you have not touched. You, over there, so deeply engrossed in prayer, fortified, inspired, uplifted by the surge of your inner spiritual life – whatever you do will be better than any advice of mine given in the dark. I submit myself entirely to your decisions; do not feel constricted by worries on my account. I shall always be happy with you.

Anyway you will know my thoughts – however fallible – when you read my letters. And if they do not reach you, it will mean that I am wrong and that God is not on my side.

We are all well, and everybody asks after you and sends you love. Mother in the first place. Konradek mentions you every day, asking, 'When shall we go to Daddy?'

Each day I commend you to God a hundred times. I am doing it right now, my dearest; be strong and persevering, and if you trust my instinct stop counting on newspapers but look for other occupations; none would impair your chances of earning money from journalism if you should feel inclined that way.

Ah! You do not know, or perhaps you do know what dreams I have about your future dramas: what a lot of marvellous scenes charged with

---

[1] Kazimierz Kaszewski (1825–1910), critic, playwright, translator, journalist. He took part in the 1848 insurrection in Polish provinces of Prussia and in the Hungarian revolution of the same year. He was active in the Polish patriotic movement of 1863–4. In 1866 he married Miłosława Sławianowska.

Truth and the Sublime are quite ready waiting and demanding their author!

Think, think of me and of what I am writing. Adolf was to telegraph Kaz[imierz], then yourself. He may already have done it. God be with you and with all that you do.

Ewelina.

Ewa Korzeniowska to Apollo Korzeniowski

Kobieta Współczesna (Lwów), 1931, no. 18

9/21 June 1861, Żytomierz

Apolek,[1] my dear, my most beloved among men, tell me how to love so as to guard you against misfortune? Tell me how to get my prayers heard so that you should be inspired and protected by God.

I am sending this letter by hand again, though you dislike it; but I cannot do otherwise. This is the third letter bearing the same news down to the last detail. Everybody is convinced that if you return they will soon take you. *Many* in Żytomierz say so and some even maintain they have seen the order itself that you are to 'be sent away on your return'. Where to? I do not know. I even doubt whether anyone really saw the order; but I feel it is true in substance.

That kind of gossip always turns out to be true. I shall give you several instances of this kind.

(1) On the second day of the holiday local officials asked Radkiewicz where you had gone to.

(2) Several days later the same officials reprimanded him for not having told the truth and, in order to prove their own knowledge, they told him that you were in Warsaw and I in the Skwira district.

(3) Later they asked what you had done with the people who worked for you and they looked for them all over town. This is the story until 17 May.

(4) Just before the end of May, Kaftiarov, the superintendent of the Berdyczów police, appeared in disguise, without ringing the bell, at the gate of Terechowa, and questioned people in the stables as to who was in the manor house, and finally, explicitly, whether you had already returned to Warsaw. Moreover, he said that he was *your friend* and wanted to see you about something; he said that you had written to him saying you would be back by then. Łukasz came by and recognized him. We learned about it all accidentally several days later.

Now you have read it, decide if it is worth returning.

---

[1] Diminutive of Apollo.

I know that if the things that happened at Zamoyski's will require your return you will not hesitate, and naturally, I am prepared for it.[1] But for God's sake do not return on account of personal matters. It is not worth it. If you should summon me, I shall come. I shall manage and find the money for the journey. If you prefer, I shall stay here – I shall stay and not grumble. In short: I do not want *to make things difficult*, I shall arrange everything just as you would, and in the name of your love for me, please take care of yourself.

Here everything and everybody is plunged in complete silence. Mourning is spreading, no one came to Wrangel's[2] farewell ball, the *hymn*[3] was sung again on Ascension Day. Well-meaning posters were put up encouraging people to persevere with clothing bodies and hearts in mourning until the day when 'Hallelujah' can be sung to our resurrected Mother.[4]

Several women's homes have been searched. I am prepared for it, rest assured. Anyway I am convinced they will not do it. They will not want to cause alarm and will wait for your return.

I keep saying that I do not know when you will return as you are about to leave for St Petersburg. I keep maintaining that you will return but not very soon. As to myself, I shall stay here one month to take the baths. If you do not want to remain over there for good, extend your stay for the whole of June, perhaps by then it will become clear what the danger here is all about, and perhaps you will get a chance to do something at the Fair.[5]

Perhaps you could sell *Hernani* and *Les Burgraves*?[6] I can manage but it would be much nicer if you sent the money!

I do not know how things are over here but Nowicka and Marylka wring their hands, convinced that a marked regression has taken place in the general sentiments after your and Nowicki's[7] departure.

Plater as kind as ever. Now he has gone to St Petersburg on account of the high school, which is constantly under attack.

[1] Almost certainly Count Andrzej Zamoyski (1800–74), a leading political personality, the unofficial head of the moderate 'Whites', who supported limited social reforms, spurned revolutionary action and demanded autonomy for Poland. He was exiled to Russia in 1862. Probably Korzeniowski negotiated with Zamoyski about his support for the planned bi-weekly.

[2] A Russian general, stationed in Żytomierz.

[3] *Boże, coś Polskę...*, the religious hymn sung on national occasions; it begins with the words 'Oh God, who for so many centuries bestowed on Poland much power and glory...'

[4] I.e. Poland.   [5] The Kiev fair, held twice a year (in February and August).

[6] Victor Hugo's plays which Korzeniowski had translated. Of *Les Burgraves* only a few scenes were published, as early as 1846; *Hernani* was just about to be published in *Biblioteka Warszawska*.

[7] Dr Fortunat Nowicki (1830–85), physician, recently exiled to Tambov for his political activities.

I have not seen any men. Rowiński is at Berdyczów, and I do not want to listen to Knol[l].[1] He shakes his head awfully whenever he speaks of you. May God protect you. May He do with us whatever is best or ordained.

Ewelina

Ewa Korzeniowska to Apollo Korzeniowski
Kobieta Współczesna (Lwów), 1931, no. 18

16/28 June [1861], Teterów

My dear Apolek,

Adolf has telegraphed about the *second* group of debtors, that means *the worst*.[2] Of the first kind neither he nor I know anything.

You must have received the letter through Bogdanowicz. Affected by the details you found therein, I wrote to Terechowa a not too cheerful letter, and Adolf was so kind as to come over with his wife to bring me consolation. For the last three days he has been constantly inventing would-be distractions so that all of us – his wife, Mrs Pruszyńka, Marylka and I – are tired to death. To prolong the entertainment he stops us from going to bed, makes us sit up till nine o'clock at night and wakes everybody up for a bath at five in the morning. But what is one to do? We play the game. Actually we did make a lovely excursion on the water. Tomorrow Adolf and his wife are leaving.

Konradek and I are both well. Bathing does me good as usual.

Do you want me to send you Fortunat's[3] letter? I have answered him on your behalf but perhaps you too ought to write. It is hard to imagine how that miserable man eats his heart out over there. Mrs Nowicka is still here, her husband keeps detaining her; she yields to him but, obviously, her health suffers through the delay.

What do you want me to do with Ohryzko's[4] books on your shelf? I have a dozen or so copies of Goethe and the same number of books on Electricity and Magnets.[5] I would like to settle everything here as well as possible. Try writing a few times direct to Żytomierz. I think it will be all right. I shall stay here at Teterów waiting for your decision.

You cannot imagine how pleased I was by what you said about Pan Andrzej.[6] My heart felt as if you gave me back a most precious and lost illusion. You must have met so many by now!

Tadeusz called on me for about half an hour on his way to the

---

[1] Ignacy Knoll, a landowner from Volhynia. [2] I.e. the police.
[3] Dr Fortunat Nowicki; see note 7, p. 46.
[4] Józefat Ohryzko (1827–90), a Polish publisher in St Petersburg.
[5] Published by Ohryzko.
[6] Most probably Count Andrzej Zamoyski; see note 1, p. 46.

Wołodkowiczs in the Tarnów district. Tomorrow he will drop in again
on me for a while *en route* to Kiev where the Credit Society is holding a
meeting.

The intermediaries in the Lipowiec district: two Czarnowskis,
Zawistowski from Troszcza;[1] I cannot recall the fourth one.

In the Radomyśl district: Dr Duszyński, Wierzbicki – the best.
Others (six of them) not so well chosen, cannot remember the names.

Yesterday two youngsters from the High School and a Kiev student
were arrested for impolite remarks made in the street about Kaniński of
the police.

Strojnowski, by the Ministry's order, removed from professorship in
Żytomierz for causing unrest among the high school pupils; sent off for
punishment to Chodorków for an unspecified length of time. One
Father Zaleski from the village taken to Kiev.

Wilga, whom I wrote to you about, is in the Kiev fortress. His wife
dying of despair.

That would be all. They keep nagging and calling so I must finish.
Ah! My embraces defy all description. Hope you can feel them –
properly too.

Ewelina

(to be contd.)

Ewa Korzeniowska to Apollo Korzeniowski

Kobieta Współczesna (Lwów), 1931, no. 19

19 June/1 July 1861, Żytomierz

Apolleczek, my dear,

You complain that I do not write often enough. Darling! Experienced people say that this way it is safer for you. So, half believing, I half
obey. Do not hold it against me.

Oh! How we miss you at home, you cannot imagine and I should
probably be unable to express it. Good Mrs Pruszyńska kinder than
ever. I spend entire days with her and one hour on my own at home is
enough to make me feel as if centuries have passed since your departure
– there is such an all-pervading emptiness at home.

Give me something to do while we are separated. I tried to set to
work on the piano but thirty strings have been missing for six months.
Apart from my ears I could damage the instrument and cause financial
loss, so it is not possible.

---

[1] Elected by the *szlachta* to mediate between the government authorities, landowners,
and the newly liberated peasants.

Make me do some translations. Find something new and readable. I should so much like to carry at least a small proportion of the cost of living. I am thinking about it particularly in the event of our settling down *there*. Meanwhile I am idling my time away and this thought is troubling me.

Ah! Here is some consolation. This very moment I have found what I wanted: the work of Lord Elgin, title: 'Narration of the Erl [sic] of Elgin's Mission to China and Japon [sic]' by Laurence Oliphant, 2 vol. Lond. 1859 – French translation by Guizot. I must have made ghastly errors in the English title but cannot copy it any better.[1] And perhaps you will find and send – not bring – something more recent.

Yesterday Bogdanowicz set off, taking another letter for you. Heaven grant it reaches you. What about the previous ones? Believe me, I am not imparting my personal fancies to you. All I do is repeat what is generally said, and relate what I see for myself.

All is quiet here. Obviously communal life is in the doldrums. One hears nothing but it seems to me that deep down in people's hearts things are not bad. However, not everybody shares my view. Mrs Nowicka is still here. She is exhausted, poor dear, and quite ill too. I visited the Pietkiewiczes; in August they leave for Wilno. Pietkiewicz is joining the *Kurjer Wileński*. He wrote to them with the suggestion and expects to be accepted.

Whom else did I see? One Mierzejewski came to see me and very kindly enquired after you. I met Cieszkowski,[2] Kraszewski,[3] Knol[l] at Mrs Mikulicz's[4] who, having seen me at Mrs Pruszyńska's, invited me to a farewell tea party with the other ladies. I heard nothing interesting from any one of those people, over twenty of them, but saw one interesting thing: a moustache on every man's face, including Cieszkowski *et comp*. Mourning is generally observed to the extent that coloured dresses can be seen only occasionally.[5] Konradek still wears our three favourite colours;[6] but he has a mourning frock which I always make him put on for church.

Today I went to Ernest's. My heart was filled with such an

---

[1] *Narrative of the Earl of Elgin's Mission to China and Japan* (London, 1859). Korzeniowska was apparently unaware that a Polish translation had already been published.
[2] Karol Cieszkowski, a local lawyer, exiled in 1863.
[3] Józef Ignacy Kraszewski (1812–87), novelist, historian and man of letters, author of innumerable works; a great intellectual and moral authority. Editor of *Gazeta co-dzienna* (later *Gazeta Polska*); owned an estate in Volhynia. Forced to emigrate in 1863.
[4] Wife of Karol Mikulicz, the highest elected representative of the *szlachta* in Volhynia.
[5] Mourning was proclaimed by patriotic circles to commemorate the people killed by Russian soldiers in Warsaw.
[6] Blue, white and red, the colours of revolutionary France.

unreasonable longing for you that to cheer myself up I decided to send you my portrait, but the pictures are so awful and so expensive that I had to give up the idea. I am very careful and so the money will last me more than a month. You must not worry.

In a couple of days Tadeusz will be here on his way to M. Żarnowski. Otherwise I am not expecting anyone, shall stay here quietly, continuing my baths so as to be in good health for you in Warsaw.

I have met Fabiański twice in the street. Mrs Glasnepow is not being received anywhere. Mrs Kulbakinov alternates: sometimes she appears in mourning and sometimes in bright colours. Mrs Niemierzycka and Malinowska have gone away, so that after Mrs Nowicka's departure only Mrs Pruszyńska will be left of the people I like.

The Mikuliczs are leaving for Odessa for a water cure. My darling – what are you doing over there? Your letters are probably at Berdyczów and here I am without any! But one must not grumble – Better to give you a long embrace for your and my consolation.

It is night-time and Konradek is asleep. He is growing up into a lovely boy.

Ewelina.

Ewa Korzeniowska to Apollo Korzeniowski

Kobieta Współczesna (Lwów), 1931, no. 19

20 June/2 July 1861

My dearest Apoleczek,

The two letters written on 6 and 9 June reached me almost simultaneously. In the first one you ask about the nature of the debtors awaiting you here; in the second you inform me that your private affairs drag slowly on.

Here my reply:

The debtors, according to your own classification, belong to the second, that is *the worst*, group.

Letters through messengers must have reached you by now. If that is so, I beg of you to consider them with all speed and to inform me as soon as possible of your decisions.

If you were to call upon me to join you, I should like to get everything ready for the journey by mid-July. On 17 July Adolf is to send horses for me: then I should like to leave here for good. I could spend a couple of weeks at Terechowa, several days with Papa at Nowofastów, several days at Napedówka, several at Palcze, at Granny's, and then just before autumn I would arrive; that is at the end of August or the beginning of September. So, as you see, we should not delay matters. I shall manage the travel expenses; all I am worried about is that in spite of all my endeavours I am now unable to send you anything at all.

Let me know what I am to do with Ohryzko's books. And how does Łęcki's account stand? Big or small? If you were to come here *coûte que coûte*,[1] then you must also let me know; I have my reasons.

You miss me; and I do not want to speak of my longing for I know that even without words you must feel it. Besides, what is longing in comparison to the constant fear of the danger that, they say, threatens you? God is our only hope. For others it is difficult to find hope elsewhere – for us it is impossible. Let us then count on Him and His inspiration.

Have you written anything of your *Father*?[2] How is the Powązki poem getting on? Did you say a prayer over A. Zagórski's[3] grave?

Nobody here has had news as yet from Jaś and his wife and we are all anxious about them.

If you were to return, I should go and meet you at Hilary's. But as long as you do not let me know for certain, I shall not leave here.

Have pity and let me know soon: if you only knew how sad I feel!

Hilary is housebound now, but if I were to leave, Tadeusz and Adolf have offered to help me.

I shall finish now. I am tired: I have been sewing all day, a mourning frock for Konradek. Everyone is in black here, *even the children*; our little one has been constantly asking to go into mourning. It was my duty to comply. A charming boy and more good-looking every day. Love both him and me. My boundless affection,

Ewelina.

Ewa Korzeniowska to Apollo Korzeniowski
Kobieta Współczesna (Lwów), 1931, no. 22

[no date]

Dear Apoleczek,

Wiszniewski left five minutes ago, exactly five minutes, so I have had no time yet to study your letter – for I have hardly read it through once.

Wisz[niewski] left on Saturday, saw you four days ago, bade you goodbye, clasped your hand! And this very same man has just been here and from his own lips I heard about you and he spoke so kindly and described you so vividly that it seemed as if he brought a part of you to our little home. It is hard to describe and still harder to comprehend how happy I feel at this moment.

---

[1] Fr.: 'whatever the cost'. [2] *Ojciec*, a drama Korzeniowski never finished.
[3] Apolinary Zagórski (1829–59), journalist, a cousin of the Bobrowskis.

With your cigarettes I shall do what you told me. I shall send some to Fortunat through his wife who is joining him the day after tomorrow. I doubt whether Kazimierz and the crosses he is bringing will arrive in time for her.

I shall carry out all your instructions and shall bear in mind *the warnings*. I have matured a great deal during the several weeks of our separation and of constant longing combined with anxiety. When shall we be together at last?

Mrs Pruszyńska is now at Morozówka seeing off Mrs Lubo-widzka,[1] who is leaving for Odessa for a water cure. I should be frightfully lonely here if it were not for dear Mama,[2] who arrived just in time to alleviate the solitude.

You do not write when you want me to come and what should be done beforehand. It is not that I want to press for definite decisions, all I am doing is asking and informing you that they are all I am waiting and living for.

I thank you, thank you for everything you have sent. My heart is in such a flutter and I am so overwhelmed with joy that even if I tried I could not list all your gifts which have already all been unwrapped and lie around me, and I have just kissed your portrait.

God be with you, God be with us. *Au revoir*, my dearest darling. Oh! If I could see you at last ... But I shall wait patiently.

Ewelina

Ewa Korzeniowska to Apollo Korzeniowski
Kobieta Współczesna (Lwów), 1931, no. 21

5/17 July 1861

My dearest! Today is 5 July. How could I not write, if only a few words to embrace you with an even more longing affection in memory of that day! Do you remember in Terechowa? ...

Yesterday as Wiszniewski was leaving I collected your letter. Every single letter that I get from you inspires me with new life, but this one brought me consolation also. All the time, and every day, I pray that your present worries be solved favourably and I trust in God that He hears these prayers and crowns your efforts. My heart is filled with peace and quiet, while deep down there is such light and serenity that something very good must be about to come. That is what I feel, what I believe, that is what I dream of ... I can already see you in that new

---

[1] Dorota Lubowidzka, mother-in-law of Tadeusz Bobrowski.
[2] Teofila Bobrowska (d. 1875), Ewa's mother.

World[1] of yours, bearing work and responsibility with integrity, in the forefront of all that tends towards our well-deserved future, gathering around you all who have higher aims, high aspirations, energy and talent, all who are young and noble... I had never before dreamt of anything as beautiful... only 'dream, come true', my beloved!

I feel that it will 'come true'... Just as once the noble call 'Unita Italia'[2] fired my heart with elation and drew me with all possible sympathy, so today my heart trembles a thousand times more powerfully, my soul yearns for that 'Young Poland'[3] of our dreams, which you will create, rouse to life and lead into the future...

Oh God, give your blessing to the goodwill, to the earnest desire of the attainment of Your holy ends! Please send the grace of Your best inspiration, instil Your pure Truth into our heart and conscience, fortify our resolve and do not abandon us in our hard work!

Pan Kaź[imierz] not here but I am waiting patiently: 'where there is faith there is patience'.

Konrad is growing into a lovely boy. He has a heart of gold and with the ground you prepare for him there should be no problems with his conscience and mind. He often goes to church with me and almost always gives alms. When he gets tired of sitting quietly he says: 'Mummy dear, let me go outside; I shall chat with the poor because I like them very much.' Then come discourses on Granny, Daddy, sometimes on horses, bears, etc.... Not a few of those poor wretches are amused and gratified. They call him 'our dear young master, our protector'. Today the same thing happened again.

I am enclosing Mr Jort's letter. I have answered it immediately on your and my behalf.

Mama is leaving in four days. I am planning to say goodbye to Żytomierz by the middle of this month. The place is deserted and silent. Apart from *Hrabiorek* nobody is here. A thousand embraces.

Ewelina

---

[1] *Świat*, one of the planned titles of the bi-weekly Korzeniowski intended to publish in Warsaw.
[2] 'United Italy', the maxim of Italian patriots striving to unite their country.
[3] *Młoda Polska*, a semi-secret organization started in 1834 in Bern as part of the Young Europe, formed by Italian, German and Polish emigrants. Their aim was to gain independence for and establish democracy in their countries.

Ewa Korzeniowska to Apollo Korzeniowski

Kobieta Współczesna (Lwów), 1931, no. 21

8/20 July 1861

My best darling,

You grumble at my not writing often enough; would you believe that since I saw good Wiszniewski this is the fourth time I have scribbled to you and since our separation I have been constantly dispatching letters at approximately the same rate. I am amazed at your not receiving them; yours, thank God, arrive most regularly down to the tiniest scrap of paper.

Although your plans are still unsettled in detail, I regard our removal as imminent and have already begun preparations for departure so as to be ready to leave the moment you call me. I calculate that I need one month to make the rounds bidding goodbye to the family. And so I shall try to leave Żytomierz around the 20th inst. so as to spend a little time with Papa[1] at Nowofastów, then at Hilary's, and to embrace you at last by the end of August.

Such is my general plan. As to the details, I am waiting for your directives. Namely: (1) what about our library, (2) our carriages, (3) the furniture in the living-room, (4) accounts with Łecki, Budkiewicz, Adolf and Kołyszkowa,[2] (5) Ohryzko's books, (6) glassware and sideboard contents in general?

Forgive the medley of questions set out in a disorderly fashion; I was jotting them down as they came to mind. Anyhow, you are not a great lover of orderliness.

Tadeusz, Pruszyńska, Hilary will divide among themselves the furniture from the rest of the house. I shall give your fur coat to Papa. [Illegible word] may perhaps be given to Hilary or Emilcia.[3] What do you think?

How are the townspeople treating you? Shall I be a councillor's wife?[4] I am terribly interested and you say nothing.

Here too the article in no. 153 of *Gazeta Polska* raised voices of discontent: it is only natural.[5] Mrs Kraszewska on her way to Kisiele is

[1] Teodor Korzeniowski (d. 1863), Apollo's father.
[2] Dorota Kołyszkowa, widow of Władysław Kołyszko.
[3] Diminutive of Emilia; possibly Apollo Korzeniowski's sister.
[4] Elections for the Warsaw city council were scheduled for September, but Korzeniowski, although politically very active, was not a candidate. He supported participation in the elections only conditionally.
[5] The editorial in *Gazeta Polska* of 14/26 June advocated a calm and cooperative attitude towards the unnamed 'new regulations', i.e. the tzar's decrees of 18 June 1861 announcing elections to local and provincial councils.

expected here today. I shall look for her tomorrow. Who knows, perhaps she saw you before she left? Perhaps she will give me some news?

Did you get the photograph? I was looking forward to sending you Konradek's as well but it cannot be done, for the little one pleads against it. He says that Antos's brother [Pietkiewicz] in Warsaw can paint better. Perhaps he is right, so I am putting it off till Warsaw but I feel sorry on your account.

Cieszkowski was to send you today a list of local events but warned that they are few and uninteresting. I met him at the baths and attacked him with my request. He promised and I hope he keeps his word!

Last Wednesday Pietkiewicz sent off his work to Wóycicki[1] but I do not even know what it is. Something is wrong with Pietkiewicz: he is terribly sour. His wife's explanation is that he is upset by the *Kurjer's*[2] refusal. Unable to do anything with himself, he is going to remain in Żytomierz.

The count and countess have been scandalizing the town by arranging *soirées* for the Glasnaps, Mrs Braunszwejg and Mr Borozdin. The lady herself never has enough of the latter's music and constantly sings for him. I listen to it from the garden. Otherwise I see no one apart from Mierzejewski and Romański. Prusinowski called today, but I was out.

It troubles me not to be able to give you the news you desire but I know and hear nothing. I would not be living in such a tomb if the dear Nowickis were here.

No one around. Even the streets look deserted.

Our whole family is well. Hilary is rooted to the estate, Adolf and his wife are there too; about Papa I know nothing because he does not write to me. As far as possible I often try to send him your news.

Dear Marcelka! I am happy about her marriage and love her friend. Your chronicles are liked here.[3] You do the right thing with *Hernani*.[4] May God keep Kraszewski in good health. I have not read yet about the 'accursed tree'.[5] Millions of kisses – pay them back with interest.

Ewelina

---

[1] Kazimierz Władysław Wóycicki (1807–79), historian and lawyer, editor of the monthly *Biblioteka Warszawska*.

[2] *Kurjer warszawski*, a Warsaw journal.

[3] Korzeniowski's accounts of cultural life 'behind the Bug', i.e., in the former Polish provinces on the eastern side of this river, published in Warsaw's *Tygodnik Ilustrowany*, were titled *Kroniki*, 'Chronicles'.

[4] See note 7 to the letter of 9/21 June.   [5] Unidentified.

Teofila Bobrowska to Apollo Korzeniowski

Kobieta Współczesna (Lwów), 1931, no. 22

8/20 July 1861

From your letter to Ewunia[1] I know, my dear Apollo, that you have written to me as well. Probably on my return to Nowofastów I shall find your precious words which are now the only link bridging the distance between us. May God sweeten it with good news about your health and success. He has already poured so much grief into my heart that by comparison everything now seems trivial or else fills my heart to the brim. Thus now my thoughts too rejoice at your decision to settle in Warsaw, and feelings seal my lips with the desire that my dear Ewunia should not be upset when leaving me ... Darling Ewunieczka[1] is in good health, bathes regularly. Since Mrs Pruszyńska's and Marylka's departure we have lived in absolute peace and quiet. I share Stefcio's[2] opinion that Mrs Pietkiewicz holds her husband on so short a leash that he is sure never to make an appearance at Ewunia's; I should also be glad to see her settled and gone from Żytomierz as soon as possible – for your sake and for ours, so that she could join you as soon as possible, because (speaking frankly), I fear the consequences that prolonged longing has on the health – but do not tell her that, as she may bear a grudge against me for presenting her to you as a weak-spirited person when in fact she does her best to derive comfort from your dear and very welcome letters. She finds comfort not the least in her beloved child: truly, no pen could catch and render all the shades of goodness that child has in him. Imagine, he has become great friends with the poor, tells them all the details of our family life and asks them to pray for his Daddy's safe return from Warsaw. I learned it from women beggars at church. When I am at the baths people kiss him for being so lovely and well behaved. Yesterday to amuse him I took him for a drive. Suddenly two ladies appear and he promptly enquires if he should make room for them. You can easily imagine how they smothered him with kisses. And his affectionate words to the Nowickis were quite un-childlike. I suspect that our dear Konradzio[3] will grow into an exceptional man with a great heart. Sometimes his tenderness towards me brings a tear into my eyes, so once he said: 'I am speaking nicely to you, Granny, and you behave like a cry-baby, it is naughty.' But he was so moved himself that his voice shook. Well, this is what your beloved boy is like and may God protect him, as well as yourself,

---

[1] Ewunia, Ewunieczka are diminutives of Ewa.
[2] Diminutive of Stefan, Ewa's brother (1840–63).
[3] Diminutive of Conrad.

my dear son, for whom I pray and send my most tender love and blessings.

Your Mother Bobrowska

PS. What does Spasowicz[1] say about Kazio?[2] He wrote to me that he
was doing well in his examinations.

Ewa Korzeniowska to Antoni Pietkiewicz

Obshchestvenno-politicheskie dvizhenia na Ukrainie 1856–1862 (Kiev, 1963),
pp. 139–40

27 July/8 August 1861

They say that a great distance separating people weakens their affection,
and may even extinguish it. I do not know if this is sometimes the case, but
I well know that your remoteness brings me closer to you both every day,
with a growing sense of attachment and heart-felt nostalgia.

I was sorry not to have had a reply from you to my June letter –
perhaps you never received it. And I am extremely sorry not to know any
details of your dear wife's journey. All that reached me is news from
Kiev; what happened later? I know nothing. I myself am on the point of
leaving Żytomierz, and for good. Today I have been saying goodbye to
friends – not social acquaintances but friends close to my heart. Of
course I paid you a call as well. I stopped by the gate, looked at the dear
little house and prayed to God for your speedy return. I have just come
back from there and I am saying goodbye to you for a second time, my
last goodbye from Żytomierz: now I shall wait to be greeted by you in
Warsaw.

Apolek never went to St Petersburg. He came to the conclusion that
it would not be possible for him to obtain a permission for a newspaper
in Żytomierz; such things, although not easy, are nevertheless more
likely in Warsaw. He decided to try his luck and after some difficulties
bought Dmochowski's *Świat*;[3] he wants to change it into a Polish
fortnightly, similar to the *Revue des deux mondes*. The new periodical will
be called *Kraj*. Apolek is the proprietor and editor in chief; other
members of the editorial staff will be: E[h]renberg,[4] Aleksander

---

[1] Włodzimierz Spasowicz (1829–1906), prominent lawyer and historian of literature, at
that time professor of law at St Petersburg University. Later he became a leading
conservative advocate of reconciliation with Russia.

[2] Diminutive of Kazimierz, Ewa's brother (1837–86). He was attempting to enter a
military academy in St Petersburg, but failed his examination.

[3] *Świat* was a short-lived periodical of which four issues appeared in 1861, edited by F.
S. Dmochowski and Z. Zaborowski.

[4] Gustaw Ehrenberg (1818–95), illegitimate son of Alexander I and Helena Rauten-
strauch (née Dzierżanowska), poet and patriotic conspirator, sentenced to death in
1839; the sentence was commuted to hard labour; he served 15 years, was released in
1858 and was arrested again in January 1862.

Krajewski[1], Kazimierz Kaszewski, and a little later Wł. Spasowicz, who plans to settle in Warsaw before the end of the year. This is all I am able to impart to you now in the way of information; you will learn more in a few weeks' time from the prospectus.[2]

I am leaving for the Ukraine and shall be in Warsaw only at the end of August. I miss Apolek more than words can express, and my heart bursts with longing after him. But at the same time I find it difficult to part with my family, particularly with my mother, who, while blessing me for the journey with one hand, holds me back with her other hand, crying bitterly.

If you want to comfort me on my new path in life please write to Warsaw – and write soon! Let your letter be among the first I get there just as it will be among the most welcome. Send it *poste restante*.

Once again I bid you farewell. Preserve the memory of us in your hearts and thoughts. God be with you and with us. Goodbye!

Ewelina Korzeniowska

Apollo Korzeniowski imprisoned
Bobrowski, 'Memoirs', II, 465

Towards the end of October 1861 news reached us about the imprisonment of my brother-in-law Korzeniowski in the Warsaw Citadel.[3] Therefore my mother immediately left for Warsaw and soon my brother [Stefan] informed me that as he desired to visit our distressed sister and mother at Christmas, he would not be coming to stay with me, which I considered a perfectly justified decision.

Ewa Korzeniowska to Mr and Mrs Antoni Pietkiewicz
Obshchestvenno-politicheskie dvizhenia na Ukraine 1856–1862 (Kiev, 1963), 175–6

19 November 1861

Dear Friends,

Forgive my long silence; if you knew how many unpleasant things have caused it, you would undoubtedly find me excused.

[1] Aleksander Albert Krajewski (1808–1903), literary critic, journalist, conspirator. In 1838–57 he served the sentence of hard labour; in January 1862 he was exiled to Tambov.

[2] The prospectus, signed by Apollo Korzeniowski, was published in Warsaw as a broadsheet and reprinted by *Biblioteka Warszawska* and *Pszczółka*. The title was finally decided as *Dwutygodnik* ('Bi-weekly'). In four sections the periodical was to publish texts literary, critical, historical and scholarly (economy, agriculture, industry, commerce, jurisprudence); and reports of travels. The first issue was to appear on 15 November 1861.

[3] Korzeniowski was arrested on 20 October 1861.

Your last letters never reached Apolek because he, with a number of others, has been locked up in the Citadel.

You have probably heard about us. I must say that on 15, 16 and 17 October we saw things here reminiscent of the April events.[1] There were probably fewer bloody victims but the external situation was the same. Even now it is terrible to think about it.

Night-time arrests began on 18 October and they have been going on without interruption until now. Several hundred people have been taken; among them old Białobrzeski,[2] spiritual and official deputy of the deceased archbishop, and over thirty Catholic priests from Warsaw itself, not counting those brought from the provinces, five of whom have been already sent to Siberia; a dozen or so most distinguished Rabbis; three pastors of the Reformed Church; people of all estates, wealth, age and situation; among them several women.

Apolek was taken on 20 October at half past midnight. We were both awake: he writing, I reading. Six minutes after the door-bell had rung he was gone from the house.

Until now I have not been allowed to see him. I go to the Citadel every day to enquire about his health and I am informed about it verbally; a few times a week I take food and linen for him, and every ten days I am allowed to submit a short note for him to the Citadel censorship; and a few days later I receive a reply through the same channel.

Every morning I find a crowd of women by the Citadel gate; they are there for the same reason as myself. Sometimes we stand there a whole day, in rain and cold, waiting for a short note, for some news, and sometimes we wait in vain. Once, to get warm and to pass the time, we counted ourselves: we were several score more than two hundred, and the group grows larger each day.

After a great deal of effort I was given permission to send Apolek a prayer-book and Robertson's text-book for learning English.[3] *Nothing else* – but even this gave him some comfort.

We ask ourselves what will they do with all those prisoners? It is certain that for the next ten days their number will increase. But what

---

[1] On 8 April Russian soldiers, salvoing into an unarmed demonstration, killed about one hundred men and women. On 15 October (anniversary of the death of Tadeusz Kościuszko) demonstrations were violently suppressed by Cossacks and people gathered in churches were forcibly removed, with 1,678 arrested.

[2] Rev. Antoni Białobrzeski (1793–1868) was administering the archdiocese of Warsaw. He was sentenced to death for refusing to reopen the desecrated churches, then reprieved and exiled to Russia.

[3] Theodore Robertson, *Nouveau Cours pratique, analytique, théorique et synthétique de langue anglaise*, many editions.

then? It is generally believed that all will be released but not before next month at the *earliest*. No use expecting any change before then.

And what is your news, my poor beloved friends? Are you both still as lonely as before? Have you by any chance seen the two Dubiecki brothers,[1] or Stefan Bobrowski? Cit[izen] Lipski? They say that many have gone to your parts[2] (from the other side of the Bug).

I clasp your hands. Enough for today. Next month I shall write again; and I am waiting for a letter from you both – and commend you to God as ever

Ewelina Korzeniowska

The three of us in good health. And you both? Write to us *poste restante* and send your exact address.

Ewa Korzeniowska to Antoni Pietkiewicz

Obshchestvenno-politicheskie dvizhenia na Ukrainie 1856–1862 (Kiev, 1963), 208–9

7 January 1862

Your letter arrived this morning: you must admit I am quick to reply to it. I received it as I was leaving to go to Apolek. I read it on my way there, and with the details presented by you still fresh in my mind, I tried to repeat all you had asked me to. Nevertheless I was unable to comply with your request: the [holy] wafer[3] was returned to me and it has to await Apolek's return home together with many other precious gifts which keep arriving for him from all sides. Only once, on Christmas Eve, we (wives and mothers) were allowed to clasp the prisoners' hands and to break wafers with them; but the regular visits are different: a closely woven wire mesh separates visitors from prisoners; words freeze on the lips amidst repeated cries of 'not allowed' by numerous witnesses, the watchful and brutal guards; there are three categories of them: clerks in plain clothes, officers and soldiers. This torture lasts five minutes *at the most*. Such are our meetings.

And how are you both and what is your news? I am surprised and sorry to hear that Owrucz is such a sleepy place; I know tiny, very tiny villages in Volhynia which are yet quite lively.

---

[1] Aleksander (1824–68), journalist, and Marian (1838–1926), historian; both took part in the 1863 uprising.

[2] The Pietkiewiczs were still in Żytomierz.

[3] The wafer, blessed by a priest, according to a Polish custom broken and eaten before the Christmas Eve supper.

Things here have not changed: constant arrests and hardly any men released; the rest, whether under investigation or not, are kept in the Citadel in complete ignorance of their fate. A dozen or so priests have been deported to Siberia. Twenty-six Warsaw youths and as many again from the Kalisz and Lublin districts were dispatched on foot as plain soldiers to join the Orenburg regiments. I witnessed their leave-taking: the spectacle was anything but joyful. I myself bade farewell to two friends.

The town is sad, black and silent: people suffer for the victims, whose number grows daily. No one remembers such a start to a New Year. Even the holiday season did nothing to enliven the appearance of the streets: silence and desolation everywhere. Only the Citadel's iron gate is daily surrounded by crowds: so serious, grief-stricken and mournful that it is neither possible nor proper to think only of one's own suffering.

Apolek's case has not begun yet, or rather it does not exist at all. He was arrested – no one knows why; during the house-search *nothing* was found; *not one* accusation has been made until now; he was not asked about *anything*. How is one to guess what they accuse him of?

I had a problem: he had been ill, poor darling, but now he is almost well again. The lack of exercise and the [word unclear] heat of prison must have affected his health. But he is in good spirits, calm and relaxed and during our short and rare meetings we can really joke about things. This is permitted. The sight of tears is not liked and I must say they are never seen. In this respect the public is exemplary: so well-behaved and unruffled.

Please do not reproach me for not having been the first to write to you: it is not possible to meet all one's obligations. Send me news of [erased]; I need none about Żytomierz; [erased] I get many letters from there.

I shall let you know if there are new developments in Apolek's case. Otherwise I shall not be writing unless to answer your letters. Forgive me but I have neither the time nor the heart for this sad correspondence.

> Goodbye and keep well; God be
> with you both and with us
> E. Korzeniowska

The investigation and the court's verdict in the case of Apollo and Ewa Korzeniowski
Archiwum Główne Akt Dawnych (AGAD), Warsaw, Sumariusz Stałej Komisji Śledczej, II, 4091

Summary of the Records of the Permanent Board of Investigation, Part II, no. 4091.

Apollo Korzeniowski, writer, born in the Province of Kiev, a resident of Warsaw.

He was arrested on a variety of charges:

1. That he maintained close contact with Leon Frankowski[1] and Kazimierz Sikorski,[2] students from the Warsaw Real Gymnasium, and with [Stanisław] Szachowski[3] and Wojciech Gliks [Glikselli],[4] students from the Art School, and with some others who, acting under his leadership and in accordance with his instructions, formed something like a committee called 'The Mierosławski's Reds' which opposed the elections to the Warsaw City Council.[5]

2. That assisted by the students from the Art School and from the Real Gymnasium, he was the chief instigator of brawls in Wedel's confectionary shop on Miodowa Street.[6]

3. That he is the author of the mandate advocating a union between Lithuania and Poland, and of an illegal proclamation entitled 'Nation Beware.'[7]

---

[1] Frankowski (1843–63) was active on the left wing of 'Reds', took part in the 1863 insurrection, and was captured and hanged.
[2] Born in 1842, Sikorski later studied at the Polish military school in Cuneo, Italy; he returned to Poland in 1863, was arrested and sentenced to twelve years' hard labour.
[3] Szachowski (1843–1906), sculptor; he later studied at Cuneo; after the uprising he emigrated to Lwów, where he became professor of Roman law.
[4] Glikselli (1841–82), was active on the left wing of 'Reds'.
[5] Such a committee never existed, and Apollo Korzeniowski did not oppose the elections to the Warsaw city council.
[6] Nothing is known about these 'brawls', which probably consisted of singing forbidden patriotic songs.
[7] In August 1861 Korzeniowski published, anonymously, a pamphlet *Co mamy z tym fantem zrobić, co go trzymamy w ręku?* 'What should we do with the forfeit we are holding in our hands?'). He advocated the idea that members of the new councils should be elected with the mandate to champion Polish national rights and also to remind people that Lithuania and Ruthenia ought to be given the right to reunite with the Polish Kingdom. He did not, however, write *Narodzie, baczność!* ('Nation, Beware!'), a highly inflammatory, radical pamphlet addressed to peasants and artisans.

4. That before his arrival in Warsaw, in June 1861, he had organized in Żytomierz communal prayers for people who had been killed in Warsaw by the Russians during the political demonstrations; and that his wife had been distributing black crape as a sign of mourning.

Although the defendant admitted none of the above charges, nor any others, indirect evidence of his activities and of his alien way of thinking was found in the letters from his wife, and from a certain [Miss] Czarnecka[1] from Żytomierz, discovered in his possession. Amongst other things those letters warn him against returning to Żytomierz where he may be arrested. When giving evidence the defendant attributed a different meaning to those letters, and his wife even denied having written them.

[Under the heading: 'Date of submission of the case and the Commission's conclusion']
23 March/4 April 1862, no. 628. To be transferred to the Military Court for decision.

[Under the heading: 'Verdict']
27 April/9 May 1862, no. 998. It has been ordered that Korzeniowski and his wife be sent to settle in the town of Perm under strict police supervision.

The Korzeniowskis go into exile
Bobrowski, 'Memoirs', II, 457–9

Meanwhile events were running their natural course. As to my family, my brother-in-law Korzeniowski was the first victim. Recruited by members of the patriotic movement, he had gone to Warsaw under the pretence of doing some literary work; he even opened the subscription to a monthly magazine *Słowo*,[2] a publication similar to the *Revue des deux mondes*; and he also took up a high position in the Warsaw movement. Quite soon, however, in October 1861 Korzeniowski was arrested and sent to the Citadel, where he was tried by a Commission whose chairman was Colonel Rozhnov,[3] a one-time colleague of my brother Stanisław[4] from the regiment of the Grodno hussars and later governor of Warsaw. Colonel Rozhnov regarded the sentencing of Korzeniowski 'only' to exile and settlement in distant provinces as a

[1] Maria Czarnecka (1842–69), later married Władysław Mniszek.
[2] In fact, a bi-weekly, *Dwutygodnik*.
[3] Evgeni Rozhnov (1807–75), later general, 1864–6 governor-general of Warsaw.
[4] Stanisław Bobrowski (1827–59), officer in the mounted guards.

sign of his particular consideration for his friendship with my brother. Korzeniowski asked to be sent to Perm, where the governor was General Lashkarev,[1] Korzeniowski's former schoolmate and friend. The general, however, on learning about the sentence, asked not to have Korzeniowski in his province. And so the Korzeniowskis (for he was accompanied by his wife and their four-year-old son), who had almost reached Perm, were diverted to Vologda, where the governor was a kindly Bielo-Russian, Chomiński[2] (former marshal of the *szlachta* in one of the districts of Mohylew Province), who knew how to reconcile the duties of his office with a humanitarian approach. On the journey, one station before Moscow, the Korzeniowskis' little son became ill, and when the escorting guards refused them permission to break the journey, the desperate parents announced that nothing short of physical force would make them continue. A sympathetic traveller on his way to Moscow promised to send a doctor and Korzeniowski, recalling that he had a friend in Moscow, Dr Młodzianowski,[3] a university professor who at one time had been his tutor at Winnica, sent an appeal for help through the traveller. Thus the kind Aesculapius arrived soon and saved the child from acute meningitis; as the doctor had wide connections in Moscow he managed to obtain permission for a few days' delay, so that the child could stand the journey. As they were approaching Nizhni Novgorod my sister became so weak that the gendarmes had to carry her in and out of the carriage, stubbornly refusing, however, the necessary respite. An officer of the Guards passing by the post at Nizhni was so incensed by the gendarmes' ruthless and brutal treatment of the escorted party, as well as by their complete disregard of his own admonitions, that he returned to town to inform the local governor and the colonel of the gendarmes of what he had seen. The colonel of the gendarmes, who was in command of the escort, instantly arrived at the post and ordered a break in the journey. Having by some lucky chance glanced at an album with photographs carried by the travellers, he learned that Mrs Korzeniowska was a sister of his colleague (once again our brother Stanisław), a discovery which made him transfer the family from the post-house to town, where they were put up in an apartment in a government house to rest and gather strength for further journeying.

[1] Alexandr Lashkarev (1823–98), general, governor of Perm 1861–5.
[2] Stanisław Chomiński (1814–86), landowner from Wilno province, governor of Kaunas 1857–61, suspected of pro-Polish sympathies and transferred to the governorship of Vologda.
[3] Kornel Młodzianowski (1818–65), professor of pathology first at Wilno and later at Moscow University.

In Vologda the Korzeniowskis found twenty-one men, mostly priests from the Kingdom and from Lithuania. My sister was the twenty-second person and their son the twenty-third to join the Vologda Polish colony,[1] and although all were quite tolerably treated by the authorities, the climate took its toll. Almost all the men suffered from scurvy; my sister and her small son did not succumb to the disease, but the unhealthy, damp climate and a changed way of life sapped their strength ... Governor Chomiński, with the help of Zorin, a colonel of the gendarmes (another comrade of our brother's), who was quite ruthless towards the other exiles, managed to arrange, by means of several reports and intercessions, a transfer of the Korzeniowskis to Chernikhov, where they arrived in the summer of 1863,[2] unescorted by the gendarmes, purely on trust, to the considerable surprise of the Chernikhov governor, Prince Golitsyn, a tolerant and reasonable man. My sister, regarded only as accompanying her husband, was given a permit to come to me for a few months for 'family reasons'. Her health had visibly weakened by then and required prolonged rest and treatment, but we were unable to provide either one or the other, for when those few months were over the all-powerful Governor Bezak[3] gave an order forbidding her to stay on under any pretext; should she plead ill-health he instructed the Skwira police inspector to transport her to the military hospital in Kiev. The inspector himself, wishing to avoid that extreme measure, warned me about it in confidence. Thus at the beginning of the autumn of 1863 my sister had to leave for Chernikhov; she was accompanied by our mother.

Apollo Korzeniowski to Gabriela and Jan Zagórski[4]

Tygodnik Ilustrowany (Warsaw), 1920, no. 4

15/27 June 1862
Vologda, Kozlinaja St
Deviatkov's House

My beloved Gabrynia and Jaś,[5]

This is our sixteenth day at Vologda. We are in good health if you do not count my homesickness. The authorities, seeing how overworked I was on the *Dwutygodnik*, bestowed upon me their tender and paternal

---

[1] In fact the colony was bigger and did not consist mainly of priests.
[2] Not in summer, but in January, before the outbreak of the insurrection in Poland.
[3] Alexandr Bezak (1800–68), governor-general of Kiev, known for his ruthlessness.
[4] Gabriela, née Poradowska, cousin of the Bobrowskis, and Jan, a schoolfriend of Tadeusz Bobrowski; they lived in Lublin.
[5] Diminutive of Jan.

care, first prescribing a seven months' period without writing, speaking or moving – and then, having realized that the dose was too strong, they helped to make me move for over two thousand versts; now they ought to show the same motherly heart and allow me to return home, even if only for the purpose of tending swine, which would surely be nicer, nobler, more virtuous, godly and admirable than to occupy a prominent place here. And I would only ask them not to assist in my return journey; you simply cannot imagine the intolerable conditions of my travel. While we were still on home territory and at every station in the presence of scores of people, the Blue Men[1] were immensely, despicably polite. But as soon as we left Mohylew Province[2] and there was nobody around, they became despicably impolite. Evidently, over there they were afraid, here they evidently turned into heroes. I shall not describe you our journey, but from thousands of more or less unpleasant facts choose the one which is most painful, representative of the civilization of this country. In the White-stony[3] the boy gets pneumonia; the doctor applies leeches and calomel. Better. Just then they start harnessing the horses. Naturally I protest against leaving, particularly as the doctor says openly that the child may die if we do so. My passive resistance postpones the departure but causes my guard to refer to the local authorities. The civilized oracle, after hearing the report, pronounces that we have to go at once – as children are born to die (sic). And so we move on and all I gained with my passive resistance was about a dozen hours. Anyhow, God must have given me His blessing and consolation for I was spared the need to be obliged to anyone here, even if only for mere humanity, and all my gratitude has gone to Him alone for having kept the boy alive during that hard journey. In Nizhni Novgorod Ewusia[4] fell ill. When they started to telegraph there and back asking if she could stay to be cured, a few days passed and, although they refused the permission, we learned in the meantime about the change in our destination. Otherwise we would have gone to Perm and thence retraced our way for fifteen hundred versts. Anyhow, on 16 June we reached Vologda.

What is Vologda? A Christian is not required to know. Vologda is a huge quagmire stretching over three versts, cut up with parallel and intersecting lines of wooden foot-bridges, all rotten and shaky under one's feet: this is the only means of communication for the local people. Interspaced along those foot-bridges are Italian-style villas on stilts, built by the provincial gentry who all live here. A year here has two

---

[1] Gendarmes, who wore blue uniforms.
[2] That is, the former Polish territories, where most of the *szlachta* were still Polish.
[3] Moscow.   [4] Diminutive of Ewa.

seasons: white winter and green winter. The white winter lasts nine and a half months, the green winter two and a half. Now is the beginning of the green winter: it has been raining continually for twenty-one days and it will do so till the end.

During the white winter the temperature falls to minus twenty-five or thirty degrees and the wind blows from the White Sea, bringing the latest news from polar bears.

According to the statistics there are seventeen thousand – of whom or what I do not know. But during the unavoidable pilgrimage which preceded our settling down, in fifteen days I saw the following live creatures: 62 cows, 17 goats, 33 dogs and 29 coffins with human remains which count here as men. The town lies on the river called Zolotukha,[1] that is scrofula, whose waters bestow that attribute on all animalcules so perfectly that everybody is scrofulous; and since they are dead as well, they are taken to be coffins with scrofula. As I don't speak the vernacular of those animalcules which I have enumerated, I am therefore unable to gather information; but I know that Vologda has been developed in a progressive, civilized fashion. I have come into contact with two most important aspects of their civilization: police and thieves. To the police I was addressed in the way of a parcel; thieves prove their existence by everyday activity. A question arises: who begot whom? The genesis is unknown. Thus Vologda as such does not exist for us. Vologda as a collection of exiles to the extent that follows: Father Suzin from Ołyka; Father Burzyński from Maciejowice; a Greek–Catholic priest, Pelagiusz Rzewuski, from Biała; from Wilno Wacław Przybylski,[2] a nice and kind man, writer and professor. Two Limanowskis from Livonia.[3] From the Crown Stanisław Kraków, the son of Paulina:[4] he runs a photographic atelier developing pictures of local scrofulas of both sexes; Libelt from Podlasie. Lastly ourselves – God knows where from.

We have founded a chapel, which we now maintain; it is the centre of our lives. We pray a lot, earnestly and sincerely.

Apart from us there are men from 1830, 1846 and 1848 who after 1856 were allowed to return home but have become acclimatized here. They have married and (what is most curious) produced offspring, so they must belong to the amphibians.

For them our arrival was like a few drops of water fallen on quick-

[1] The official name of the river is Vologda.
[2] Przybylski (1828–72) was shortly released, played a prominent role in the 1863 insurrection, and later emigrated.
[3] Józef and Lucjan, exiled for singing *Boże coś Polskę* in Wilno cathedral on 8 May 1862.
[4] Paulina Kraków (1813–82), writer and educationist; Stanisław emigrated later to Paris, where he also had an atelier.

lime. They recall their language, customs, religion. Priests teach the
children; we urge them to attend communal prayers and gatherings
because it would be a pity if those sheep went astray. Vologda is a place
of exile for men who love their country and wish to work for it, for
women of easy virtue and for thieves. Our group, therefore, is as
numerous as it is ill-assorted.

Thus you know all about Vologda. When we were approaching it I
asked some local savages about Vologda; at my question all *rozhas*[1]
(*rozha* apes human countenance) would light up and I would always
get one and the same answer: the governor-general is kind and fish is
cheap. As you see, the alpha and omega of happiness. The governor-
general may indeed be kind, for he has not done us any harm: this is
exceptional here, as it is in fact at home. About fish I know nothing.
But that would not concern you, anyway. The air stinks of mud, birch
tar and whale-oil: this is what we breathe. One is not inclined to talk
because it seems that one's voice will disperse and fail to reach the
listener's ear; one is not inclined to write because it seems that ink will
not leave a trace on the paper. All one does is pray with confidence and
blind faith, although common sense says that prayers from here can
never reach heaven and that God always looks another way, or else the
view of the world would become too repugnant for Him. We have not
had a single letter yet from anyone. We have written a great number to
many.

Having unpacked our oddments, we feel very close to you. Your
pictures and Gabrynia's[2] affectionate letters bring you constantly to
mind. So do also Ewincia's[3] recollections of the days when I was
buried under the towering monument of the frog-like and bird-like
figure of Rozhnov. All conversation is about you; for us only the past
exists, today falls into oblivion, of tomorrow we dare not dream. Even if
– what use would there be for men creeping out of the grave? Only one
such man was needed as Saviour; but he was God–Man. I know from
experience that others are good for nothing and that's the way I shall
probably be. Is it not better to die here? As a memory, exile and death
will provide a better and more substantial evidence of service to the
cause of truth and of one's beloved country than the return of someone
driven to desperation by homesickness, rotten, and carrying that rot-
tenness back home. And as I have with me a handful of our native soil,
death does not frighten me because at least accursed local earth will not
touch my cadaverous eye-sockets or my stilled heart. Anyway we do
not regard exile as a punishment but as a new way of serving our
country. There can be no punishment for us, since we are innocent.

[1] Mug, snout.   [2] Diminutive of Gabriela.   [3] Diminutive of Ewa.

Whatever the form of service may be, it always means living for others – so let our Lord Jesus Christ be praised for having rewarded us more than we deserve! Our serene faces, proud bearing and defiant eyes cause great wonder here: because after what we have seen and what God saw a luminous glow has remained in our eyes, a glow which will not be dimmed by anything and which will stay with us like a testimony when one day we appear before God's tribunal. So do not pity us and do not think of us as martyrs. We are servants rewarded above their deserts. Thanks to our present life I have got to know an illness new to me. I suffer from nostalgia – what is the Polish word for it? You can't imagine how tiring it is and yet I don't want to be cured. I would rather die from it.

May God bless you and keep you in good health.

Yours – always yours – as of a
part of our Country.
A.K.

Apollo Korzeniowski to Gabriela and Jan Zagórski

Tygodnik Ilustrowany (Warsaw), 1920, no. 20

Vologda 2/14 October, 1862

My best and dearest,

Talking about you both constantly was our way of celebrating here Marcelka's[1] wedding anniversary and our stay with you; and, therefore, when you sent us a souvenir of that day, showing that you too remembered this anniversary, we took great comfort at the thought of the power instilled by God into the human heart: in goodness the heart is strong, but for solace it is omnipotent; neither dank dungeons, nor northern blasts, nor life in an echoless land, nor mighty pressure can break it or cramp it. And the godliness of human nature is equally strong in poor and rich, wise and stupid; and yet there exist people who repudiate or disregard this gift of the Father, the Son and the Holy Ghost, robbing themselves wilfully of that most laudable attribute of humanity. Such are the thoughts that fill me as I write to you both, my dear Gabrynia. Having entrusted photographs and messages to a priest's hands, I assumed that they would reach you in a cassock. It was, therefore, no little surprise to read that you had received them through the devices of human civilization. No doubt, however, that the dear and kind Father Jan acted as he thought appropriate and,

---

[1] Marcelina Ołdakowska, daughter of Aleksander Poradowski (d. 1844), general in the Russian army.

anyhow, they did arrive; thanks be to God. Do you know if the word I sent to Arct's,[1] commending me to him, did reach him also? Father Jan wrote to me from Garwolin but never mentioned my commissions. You have probably met him. He is a most kindly person, but still quite a child. We are bitterly cold here. For the last couple of days we have had plenty of snow. Firewood is as expensive as in Warsaw, and the number of stoves equals that of the windows, so we must heat furiously; but even when the stoves are red-hot, after several days of frost a white moss appears in the corners of the warmest of dwellings. We shall become capital preserves. Did I write to tell you that a couple of weeks ago, on 2 October, the governor gave permission to move us to Chernikhov, but it is impossible on account of our health and the state of local roads. *Tandem*[2] thus (let Gabrynia explain *tandem* to Jaś) – we stay put.

One thing is invaluable here – the quiet.

It could make a *nec plus ultra* cemetery. But this stillness without doors, windows or other openings makes one feel that nothing will ever escape from here. If the Pharisees, having tortured Christ to death, buried him in Vologda, there would be no need for seals or guards – the act of our redemption would be still lying in cold storage, the Resurrection would not have taken place. This is probably why the God of the Old Testament did not let humankind expand its knowledge of geography. Yes, there would be no Resurrection, no Easter holidays, no Easter cakes; but at least we, human beings, would be spared the painful sight of the frequent, so very frequent, crucifixions of Christ in humanity. However, as God ordered things thus, it is obviously necessary.

Ah! Poradowski girls! Where are your dainty hands and feet, graceful Marcelka and Ewunia?[3] Those lovely hands – small, wise, witty, affectionate. Judging by myself, the exile to Vologda is a punishment for people with aesthetic taste, for looking at those mutton-fists and clumsy stumps, at the rampant repulsive ugliness all round, offers constant temptation to hang oneself. And in the First Chapter of Genesis it says that man was created in God's image: I believe in it because it is written; but here my belief is put under a serious test. Take an hour-glass where scrofula runs instead of sand; throw over it something coloured, set it on two abominable tortoises wrapped in filthy rags and let it waddle along; fasten to each wrist a badly baked brick to which five rotten carrots are attached – and there you have a Vologda

---

[1] Michał Arct (1840–1916), eminent Warsaw publisher.

[2] Finally (Latin); *tandem tedy* (thus finally) was a jocular Polish expression.

[3] Marcelina Ołdakowska and her sister Ewa Poradowska (d. 1868).

woman with arms and legs. Horrible things. I am not enclosing the portrait of a native creature, because I know, dear Gabrynia, how dearly you wish for a daughter; my letter could arrive at the blessed moment and it would be dangerous to let your gaze fall on a monster. And besides, the local males and females in their moral aspect remind one of uncorked bottles. Sometimes, in conversation, a drop of thought will leak out, but then something inside will block its way again, and I know not what should be done to pour out a sentence. Why am I writing all this to you? Because I am afraid of falling back on memories, like people who refrain from touching the bones of the dead; and the present is such a huge nothing, it is awesome. Konradek remembers you very well and loves you more than his age can warrant. I kiss your hands, dear Gabrynia, and all three of us embrace your little brood. Let us hope that the youngest of us will live to see happier days – together with your little ones. My warm embraces for dear Jaś, as to my friend and relative, and as to someone who is to me more than that; but human speech cannot express it, because people in everyday life pay too little attention and care to their feelings to find names for them. Not till after I had dispatched my previous letter to you did I recollect, or rather, not until I had re-read your letter for the fourth time (three times always is a gallop through) did I notice that your estate is not called Dry Willows.[1] So much the better: I do not like unpleasant appellations. Please tell me if Oleś[2] received my letter addressed to Białystok, to Marcelka? It is my heart-felt problem that I do not know how to tell him or show him my devotion and my gratitude for the brotherly care he bestowed upon us during the last days before we were taken away. My humble and loving regards to Aunt,[3] embraces for Marcelka, her husband and child. To Ewunia and Żancia[4] – I do not know what to say but I would like it to be something very affectionate. Why do you never write about Ewunia and Żancia? You mention sometimes Marcelka but never the others. God speed Mr Konstanty in his idea of a spouse! Please give my brotherly regards to all Lublin dwellers who remember me. And to all known and unknown men, wherever they may be and as far as your voice can reach, please convey my constant and unim-paired love and faith. The other theological virtue does not even appear in the local cold – but some day we may induce it by the

---

[1] Such a name would be a bad omen.
[2] Aleksander Poradowski (1836–1890), brother of Ewa and Marcelina, officer in the Russian army. He joined the 1863 insurrection, and later emigrated. Husband of Marguerite Poradowska, née Gachet (1848–1937).
[3] Poradowska, widow of the general.
[4] Joanna Poradowska, sister of Ewa and Marcelina.

sadness of our hearts and by our ... prayers; and work will make it a living reality that exists among us.

Yours

Apollo

Stefan Bobrowski's character

Bobrowski, 'Memoirs', ii, 463–4

It is now time to mention my youngest brother, Stefan, who held an important position in the 1863 movement, for which participation he paid with his life, leaving a kind memory even among his enemies. I shall relate all I know directly from him, and what I regard as trustworthy in the accounts of various competent and incompetent persons who claim to have been close to him at that time.

He [Stefan] was a young man (barely twenty years of age, as he had been born in 1841, on 10/22 April)[1] of unusual ability and, for his age, exceptional education, mostly in history, philosophy and politics. The range of his reading was enormous, and his memory even more capacious – but above all he had an extraordinary, almost intuitive, knowledge of people, and a great facility in establishing and using human contacts; in this respect he was a born conspirator. A man of the most noble and deep feelings, personal integrity and sweetness of character; devoid of the least sign of egoism; of pleasant and attractive bearing; enriched by eloquence and natural wit and overwhelming kind-heartedness, he was loved and welcomed by everybody – particularly since, in spite of his shrewd mind, he was never sarcastic or given to displaying his superiority. With a strong will and tenacity contained in his seemingly frail body, in which nerves played the predominant part, and with his extremely weak eyesight (he used to read with each eye in turn, holding the page almost against his nose), the above qualities produced a forceful personality which attracted almost everyone who came into contact with him, irrespective of that person's education. I met people of dull intellect, poorly educated and rusty in their feelings, whom my brother later turned into active supporters of his ideals, or even, without their realizing it, into his blind instruments. He never used unpleasant arguments *ad hominem*, nor was he given to offensive insinuations as is common among mediocre agitators, for he knew how to listen to contrary opinions; he would ascertain at once if his interlocutor might be won over, and, if not, he would leave him alone: a fact which accounted for the favourable impression my brother

---

[1] In fact on 17 January 1840; killed in a duel 14 April 1863.

would leave on his opponents. He knew me and my views too well not to realize that if I heard about his revolutionary activities I would try to discourage him. This was probably why he never confided in me on the subject; other reasons being the considerable difference in our age, and a younger brother's respect, which he invariably used to show, for his elder tutor ... Now and again we engaged in academic discussions on national and political issues, but it seemed that our difference in outlook was not really fundamental, only due to our age and milieu. Aware of his ability, intelligence and propensity for learning, and faithful to the principle which I uniformly applied to all my charges, I saw no reason for exercising a detailed control over their occupations and way of life, and was only careful that their conduct should, on the whole, be beyond reproach; my main concern was with their character and inclinations which I tried to influence by means of conversation – if I met my charges often – or by letters, of which I was not sparing, observing at every opportunity, and with real fondness, the ways and stages of the development of each one of them; this was the method I applied with an even greater thoroughness to my brother.

An incident in the 1863 insurrection

Bobrowski, 'Memoirs', II, 489

Allegedly engaged in the pursuit of insurgents, the peasants raided and robbed houses, as the following incident, which was well known to me, testifies; its victim was my seventy-year-old uncle, Mikołaj Bobrowski, former captain in the erstwhile Polish Army, resident of Sołotnin near Kodnia (Żytomierz district). In his absence a patrol of Cossacks arrived at his homestead, and the officer in command asked about the master. The servant answered that his master had gone to Berdyczów; asked whether he had not perchance gone to join the insurrection, the same servant replied: 'Our master would be too old for that, as he is over seventy.' 'Have you any arms in the house?' 'Yes, we have,' and he showed the officer an old sword and a couple of flint-lock pistols from Napoleonic times (my uncle was a Knight of the Legion of Honour and he valued the decoration very highly, although he never wore it). The officer ordered a retreat from the manor and the hamlet and the patrol rode away, but the mob of peasants invaded the house, telling each other: 'The old man must have money somewhere.' Suddenly somebody accidentally overturned a small writing-table and as it fell a chink of gold was heard; the writing-table was instantly smashed and the contents taken. The search raised the peasants to such a frenzy that they smashed every single piece of furniture, including even the

mirrors which they broke for the sheer pleasure of destruction; they
filled several cart-loads with anything they could lay their hands on,
and drove away to the nearby village of Cudnowo. They took about
eight hundred half-imperials, twelve hundred roubles in silver and
notes, over two thousand roubles' worth of possessions, not counting
the damaged furniture and the broken mirrors, which were of considerable value. Among other things there was a small box containing the
insignia of the Legion [of Honour] and of the Polish Military Cross. At
the sight of this last piece of booty the peasants took fright and,
thinking that it might have come from none other than the Tzar
himself, they threw the box into the garden, leaving inside it seven
hundred and twenty roubles in notes – apparently they searched in
haste and carelessly. As soon as my uncle was informed about the
robbery, he went straight from Berdyczów to Prince Drucki, the
Governor of Volhynia Province, to lodge a complaint. The Prince
answered him: 'What do you expect? This is war and you as a former
soldier ought to know what that means! Anyway you all asked for it.' So
my uncle was sent away with nothing. And the peasantry, running wild
after having once got away unpunished, enjoyed themselves in the
neighbourhood of Sołotnin along the postal track between Berdyczów
and Żytomierz, where they prowled at large, stopping and robbing
travellers, among them an envoy of the governor-general, so that the
latter was informed of what was going on near Żytomierz ... Thus the
Governor was given a dressing down and an enquiry began; peasants
were summoned, but neither punished nor forced to compensate for the
damage – and that was the end of the affair! ... It was characteristic
that out of all this considerable loss my uncle most regretted the torn
Patent of the Legion [of Honour], whose preamble he knew by heart
and used to recite almost with tears in his eyes, while he would not
mention other things at all.

Thoughts on chauvinism
Bobrowski, 'Memoirs', II, 518

Anyhow it is obvious that chauvinist trends have nowadays spread to
governments and peoples all over the world, superseding the lofty
humanitarian slogans proclaimed at the close of the last century, after
their short-lived and ostensible career! Could this mean a regression in
humanity's ethical development? I do not believe this to be the case,
although what we see, hear and experience suggests precisely such a
conclusion. The reason for this, if I may so call it, 'bestialization' of
governments and peoples is their mania for grandeur, their exaggerated

national egoism, their disregard of principles for the sake of gain, their worship of power and success justifying the use of all available means! Such tendencies must surely be only temporary phases in the general evolution of mankind, and it seems to me that this detrimental tide, pushing mankind many centuries back, like other similar tides which had seemed to arrest progress, following the cataclysm of the epoch of 'blood and iron'[1] and – let me add – of 'mutual hatred' as well, will pass … and must pass … and after an era of moral and material exhaustion there must come an 'epoch of peace and reconciliation', an epoch of reflection on the part of the strong and mighty, that will enable the weak and oppressed to live and rise in the name of the holiest interests of mankind and of nations, based on experience; and with this conviction I look to the future which I shall not live to see, but which I expect to come and in which I trust!

'Poland and Muscovy', by Apollo Korzeniowski

Polska i Moskwa. Pamiętnik xxx zaczęty 186…, Ojczyzna (Leipzig), 1864, nos 27–9, 34–6, 42–52

POLAND AND MUSCOVY
Memoirs of xxx*
Begun in 186…

'Vitam impendere vero'
Introduction

Last morning in the Citadel. – A *tableau vivant* of Muscovy-style social order. – Captain Żuczkowski. – 'Paper' from Muscovy. – Verdict.

The Citadel clock struck the fifth hour of the day.

Warsaw Citadel is the city's ever-ready machine of destruction, and at the same time an immense dungeon where tzardom buries Polish patriotism. As a machine it simply awaits the whim of some satrap. As a dungeon – opening and closing in turns – it devours thousands of innocent victims. The Citadel was built by Tzar Nicholas [I], who named it the Alexandrian Citadel after his brother and predecessor.

Following the great national cataclysm, some Poles who saved their property and titles called Alexander I 'the benefactor, renovator and

---

* Although the author of this diary is no longer alive, we refrain from printing his name from fear of rousing Muscovy's wrath against his surviving family. (ed.)[2]

[1] Allusion to Bismarck's words of 30 September 1862 in the Prussian Chamber of Deputies: 'Not speeches or resolutions of a majority will decide the great problems of our time – that was the error of the years 1848 and 1849 – but iron and blood.'

[2] Undoubtedly the editors knew that the author of the anonymously published 'memoir' was alive, but under police supervision in Russia.

reviver' of Poland – names lisped out by renegades; Tzar Nicholas, after the 1831 Revolution, fomented and provoked by the tzar's 'charity', built his comment in stone and dug it firmly into the ground – heap of boulders, bristling with guns and crawling with vermin of thugs and torturers. This 'charity', bearing the name of our Renovator and Reviver, Tzar Alexander I, presents a constant threat of extinction to the Polish capital and inside its walls throttles one generation of Polish patriots after another.

Such is the Book of Genesis of the Alexandrian Citadel in Warsaw.

The last chime of the hour died out. Suddenly the double bolts moved with a grating sound. The key rattled in the lock. The door of my cell opened with a bang.

A new day of the second half of my eight-month stay in the Citadel began.

I had been lying for a long time on my bed wide awake and fully dressed. Through the open door of my cell, as if from a theatre box, I saw a *tableau vivant* of the 'Social Order'. I was to pay for that theatre box with many days of my life.

At the end of the corridor, opposite my door, stood four *soldats*. Holding their rifles they stood as stiff as pokers, stone-like. Their chests, faces and guns were directed at me; but their gaze turned suddenly cross-eyed as they looked towards the end of the corridor, whence a noise of steps and a rattling of swords was approaching.

I am using the word *soldat* instead of soldier. The concept 'soldier' invokes noble-minded courage and valour ready for self-sacrifice. Muscovy never had nor will have any soldiers. Poland, whether flourishing or fighting deadly battles, has always had armed citizens. Other nations have soldiers. A *soldat* is a product of Muscovy. *Soldats* are armed and organized plunderers and bandits, from the commander-in-chief down to the last camp-follower. Their civilian status – thievery in uniform and without arms; military status – the same thievery only armed for plunder.

I raised myself and sat up on my bunk. Through all that noise of clattering and banging in the corridor I could somehow sense an imminent and unknown crisis in my life as a prisoner. Social order would not exert itself with such pomp and circumstance for nothing. Thus the *tableau vivant* was gradually becoming more complete and perfect.

In front of the afore-mentioned wall composed of the four *soldats* two gendarmes passed and took up guarding positions by the door of my cell; Muscovite gendarmes are but armed spies.

Between that main wall and the two supporting pillars of tzardom slid into the cell the captain of the gendarmes – a man named Żucz-kowski.

He had been for many years host, steward, administrator, house-keeper, watchman, spy, torturer, master of ceremonies, in the dungeons of Warsaw Citadel. Prisoners unknown to each other and unable to communicate referred to Captain Żuczkowski as 'Morok'.[1] The more appropriate name, however, would have been 'Judas Iscariot', for the man was a Pole.

He was an example of the effect that the Muscovy spirit had on human nature. Later I shall try to show the effects of that spirit on the already degraded nature of the Muscovites themselves. In my memoirs, devoted to the Polish question which for countless years has had to force its way through the dense jungle of ignorance and Muscovite tyranny, I shall aim at presenting the spirit of Muscovy, their customs and way of life. It is important, however, to make clear right from the beginning that Muscovy has its own, special civilization: terrible, depraved, destructive. To that civilization, nurtured under the Tartar whip and tzarist knout, Muscovy swears allegiance; but she does it surreptitiously, under a cloak of affected Western refinement.

The aim of Muscovy's development is to bring to a standstill all progress of humankind. So there is nothing surprising that Muscovy should keep this aim secret, and if it were not for her history I could be accused of exaggeration. Muscovy's history, however, shows that ever since she wriggled her way into European affairs, she has launched passionate attacks against every holy principle which happened to bloom in the civilized world, devouring or maiming it dangerously. As soon, however, as she became defeated, she would go under cover and whine in all possible human languages, imitating all nationalities in turn, so as to convince humanity of her own human nature.

It is not my intention to write a dissertation about all that. The very subject of these memoirs will bring to my mind thousands of events which, related dispassionately, will clarify, justify, explain and prove that Muscovy is now the plague of humanity and that her civilization means envy and negation of human progress; that it has been more than once dangerous to that progress but may in the future cause its arrest and ruin.

Let me go back to my last morning at the Citadel prison.

Right behind Żuczkowski there entered a military man of higher rank, a *geroy*[2] not known to me by name. In his hand he held a sheet of paper.

---

[1] 'Darkness' (Russian).   [2] 'Hero' (Russian).

The 'paper' is an official document of Muscovy, printed or hand-written. The significance of Muscovy 'paper' could not be described in several extensive volumes even if they were written with poisonous bile and with the spit of the most terrible scorn. France paid for the destruction of the Bastille and of what were called *lettres de cachet*[1] with the lives of thousands of her citizens. What would have happened if but one Muscovy 'paper' landed there?

We Poles have suffered slaughter, conflagration, robbery, rape and torture in the hands of Muscovy. We have perished by their sabres, bayonets and guns. Our defenceless chests were targets for their rifles. We are familiar with their truncheons, knouts and nooses. We got used to their prison dungeons, to the foul mines of their Siberia. We have seen the greatest disgrace of all: our human shoulders clad in their uniforms. We neither turned deadly white nor shook from fear of their scourge. The past ninety years of our existence have proved our civil courage. Nevertheless, the very sight of Muscovy 'paper' makes us shake with uncontrollable indignation. We cannot get used to it. We cannot bear the sight of it and we cannot bring ourselves to look at it with proud indifference, in spite of the strength of our spirit hardened by a century of suffering. He who has not been a Pole under the tzars cannot possibly understand and divine the magnitude of that official ignominy, whether handwritten or printed.

Ever since that pack of patient jackals called itself *hosudarstwo*[2] (not daring to use the word 'nation'), and ever since they mastered the art of writing, beauty, goodness and truth have never appeared on any piece of paper whether covered with handwriting or print. Lies, brazen and rousing lies have been the contents of their official documents from the first to the last letter...

But then, the whole of Muscovy is a prison. Beginning with the Ryryks, and then with the Tartar thraldom, the oppression of Ivan, under the knouts of various tzars and empresses and so forth, Muscovy has been, is and always shall be a prison – otherwise it would cease to be itself. In that prison committed crimes and flourishing deceit copulate obscenely. The law and official religion sanctify those unions. Their offspring: the falseness and infamy of all religions, of all social, political, national and personal relations.

If by some miracle prisons and penitentiaries all over Europe opened up suddenly, and if criminals armed, organized and ready for everything, were to flood society, peoples and governments would tremble

---

[1] 'Sealed letter', an envelope sealed with a royal seal and containing an order of imprisonment or exile.
[2] Russian *gosudarstvo* (Korzeniowski uses Ukrainian spelling), 'state'.

with fear and make superhuman efforts to save themselves from impending extermination. The supposition is impossible but its results cannot be denied.

And yet governments and peoples watch Muscovy without anxiety... Governments and peoples look at Muscovy, and although she makes them sometimes shudder with disgust, they fail to notice the urgency of danger. Meanwhile, in all likelihood, the release of the world's criminals is but a trifle in comparison with Muscovy, standing unrestrained, organized and ready to spew out millions of her criminals over Europe. All prisons of the world, taken together, do not hold forty million convicts; looking through all the prisons and their worst criminals it would be difficult to find even one who could equal the Bibikovs,[1] Muravevs,[2] Bergs[3]... Countless swarms of Muscovites, corrupted and infested with vermin, are out to destroy everything that man, conscious of his human dignity, has built, in the course of a centuries-long effort of mind, and at the price of blood. These swarms, consisting of government, clergy, bureaucracy, army, and all social classes, wait, ready to attack Europe. Meanwhile, to keep in training, Muscovy chews living Poland as if she were dead. Poland has been swallowed but not digested. The process of digestion has just begun. When it ends, the turn of other nations will come. The most hideous slavery, because inflicted by a debased hand, hangs over Europe. The portents of things to come are already visible. Where? In that fear and horror of Muscovy displayed by the English government in its dealing with the *hosudarstwo*; in that docility towards Muscovy shown by the governments of Prussia and Austria; and lastly in the vacillation and wavering towards Muscovy so characteristic of the attitude of the most noble government, the government of France.

The design of Muscovy's civilization is to smear her own deceit over the rest of humanity.

Holding such a 'paper' the afore-mentioned *geroy* stepped into my cell. Next to him stood the prison warder, Żuczkowski, and behind him the *soldats* and gendarmes – to make sure that Muscovy's falsehood became truth and reality for me.

The *geroy* bowed.

Ever since European journalists tried to console Tzar Alexander II and sweeten the bitter taste of his defeat in the Eastern [Crimean] War,

---

[1] Dmitri Bibikov (1792–1870), 1837–1852 governor-general of Kiev, 1852–5 Russian minister of the interior, an arch-reactionary.

[2] Mikhail Muravev (1796–1866), 1863–8 governor-general of Wilno, famed for ruthlessness, nicknamed *Veshatel* ('hangman' in Russian).

[3] Fyodor Berg (1790–1874), 1863–74 the viceroy of the Polish Kingdom.

they have kept calling him progressive and liberal; Muscovy seized on
that name as a means of pulling wool over Europe's eyes.

All cogs and wheels in the government machine received orders: to
carry on as before all the crushing, smashing, breaking, torturing and
robbing but to do it with propriety and, as far as possible, politeness.
The name given to that scheme was 'concessions' or 'tzar's own noble
impulses'. Wielopolski[1] supported that scheme, and among its representatives were Sukhozanet,[2] who boasted that he 'could not be called
murderer', and Lambert,[3] who used to faint when given orders to
slaughter defenceless people in churches, and also the tzar's brother
Constantine.[4] To this day the Muscovites cannot forgive their ruler
his 'kindness and the policy of concessions'. Anyway, it has all come to
an end, and now we have another scheme which cannot be described in
human language because no precedent for it exists in world history. By
comparison Ivan the Terrible appears but a tame figure; the new
scheme bears the most contemptible and despicable name: it is called
the Muravev system.

At the time of my arrest the operative scheme was the 'tzar's goodwill towards the Polish nation'. And so it was fully expressed by the
geroy's bow. As to the 'paper', it expressed Muscovite nature in its pure
form.

I sat immobile.

'Please be so kind as to stand up and listen while I read out the
sentence,' said the *geroy*.

A long time ago we decided that all our relations with Muscovy were
to be determined by orders and compulsion. Without orders or compulsion neither Muscovy nor her government would exist for us.
Anyway, this is part of our general cause. At the present moment,
however, the order was given and it was enforced by the presence of
armed men, therefore I stood up.

The *geroy* cleared his throat.

'Your name, Sir?' he asked in an official voice.

One wonders at the number of voices the Muscovites have! They
have a special voice to address their inferiors; another one to talk to

---

[1] Aleksander Wielopolski (1803–77), Polish conservative politician and the main prop-
onent of appeasement of Russia; 1862–3 head of the civil government in the Polish
Kingdom.
[2] Nikolai Sukhozanet (1794–1871), Russian minister of war, May–August 1861 acting
viceroy of the Polish Kingdom.
[3] Count Karl Lambert (1815–65), general, acting viceroy of the Polish Kingdom from
August to October 1861.
[4] Grand Duke Constantin Nikolaievich (1827–1892), brother of Tzar Alexander II,
viceroy of the Polish Kingdom June 1862–August 1863.

superiors; another in Moscow; still another in Europe; a different one in salons; and a different one at home. The *geroy*'s voice was official.

While imprisoned in the Citadel I heard that question at least a dozen times; and my answer was always put down in writing. If my name does not pass to posterity, it will not be the fault of Muscovy's military bureaucracy.

I gave my name.

There must have been a note of surprise in my voice, for the *geroy*, apparently always set on keeping up appearances, considered it necessary to offer an explanation.

'Even at the Citadel the government may be deceived' – his voice sounded dogmatic – 'somebody else might have been substituted for you and although innocent, subjected to punishment. A just government does not wish it to happen.'

'The justice of the government is known to all,' I replied, 'but the sensitivity of its conscience may, under the circumstances, concern only the present Captain Żuczkowski, the omnipotent ruler of the Citadel's inmates. He is the only person able to exchange prisoners. It is therefore he who must be left to ponder the sensitivity of the government's feelings and his gratitude for the recognition of his many years of meritorious services.'

The *geroy* spoke in Muscovite, I in Polish. Under those circumstances there was no reason for anyone to feel dissatisfied: each of us had the right to understand only what he wanted.

Żuczkowski, as a Pole in Muscovy's service, did not have that advantage; and as one of the 'faithfuls' he was just about to open his mouth to point out to the *geroy* the immoderation of my style, when the latter stopped him by a gesture. Obviously he was pressed for time and the paper he held carried replies to everything I could say either now or later.

Thus he unfolded several sheets covered with beautiful handwriting and started reading out the verdict!

I should have been able to judge the time the reading would take by the thickness of the scroll. However, I was disappointed.

The *geroy* read:

'Such and such (here came my name), as the authorities are well aware, was not only a participant in but the principal leader of the entire rebellious movement and the demonstrations designed to overthrow the government of our most gracious tzar. Moreover he presided over a clandestine committee, distributed brochures, and gave rebellious orders; he maintained criminal relations with Galicia and the Great Duchy of Poznań, and by perfidious endeavours instilled in the

population of Warsaw and the Congress Kingdom of Poland a conviction, an unshaken belief, that Lithuania, Bielo-Russia and the western
provinces of the tzarist empire, Volhynia, Podolia and Kiev, form an
inseparable part of Poland. Therefore, although the court martial
commission of enquiry is not in possession of any evidence against the
accused, could not find any witnesses against him in the misled populace, was not able to extract any statements from the accused – nevertheless,
relying on its moral conviction and bearing in mind the brazen
answers of the accused as well as his written statement that he is a Pole,
always has been and always will be striving for Poland's happiness, the
commission has ordered the deportation of such and such (name), to xxx
(name of place), under the strictest military escort during the journey
and then under constant police surveillance in the place of his exile.'

That was all. The Muscovite reader lapsed into silence. I looked up,
surprised. His eyes rested on the first half of the first sheet; and I had
made out four or six sheets covered with writing.

'That's all,' said the *geroy*, noticing that I expected him to continue.
'You have to sign the verdict to show that you've heard it.'

He turned over to the last page and at the bottom of the fourth or sixth
sheet pointed out the place where I was to certify with my own signature
that I had been made familiar with the Muscovite lucubration.

However, before I picked up the pen the *geroy* asked me:

'Have you anything to say against this verdict, Sir?'

I answered with a question.

'Is my reply going to be put down on paper?'

'Indeed not. But you can speak up. Higher authorities will be informed.'

'Oh, I am not concerned with such publicity. I am only surprised at
the eight-month-long interrogation when such an arbitrary verdict could
have been written beforehand,' I said, and took the pen to sign. 'But I
wish to make clear that the only place that I can put my signature is
below the sentences which have been read out to me and not at the end of
the verdict which as I see runs over several pages.'

The *geroy* thought a while. Żuczkowski signalled negation with his
head and eyes. The *geroy* either did not see this or chose to disregard it.
Having pondered over the problem, he said: 'All right.'

He handed me the paper. Half of the page which had been read out to
me was left uncovered. Over the rest he carefully placed his hand.

Thus I signed below the words 'of his exile', having splashed some ink
over the *geroy*'s fingers which kept from me the secret of the verdict. It
seemed that the pen itself spat with the utmost contempt.

'Come. Get going. You're coming with me,' said the *geroy* and made a sign to Żuczkowski. Żuczkowski in turn made a sign to the gendarmes, who removed my few belongings and bedding from the cell.

Glancing round I bade farewell to the walls of my prison. There floated my thoughts of the past eight months – my dreams – my intentions – my memories. But there was not a single tear anywhere; for we are not allowed to weep, unless with tears of blood that pour over Poland.

Żuczkowski's voice roused me from this momentary meditation.

'Goodbye, Sir,' he said with a kind of venomous sweetness. 'I suppose you are satisfied with your stay here, for I did everything possible to render your imprisonment more pleasant.'

'I hope that God will measure out the same solace and favours as I have enjoyed in this dungeon, if not to yourself, then perhaps to your children.'

And I walked passed the *geroy* and Żuczkowski, in front of the *soldats* and gendarmes, holding my head high with Polish dignity.

Surrounded by the guards we entered the carriage.

It was an old-fashioned four-wheel droshky, a Warsaw cab, summoned by the police. I shall never forget the driver's eyes. He looked at me with pain and – gratitude. The people of Warsaw made no mistake in judging the conduct of those whom the Muscovy government decided to eliminate first, as leaders.

It was daybreak. The city was still asleep. In the empty streets leading to the Warsaw–St Petersburg railway station and in the Old Town Square I saw only a few female street-vendors and a few cooks wandering about. The look the cab-driver gave me repeated itself in the eyes of those miserable women. I drank in those looks, aware that they were the only farewells I was to get from my beloved country.

Zsylka[1] awaited me. It would be pointless to search any other language for the exact meaning of Muscovy's words and I have therefore left some of them in their original form. All I have allowed myself is the right to provide an explanation. *Zsylka* means imprisonment in the wilderness, among wild animals and without means of defence.

In spite of my knowledge of *zsylka* – a family knowledge, inherited from the days of my grandfather – I was delighted to be leaving the Citadel. I thirsted for air.

I was going to depart from my country: everything which quickens my heartbeat and everything I stand for would be torn away from me. Nevertheless I was not sad. True, I had been denied an open trial which even if it had led me to the gallows would always have been a triumph for the national cause. Instead I was going to the *zsylka*, but to

[1] Russian *ssylka* – 'exile', 'banishment'.

me it seemed as good a way to serve my country as any other. The sentence lay heavily on my breast, stifling my breath and thought; but at the same time it shone like a sign of merit, branded by the enemy but awarded by my country.

Those were the thoughts which gave my face and eyes a look of serenity and pride as I stood in front of the *geroy*, who to me at that moment meant Muscovy!

In the railway-station yard we were surrounded by gendarmes. A special train waited on the platform. I was to depart at once.

Let me leave for the moment the description of the preparations for the journey, the farewells, the voyage itself, the arrival at the place of *zsylka*, my stay there and my personal life; I am putting it off in order to occupy myself with the immortal cause of Poland which produced the trifling grain of sand in the form of my *zsylka*.

After all, it is such grains that make up a great expanse of sand, which sometimes, when breathed upon by God, is stirred up and buries those who dare to tread on it.

A sudden arrest at home during the night. Eight months of unlawful imprisonment. Then surreptitious interrogation at night in a dungeon. The working of the predatory court which calls itself martial, finally the sentence, partly disclosed and partly concealed, which fell upon me. For each one of those things there must have been some reason, and however varied those reasons might be, they can all be reduced to a common denominator.

The denominator is the theft (fraudulent acquisition) of Poland by Muscovy, with the consent of the nations of Europe and their governments.

The individual numerator of this denominator is my fate.

The national numerator is the martyrdom of millions of Poles.

The general numerator is the suffering, bullying and tormenting endured by those European nations which silently acquiesced to the most shameful crime that has occurred since the days of Christ.

Ninety years ago the European governments and nations looked on impassively as swarms of locusts descended on the most fertile fields, as the miasma of the most sordid and lethal plague spread, as seas of foul muck poured over the fruits of the earth, as barbarism, ignorance, renegation swallowed up civilization, light, faith in God and in the future of mankind; in short, it all happened when Muscovy seized Poland.

And here we have Austria, which in exchange for a hunk of a territory taken illegally has served Moscow for the past ninety years; having lost her dignity and respect in Europe she finds no peace in the present and sees only uncertainty and fear for the future.

And here we have Prussia, an outgrowth of former vassals of Poland and now servile to Muscovy, against all values that humanity in its earthly existence regards as holy and fundamental.

And here we have the German Reich searching in vain in Austria and Prussia for signs of the unfettered and impeccable dignity indispensable in the creation of that much-cherished and beautiful German unity which was to be built upon those powers; that unity, depending on the winds blowing from Muscovy, is constantly tossed between the despotic Prussian government and impotent Austria, and thus the German nation is prevented from rising like a great and uniform wall that would face Muscovy's Mongolian hordes.

And here we have England – that same England justifiably proud of her liberties that blossomed in the work of ordinary people; for the past ninety years she has been yielding to Muscovy in Europe; she quails before Muscovy in the East; she was seized with fear of Muscovy at the Congress of Vienna; in 1831 she was forced to acquiesce to Nicholas's lawlessness; the Sebastopol War[1] did not give her the advantages she was entitled to, and, finally, in 1863, she was made to watch her leading statesman being slapped in the face by a Muscovite minister.[2] Till now England has had to bear it all out of fear, but tomorrow – tomorrow – she may be forced to put up with the ruin of her own interests in the East.

And here we have France – that same France where a Polish noblewoman was at one time the queen;[3] that same France whose noble daughter sat on the Polish throne under the garland of the rescuers of Christianity;[4] that same France whose sons side by side with thousands of Polish children shed their blood, fertilizing the soil of Europe for the rich crops of freedom and equality; that same France, after the annihilation of Poland, saw her own lands and capital defiled by Muscovy's invasion and has been writhing for many years under the yoke of the Congress of Vienna, which will hold legal and strong till the day when Poland comes between Muscovy and Europe. That same France which even after the Sebastopol War has kept up the appearance of friendship with the hordes of the North. Today, therefore, France cannot lay claims, clear and constant, to all that she believes in, to all that she has got in her blood and spirit – to freedom and

---

[1] I.e. the Crimean War (1854–6), with the siege of Sebastopol.

[2] Korzeniowski seems to be referring metaphorically, to Count Alexander Gorchakov's contemptuous rejection of Lord John Russell's note of 17 June 1863, in which Great Britain demanded autonomy for the Polish kingdom.

[3] Maria Leszczyńska (1703–68), daughter of the Polish King Stanisław Leszczyński and wife of Louis XV.

[4] Marie Casimire d'Arquien (1641–1716), wife of King Jan III Sobieski.

independence. She is smothered by Muscovy. And tomorrow – tomorrow – maybe she will again see Muscovy's rabble trampling down
her lands and their great destiny.

Let us not talk about other European states. But when we catch the
glimpse of Europe as a whole – of that area representative of the
greatest progress of God and man, it seems to us like a man–giant
bending down before the axe of the executioner, Muscovy. Such has
been the state of Europe for the last ninety years, since Poland ceased to
stand between her and Muscovy.

However, as this introduction is meant to be personal, I am going
back to the subject of myself.

In physical birth we observe inherited characteristics. We are often
struck by the way the blood carries the character of the forefathers into
succeeding generations. There is nothing to contradict it in the material
world and in the sphere of morals it is equally undeniable. The cruel
and foul crime breeds millions of minor crimes just as sordid and cruel,
albeit on a more limited scale.

Muscovy has stolen out of mankind's treasury a precious stone: Poland.
Now, even if reluctant – but Muscovy is not reluctant – it has to build
gallows, to bury people in underground dungeons, to destroy, rape, burn,
rob, torture, plunge knives into helpless breasts, annihilate the Poles;
otherwise the precious stone may be torn away from the robber.

Thus my exile into slavery is the obvious result of the foray on
Poland.

I have said already that such an exile is called *zsylka*.

The arrested victim walks or is transported with or without handcuffs and chains.

I was supposed to be driven fetterless, as a consequence of the
introduction of that system which the Muscovites call today with
indignation 'the concessions and benefits' for Poland.

During the entire journey, which takes him for over a thousand
versts, the convict, driven or led on foot, appears to the population of
the lands he crosses as a wild beast, as a raving madman – in view of
the vigilance surrounding him and the closeness of the surveillance
practised by the guards.

On reaching the place of his *zsylka* – be it Siberia or Muscovy proper
– the prisoner is left with an accompanying huge bundle of papers, at
the mercy of the local authorities.

Those authorities extend a most harsh guardianship over their prisoner in respect of his contacts, his correspondence and all the most
private aspects of his life.

In my case it had been decided that I should go to the province xxx,
the town of xxx.

In the European part of Muscovy some provinces are called Siberian. Although the whole of Muscovy is in fact a place of *zsylka* – prison
and exile – those particular provinces are the government's favourite
choice. Firstly because they are the farthest removed from the world of
people and secondly because the inherent characteristics of the local
inhabitants, well known for social robbery, are most deadly and
poisonous. More often than not, therefore, the exiles are doomed to die
in one of those provinces, if not in Siberia itself.

What are we to think of a nation which not only consents to, but is
well-nigh proud of, the fact that their entire country serves as exile for
various kinds of criminals? The entire Muscovy nation regards itself as
naturally chosen for such a fate. Parricides, murderers, thiefs, crooks,
incendiaries, law-breakers, political criminals – all of them get absorbed in Muscovy's immensity. Except for one particular type of exile,
none of those criminals offends with his presence the society which
accepts him – owing to their mutual understanding they quickly merge
into that society. The only exception is the political 'criminal'. He is the
only one who evokes horror, repugnance and fear; watched by all eyes,
listened to by all ears, he finds himself, possibly for his entire life, not
only under police surveillance but under the closer, more unpleasant
and humiliating surveillance of the local criminal populace.

As I have already mentioned, my sentence had been decided in
advance. The actual arrest was like an act of brigandage; the search of
my home like an act of robbery; the eight-month-long imprisonment
like a burial in a grave; the interrogation and trial like acts of lawlessness designed to intensify the punishment.

Several hundreds of Warsaw citizens shared at the same time my fate
at the Citadel. Then came the handcuffs, the dungeons, *zsylka*, the
gallows, executions by a firing squad, hard labour in the mines and –
the worst, because the most infamous of all – Muscovy uniform, worn
not by hundreds but by tens of thousands. The Muscovites soon
realized that it was not a case of several hundred influential persons
being dedicated to fight for the great and godly cause of Poland, for her
freedom and independence; but there was something more sublime,
something that even a Muscovite cannot destroy: the Polish spirit
which shines just as brightly whether under a velvet cape or a peasant's
coat.

My personal fate, like that which befell hundreds of thousands of my
countrymen, would not give me the right to dwell upon it. But when
thoughts, actions, lives, tortures, bloodshed, deaths of all those
brethren taken together form the character of a particular epoch in the
history of Poland; when that epoch towers above all that is most laudable
in human history, I believe that I have the right to tell it. In my story,

however, I cannot leave out details that go into the making of the Polish spirit and of the mystical body that forms it.

The greatness of those last days of entombed Poland has only one expression worthy of itself: a confession based on nothing but the life-giving Truth.

That is why my diary is a Confession.

The superhuman and God-given sacrifice of the Poles in order to be understood in the political world of Europe must be recorded not only in the final act but also in the preceding preparations.

I am, therefore, leaving aside, for the time being, the story of my *zsylka*, which in every detail of its domestic life will testify to the truth of what I am going to say about the political aspect – and I am going to devote the following chapters to the Polish cause that is entangled in Muscovy's hell.

In the name of our Father and our Country I begin.

Reducing to words the stipulation of the Vienna Congress on the Polish question, we find the following particulars. England wanted an independent Poland; Austria, fearing Moscow, was ready to give up Galicia; Prussia, whose greed overcame fear, reconciled the one with the other and wished only for a few obstacles and restrictions to be set up against Moscow. England at that time could not back her demands and general policy by force of arms. Although a free and undivided Poland was for England like an open larder with the basic product: bread; like a shop counter ready to receive all English products without any restrictions and in the greatest possible freedom of trade; still the power of exhausted Britain could not throw itself against the power of Muscovy, particularly since it could be foreseen that, under Moscow's pressure, Prussia and Austria would soon change from friends and allies into England's enemies.

Tadeusz Bobrowski's dedication on a book given to Konrad Korzeniowski, 1 January 1863

Rosenbach Foundation, Philadelphia

1 January 1863

This book,[1] which used to belong to your aunt, my wife, I am now giving to you, my dear Konradek, as a threefold remembrance – to remind you of a dear person who loved you, but whom you did not

---

[1] M. A. E. de Saintes, *Les Anges de la terre, personnifiés par leurs vertus et leurs belles actions, publiés et illustrés avec le concours de plusieurs gens de lettres et artistes distingués* (Paris, 1844). Included are, *inter alia*, Charlemagne, Saint Louis, Columbus, Bartolomeo Las Casas, Mme de Sévigné, Maria Leszczyńska.

know; to remind you of the year of your life which began in exile with your parents but far from your relations and which, God willing, may not end in exile; finally to remind you of your uncle who, wherever you are or will be, will always love you with all his heart just as he loves and blesses you now.

Tadeusz Bobrowski

Apollo Korzeniowski to Gabriela and Jan Zagórski

Tygodnik Ilustrowany (Warsaw), 1920, no. 20

15/27 March 1863

My beloved,

I do not know when and about what I wrote to you last: all life within us has come to an end, we are stunned by despair.[1]

The persecutors of the first Christians were indeed generous: they would throw a whole bunch of them into the arena of the circus to be torn to pieces and devoured all together: children with parents, brothers with brothers, sisters with sisters. Modern times have inspired people with a greater power of inventing torments: let the bloodstained pieces of brothers, sons, daughters and mothers, mauled by the furious teeth, fly over the arena in the full view of their beloved, who, bound and chained, sit in this holocaust of a theatre looking at the tortured. How long can eyes bear to look? The eyes are fixed constantly and for ever, because the lids cannot shut out this view; the time will come when, through the pupils stained with our brothers' blood and their last gasps, a frenzy of despair will sink into our hearts and make them burst – but only God, He who measures out their strength for bearing crosses, knows when it will happen. I know not when; but I know it will be soon.

Here in short is the state of mind, heart, soul and even, not the least, of that foolish body which acquires sense only under such lashings.

We have received your most kind letters and pleasing gifts. We thank you for ... well, for everything. Your words are for us like drops of liquid quenching our everlasting thirst. And so we do not read your letters – we breathe them in.

We pray to God for your health. May His blessing be amongst you both and your children. But do you know, my dearest, that we are overcome by a certain indifference, probably sinful, towards all those

---

[1] The insurrection in Poland began on 22 January. The outbreak, much earlier than planned, was prompted by the announcement of an enforced conscription into the Russian army. In the middle of winter the insurgents, operating mainly in the field, found themselves at a great disadvantage and suffered heavy losses.

troubles which are of a personal and intimate but merely family kind. Some disturbing but personal news arrives: the head bends down slightly more – that is all. And again after a while the eye and the heart take up their old position and in an ultimate effort of the mind observe and become conscious of current events.

The imprisonment of my brother, Hil[ary] (23 January in the Kiev fortress), the wounding and captivity of Leonek, the death of Franciszek – like small episodes, like strophes, rang out painfully and grew silent in the soul, which again looks at those still living and listens to that infernal poem where passages are made up of violence and slaughter, rhyme of the singing of bullets, and stanzas of heroic death; the poem whose syllables show through a pile of falsehood; whose forgotten and by now redundant preface is us, but whose epilogue will be God! Only this thought gives one strength...

Yesterday local newspapers arrived with dispatches of 7, 8, 9 and 10 March.

Newspapers are like opium; we know they will kill us and yet we go on reading them. Moreover we live from one postal delivery to the next.

What else is there to write? The heart is full but the mind is poor – in rags; all it can do is beg for news. Nothing else. May God protect you. May He have mercy on you and guard your steps as the road is full of sharp stones.

The hope of getting permission to travel abroad for the sake of my steadily worsening health has as yet not been taken away from us. Ewunia could settle down in some quiet spot and I would nurse myself, nurse myself – nurse myself until complete recovery – in this world or in God's.

On 19 March we are celebrating the name-day of our good Father Józef Burzyński (from Maciejowice), who is our source of religious consolation; lately he lost two of his brothers and his mother died suddenly. But is there anyone here who does not weep because of something or someone? My letter is sad – please forgive me but being away from you is too hard to bear and this drop of bitterness causes the chalice to overflow.

I embrace you wholeheartedly

A.K.

I am enclosing a portrait of myself, Father Burzyński and Stanisł[aw] Kraków. Why? Just so that my likeness makes its appearance amidst you all.

Ewunia and Konrad send kisses to your little ones. Ewunia is just writing to her mother but will send you a letter by the next post.

Winter is here. Snow.

Apollo Korzeniowski to Kazimierz Kaszewski

Biblioteka Jagiellońska, Cracow, MS 3057

[Chernigov, 26 February 1865]

Dear Kazimierz,

This is the third time I have written to you since the arrival of your most beloved letter together with the money. I expected to get news of you from various people I had written to in Warsaw. Suddenly, several days ago, words reached me from the good Ludwik[1] and Władysław-Kazimierz,[2] but as they had been scrawled as long ago as last November, I still learned nothing about you. Finally the editors of *Kłosy*[3] mentioned you, but all I gathered from them is that you are unceasingly kind in remembering me and that it is most certainly to you that I owe the editors' note – but nothing about yourself. So I am sending this word care of them, particularly since I do not have your exact address. My news is very sad.

My poor wife, who these last two years has been destroyed by despair and by the repeated blows that fall on the members of our joined families, for the last four months terribly – gravely ill, has barely the strength to look at me, to speak with a hollow voice. This state has been caused by the lack of everything for the body and the soul – no doctors, no medicines. Today she is allowed to go for treatment to Kiev but her lack of strength makes it impossible. May God be with us, for now people cannot be of much help. For several months I have been everything in the house – master and servant. I am not complaining about this burden but about how often I am unable to satisfy, help or console my poor patient. Konradek is of course neglected; the present is so hard that the future may be even more frightful.

The letter from *Kłosy* has enlivened her for a while and as there is a mention of you, and as she ascribes all remembrance of us to your loving friendship, she has ordered me to sit beside her and to write reproaching you for your silence, knowing however that it is not due to forgetfulness.

And thus we send you our most faithful and affectionate greetings. We send our blessings to your Bronek;[4] we wish you health to work and work to live, and we ask you to keep us forever in your dear hearts and kind memory.

---

[1] Ludwik Jenike (1818–1903), translator and editor of the weekly *Tygodnik Ilustrowany* in Warsaw.
[2] Kazimierz Władysław Wóycicki.
[3] A Warsaw weekly.
[4] Bronisław, Kaszewski's son from his first marriage.

I shall end now because I am by the invalid's side. We shall wait for
your news with heart-felt impatience. Do not delay –
                              Your
                                                              Apollo

Apollo Korzeniowski to Kazimierz Kaszewski
Biblioteka Jagiellońska, Cracow, MS 3057

                                                     28 Feb[ruary] 1865
I think, our dear friend, that two or three days ago I sent you a letter,
care of the editor of the illustrated weekly *Kłosy*. I think – for I do not
know what I do – or feel – and I remember nothing. You will understand when I tell you: my wife is very, very, very ill – the only hope is in
God. People who for some reason refuse to give alms tell the poor: 'May
God help you.' Our doctor tells me the same – and it would be hard to
find such a beggar as I.

Despair has been slowly eating like rust into the physical constitution
of my wife. For eighteen months the poor girl has been putting everything down to nerves; the local doctors – are they doctors? – kept saying
'nothing, nothing, it will pass'. I, anxious – never having done anything
for my own benefit – cringed, pleaded, begged for a year to change our
place of exile so as to get a chance to find doctors deserving that name.
Constantly let down and deferred, I lost hope. And a couple of months
ago a sudden consuming fever, a lung condition and an inner tumor,
caused by an irregular blood flow, requiring removal. An old friend – a
doctor – from Żytomierz, where, as you know, we lived at one time,
having accidentally heard about my wife's illness, came to us; he has
come for the third time, this kindest of men. He sees the operation as
imperative but cannot perform it owing to her lack of strength; he
wants to increase her strength – the lung disease becomes more menac-
ing; her strength is greater – haemorrhages take it away. There is a
threat of death from every side so that her life is in God's hands alone.
If He does not show mercy there exists no human sympathy great
enough to bring salvation to my wife.

Would you recognize her – you – such a good friend of hers? Only her
spirit is intact. Is she not aware of her state or does she bear it bravely –
who could read the answer in her eyes, when I, for whom they were like
an open book, cannot read anything? Only occasionally a stronger
embrace for myself or Konradek tells of her courage. Oh God, what else
can I write to you ... I believe in God and patiently carry this stone in
my heart: days and nights beside my wife – sometimes even without a

servant, for that is difficult. Our mother came yesterday, as soon as she herself could get out of bed.

In this black sorrow of mine, amidst the sufferings of my Beloved, your letter, my dear friend, was received by both of us with joy. She was enlivened for a while, took a long time to ponder over your letter and then insisted on my writing to you to infuse you with courage – courage, strength and particularly to make you entrust man's fate to God; for a Christian such an act of trust does not exclude either caution or consideration or personal initiative.

My wife maintains, and so do I, that when the soul feels despair – when it is pining – it must find consolation even by drinking poison. Satan offers it many times; but next to that cup overflowing with delusion and outward sweetness an invisible hand holds another cup offered by Providence. The art is in choosing. While the first deceives a man's reason, the second often does not suit man's reason, but his heart trembles towards it with a strange inclination. I said the art is in choosing; no, my dear friend. It is easy – providing that no disappointment, no misfortune causes that other soul which is welded to yours to shirk it. She and I have both acted in this way. We are very miserable and unhappy today, but even had we been fully aware of the fate which awaited us, we would have acted in the same way. We are very miserable and unhappy – but we praise God for letting us carry our destiny together. We pray to Him to withdraw the cup of bitterness from our lips, for we have already imbibed too much and too often; but we thank Him that our lips can jointly drink that liquid. We would not exchange it for nectar if we were to drink it separately. And all this has resulted from unity – not of ideas but of principles; from unity – not of tastes but of a sense of duty; from different feelings but such that they are like different notes linked together in one chord of unshaken love. We have never been blinded by one another; we loved each other not because we were perfect in one another's eyes but in spite of our shortcomings and defects, which nevertheless never concealed my heart and soul from her nor her heart and soul from me. Writing to you about happiness while crushed down to the ground, crushed and hardly able to breathe under the weight of my cross – I believe that we have been happy, that until this day we have lived in a superior glow of happiness, never obscured. And so if you have found, without being blinded, another soul prepared to give itself up to you – that is enough. There is nothing to hesitate about. But remember, my dear friend, that in matters of happiness as in matters of faith, it is not absolute reason but the heart that does not err.

That is all I can write. You would understand me a thousand times better if you could see us today; if you could feel the clasp of our hands – hers, although powerless, and mine, although trembling with anxiety.

My poor darling wants to dictate a letter to you – she wants her words to be transmitted through my writing and so you may get a second letter; this one I am writing to you – *tibi soli*[1] – and when you write back to us, disclosing your knowledge of her illness, do not mention my suffering and fears. The lie of peaceful serenity in my eyes and on my face remains throughout day and night; my terrors are all within me and until now none has crept over my countenance. For she might be looking at me. Whatever happens, may she believe that our parting is inconceivable – otherwise she might not have the strength to bear anything.

I embrace you – my blessings to Bronek – what a fine boy – his portrait beside my poor darling. A handshake for my best friends; I shall never forget you – forever your faithful and devoted friend.

Waiting for you in a letter.

Your

Apollo

Apollo Korzeniowski to Kazimierz Kaszewski

Biblioteka Jagiellońska, Cracow, MS 3057

29 May/10 June 1865

My best friend,

At last I have recovered sufficiently to be able, to know how, to write to you. Where my soul has been I do not know but it is returning dreadfully exhausted, as if not mine, enveloped in manifold shrouds, bearing a cross so heavy that I tremble at the thought of some friendly eye looking at it and turning away in terror. That is why until now I have not dared to speak to my two best and most beloved ones, to my brother and yourself. Today I am writing to you both. I do not like to throw pearls of a holy and lifelong sorrow on to the rubbish heap of everyday life; but unfortunately live I must! And in order to live one has to speak sometimes to loving hearts able to understand and sympathize with such pain as mine. And I am here so very much alone: no other company but this silent grave, bewitched in silence, deaf to prayers, unresponsive to tears, harder even than Adam's stone, for a tear will not seep through it.[2] I spend the greatest part of my days by the grave, but what am I to do about it – how am I to rid myself of

---

[1] Lat.: 'to you alone'.
[2] Allusion to a passage in Adam Mickiewicz's poem *Dziady* ('The Forefathers' Eve'), part IV (1823), about a stone crying at the sight of changes caused in Poland by the partition of the country.

the remaining hours of vigil or of sleep? Tell me, my best friend. My deepest beliefs are shaken; doubts consume all my thoughts. When She is not here, when all I dream about is to see her again – this creature without a blemish, who constituted the entire delight of my existence – doubts overwhelm me and call out: and if my faith is but deluded imagination? If my mother's teaching about another and better life for the soul was only her heart's mistake? If death does end everything? If I shall never see her, never?! Ah, my dear friend, what torments! ...

Forgive me, my best friend! Ludwik has written that you are ailing and here I pester you with my suffering. But what else could I be writing today to those I love? I feel such a need to send you a word and to read yours, when it is not God's pleasure to allow me to hear it live and pulsating from that heart that issues it. Anyway, in expectation – for it is difficult not to expect departure when the only thought is to depart – and mindful of your friendship for us, mindful of your precious words at our parting, I even have a request, nay, a prayer to you. Although I am writing this myself, we are writing together – she from her grave and I without it, above her. We write together whether in her or my hand – as we always used to do in her lifetime. Oh! I have not parted with her: I just cannot see or hear her. In order to make my request clearer and more comprehensible, I wish to remind you, my friend, as in the sadness of our parting, gazing at our tiny one, Konradek, you said: 'If you were not to return for a long long time, send him to me and I shall look after him as I do after my Bronek.' Well, she will never return, and perhaps I shall never return either; and Konradek is growing up at my side and by the time he is grown up I shall not be here. Please fulfil your promise. I want whatever of hers that remains on this earth to bear proper testimony to her in the eyes of those who will never forget her; and who is better able than you, my dear and noble friend, to clothe him with full morality? I repeat: this I am writing in anticipation and therefore ahead of the time which may come in a year, but, who knows, may be tomorrow. I should not like to worry on that score. She used to pour out her heart and soul on to the child and now to leave him without any assurance or to dismiss him without any hope would seem to me to be disloyal to Her heart and soul. I have arranged for Konradek to have a provision until the end of his schooling, small but sufficient for his upkeep and education; in addition to some crumbs inherited from his mother. I have made all necessary sacrifices today to ensure his tomorrow. So he may be for you a bother, but not a material burden. Please tell me, my dear and best! Is it yea? Will you do it for me? I must know what to tell the people who, under the circumstances, will take care of Konradek during the first days of his complete bereavement.

A couple of months before her death I wrote to you two letters; to the second one she added a note in her almost dying hand about what was sustaining life in her – about her hope of return. Have those letters reached you? Have you answered them? We received nothing. My Unforgettable one, dying, a couple of hours before she changed from a martyr into an angel, when white wings of immortality seemed to flutter from her shoulders, surrounded by portraits of all those who had been close to her heart and memory, kept mentioning you, asking constantly whether a letter from you had arrived; and in her final days, her dreams affected by hallucinations, whispering continually prayers or hymns, surprised, she would ask dreamily after you: why have you not come, knowing how sad and forlorn we are? I am writing all this so that you should know how dear you were and still are to our hearts – need I tell you? – and thus you shall remain. Our faith in guardian angels is beautiful – oh, if it is not illusory I am certain that today she is mine. I shall wait impatiently for your reply; do not write at length but answer in a few words. Apart from that main request I have yet another, concerning the memory of my Beloved and her last will: it is not difficult to fulfil but can only be done where you are. I shall write to you about it as soon as I receive your letter. Now, my – our – dear friend, I bid you goodbye – that sorrow which will keep me upright till my very last breath, with that sadness which speaks to me about the immortality of souls, with that memory which is my only love and farewell to life on earth; my blessings to your Bronek; and as to myself, the only comfort I now need on this earth may be found in your handshake.

                                                        Your Apollo

A handshake to those who remember kindly the dear one I have lost. Please answer. I devote myself much to Konradek's education; if only I could have the school syllabus used in the Kingdom! And several schoolbooks for the first and second class – could you, please? – and I shall think about repayment.

There is nothing I need now and therefore hardly think about means of support. The Weekly *Kłosy* has ordered, and I have supplied, three dramas by Victor Hugo and now, as soon as I have copied them out I shall send them Shakespeare's *The Comedy of Errors* and Dickens's *Hard Times*.[1] If you could glance at the *Comedy of Errors*, judge it; if bad, take it and do not let them print it.

I shall send you – as to all her blood-relations – a memento of her.

[1] *The Comedy of Errors* was published, as *Komedia obłędów*, in *Kłosy*, 1866, nos 36–41; *Hard Times* as *Ciężkie czasy na te czasy* in *Gazeta Polska*, 1866, nos 267–83, 292, and 1867, nos 1–2, 14–20, 26–7.

Apollo Korzeniowski to Kazimierz Kaszewski
Biblioteka Jagiellońska, Cracow, MS 3057

6/18 Sept[ember] 1865

My own best friend, blessed be your letter which gave me strength and comfort; for I know that those severe words come from a heart which understands the immensity of my loss, sympathizes with my grief and sadness. Your letter was just what I needed. I have enough and more than enough of thoughtless indifference and deathlike solitude. And that letter of yours – although written with syllables of pained compassion – pulsates with life and stimulates to life. That is what it means to me; and I had to wait with my reply until your expected return from your excursion. Have you had a respite from work? Has the air strengthened you for the future toil? How is your health? Do I have to thank you for your good intentions towards my little orphan? Your promises are what we were constantly dreaming of in the troubled days and they gave us courage in the expectation of an even worse fate to come. She departed into a better world with that hope of a sheltered future for her child; and I live with that assurance till this day. Perhaps I shall send the little mite away for the next school year: my mind is set firmly on it, but for a man whose life is as disrupted as mine everything is governed by circumstances; that is why I say 'perhaps'. In any case your promise to send the schoolbooks and the syllabus made me happy and I am looking forward to their arrival. To cover the cost of the books please sell my secretaire: it used to be a favourite of hers, but she will never see me behind it. Since your letter several new and painful blows have fallen on me: albeit the first thunderbolts had left but little work for those that followed. My younger brother has started on a sixteen-month walk;[1] any day now my sister will begin her walk – perhaps not exactly along the same road, but just as long.[2] This has caused the loss of everything we have which was kept undivided, since we loved each other; and two beggars have joined in my wealth. May it all add to God's glory if He should lend us the strength to carry our burden. That is why I am exerting all my energy (until now to no avail) to find a private paid job, as well as any literary work which does not require ready inspiration – e.g. translations from Fr[ench] Eng[lish] Germ[an] will be gratefully welcomed. Thus you see, my best friend, that I am most anxious for what you justly call substitutes, and even if not to delude my lifelong grief, I shall work out of sense of duty.

[1] Hilary Korzeniowski was exiled to Tomsk, where he died in 1873.
[2] Apollo's sister (married), of unknown name; this is one of three extant mentions of her existence.

Konradek's education as well as his amusement take up a lot of daylight hours. Poor child: he does not know what a contemporary playmate is; he looks at the decrepitude of my sadness and who knows if that sight does not make his young heart wrinkled or his awakening soul grizzled. These are important reasons forcing me to tear this poor child away from my dejected heart. As I write to you, my most faithful friend, words of gratitude fight for priority in my thoughts with new requests. Both spring from the heart. And in addition to the old ones there is a new request: you have a photograph of my Beloved in heaven; I have here a very similar picture, larger, but not as good as a photograph. Might I send it to you in the hope of one of the painters making from it a large portrait of which several photographs could then be taken? In the first place I want to have it for myself and the child; then for several members of the family and a few friends. My dear, you will not refuse your cooperation in this matter: please, let me know and I shall send the photograph at once. What might be the cost for the execution of a pencil-drawing? Tell me.

Kłosy has announced its intention of publishing my translations of Dickens's *Hard Times* and Shakespeare's *The Comedy of Errors*; I have dispatched both. The comedy is excellent and ready for the stage. I have tried to preserve not only the thought but in certain respects the literary meaning and shape of the verse. Shakespeare puts serious or pompous conversation into unrhymed verse with occasional rhymes in more prominent places – my translation is done in rhyming lines of thirteen syllables. His lively, witty or jocular conversations run usually in prose – mine are in rhyming lines of thirteen syllables. Shakespeare's love scenes are in mixed verse, rhymed (longer and shorter) – I did likewise, alternating lines of eleven and eight syllables. I have asked the editors to show you the translation. It was my first attempt at translating Shakespeare and I do not feel confident. Please look at it.

Little to write about myself. My teeth have been clenched for a long time; as you know, words do not get through clenched teeth; only moans escape. Thank God, however, those who are indifferent did not hear them, just as no one in the worst moment saw my tears; the scorching drops from my eyes would sink into my heart leaving it scarred forever.

Let your words about my Unforgettable one return in the form of blessings upon your Bronek. I have sent them on to our unhappy mother: she thanks you by prayer. Poor mother is in the country with her son; she is well-nigh bed-ridden, longing and waiting for the moment when she will see her beloved children who departed from her. Very unhappy. As to myself, I believe that if I am alive it is because, as you yourself say, the One Who is in heaven looks down upon me. I am possessed by the desire to ensure her immortality. As to eternal immortality – she has found it in God's blessing; but I want her to be immortal in the hearts of those she loved in her lifetime. Yours is one of them.

Nothing but this is dear to me. My feelings must be such as were experienced by a lonely barbarian dying in the arena in the unfamiliar town of Rome; but, may God be my witness, I do not call for death and while there is life in me I shall, I shall go on living. Some trace, if not today – then tomorrow; if not for myself – then for others. I shall never lack this kind of work; no one will give it to me because I have taken it myself – it comes foremost. But I ask and try for another, as I do not want to be a burden to anyone and wish to carry alone all my dearly beloved burdens, particularly those sent by God. I embrace you and Bronek and commend my Konradek to your love. Pass my respects to Mr Aleks. Brotherly regards to those who know me and are sympathetic.

Your Apollo

Friendly regards to Ludwik and to the Reverend Ed.[1]

Apollo Korzeniowski to Kazimierz Kaszewski
Biblioteka Jagiellońska, Cracow, MS 3057

19/31 Oct[ober] 1865

My best Kazimierz, having guessed at your return to work from the excursion, I have dispatched one letter already; I am writing a second one, not to force a reply from you, as it takes time and I know how busy you are in your work. But one affectionate word by post would bring me great consolation, for your health is a worry to me and my heart has not yet learned to do without news from those it loves. Moreover, I have something to ask of you – for three years I have been flooding you with requests. First of all, I wish to remind you of the promised school syllabus and classical books for Konradek; I should like to prepare him a little in accordance with the requirements. Secondly, my dear friend, if there is a buyer for the secretaire, please sell it at once, and after deducting the money for Konradek's books, send the rest to my address. I counted a little on receiving a payment from *Kłosy*, as they had informed me in ink and print of their decision to publish my translations of Dickens and the *Comedy of Errors* – Dickens at the end of

---

[1] Unidentified.

September and *The Comedy of Errors* at the beginning of November – and asked me how best to send me the dues. I answered immediately; that was at the beginning of August. Since then I have not had a word from them and last month even the weekly *Kłosy* stopped coming. Today I wrote them a letter. But it is all rather disappointing. In order to explain my needs I would have to write at great length, recounting an entire chapter of my hard life; thus only the outline: 'Brother – Sister – their unexpected and trying journey – my bereavement. The annihilated brother becomes the head of the family and its support, himself having nothing to support himself with! These, my best friend, are the reasons why every penny is forty-eight times dearer to me now than ever before. Of course as long as the secretaire is not sold no money is due to me; unless *Kłosy* pays for the MS according to its rates.

To turn from my troubles to the holy memory, I am sending you, my dear friend, the picture of the grave, the only thing that is left from my entire happiness. I have a heart-felt obligation to send the picture to you, who were such a good friend of my Dearest One in heaven – or rather, to send the picture of the grave of someone who was such a good friend of yours. Since last autumn my health has been declining badly and my dear little mite takes care of me – only the two of us left on this earth. I need never be ashamed on account of his heart – he inherited his gifts from his mother – but his head is not to be envied – it is mine. And your Bronek? Robust? To Konradek he always represents the quintessence of all wisdom. I live in the hope that near you and close to your heart, my Konrad will become humanized in human surroundings. I embrace you time and time again. Best regards to friends.

Your

Apollo Korze.

Chernihov District
Apoll, Korzen.

The inscription on the back of the photograph may be found on a marble plaque in the local church.[1]

---

[1] The Catholic church in Chernihov (Chernigov) has been destroyed; the cemetery where Ewa Korzeniowska was buried was turned into a collective farmers' market.

Regina Korzeniowska[1] to Konrad Korzeniowski

Beinecke Library, Yale University, New Haven, Conn.

> Win[n]ica 1865,
> on St Konrad's Day [26 November 1865]

My beloved Konradek,

I hasten to send you my most loving and affectionate wishes: may you grow up to be a comfort to your father and your devoted relatives. May you always enjoy good health and make slow progress in your studies, for a smaller amount of knowledge becomes more firmly fixed in one's memory.

I would be glad to see you in robust health, but having encountered frightening examples of careless mothers and nannies, I refrain from any suggestions, particularly since I am not familiar with the temperature in your part of the world. Here I watch a group of ten young children being taken out for a walk every day, before lunch, while their rooms are being aired, twice a day, even in bad weather. The lady is very young, slim and pale, but the children are robust and plump, constantly on the move and well used to the cold. Their sheep-skin coats are close-fitting, boots are warm and bonnets well made to protect them against blizzards.

And so I have decided to equip you in the same way for life, by bequeathing to you, together with my sister, one thousand roubles – for boots, galoshes, and a fur coat; when I am gone you will collect the same interest as I have been getting during my lifetime, from the few thousand roubles which represent my entire capital. I am happy to bestow upon you today this gift and best wishes with a request that you should now and then say the Angelus for my soul.

> Regina

Apollo Korzeniowski to Gabriela and Jan Zagórski

Tygodnik Ilustrowany (Warsaw), 1920, no. 20

> 6/18 January 1866

May God's blessing be with you, and may peace reign in your house, my beloved Gabrynia and Jaś. May your own and your adopted children's good health and kind hearts lighten and sweeten the burden of parental responsibilities. If there is a smile anywhere in our country, may it light up your life; let tears not scorch your hearts but bring relief

---

[1] Regina Korzeniowska (1793–1874), editor of geographical atlases, and Conrad's great-aunt. See Jan Perłowski's essay in this volume, p. 156.

to your tormented souls. God is so great, merciful and compassionate, that we – even we, who are surrounded by boundless cruelty and pitilessness – may still exchange wishes, hopeful that they, like our daily prayers, may be heard in heaven. May this New Year – I know not which of the many years of sorrow and grief – spare you further suffering so that you will at least be able to cherish quietly and peacefully the loving memory of those who are far away and those who sleep in their graves, but live for ever in God's mercy. I have lived through them with God-given strength, not my own. Undoubtedly I have never suffered nor could suffer as much as our Saviour did – but I am only a man. By looking continually at the Cross I kept fortifying my enfeebled soul, my confused thoughts. And thus the holy days of torture had passed, and I, feeling slightly broken but still alive and breathing, rose to meet my everyday existence. The little orphan keeps clinging to me and it is impossible not to be constantly worrying about him. And so, my beloved, I continue living and loving whatever is left to love as strongly as before, except that in the past I could give something, sacrifice something, to the objects of my love, and today I cannot. Whatever I do in life I can neither give nor sacrifice anything; for I have nothing left to give or to sacrifice. It is a sad state for a man to be in when the only two ways to dignity, and to being in God's image and likeness, are closed to him; but such are the decrees of Providence.

When bitter misery chokes me and a kind of godly sadness – not proud despair – descends upon me, I read your dear letter again and again; tears will stream down, thoughts will flow away, and slightly calmer I begin once again to tackle my life, which is, at present, confined solely to Konradek. I teach him all I know myself – alas, it is not much; I guard him against the influence of the local atmosphere and the little mite is growing up as though in a cloister; the grave of our Unforgettable is our *memento mori* and every letter from the East, West, South or North brings us fastings, hair-shirts and flogging. We tremble with cold, die of hunger, struggle in abject poverty with our brethren; and in our prayers, God knows, we put only a couple of words about ourselves.

I am here as though behind bolted doors where a beloved being is dying and we cannot as much as wipe the mortal sweat off her forehead; on the other side there is a wide open door through which we cannot enter but are permitted to look at something that Dante never described, for his soul, stricken with countless horrors but none the less Christian, could not have had such inhuman visions.

That is our life. Does not love have a strange power to be able to lead my thought out of this abyss to visit my dear, beloved and only friends, and then bring it back here – if not comforted then at least appeased?

After the embrace which I send on paper to you and your children, I feel more brave in my fear, more dignified in my nonentity, more saintly in the penance which God has assigned to me.

How stupid man's language is; having written it all I see that I have not said anything, either about my terrible sadness, or about my devotion to you both – to you, whom she loved; to you – whose kind and saintly hearts she brought me in her dowry, and, I feel sure, did not take away with her when she departed to God. But I love you very very much, believe me. I feel the same anxiety about your children as about my Konradek; thoughts about you exorcise the loneliness of an orphan and exile. May you find your reward in God, as my love is not of my will's but of your hearts' doing.

Please tell your family, all of them, that I am faithful in my attachments; and tell others that I am as fond of them now as years ago when I was rich in love; today I have nothing left for myself – but for others my heart has not diminished.

I shall end as I began, with the name of our Blessed Saviour who died so as to make us happy, and who can see that we are still waiting for the happiness to come.

Your one and always the same

Apollo

Apollo Korzeniowski to Kazimierz Kaszewski
Biblioteka Jagiellońska, Cracow, MS 3057

20 January/1 February 1866

Poor you, my best Kazimierz, because all the trust I have in your friendship for our deceased and for us the living, and my gratitude for your kindness, fall on you in a shower of letters when you stand anyway under the drainpipe of your daily toil. But what am I to do? I have just collected your gift: books for Konradek – am I not to thank you? And in your letter there is news about the only thing I care about: the likeness of my Beloved who is in heaven – and ought I to keep silent too? Bear with me, my dear, with the results of my misery, and some day God will reward you.

I thank you for the books, but I blame myself for not having told you more explicitly what I needed and thus having put you to extra expense (French method). The rest will be most useful. I myself have arranged the French method following the pattern of Robertson's English method and can marvel now at its excellent results upon my boy. I am convinced that he, who knows only the grammar of his mother tongue, will learn in one year, without a teacher, to pronounce fairly well, to write correctly, to understand everything, and will be able to say a lot. But, my dear friend, what I now urgently need is the geometry book. If you could find the old book used by district schools rather than the present-day lucubrations I would readily kiss hands for it. Nowadays when they want to popularize a subject, they destroy all common sense in the head – the thing which ought to be more 'popular' than anything else. Apart from that I need nothing else for Konradek's education. Your observation went straight to my heart: indeed we are both without any points of comparison; I teach and demand too much and the little one, seeing nobody, burrows too deeply into books. Thank you for the warning.

Ah! my best friend, what a bother for you with that portrait! But it is all I have apart from my heart and soul. That is why I conceived the idea of having a beautiful pencil-drawing made from those photographs and then having the drawing photographed. I know the problems of enlargements, particularly when the original portrait has defects, and that is why I wanted a skilful drawing made for the photographer. Please forgive me, my dear, and accept my sincere thanks; but how am I to thank Beyer?[1] Perhaps he pays with kindness for the respect evoked by his good life. But the thought of having the photograph coloured never crossed my mind. Even *retouching* may damage a photograph, let alone colouring. A couple of days ago I dispatched to you *one* act of the play *Bez ratunku*.[2] The work is completed and it may suit the magazine; do not print my name for the reasons previously stated.[3] I expect no payment for it – anyway I shall always remain indebted to the magazine.

I embrace you very, very warmly. My health has again deteriorated – I can hardly write and scarcely know what I am writing; that does not prevent me from feeling very strongly the kindness of you *both*. Kiss for me those good hands that care for you. Let my kiss bestow a blessing on Bronek's little head. Ah, my dear – it is hard to be so old; the soul does not want to remain in the shattered machinery; I would not wish for more than to help Konrad stand on firm ground among decent people; to weld his body and awakening soul to the body of our society; also to take Her ashes from that alien cemetery to the family grave, and to put my foot on my native soil, to breathe its air, to look into the eyes of those I love and to call out: now, please God, receive your servant, for he is very very weary.

---

[1] Karol Beyer (1808–77) in Warsaw, one of the pioneers of photography.
[2] *Bez ratunku, urywek dramatu nieoryginalnego* ('Beyond Rescue, Fragment of an Unoriginal Drama') was published in *Tygodnik ilustrowany*, 1866, nos 339–41.
[3] On 19/31 January 1866 Korzeniowski wrote to Kaszewski that he thought he had taken the idea of that piece from somebody, but could not remember from whom.

Modest and yet so unlikely *pia desideria*.[1] I embrace you, thank you and ask to be remembered.

Apollo

Apollo Korzeniowski to Kazimierz Kaszewski
Biblioteka Jagiellońska, Cracow, MS 3057

10/22 November 1866

My best Kazimierz, I was eighteen years of age when I read in some book these three words: 'despair and die'.[2] The language was then unknown to me, and yet, those incomprehensible letters, those strange sounds, inflicted such a pain in my heart that today, suffering from genuine heart trouble, I experience a similar pain from time to time. I did not ask anyone then about the meaning of those words and they remained in my memory as inscrutable hieroglyphs. Today, however, aware of their meaning, I see that they were like a prophecy of my future life. Only my Christianity makes me reject the first word – but in the second one I await my end in peace. Let this tell you about my present life: millions of small details would not present a more accurate picture.

This letter of mine ought to be directed to both of you since your good wife was kind enough to send me the alms of her best thoughts, words and sympathy. How grateful I am to you both! May neither of you, nor your loved ones, ever experience such a Sahara-like drought when every little drop of life-giving dew is received by the lips with as rapturous a pleasure! I am lonely. Konradek is with his granny; his first month away was at Kiev visiting the doctors, then, on their advice, he went to his uncle in the country.[3] We both suffer equally: just imagine, the boy is so stupid that he misses his loneliness where all he saw was my clouded face and where the only diversions of his nine-year-old life were arduous lessons; he misses me in the clean country air, amidst amusements with his first cousin,[4] his contemporary, under the caressing wings of his granny, with his indulgent uncle who has transferred all his love for his sister on to her son, upon whom he looks with tender respect as upon the child of an unforgettable and superior being. And the boy pines away – he must be stupid, and, I fear, will remain so all his life! He has grown, his little face has altered, he begins to look very much like his mother. May God bless him; I cannot do anything for him now nor in the future.

---

[1] Lat.: 'pious wishes'.　　　[2] English in the original.
[3] In Nowochwastów (Nowofastów), the family estate of the Lubowidzkis, Tadeusz Bobrowski's parents-in-law.
[4] Józefa Bobrowska (1858–71), Tadeusz's daughter.

I am grateful to you, but at the same time sorry, that you used my letter to Ludwik as a bullet to shoot at the *Kłosy* phalanx: you must have caused quite a panic there, for I received a letter from Kaz. W. Wóycicki with fifty roubles as payment for *The Comedy of Errors*. But those fifty gold coins are too dear when bought with your words. For you ought to know that I have preserved quite an interesting collection of letters from them. They used to press for every manuscript as if unable to survive without it; on several occasions they wrote down the date of the commencement of printing; a couple of times they informed me of having sent me the fee, and so it went on for a full two years. At first I was surprised, then rather shocked, as I had already answered a touching letter from them and in all good faith I had rashly described my position, explaining why I care about the fee. In any case it is most kind of you to have intervened; I do not know if I wrote to you that my brother, with whom we had never divided our property, has gone far, far away; he trades in tea and runs a slaughter-house employing four priests extricated from their jobs as innkeepers. But that does not alter the fact that with my brother's departure, our little estate departed in the opposite direction; and to no avail were my protests that half of it was mine. Thus our joint means of support has vanished; and being nearer myself, it has become my duty to help my brother. This concerns my own brother, but what about all those who are not my own but equally dear to me and who parade before me in utter poverty? It is hard to meet the demands – but it must be done.

Believe me that since the death of my Unforgettable I know not what a servant is, and the world of architecture is reduced to my four bare walls. I am not complaining, God forbid! At times so ill as to have to lie down, I lie alone, quietly, without a murmur, and when God permits me to move about, I thank Him profusely. I live on various moneys owed to me and sent by various people according to their memory and capacity. I never know what I have or could have. Because all I managed to accumulate that is durable remains untouchable – for Konradek, whom I do not want to go through my experience after my death.

This brings me to your question how to dispose of our things. I shall let you know shortly: the list is with our mother, so I must ask her for it. Unable to keep them I am burning most momentoes of her. Some of the things I shall ask you to sell; but first of all, when you have time, do me a favour and inform me of the state of our accounts. How much do I owe you? Please do it for me, my dear friend. Add up the credit from the sales and the expenses since our departure. It will be a weight off my heart.

I imagine your life, the troubles which I – remote and blindfold – do not experience here, your work frequently seasoned with bitterness which ought not to exist in work, and that kind of discouragement – nay, such as yourself do not get discouraged! – but that disgust which comes from forcing on to the *populace* something good when all it wants and thirsts for is dregs. You are right to use the word *populace* instead of *public*. In the olden days the first word had the meaning best suited to a society that grows in a foggy and damp atmosphere. This sad truth applies no doubt to all parts of our native land; letters from opposite ends of the country seem to confirm it. May God give you perseverance, for that in itself permeates the air with goodness and enters human lungs even in spite of and against their will. May Cicero sweeten the hours for you, and the public lecture at the Main School[1] bring as much good to some as we should wish for all.

I have sent Jenike my translation of Shakespeare's comedy *Much Ado About Nothing*.[2] I really cannot give it away for nothing. Let him sell it even if only for a little; the Charitable Society which has taken root in my heart suffers many needs. *Kłosy* has other manuscripts as well, and in my next letter I shall send you a list authorizing you to take them; you can do with them whatever you think suitable. For two years *Kłosy* pressed for the novel *Hard Times*, making me hurry furiously; my apprehensions concern not so much inaccuracies as flaws of style. But the translation is certainly not worse than that of *Les Misérables* and of *The Toilers of the Sea*.[3] Do not haggle over terms out of kindness towards me, but accept whatever they offer and be done with it.

You know, my dear, that I taught myself English following Robertson's method. So I know how much easier it makes learning. Konradek is another case in point: I taught him French by the same method and every day has brought new progress. The French governess is amazed by his knowledge of French after only one year of lessons. I myself worked out for Konradek a French method based on Robertson's, and adapted it to the Polish language; but it could also prove useful for other young people, particularly those who are already acquainted with Polish grammar, like Konradek. Would any publishers be interested in it? Write, and I shall send you the first lesson as an example. This method allows one to dispense with a teacher. Such an elementary course could be quite useful. Ohn's methods cannot stand comparison. I claim no other merits apart from tedious work and

---

[1] Kaszewski gave a lecture about Cicero at Warsaw's *Szkoła Główna*, equivalent of a university.
[2] This translation was never published and the MS has been lost.
[3] Also never published and lost.

a great deal of writing. There could be two volumes. But it is certain that having worked his way through the forty lessons (forty make up the total) the pupil will understand and write excellent French; and he will speak in proportion to the amount of work put in, as nothing can be done without it. Please answer me. All I have said here is based on experience.

My dear, perhaps you will not have enough time to read this letter, and yet I cannot bring myself to end. As soon as I leave off I become so lonely – do not hold my endless chatting against me! Your letter gave me the impression of saying in a manly voice: 'Well, my dear, we shall probably never see each other again – be brave and persevere till the end.' I think likewise and shall act accordingly. I shall take with me the memory of you – of you both – to that place where we shall all eventually go – as the greatest asset of my lifetime. If I had the certainty that my boy would follow the footsteps of good and honest people, that in him would live those qualities which make his father love people like yourself, how very peacefully would I be leaving this world and how confidently would I look into the eyes of my Unforgettable in heaven! Although everything around forces me to doubt God's omnipotence, in Him I place all my trust and leave the fate of my little one in His care. Meanwhile the only happy moment left to me will be when my boy stands before you. This year and its attendant circumstances have hindered my projects, but have not impaired or eradicated them. It is a great consolation to me to keep always in my heart your promise in which My Unforgettable placed her trust.

I embrace you most tenderly and kiss your wife's hands. Bless Bronek from me most tenderly. Regards to all who remember me kindly; I have not forgotten anybody or anything; always faithful – always the same.

Your friend,

Apollo

Apollo Korzeniowski to Kazimierz Władysław Wóycicki

Biblioteka Jagiellońska, Cracow, MS 7832

2/14 December 1866

My esteemed and always dear friend, I expect you will believe me when I tell you that your last letter was precious and beneficial to my heart. Everything you told me as a friend – irrespective of paper, ink and quill, those literary paraphernalia – I have accepted with open arms into my soul; and God sees that all you do is to give me back, tit for tat, your kindness and goodwill. And your friendly words and your dear wife's thoughts, little deserved but not through ill-will, I regard as bread for the *bene merenti*,[1] and as such it not only enlivens my spirit but also brings me honour.

Amidst the small troubles of working life which many of you share, little attention is paid to words; and more lively expressions are always suspected of being mere rhetoric. Such is not the case with mine. But when having been silent for days and months on end I happen to make a pronouncement, words fly out like a suppressed charge: yet you may believe me that the explosive must have been of good quality, since it has retained its properties until now! I suppose it is enough for you to get a clear picture of my existence here. Poor Konradek is ill and receiving treatment at his uncle's country house; as to myself, without exaggeration, I doubt if I have spoken a thousand words in the last two years. Lonely in my lodgings; in the morning the caretaker of the house brings me that palladium of the local life, the samovar; he sweeps the room and brings a supply of water. I pay him on the condition that he does not bark at me. At church I pray silently and the local Catholics, our self-confessed countrymen, are not worth knowing: they are frightened of me and I, well, I just hardly pay attention to their crawling movements.

Enough said of this.

But, my dear Pan Kazimierz, as to literature: all of you editors behave like kittenish old women; it is so important to you to have an *entourage* for distributing your smiles left and right in order to attract. And this is the spirit in which I have received your flattering words as to what I *can* or *could* achieve with pen in hand. Nevertheless I have heard those words with gratitude because they came from friendly lips and were written by a hand I would gladly clasp in mine.

I shall wait for your prospectus – not as a wholesaler who has a lot to dispose of, but as one who wants to send you something suitable.

According to the weekly *Kłosy*, two years ago *Ruy Blas*[2] did not get passed by the censors. Now you say that it is uncensored. At the time I half believed; today it does not seem to me that there should be any difficulties with the censorship. Apart from noble, well-expressed thought, there is nothing there to shock. But let it be as you wish.

I confess I find the dispute which you describe between *Kto[sy]* and *Tyg[odnik] Il[ustrowany]* puzzling – believe me, I never received a single unfavourable word about *Kłosy* from Warsaw.

It is not feasible to put down on paper everything I hear about *Kłosy*. As I am regarded by old, non-literary friends as a man of letters people write to me from various corners of the earth, thinking it essential to

[1] Lat.: 'the well deserving'.   [2] Never published and lost.

discuss literary matters with me, and I could present no mean mosaic of public opinion about *Kłosy* in the form of ? or ! To my mind your editorship bids well for the journal – do sign yourself clearly in capitals on the prospectus – and without that obviously mercantile 'so & so & Co.'.

Getting near Christmas, from my loneliness, dumbness, deafness, extinction, from this grave of mine, I send you all that which does not die or get killed: my best wishes from the depths of my soul for you, yours and those you love.

Your servant and friend,
A. Korzeniowski

Apollo Korzeniowski to Kazimierz Kaszewski

Biblioteka Jagiellońska, Cracow, MS 3057

7/19 February 1867

Reconcile yourself, my best friend, to receiving a letter from me once a month. You may offer it to God as punishment for, at least, your venial sins, as it appears to be the only possible use to be made of my correspondence. And I find it so very hard to remain for you both remote and invisible! Let at least those few drops of ink keep my presence in your small circle. As to your kind and brave offer to attend to my odds and ends, my answer, based on exploiting your own and your wife's goodwill, was definite. It may be a selfish way of showing gratitude: simply to accept what kind-hearted people offer; but I have no choice.

My days grow longer, my time runs shorter; the former, as if each day was a day of fasting; the latter, like a sleep of death. Everything contributes to it; and amidst my suffering it is my sole diversion to remain vigilant so that the indifferent and ill-disposed do not see my exhaustion and collapse. My poor Konradek still ill – undergoing treatment – far from me. And I am getting weaker and weaker, every day one hour of fever, completely alone (this I am not complaining about because I always feel ashamed of ailing), cut off from everything that concerns me, insensible to the murmur of life, which reaches my ears but penetrates neither my mind nor thoughts – as if they were temples of an alien denomination.

What strange conceit to be thus chatting to a man like yourself from a place as sordid as this one, and from an equally detestable personal position. Admittedly, Job spoke from under the dung, but he was heard by all the peoples; he did not whisper into individual ears what no single human ear on its own can bear to listen to. And so I am restraining my outpourings. Do not think, however, that I want to compare myself with Job: you know how I dislike all ornamentation for my heart and soul.

I do not remember if someone told me this – who could it be? – but I know or seem to know that you have written an original comedy. If it is true, let me know something more definite about it. As you are one who feels everything, you should also be able to feel the extent of the interest I take in every word of yours, whether directed to me or to people in general. Apropos of originality, tell me how Wacław Szymanowski[1] has offended Jenike and possibly others as well, as I read twice (once in Jenike's article and the second time in someone else's, I cannot remember where) that Wacław Szymanowski is the *author* of *Paria*.[2] It must be very painful for Casimir Delavigne to be thus *de propos délibéré*[3] stripped of his laurel leaves, which anyway were not too many. But Szymanowski has been wronged all the same.

There is still some strength left in me; how gladly would I use it to make my boy's future more secure financially! That is why I have worked out that French–Polish method which required me only to recall the old skill and to drive my quill energetically. And that is why I should be willing to translate everything possible from French and English – when commissioned. And since I can spend entire days working, the job would be completed no less quickly than if it were done on the spot. Should some merciful daily newspaper send me, at my expense, a work requiring translation, I would not fail to complete my task on time, by dispatching every week a sheaf of pages. Please, would you consider the possibilities of finding me that kind of occupation?

I have certain pieces already translated but some are unfinished and others require careful checking on account of what you call 'unforseen circumstances', and really my mind is not fit for it today. If only I could take a deep breath, a hasty look and embrace another in my arms – ah! I should probably revive and be cured. I know, I know what *Heimweh*[4] is. My doctors here keep telling me that local chemists do not have medicines for me; that I am not ill but involuntarily slipping away from life without bidding goodbye. I have two doctors – both have lived here for many years – both friendly towards me, but both complain that the sight and treatment of my afflictions shake their long-lasting quietism and now they are constantly making plans to

---

[1] Wacław Szymanowski (1821–86), journalist, editor, translator and minor poet.
[2] *Le Paria* (1821), a tragedy by Casimir Delavigne (1794–1843), French poet and dramatist.
[3] Fr.: 'on purpose'.   [4] German: 'longing for one's country'.

leave; but in view of the many invisible and yet steel-like threads that keep them here I doubt whether they will ever take themselves off.

I embrace you and Bronek and kiss your wife's hand. I commend myself to your memory – very earnestly.

Always your devoted

A. Korz.

Apollo Korzeniowski to Stefan Buszczyński[1]
Biblioteka PAN, Cracow, MS 2604

5/17 March 1868
Wegieł Szeroki, Penter's House, No. 804 [Lwów]

My dearest Stefan,

What a great, unexpected and undeserved grace of God: we may openly write to each other; we may cherish the hope of seeing each other some day; I may discharge straight to your heart my tender gratitude and love for your kindest of daughters who, lonely forlorn orphan that she is, has found the time and strength of heart to send her old friend a ray of consolation by her words...

However, the circumstances happen to be untoward – something I am quite accustomed to – and prevent me from hasting away to Cracow, where sooner or later I shall go. Apart from those circumstances I have not yet had time to acquaint myself with Lwów, or rather the Lwowians, in order to form a clear idea about the present situation and to answer for myself the two questions: shall I be able to find work to support myself in Lwów and shall I at my last gasp be of any use to the community? Let me tell you openly, to no one but yourself, that until now Lwów has not succeeded in winning my allegiance. In the first place I was struck by the local envy directed at Cracow, which Lwów would willingly flay of everything possible.[2] Cracow and Lwów are like a father and his scamp of a son: the first is an old, respectable, pious man of high desert; the latter, brought up abroad, a Hegelian, Kantian, Spinozist, political economist, accountant, but mindful of public opinion, simulating respect for the old man on condition that he does not join the guests, does not speak, only sits in a corner praising God to avoid possible embarrassment to his educated son. I do not like it. If only one could find in Lwów a trace of some great idea born and nurtured in the city's own heart and able to grow, flourish and shine out,

---

[1] Stefan Buszczyński (1821–92), Korzeniowski's closest friend, liberal–democratic political writer, active in the 1863 insurrection, an enemy of appeasement.
[2] Cracow was historically the main centre of Polish cultural and political life outside Warsaw. Lwów was the capital of the Austrian part of Poland and a rapidly developing administrative centre.

for the public weal! And that is precisely what I do not see. Roused from my long sleep, I am struck by [fragment destroyed] the sight of people who, amidst their semi-torpid floundering, happen to find a bone and in no time sit down as calmly as could be to pick at it till the end of their days, watching only that no one should come and take it away from them: that is why they snarl at one another. This selfish snarling is, as the English would say, the Lwów 'keynote'. Having overcome certain difficulties and having given assurances that my appetite is poor I could probably lie down next to someone with his bone – but it is not my wont. All this confirms my belief that I will not be of any use here, nor will I find means of support; although the material needs of one who survived several years of Muscovy's exile are very, very, very small indeed. Anyway my second, if not my first object is to bring up Konradek not as a democrat, aristocrat, demagogue, republican, monarchist, or as a servant and flunkey of those parties – but only as a Pole: and I doubt whether that is the intention behind the present educational system in Lwów. One could write about it at great length – indeed there is much to say. It is very likely that I shall eventually move to Cracow: if I am to carry my life's heavy burden it is certainly better to do it in the vicinity of that Holy Sepulchre which may become my child's cradle – his holy, royal cradle! The next couple of months will be decisive. What keeps me in Lwów is that this is a providential city where although Polishness *is lacking* today, it may still find its expression. Close to our provinces,[1] it could radiate onto them and at a given moment it could even reveal to the Austrian government that the strength and power of the true *Oest-reich*[2] lies there. But will you believe me that at twenty public meetings here I heard the word *Poland* only once (from Mr Bielowski).[3] [Fragment destroyed] ... I tell you that my health is like a thermometer of the local Polish spirit – it rises in strength at the least ray of this sun of ours; it declines – freezes – dies at every repeated eclipse. One day will suddenly bring the final fall.

I have received some news of you from Mieczysław Pawlikowski.[4] Apparently you have written a book, very close to my heart according to what I have understood; its title, I believe, is *De la Décadence de l'Europe*[5] – am I right? But even if I had everything you have written

---

[1] That is, the former Polish south-east provinces under Russian rule.
[2] A pun: Austria is Österreich in German, *östlich* is 'eastern', *Reich*, 'state'.
[3] August Bielowski (1806–76), historian, editor of *Monumenta Poloniae historica*.
[4] Pawlikowski (1843–1903), politically active aristocrat, imprisoned for taking part in the 1863 movement, a liberal, later coeditor of the weekly *Kraj*.
[5] *La Décadence de l'Europe* (Paris, 1867), Buszczyński's best-known work, praised by Victor Hugo and Jules Michelet. He predicted that the democratic United States would overtake Europe both economically and politically.

within reach, I would give it all up for one clasp of your hand, for one look into your eyes.

I embrace you affectionately. Write to me of Cracow. My little one is with me. His illness of two years' duration is not over yet; but I thank God even for the present improvement. I have begun to teach him German so that he could attend local schools. I wish you could lay your kind hand upon his little head. Once again I strain you to my heart as a friend and a brother – I kiss your Ofelka's[1] hands. I was already here when she passed through Lwów. That is what old Krechowiecki[2] told me recently – but others say that the old man lies frequently. Goodbye, my only and dearest friends. My heart, until its last beat, will be always yours, faithful and unchanged.

Your

Apollo

Apollo Korzeniowski to Kazimierz Kaszewski
Biblioteka Jagiellońska, Cracow, MS 3057

11/23 March 1868

My dear Kazimierz, my only true friend,

I received your letter written to Nowofastów, but only yesterday – here – in Lwów. If I had expected a life-giving shower of affection on my return, I found it only in reading your letter. I wrote to you why I had been unable to go through Warsaw: the cost of it was prohibitive for me and even a short glimpse of you could not justify it. Now my weak condition and the rather unfavourable weather keep me in Lwów, and I am not even speculating as to when the doctors will give me their blessing for another journey: that is why all letters to me have to be addressed *poste restante* Lwów – at least for the time being. Wild's bookshop may also be used as an address. Enough of that. And so, my best friend, I have been two months in Lwów: I am as if I were not: not the I you knew of old. Many things have oppressed me, pushed me down, and the last one which troubles me is this permit exclusively for myself: by taking advantage of it I have deserted all those who suffered faithfully and patiently together with me, and moreover, I have parted with my grave. I am telling you all this because I want at least one other heart to know what is going on in mine. The thought of my disloyalty troubles me all the more as frankly speaking, deep down, I am not at all convinced that I can be of any use here to anything or

---

[1] Ofelia Buszczyńska, Stefan's daughter.
[2] Jan Krechowiecki (1805–85), a landowner from Volhynia, 1839–43 exiled to Siberia, after 1863 a political *émigré*; historian.

anybody. My only excuse is Konradek's upbringing. Thus, my dear, whenever things go wrong, a nagging thought comes to mind: it is God's justifiable punishment for deserting my post. Of course I mean general things, because having gone through my experiences, I do not expect anything personally from the world. I thank you very much for your willingness, over so many years, to assist me with my odds and ends. To tell you the truth, I should like some of them to help me pay for my needs and the remainder – to look at when I am dying. It is written upon my forehead that I am departing; perhaps it accounts for the Galileans[1] bearing my presence patiently: I will not take away from anyone the bone he is picking. This disinterestedness makes me strong to tell them the truth occasionally to their faces. What is so hard to come by came to them from above and without any merit on their part, and maybe precisely because it is undeserved they do not have the ability, nor, what is worse, the desire, to make proper use of it. Few peoples in Europe can boast of such freedom of expression as they have here today; but what of it if the *word* has long since died in them and only empty phrases remain for barking and growling at each other? Believe me, I am not exaggerating, I look at it soberly, because my love is deep and boundless. Although personal love may be blind, general love gives second sight. Oh, how selfish, selfish to the tenth degree are those inhabitants of the Kingdom of Głodomeria and Golicia![2] When I tell them about other parts of the country it is a contemporary cock-and-bull story to them. One may find a human being here and there, but they are like pearls on a rubbish heap and my eye-sight is too poor to pick them out. Miłaszewski[3] is a theatre manager here; he appears to be the only person glad to see me (although the wise and the simple, the small and the great keep telling me that I came just in time; they think probably that this empty phrase will lull me to sleep), but I have been disillusioned so many times that I still keep watching him before establishing firmer links with the Polish stage. Yesterday Mr Zielinski junior called on me, mentioning you as his reference. I was of course ready to take him to my heart and soul. He comes from Lublin district, but his father lives here. His father is a clever man, but not very popular among the local population. We talked a great deal about what one ought to do. And so, if I could obtain from you detailed reports, such as I have secured from other districts, *des gestes et des faits*[4] both about those who sit on top of others and those who

---

[1] Inhabitants of Galicia (jocular).

[2] A pun: the official name of Polish provinces of Austria–Hungary was 'the Kingdom of Galicia and Lodomeria'; *głód* means 'hunger' in Polish, hence Głodomeria = 'land of hunger'.

[3] Adam Aleksander Miłaszewski (1827–93), actor and stage producer, 1864–71 director of the Lwów theatre.

[4] Fr.: 'doings and exploits'.

serve as seats, then, slowly, drop after drop, one could bore a hole in that Galician rock. My lack of funds is, as you know, another obstacle in my way; for I shall not touch anything that is Konradek's, and all that was mine is either finished or on the eve of running out. If I were but a little stronger – perhaps – perhaps I could manage. I am over-writing myself; but your words are like an invigorating tonic to me – believe me, my best, dearest, only friend. Have you received my letter from Lwów? I doubt it; that is probably why I have repeated myself in this one. I thank you for placing my essay in *B.W.*[1] I am asking for *Ruy Blas* because it will be staged here shortly and could be published, which would give me a little respite to sort out my other things that were crushed and pulled about on the journey. Probably my old, old poems, hitherto unpublished, will be issued by Brockhaus; but I wonder myself whether they deserve to see the light of day since their time has passed; although who can say in this country 'the time has gone'?

I shall be sending Konradek to a Polish high school here, although the syllabus is not to my liking; as to the teachers, with two or three exceptions they have no good influence upon their pupils. I was on the point of sending the boy to Cracow, but have put it off for the time being. That is all. Please give a thought to the written reports I need. Perhaps some sympathetic and intelligent person will consent to cor-respond with me, directly with me. Please, dear Kazimierz, it is easy for you, your wife and Bronek to imagine that I have invented some new form of expressing my attachment and love, telling you openly, show-ing explicitly these feelings of mind which I shall cherish for you till the end of my days and which I would willingly take with me to the grave – as the best that life gave me.

Your

Apollo

Apollo Korzeniowski to Stefan Buszczyński
Biblioteka PAN, Cracow, MS 2064

Przemyśl – Kruhel Wielki
10 May [1868]

Konradek kisses his uncle's hands – and bows his respects to his aunt. He intends to write to you. He writes well, without any help from me –

---

[1] *Biblioteka Warszawska*, a Warsaw monthly. *Studia nad dramatycznością w utworach Szeks-pira* ('A Study on the Dramatic Element in the Works of Shakespeare') was published in it in 1868, vol. 2, pp. 1–17, 219–32.

and as to loving, he loves those whom I point out to him as worthy. May God bless you and shelter you under the wings of his providence.

Your

Apollo

Apollo Korzeniowski to Stefan Buszczyński
Biblioteka PAN, Cracow, MS 2064

29 May 1868
[As before, Kruhel Wielki]

I have written two letters to Prince A.S.[1] But do you not know Galicia? If my health were good and if I could pursue some people by turning up constantly before their eyes, many good things could be brought to this land; but the Austrian agriculture has made them so rotten through and through that even the best men keep putting off their good intentions. Will mankind never learn what wasting time means? Is not this calm before the storm the right time to prepare Galicia for the good? When she is taken unawares by the hurricane, stupidity, baseness and treachery will appear, ruining everything; God grant I may be wrong, but neither at home nor at school nor at Church do I see any evidence of sacrifice and readiness for the opportune moment, or of the strength and salutary power of exerting influence upon the weaker, more crushed parts of the country. In that best paradise the storm will find nothing but a chaos – and who knows how much time we have to set in order and prepare in our consciences everything that may be needed for our salvation.

That is why I considered as absolutely necessary a new press organ, entirely permeated by the new spirit befitting the time before the storm – but I see it moves at a snail's pace...

Apollo Korzeniowski to Stefan Buszczyński
Biblioteka PAN, Cracow, MS 2064

[13 June 1868]

But, my best friend, I am a monk and moreover a simple *frater* in the Polish Order. I have hitherto confined my thoughts in a small cell of patriotism; I am moved only by what directly leads me and everybody mine towards the desired goal. Of what excellence must your humani-

---

[1] Prince Adam Sapieha (1828–1903), 'the Red Prince', descendant of one of the greatest Polish noble families, a liberal–democratic politician, strove for the autonomy of Galicia and the reconstruction of Poland; he was to finance the weekly *Kraj*.

tarian, or at least European, thought be, to absorb and move me, the confirmed and sworn simpleton, to such a degree? Believe me, if you knew me as I am today you would realize the extent of my praise for your work. . .

Apollo Korzeniowski to Kazimierz Kaszewski
Biblioteka Jagiellońska, Cracow, MS 3057

[24 June 1868]

My dear and best Kazimierz,

Please do not hold it against me that I, who normally indulge in an orgy of letter-writing to all my beloved, have remained silent for such a long time after receiving your last letter together with 20 roubles for my article. In addition to my illness I was thrown into confusion by all the things I neither wanted nor expected to find in Galicia; right at the beginning, in the moment of perception, everything that I had dreamt of in the solitude of exile, particularly since my bereavement, crumbled away, and thus, morally and physically broken down, I could not glue myself together into a whole that could write to you and be worthy of sharing thoughts with you. Now I have given Galicia up and retired into my shell to devote myself to the improvement of my health and to watching over Konradek's. The two homeless wanderers need one another: I as his miserable protector, he as the only strength that keeps me on this earth. For ten days now I have been in a little mountain hideout at Topolnica ([Address:] Galicia, – via Przemyśl, Stare Miasto – Łopuszanka – Korzeniow. at Topolnica; or in two envelopes the way I write to you, the top one addressed to Mr Stupnicki). I drink sheep whey with such determination that when the I[mperial] and R[oyal] police enquired as to what I was doing in Galicia, I answered with a clear conscience, 'I am drinking sheep whey.' If there is any improvement, I have not perceived it yet, but since I can drink from this source of health without any repugnance or ill-effects, the experts regard it as a proof of the restorative properties of sheep whey. The air obviously does me good. Topolnica is an obscure hole, very beautiful and quite deserted; with me, and following the same treatment, are two colleagues *eiusdem farinae*[1] and all three of us had to renounce all ordinary comforts of life, however modest, for the sake of this beneficial drink. The roof over our heads is passable, but as to food – in order to find it in this remote nook we exert ourselves like Adam and Eve after their expulsion from Paradise. This is an undeserved situation, for it was not

---

[1] Lat.: 'of the same kind' (lit. 'of the same flour').

from Eden that we came here. My little one suffers from a new onset of his old illness typical of children: urinary sand forms in his bladder causing constant cramps in the belly. In such a state of health it is difficult to make him do his lessons, and yet he is already eleven years old and for the last two years has hardly studied at all. Kind as always, he kisses your hands because he knows well how grateful he ought to be for your love for us that since the sad day of our parting has never left us, lighting up like God's blessing our frequently hard and constantly sad days. I shall stay here till the end of July, so should you write to me, your letter will find me here. Most probably I shall live in Cracow: at least there will be good schools and an atmosphere of tradition emanating from almost every building. If you have friends in Cracow, please mention me to them. Never before did I need so much to see at least a few kind faces; to clasp a few kind hands.

It is difficult to write more extensively from this wilderness, but eleven days ago, when I was still in a busier world, my pleasures were few. Whatever one says there, every one agrees; but when it is a question of transforming the best words into action – nothing gets done ... and so with the new press organ which very nearly came into being since everybody had felt that *Czas, Narodowa Gazeta, Lwowski Dziennik* and others do not bring any credit to the province. Every one of them has its worm that gnaws it: *Czas* – church supervision; *Narodowa Gazeta* – non-national supervision, to which they have sold themselves; *Lwowski Dziennik* – mendicancy, which is their means of existence; and generally speaking all of them, without principles, without love of their country, are directed by men who, some slightly and others up to their necks, are smeared with mud, and, lacking moral strength, cannot wash it off. Just as a very important issue failed although desperate efforts had been made to choose the lesser evil from various bad positions. It concerned the sale of national property[1] – illegally – but nothing could be done apart from minor protests; the sale had to take place. The property ought to have been divided into small parts that would find their way into hands of many decent people instead of large portions going to German capitalists. Local landowners worked it out differently: they purchase huge lumps for themselves, and poor people will have nothing from it: all profits go to the wealthy and the problem of attracting a healthy element has been shelved. And so it is with everything. It happens sometimes that one first learns something interesting about Galicia from the Hungarian rather than from the local press. The Hungarians, prompted by friendliness, caution the Gali-

---

[1] That is, of the estates belonging to the government, which were sold, over local protests, to cover the debts of Austria-Hungary.

cians not to slacken off in trying to build up material and moral strength – but all to no avail.

Enough of that. It is hard for me to write; and all I have said will not remedy the evil, nor is it worthy of the brotherly embrace I send you and Bronek, nor of my heart-felt devotion to your wife and yourself. I bid you to accept all these from your always faithful friend.

Apollo

Konradek kisses your hand and embraces Bronek.

Apollo Korzeniowski to Stefan Buszczyński
Biblioteka PAN, Cracow, MS 2064

Monday [12 October 1868]

My favourite brother Stefan,

Your dear child tells me that those you love are never forgotten: I believe her ... but as I am filled with distaste for myself (not on account of any Giaourish[1] reason), forgetfulness, when encountered, does not surprise me in the least. A life of tiresome struggle – you remember we embarked on it fourteen years ago – the imprisonment in a rotten Muscovite dungeon, the foul Muscovite exile and all the personal anguish – you know their measure; all of it has not achieved what a six-month stay in Galicia has done: I am broken, fit for nothing, too tired even to spit upon things. In four days I am going to Lwów, where I shall retire from sight and occupy myself with one thing only: the education and upbringing of Konradek. In the nature of writing I shall only reserve the right to write rare letters to even rarer friends. By Saturday I shall already be in Lwów. I was glad to learn of your wayfaring in the mountains, where, upon hearing of the stupidity and foulness of the whole great province, you may with Heine call out: 'Auf die Berge will ich steigen.'[2] I too have been avoiding Lwów, but, living in the country among the *szlachta* of the Przemyśl region, which considers itself the greatest *szlachta* of all, I have suffered tortures. As you probably noticed, the Galicians know best everything except their own extreme stupidity: thus there was no way to make them see that such expenses are a sin in the face of the destitution of their compatriots; that such a jubilation is an outrage on all those tears still flowing;

---

[1] Allusion to Byron's *The Giaour* (1813), popular in Poland thanks to Mickiewicz's translation of 1833. The hero suffers from a mysterious guilt.

[2] 'I want to climb the mountains', from 'Prolog' to the collection of poems *Aus der Harzreise* (1824). The author announces his departure from the world of bourgeois superficiality.

that the masquerade in the robes of the old Polish *szlachta* with the Wittelsbach colours[1] is not, as the esteemed Mr Dietl[2] maintains in his proclamation, a proof of the chivalric spirit, but an ultimate form of making fools of themselves; that ... but it is all to no purpose whatsoever. What is even worse, my dear friend, is that looking at it from behind the scenes I have become convinced that everything in that serious *sejm*[3] is insincere, done without conviction, for effect – like the pronouncements of Smolka,[4] Zyblikiewicz's[5] amendments, Adam S[apieha]'s rhetoric or the gloomy platitudes of Adam P.[6] And all of them have such a fear of Moscow that they would let her devour their own children providing she would not interfere in Galicia with their parading of horses, leading of dances at balls, *gründening*[7] of partnerships etc. They have forgotten what it is to feel – they know not how to speak – they read nothing. Customs, language, religion mean nothing to them. One could get at their heart through business, but from the very nature of things business is variable and unstable and so too would be the actions it produced.

Galicia weighs on me heavily like a presentiment of my tombstone; and should my grave have no stone, I expect to feel there less oppressed than I do today in Galicia.

Your dear child writes to me also about her Warsaw friend. The very mention of Warsaw or Varsovians makes my heart beat faster: I have never met people more alive and honest. The time I spent there I count as the most beautiful moments in my life as man and Pole. For one Varsovian I could give away many many Galicians and the rest besides. Let your darling child tell her friend that in conveying my greetings to her, I send them to everybody in the Kingdom for whom I shall always remain a loving, sworn brother. Write to me now to Lwów, to my temporary address: Ormiańska Street No. 104, the house of Tokarski, the Hon. Tokarski, for Korzeniowski.

In any case, I shall be here till the 15th and by the evening of the 16th I shall be back in Lwów.

You have said that you would like to see me – and I? If I have to

---

[1] Allusion unclear; the colours of the Wittelsbach dynasty, ruling in Bavaria 1080–1918, were blue and white.

[2] Dr Józef Dietl (1804–78), eminent physician and conservative politician, 1866–74 President of the City of Cracow.

[3] The Polish parliament.

[4] Franciszek Smolka (1810–99), lawyer and liberal politician, leader of the autonomists in Galicia.

[5] Mikołaj Zyblikiewicz (1825–86), a moderately conservative politician.

[6] Count Adam Potocki (1822–71), great landowner, leader of conservative aristocrats.

[7] From the German *gründen*, 'to found', 'establish'.

measure your friendly desire by my attachment to you both then I shall say with all confidence, when you see me, that no one loves you better, more faithfully and affectionately than myself.

Do you think that anyone will want to publish my poem *Grzech i śmiech?* Possibly only the *Dziennik Lwowski*, the democratic paper, but even that is not certain; but I shall manage somehow: by including *Grzech i śmiech* in the short correspondence I shall circulate it anyway. Alas, one cannot even count on women here – but perhaps it is my age and I have no right to count on anything.

Three cold days seemed to have ruined my summer cure and again I feel a heavy weight on my breast and a fire inside – but this fire is smaller than the one burning in my soul, in which all of you live like beautiful and beloved salamanders in the flames of my affection.

Your Apollo

Apollo Korzeniowski to Stefan Buszczyński
Biblioteka PAN, Cracow, MS 2064

[19–29 October 1868]

If my health permits I might write something, and a long Polish novel is in my head – about the depravity flowing to us from Moscow through the Asiatic splendour, the bureaucratic honours, the disbelief inculcated into public education, the baubles of civilized fashionable Muscovy, and finally by penetration through intermarriage. It would begin in '54 and end in 1861.[1] That is all very well, but will anything come out of it? I have also finished the translations of all Victor Hugo's dramas (apart from *Cromwell*), so that I could publish them with an introduction about Victor Hugo: citizen–poet.[2]

Usually those at the end of their tether keep making plans: I suppose I am not unlike them...

Apollo Korzeniowski to Stefan Buszczyński
Biblioteka PAN, Cracow, MS 2064

[24 December 1868]

The New Year is round the corner – may it bring us that which we are awaiting and the fulfilment of our cherished dreams! Ah, dear Stefan, how wonderful it would be, how sweet death would seem, if one could say with Simeon, 'Lord, now lettest thou thy servant depart...'! Mean-

---

[1] The project was not realized.
[2] Of these translations *Les Burgraves, Hernani* and *Marion Delorme* were published during Korzeniowski's lifetime; the rest, in Stefan Buszczyński's hands after Korzeniowski's death, have been lost.

while all memorial and festive days are a torture to me. When I recall my losses, I cannot even accept the possibility of recompense. The demon of grief wrings my heart, extreme prostration confuses my thoughts, tears refuse to flow, my breast cannot heave a sigh – I am a stone, the most miserable stone one feeling its own stoniness. The dead will rise one day but stones will crumble into dust. Better leave it untold...

Apollo Korzeniowski to Kazimierz Kaszewski

Biblioteka Jagiellońska, Cracow, MS 3057

24 Dec[ember] 1868
11 Szeroka Street
Lwów

Konradek and I, like two orphans, had just broken the holy wafer (leaving a small piece to send to you) when the doctor brought your letter, my dear Kazimierz. It is news from better spheres and I am grateful beyond words. My whole life consists of memories of you and those like yourself, beloved by heart and approved by conscience. Neither the presence of others nor the present time can dim or eradicate old memories: I am at that stage of life when everything that is God's comes to mind 'nella miseria'. All my feelings were stirred by your description of Bronek. Ah well! As to his ultra-lofty inclinations, which you rightly wish to bring into balance, are they not better than the carnal appetites of today's young generation? Although no province of ours produces specimens equal to those of Galicia, believe me, their future can be nothing but awful, wasted, rotten. My Konradek is in good health. And this pleases me more than anything else, for his nerves were shaky. He is receiving formal education in accordance with the local school syllabus, although this year he will not attend classes. He is quite capable but has as yet no taste for learning and lacks stability. Admittedly he is only eleven. But before I close my eyes I would like to forsee the course he will follow. He likes to criticize everything from a sympathetic standpoint. He is also tender and good beyond words.

I have deteriorated since the autumn; I keep to my room and participate in nothing; even the announcement of my collaboration with one of the periodicals was declared an indiscretion on the part of the editors. I do not even know if it was the *bell* or the *ant*[1] that brought you the news. Anyhow the bell died before birth. The editors have left Lwów. Literature here is in a very poor state, which can only

---

[1] *Dzwon* ('The Bell') was the title of a weekly, plans for which fell through. *Mrówka* ('The Ant'), an illustrated Lwów weekly, started publication on 5 February 1869.

be compared to that of the schools and the Church. No spirit anywhere, a lot of cant but all insipid; even humorous literature is insipid. If it were not for my belief in progress, I should say that Galicia has no future.

Whence and why are you sending me *100* zlotys? I have no doubts that it will be paid out to me; but it is holiday time now and therefore I am unable to send you the receipt.

Poor mother, because of her health she cannot get to Warsaw to see you and to relieve you of the trouble of disposing of my belongings. Anyway she will come to you. Through the kindness of your hearts you have become involved in all our emotions, many of them mournful and yet so precious to the memory.

If God wills me to last till the spring I shall probably be drinking sheep whey again; it did me good: but the autumn has ruined it all. I cannot say I am worse than last winter, but certainly I am not better.

My life here is funny: I do not feel drawn to the local population, nor they towards me. I have neither friends nor enemies: all are indifferent. Having become myself unfit to teach, I found a tutor for Konradek from the 8th class of the high school; all I do is watch that he does not convert the boy's Polish into Galician. Ah! what oysters people are here; it shows how science lies: natural history tells one to look for oysters in the sea: no sign of sea here and yet oysters at every step. Wieliczka goes down the drain, but, God willing, not entirely. And so with everything – impossible to find any of the old wealth. I was very keen to move to Cracow just to be near you all, but it was impossible: the journey is costly. As it is, thanks to the railway I am not far from you, but thanks to my fate I am separated more effectively than by the Atlantic Ocean. Tell me, please: who is Mr. Wł. Górski?[1] For a time he edited the *Wędrowiec*.[2] Finding himself in difficult, truly destitute circumstances, he came to me: what was I to do? I did not let him die, and God is my witness that in Lwów the situation was desperate; I managed to find him – quite by chance – a job at 600 florins, i.e. 2400 zlotys. But I do not know who he is and my involvement worries me. If you can, please write about him.

I am still sorting my old papers; perhaps I shall at last publish something. To *Bez ratunku* I have added a second and last act.[3] But

---

[1] Włodzimierz Górski (*c.* 1824–78), editor of *Wędrowiec* 1864–7, in Lwów since 1867.

[2] A lively Warsaw weekly magazine, specializing in reports on travels, discoveries, and new developments in the natural sciences and technology.

[3] *Bez ratunku* ('Beyond Rescue'), first published in 1866, was just about to be reprinted, in a slightly changed version, as *Akt pierwszy* ('The First Act'), Lwów, 1869. It was supposed to form the first part of a trilogy; however, only the opening scenes of the second part, *Ojciec* ('The Father') are found among the extant MSS of Apollo Korzeniowski.

everything is an uphill struggle for me and nothing runs on a simple and straightforward path. Well, perhaps by next spring I shall find such a path. It would be pleasant to recover one's breath at last.

I share the holy wafer with you and yours, and may God answer all my prayers for you, giving me the proof that I have loved you like a friend and a brother.

Yours always

A. Korzen.

I kiss your wife's hand. Oh! if we could meet ... if I could just sit in some little corner in your home, chat or even weep together. Kisses and blessings for Bronek. I commend my Konradek to your loving hearts.

Apollo Korzeniowski to Stefan Buszczyński

Biblioteka PAN, Cracow, MS 2064

19 Jan[uary] 1869

All well and good, but why are you not writing to me? God forbid that anything should have befallen you! My last sign was the despatch of my short play. Did you get it? Lacking in strength I enclosed no letter. Waiting to hear from you I have been delaying writing, although, dear Stefek, I am like a blind hen that found a seed on a rubbish heap. That it is a rubbish heap I know for sure, because it is Galicia; but whether it is a good seed or a sterile seed of couch-grass remains to be seen. I have been invited to join a periodical which is supposed to start on 1 February in Lwów.[1] The invitation is both in writing and personal; and since the inviting person provides money, it is valid and serious. *En principe* I accepted at once. But I put forward the matter of principles and obligations to be undertaken – and therefore of the rights I shall acquire. You remember how on two past occasions you coerced me into writing to Prince Adam [Sapieha] on account of those debates in Cracow about the periodical, and even gave me his address. Well, he says he has never received my letters; but all the principles that he laid down *de son chef*[2] for the paper are not a paraphrase but an accurate reproduction of what I had written to him. To the extent that when speaking of the title (I suggested Polska v. Unia) he tried to explain that perhaps it had better not be *Polska* but *Kraj*, since certain people who might willingly join *Kraj* would be put off slightly by the title *Polska*. Thus the matter of principles was quickly solved and in good conscience I neither can, nor have the right to, refuse to participate. So the

---

[1] Probably the *Mrówka*. [2] Fr.: 'of his own accord'.

question of *duties* arises and that is precisely *hic*; they let me choose for myself the duties I wish to undertake but they do not specify clearly my *rights*, nor my authority; my only plainly stated right is the right to financial remuneration. To me – although I closely resemble some poor church mouse – the matter is of secondary importance. That is how things stand at present. The state of my health is preventing me from going to Cracow, so the discussion is by letter: during the first talk and in two of my letters I put forward your name, precisely as follows: 'For the literary and political success of the periodical, for the radiance of integrity lent to the publication by the names of contributors, I strongly advise and recommend to you, Sirs, to *try and secure* the regular cooperation of Mr Buszczyński, a publicist, writer and well-tried patriot.' In conversation the suggestion was received favourably; as to my letters, no reply has reached me. Have any overtures been made to you? Please regard my letter about the daily as confidential: you cannot imagine what the honest people from various democratic parties here can make out of well-meant words, which having entered their ears accidentally leave their mouths later by design.

In the event of the arrangement being concluded I shall have to go to Cracow. I do not know to what extent this will be possible for me. I am waiting to ask the doctor who advises me occasionally. Who knows if the offer has not come too late. I am consumed by fever daily; I need not only a warmer climate but also a better life, and particularly fare that I am unable to have. Anyway, even that may not be helped.

Half of Lwów calls on me: the day after tomorrow patriots, democrats, aristocrats hunting for literary sinecures; they all know I have been invited; they marvel at it, but cannot find out anything more from me. Otherwise who knows if this threat of my grabbing the bone from under their noses would not stir up intrigues that would render my stay in Galicia impossible while I have neither money nor strength to leave.

I was told, and had it written to me, that every one of us joining the paper ought to make small sacrifices, as at the beginning he could not be paid according to his worth – but any measure of success would at once improve the position of all the contributors. To me it all sounds like Ossianic arithmetic. But in no case shall I refuse. If only I go to Cracow I can live there on what I live on here. I did not, however, disclose to them that innocent side of my character.

And thus, dear Stefek, I have enlightened you on everything that happened to me from the 12th to this day. If the business is settled I shall write to you at once requesting you to do some things for me in

Cracow. Well, perhaps at last we shall be both in one nest! We shall see. God's will. I embrace you and kiss your maiden's hand.

Your brother

Ap.

Did you like my Act I?[1]
Your article 'Reply' was published the very next day.

Apollo Korzeniowski to Stefan Buszczyński

Biblioteka PAN, Cracow, MS 2064

[7 February 1869]

My dear Stefan,

Chłapowski[2] was here yesterday; an understanding was reached to the extent that I promised to come to Cracow about the 20th; that I shall join the editorial staff;[3] that I shall be *ex officio* responsible for Muscovy, the territories annexed by her, and for England; that if I deem it necessary I shall write one leading article per week for my section; that in case of need I shall not refuse to write literary articles, but shall only do so occasionally. All that is neither committed to paper nor guaranteed, and as far as I am concerned it has been adjourned until my arrival in Cracow. Therefore I want to be there about the 20th, as I am to begin on 1 March. I told him that your participation in the venture is a great incentive for me. I have a favour to ask of you: I am ill and move only with difficulty – please find, or order someone to find, me a billet. 1. Near, as near as possible to the office; 2. on the ground floor, at most on the first; 3. dry; 4. warm; 5. if possible furnished; 6. with a kitchen, since cook-shops (forsooth) poison my remaining strength. There may be three rooms, or, at least, two. Chłapowski promised to look for it, but it would be over-presumptuous of me to believe him. Ah! If I could live in the office paying my share, that would be something! I find walking difficult – working in my room more easeful. At last, Stefan, we shall be together.

Health is the only trouble. I now need a bit of comfort and home care and that is precisely what I lack – all those activities prey upon the remainder of my strength. I am like you: both father and mother, moreover, my child is small still and ailing.

---

[1] See note 3, p. 124.
[2] Karol Bodzenta Chłapowski (1840–1914), landowner and journalist, insurgent in 1863. 1868 married Helena Modrzejewska (Modjeska), the famous actress. Editor of *Kraj*.
[3] Of the irredentist and progressive daily *Kraj*.

Vivat! We shall see each other. You cannot imagine my joy – may God allow it to come about!

Your

Apollo

Apollo Korzeniowski to Stefan Buszczyński
Biblioteka PAN, Cracow, MS 2064

17 February 1869

My dear Stefek,

Sabowski[1] horrified me on his return from Prince Adam, who had received a letter from Cracow with the news that the first issue is to appear on 20 February. All of us have been wronged in our absence. Not to start together is to risk the sequel being a broken rather than a straight line. I wrote to Maciejowski,[2] and please use your influence for them not to mind now about the eight days. Sabowski writes along the same lines, Prince Adam too. In 3–4 days I shall be in Cracow. Maciejowski writes that they have several flats close by, so that when I arrive I shall choose. The first clear day and a few troubles resolved here and I am on my way.

I embrace you warmly and kiss your maiden's hand.

Always your devoted

A. Korzeniowski

An immediate reply will still find me here. My journey will take two days as I can neither leave very early nor travel at night.

Apollo Korzeniowski's death certificate
Biblioteka Jagiellońska, Cracow, MS 6391

No 298

The Austrian Empire
The Grand Duchy of Cracow – City of Cracow
An Extract

from the death certificate in the I[mperial] and R[oyal] Public Registry Books of the Collegiate and Parish Church of All Saints in Cracow.

---

[1] Władysław Sabowski (1837–88), journalist and novelist, using the pen-name Wołody Skiba. Took part in the 1863 uprising.

[2] Ignacy Maciejowski (1835–1901), pen-name Sewer, novelist and journalist, insurgent in 1863, coeditor of *Kraj*. Lived in England 1871–8, sending correspondence to Polish periodicals.

In the year one thousand eight hundred and sixty-nine on the twenty-fourth day of May, at eleven o'clock in the forenoon, the Dean of the Collegiate and Parish Church of All Saints, the Public Registrar in Cracow, received Mr Piotr Gałuszkiewicz and Mr Kazimierz Giergiel, both of full age and of sound mind, both in the service of the Church, residing at 139 Poselska Street, who stated that at 136 Poselska Street, on the twenty-third day of May this year, at the hour of three-thirty in the afternoon, the death occurred of Apollo Nałęcz Korzeniowski, fifty years of age, landowner from Volhynia, under Russian dominion, predeceased by his wife Ewelina Bobrowska. The certificate was read out to the witnesses, and since they were unable to write, it was signed on their behalf by the Public Registrar, Father Waleryan Serwatowski.

I certify that the above extract conforms to the original on page eighteen, the serial number of the certificate entry being ninety-eight.

Cracow, 9 November 1872
Father Franciszek Madejski, Deputy of the Public Registrar

Description of Apollo Korzeniowski's funeral
Kraj (Cracow), no. 68, 25 May 1869

Yesterday, at six o'clock in the evening, huge crowds filled Grodzka and Poselska streets to pay a last tribute to Poland's great son, the untimely departed poet. Clergymen, city guildsmen with banners, university professors and school-teachers, students and schoolchildren, members of academic and educational societies, and members of the 'Mrówka'[1] and the 'Muza'[2] surrounded the hearse; several thousand people followed the coffin in silence. Everyone was struck, however, by the absence of what is called high society, which was represented by barely two or three people.

The procession advanced solemnly to the place of eternal rest, to the accompaniment of religious songs and the tolling of the church bells. A deep sorrow and reverence was manifest on all the faces for the new victim snatched from the patriotic host; for the man who had set the seal of death on his life of sacrifice for the Motherland.

The members of the 'Muza' association sang *Salve Regina* at the grave, and Mr Wiktor Bylicki[3] delivered a moving speech paying homage to his dead colleague from Siberia[!] The crowds dispersed in deep silence. It has been a long time since Cracow has seen such an

---

[1] Self-education association.   [2] Musical association.
[3] Wiktor Bylicki (1817–93), from Warsaw, for conspiratorial activity exiled to Siberia 1863–4.

impressive funeral – not so much because of the external pomp, but because of the participation and tears of the inhabitants. The ceremony could only be compared to the funeral of the seventeen victims killed on 26 April 1848.[1]

Teofila Bobrowska to Kazimierz Kaszewski
Biblioteka Jagiellońska, Cracow, MS 3057

Cracow, 12 June 1869

Dear Sir,

Our beloved late Apollon, sensing his approaching end, prepared me for it by letter, his only child by word of mouth; and to his schoolmate and constant friend from boyhood to the grave he passed on his thoughts and wishes concerning his remaining manuscripts. Mr Stefan Buszczyński, an intimate friend, having moved all noble hearts to pay homage to the late wanderer, having surrounded the orphan left in his care with the greatest possible affection, as a most worthy and kind man has embarked with energy upon the tedious work of sorting out the remaining papers, some of which have to be collected from all over the world. Thus on behalf of the executor of our beloved Apollo's last wishes, the guardian of our poor orphan, and for my own sake, I beg you, dear Sir, as a friend of both the deceased, not to refuse your help in forwarding all the manuscripts which I put into the folding table stowed away inside the trunk many years ago; I assure you that everything reaches Cracow without being checked, so all depends on whether you think it can be done from where you are; if so, I would ask you to make available any letters written by the deceased which may be in your possession and which you, as a friend and a writer, consider as containing thoughts representative of the enormous wealth of that noble soul. There were once a great many fragments of occasional poems scattered about, and there is no trace of them here – perchance some have been preserved – I entrust you with my request, dear Sir. Do you remember in whose charge that elegant embroidery on canvas was left? It would be a pity to lose it – don't you agree? In view of the difficulties in our part of the world I am sending you below two addresses. Mr Mirecki,[2] the artist, put the finishing touches to Apollo's portrait a couple of weeks before that unhappy day of 23 May; in this artistic likeness the troubled forehead seems to radiate spirituality. Apollo regretted immensely that for reasons of frugality he was unable

---

[1] During the short-lived popular rebellion in Cracow the Austrian general Heinrich Castiglioni had the city shelled.

[2] Kazimierz Mirecki (1830–1911), painter active in Warsaw and Cracow.

to purchase this souvenir for Konradek. I did that, however, and photographs are being printed, and it will be the duty of close relatives to send them to intimate friends. The newspaper office where the poor fellow worked acquitted itself admirably by contributing towards a more elevated atmosphere in the funeral *cortège*; it was on their initiative that a collection for a monument was organized, and since there is a balance left, our kind Mr Buszczyński is thinking of busts and medals – a death-mask was taken.[1]

My beloved orphan, in accordance with his father's wishes, has been placed *en pension* with Mr Georgeon[2] in Cracow. The boy's ignorance of the German and Latin languages prevent him from attending the second class; we hope he will go into the fourth class next year, since his headmaster and the teachers praise his industry, comprehension and application – providing God gives him health – to which end I shall devote myself in his free time. His guardian maintains that he does not know another child so easy to bring up and with a heart as noble as his; he had surrounded his poor father with the most tender attention and prayed for his soul, in a flood of tears, kneeling between the priest and nuns, before they all came to their senses and called for Mr Buszczyński, who took the boy and strained him to his heart – and so, together with Mr Buszczyński, his daughter and Mr Mniszek, he walked at the head of the enormous procession. (The latter is the husband of Miss Czarnecka, close friend of my Ewineczka, who always spoke of her.) Please, my dear Sir, forgive this long passage about my sorrow and about Konradek, whom I commend to your and your wife's blessing, for I value greatly your wife's sympathetic heart. I commend him to Bronek's heart – perhaps one day they will meet and embrace each other – because for the orphan of a homeless exile there can never be too much human affection. And as for me, I shall never tire of repeating what great respect I cherish for yourself and your wife, your kind mother and sisters. I kiss Bronek and forever commend myself to your memory.

With best regards, respectfully
yours
Bobrowska

The address of Mr Stefan Buszczyński: Floriańska Street, Mr Ziębow-ski's house, No. 366.

[1] The monument on Korzeniowski's grave was designed by Walery Gadomski (1833–1911), at that time the most eminent Cracow sculptor. The other projects were not realized.

[2] Ludwik Georgeon (1832–79), born in Cracow, son of Joseph Georgeon from Dôle, insurgent in 1863. From 1867 he directed a four-class boarding school for boys. His wife, Marianna Mohr, was also known for her patriotism.

The address of Ludwik Georgeon: Floriańska Street, Mr Fajll's house, No. 300

Kazimierz Bobrowski[1] to Konrad Korzeniowski

Biblioteka Narodowa, Warsaw, MS 2889

13/25 December 1869
Łomża

Dear Konrad,

What unspeakable pleasure has been afforded us by your scroll as an indication of your feelings for us. We thank you for them most cordially, although we have never doubted them. Your letter gave us double pleasure as additional proof of your recovery, a fact of great value to anyone – and all the more to yourself.

We are taking away from you your best and most beloved Granny! I know that you were the first to say, 'you must go away, Granny, to nurse the sick' and therefore I am not asking you, 'please forgive us for taking Granny away', but saying, 'May God bless you for giving what is most precious to us all.'

When Granny returns here, we shall get more frequent letters from you – although not necessarily written specifically to us, your aunt and uncle, but jointly to us all; for I know that as you love us you will always include a warm word or two for us in a letter written principally to Granny.

Keep your spirits up, dear child, and, God permitting, Granny will visit you next spring and get pleasure out of spoiling you again – but God forbid there should be any need to nurse you, as there was this year.

Both Aunt and myself send you kisses and blessings. Staś and Zuńka[2] 'kiss their little brother' and we all wish you all the best, particularly good health for the coming year.

Your devoted uncle
K.Bobrowski

---

[1] Kazimierz Bobrowski (1837–86), Ewa Korzeniowska's brother. A captain in the Russian army, imprisoned in 1863 for conspiracy, he managed to destroy compromising documents. He worked as a railway station-master.

[2] Stanisław (1865–1939) and Zuzanna (1866–1942), Kazimierz's children.

Stefan Buszczyński to Józef Ignacy Kraszewski
Biblioteka Jagiellońska, Cracow, MS 6490

19 January 1870
Floriańska Street, the house of Nitsch

Sir,
I am in possession of all the hitherto unpublished manuscripts left by the late Apollo Korzeniowski, whom you honoured with your friendship. If publishing poetry (in exceptional cases) fits in with the *Tygodnik*[1] editorial policy, please consider me at your service. This is why I am sending you this information.

There are many beautiful things; apart from his own poems there are translations of Shakespeare's and Victor Hugo's plays. My deceased friend left all his works in my care. I would like to find a publisher for them...

Nomination of Conrad's legal guardians, 2 August 1870
Biblioteka Jagiellońska, Cracow, MS 6391

L. 14844

The I[mperial] and R[oyal] City Court of Justice in Cracow appoints Mrs Teofila Bobrowska to act as Guardian to her grandson, Konrad Nałęcz Korzeniowski, a minor, with Count Władysław Mniszek as co-guardian. The Court informs the child's Guardian that it is her duty to bring up the minor well, to inculcate in him virtue and piety, to appear on his behalf and to defend him in court and elsewhere, to observe carefully all the regulations of Chapter IV of the Civil Code, to administer faithfully and fairly the minor's estate and conscientiously to inform the court at least three months prior to the minor's coming of age, if in her opinion there exist serious reasons requiring an extension of the guardianship in accordance with § 251 of the Civil Code.

Finally, in accordance with § 255 of the Civil Code, the Guardian is under obligation to inform the Court without delay if she intends to remarry.

Cracow, 2 August 1870

(signature illegible)

---

[1] *Tydzień* (not *Tygodnik*) *Polityczny, Naukowy, Literacki i Artystyczny* was a weekly, edited in Dresden by Kraszewski, who had been forced to emigrate from Russian-held Poland.

From the President of the City of Cracow to Teofila Bobrowska, 28 December 1872

Biblioteka Jagiellońska, Cracow, MS 6391

No. 28175

The President
of the City of Cracow
                To
                The Hon. Teofila Bobrowska
                c/o Dr Wilkosz, Solicitor.

In accordance with the resolution of the City Council of the 23rd inst., it has been decided to guarantee the admission of Konrad Korzeniowski, a minor, to the local commune, with exemption from taxes, on the condition that he be granted Austrian citizenship, for which a separate application with a stamp duty of 2 Złr [Rheinish Zlotys] ought to be submitted to the I[mperial] and R[oyal] Governor, through the offices of the Municipality.

This is for your information, Madam, as the guardian appointed by the Court for the afore-said minor. Please find herewith returned the enclosed petition.

Cracow, 28 December 1872

(signature illegible)

'Conradiana', by Stanisław Czosnowski

Epoka (Warsaw), 1929, no. 136

I heard of Conrad for the first time when I was a very young child. There were close family links between my family and the Bobrowskis. Tadeusz and Stefan Bobrowski, as well as Conrad's mother, were first cousins of my grandfather, Wacław Czosnowski (his mother's family name was Bobrowska) and as children they were for a time brought up together. My grandparents were on quite close terms with the Bobrowskis. I remember seeing in my father's desk a parcel containing Tadeusz Bobrowski's letters and old yellowed photographs, among them those of Conrad's parents. Those documents and family souvenirs were lost during the Bolshevik Revolution.

Conrad used to be referred to as that 'crazy' cousin who preferred to sail far away in foreign service rather than to plough peacefully the rich paternal acres. Thirty years ago he was neither known nor famous as a writer.

Encouraged by Zygmunt Kisielewski,[1] who found in Bobrowski's

[1] Zygmunt Kisielewski (1882–1942), prominent socialist intellectual.

memoirs some reference to a kinship between our families, I have sent letters to several persons related to Conrad through the Bobrowskis, asking them to write down either their personal recollections or those preserved in family tradition; in short, to contribute details which would throw some light on Conrad's childhood. My letters have remained unanswered except for one which I sent to a very aged cousin of mine who died several months ago, Mr. Zygmunt Radzimiński, a former landowner from Volhynia, historian and heraldic expert.

Here is what the late Mr Radzimiński wrote on 17th June 1927 in reply to my letter:

'I knew personally not only his [Conrad's] uncle Tadeusz Bobrowski but also his uncle's paternal uncle Mikołaj Bobrowski, who paid several visits to Matwijowice and Słotwin; and also Tadeusz's younger brother Stefan, who was with me for a certain time at Kiev University. I can also remember Conrad's father, Apollo Nałęcz Korzeniowski, as well as his hunchback brother, Hilary, the great 1863 activist in the Zasław district. And I also met Conrad as a youngster in Cracow; if my memory does not deceive me the meeting took place at the home of his cousin, Mrs Falkenhagen-Zaleska.[1] Conrad's departure, or, as some used to call it, his escape, from Cracow to go to sea, was an event talked about for a time by his close friends and relatives. Eventually it was forgotten.'

Then follows an account of the genealogical background of the Nałęcz Korzeniowski family and a long excerpt from a letter from Mrs Tekla Wojakowska, née Syroczyńska,[2] Conrad's cousin thrice removed, to whom Mr Radzimiński had addressed his request for information and recollections.

Here is what Mrs Wojakowska wrote:

'I met Konradek for the first time fifty-seven years ago and then saw him frequently during his eight-month stay in Lwów. I used to come on Thursdays and Sundays to take the eleven-year-old Konradek to our house where we also had the lease of an enormous garden with beautiful flowers and trees. We tried to amuse the pale and delicate little boy and cheer him up. His father, Apollo, a very sensitive poet of melancholy disposition, depressed by the failure of the insurrection and by the recent death of his wife, arrived from Vologda in 1869 and rented in the Żółkiewskie suburb two rooms which the sun never reached.[3] He personally took care of his son's tuition, but apart from that did not

---

[1] Daughter of the writer Józef Korzeniowski (1797–1863), not related to Apollo.

[2] Daughter of Antoni Syroczyński.

[3] The address given by Korzeniowski in his letters was quite different; he lived in the very centre of Lwów.

know how to look after the boy – perhaps in his state of apathy the task was too demanding. I remember noticing in their flat a great quantity of books which Konradek read as he pleased. At that time he had written a short play which he wanted us to perform, but somehow it never came about. Once, when I was visiting them, I found Apollo sitting motionless in front of his wife's portrait. He never stirred on seeing us and Konradek who was accompanying me put his finger to his lips and said: "Let us cross the room quietly. Father spends every anniversary of Mother's death sitting all day and looking at her portrait; he does not speak or eat."[1] Konradek recalled with enthusiasm his two-month stay at the seaside (when nine years old he was taken by his uncle Bobrowski to Odessa's coastal salt lake). He told me that he wanted to be a sailor and to do a lot of travelling; with that object in mind he applied himself to geography and languages. From Lwów they moved to Cracow, where his father died from pneumonia. Then his grandmother Bobrowska, Tadeusz's and Stefan's mother, moved to Cracow, where she took a comfortable first-floor flat, especially for the sake of her grandson. Konradek attended the local school for several years[2] and Mr Pochman,[3] whom he was very fond of, acted as his tutor. We used to visit him there, and after the death of his grandmother, in 1873,[4] Konradek came to live with my father. He stayed with us for ten months studying in the seventh class at the High School. Intellectually he was extremely advanced but he disliked school routine, which he found tiring and dull; he used to say that he was very talented and planned to become a great writer. Such declarations, coupled with a sarcastic expression on his face and with frequent critical remarks, used to shock his teachers and provoke laughter among his class-mates. He disliked all restrictions. At home, at school or in the living-room he would sprawl about unceremoniously. He used to suffer from severe headaches and nervous attacks; the doctors thought that a stay at the seaside might cure him. This helped to overcome the objections of his uncle and guardian, Bobrowski, who hitherto had not wanted to let his ward become a sailor. At sea Konrad was seldom affected by illness, but on one occasion he had an attack when at the masthead: he fell to the deck and broke his leg. After that he walked with a limp. His hair and eyes were black and his complexion dull. There was something original and distinguished in his ugliness. All my souvenirs of him were lost during the war except for the

---

[1] Apollo and Konrad did not spend in Lwów any anniversary of Ewa's death.
[2] There is no evidence for this.
[3] Correctly: Pulman; see his letters in this volume, pp. 145–7.
[4] Actually only in 1875.

table at which he used to study, and for the Erazm Dionizy Korzeniowski's lithograph on stone.[1] The details of Konrad's early years
are well known to Mme Marguerite Poradowska, née Gachet, who lives
in Paris, and those of his later years to Mrs Aniela Zagórska, in whose
pension "Turnia" in Zakopane Konrad Korzeniowski spent several
months before the outbreak of war.[2]

'Well, that is all,' concludes Radzimiński, 'just a batch of minor
facts, but even such as they are they might throw some light on the
disposition of our outstanding countryman and your relative who spontaneously converted himself into an Englishman.'

And I too shall bring my account to a close. I have not succeeded in
producing a rich harvest of reminiscences and I offer no comments on
the bits of information I have gathered, hoping however that, although
insignificant, they may prove useful.

'From Conrad's Youth', by Roman Dyboski

'Z młodości Józefa Conrada', *Czas* (Cracow), 1927, no. 296

I

When one of the greatest contemporary English writers passed away in
August 1924, people in Poland were well aware that they might mourn,
side by side with the English, the departure of a son of Poland, who had
never renounced his country although he had made England his second
home. Two years earlier Stefan Żeromski, in his foreward to the Polish
edition of Joseph Conrad's selected writings,[3] included a number of
details about the tragic exile of Conrad's parents, found in the forgotten
'Memoirs' of his uncle Tadeusz Bobrowski, and added some new facts
in two articles written after the author's death. Żeromski also included
Conrad's own recollections of his sad boyhood in Cracow, spent at the
side of his dying father after he had returned from exile. The affectionate terms used by the great novelist to describe Cracow, that 'old royal
and academic city', appear in gold letters on the commemorative
plaque on the house where he then lived with his father.

Conrad, having revisited Cracow with his sons on the eve of the
1914–18 war, has provided a written account of this moving experience
and acknowledged a strong spiritual bond between himself and that
city. However, the two visits paid in his early years to another Polish
town – Lwów – apparently escaped his memory, crowded with count-

---

[1] Conrad's great-grandfather.
[2] In fact in 'Konstantynówka' and after the outbreak of war in 1914.
[3] Józef [sic] Conrad Korzeniowski, *Pisma wybrane*, vol. I, *Fantazja Almayera* (Ignis:
Warszaw, 1923), pp. vii–xxxiii.

less impressions of his later travels over distant lands and seas. Over two years after the writer's death, and thanks to an unusual and pleasant coincidence, I came across some very characteristic facts relating to the time he had spent in Lwów.

It so happened that once, when I went to Bielsko in Silesia to give a lecture on Conrad, I heard an old lady living in the vicinity, who in her youth had known Conrad. In reply to my enquiry Mrs Jadwiga Kałuska, born Tokarska, was kind enough to write down for me at length her reminiscences of the young Józef Teodor Konrad Korzeniowski. Having received the lady's permission to publish I wish to invite my Polish readers to partake at Christmas time in the enjoyment of the following scenes from the Polish youth of the great English writer.

2

My esteemed informant was brought up in a small Ukrainian town, next door to Korzeniowski's relatives.[1] She met Konrad's father and little Konrad in the autumn of 1867 when her own father, a doctor, moved permanently to Lwów. One day they had a visit from Apollo Nałęcz Korzeniowski, an exile recently returned from Russia. He had ruined his health in the ice-bound Vologda, buried his wife in Chernihov and now arrived with his little son in Lwów animated by the sole desire – as he wrote to his friends – for his son to live among his own people and be brought up as a Pole. That wreck of a human being accompanied by the motherless boy presented an image worthy of Grottger's[2] pencil and like one of his drawings became engraved on the memory of the lady whose eyes had beheld the scene some sixty years earlier.

'Released as the result of an amnesty, he came to Lwów to look for some work as a writer because the Muscovites had confiscated his estate. He was a man ruined both physically and mentally by suffering. Pale, dark-haired with a long beard, extremely wan and sad, he could have been around forty-five years old. As for the eleven-year-old Konrad, he was lively, cheerful and extremely bright. He proudly wore his square-topped cap bordered with white sheep-skin fur...'

Conrad, in his posthumously published short story 'Prince Roman', tells in moving terms of the respect he felt when, as a small boy, he saw the majestic personage of Roman Sanguszko, hero of the 1831 insurrection and a long-term exile in Siberia. What a strong imprint must have

---

[1] She was probably a daughter of Dr Tokarski, family physician of the Lubowidzkis in Nowofastów.

[2] Artur Grottger (1837–67), a Romantic painter and engraver, famous in Poland for his scenes of the 1863 insurrection.

been left on his mind by everything he had heard from his father about the recent tragedy of 1863 and by its consequences, which he himself witnessed! The young boy, whom we get to know better in the following extracts taken from Mrs Kałuska's memoirs, appears to have been completely overwhelmed by the heroic and poetic aspects of that tragedy. The most interesting are those scenes which depict the awakening of Konrad's literary gift.

'My mother, wishing to alleviate the burden of looking after a lively child, suggested that in the time free from studies he should come and play with us children. I cannot recall if Konrad attended a school then or if he was taught by his father. Thus Konrad used to spend all his holidays with us, and when it rained, stayed the night. We were all impressed with his memory: he knew long passages from *Pan Tadeusz*[1] and Mickiewicz's 'Ballads'[2] by heart. His gift for writing began to show at that time. He was the author of a number of short comedies, which he used to bring along and then distribute the parts between my brother and me; and if we did not learn our lines he used to get angry. Large cardboard boxes served as stage settings and a blue and red pencil represented our only paint. The themes of those plays were battles with the Muscovites. To rise to the occasion I had to dress in my brother's clothes ... "Insurgents" sat round a camp fire with their commander (in the red square-topped cap) and sang patriotic songs. Konrad knew those songs and made us repeat the last stanzas. Then the Muscovites crept on us noiselessly. A fight would follow with the breaking of chairs and stools... I remember it all so clearly – those were merry, carefree days ... The little tyrant ruled over us and we obeyed our commander-in-chief. The best play was entitled 'The Eyes of King Jan Sobieski'.[3] Konrad's every action was coloured with love for his unhappy motherland. His father transmitted to Konrad everything he felt himself.'

Here end those lively recollections of the childhood years of our great author. Mr Apollo Nałęcz Korzeniowski moved to Cracow, taking his son with him, to 'our as well as Konrad's great sorrow'.

3

One more meeting was to take place in Lwów between the childhood friends. This time Mrs Kałuska's reminiscences show Konrad in a different phase of life.

[1] The most celebrated work of Mickiewicz: a national epic (1834).
[2] *Ballady* (1822).
[3] Jan III Sobieski (1629–96), King of Poland from 1674, outstanding military leader (battle of Vienna, 1683).

In September 1873, Konrad, as an adolescent boy, was brought again to Lwów at the instance of his uncle and guardian Tadeusz Bobrowski, to whom he later dedicated his first English novel. His uncle, as Mrs Kałuska informs us, 'placed him with Mr Syroczyński who kept several boy lodgers from landowning families. They were well cared for and supervised there. Mr Syroczyński[1] must have been an *émigré*, for the conversation at home was in French.'

On a par with the moving picture from the life of the insurgents' children, those inheritors of romantic heroism, the following account gives us a lively description of the adolescent youths in the first ten years after the January debacle.[2] They were unusually serious for their age, pensive, devoured by some inner anxiety, committed to new intellectual trends which, brought by Western winds to the ravaged country, held a promise of revival by means of 'organic work'. And in an atmosphere of a close family circle Conrad witnessed that stage of Polish spiritual development.

'Konrad had not forgotten us,' continues Mrs Kałuska, 'and came to see us a few days after his arrival. At first I did not recognize him: he had grown taller, his hair was long, brushed back, a trace of down announced an incipient moustache. He was in the habit of screwing up his eyes and looking through narrow slits. It gave him an air of slight haughtiness. His attitude towards me was unchanged: he was a good friend. We were on a Christian-name basis. In those days a girl of seventeen and a boy of eighteen or nineteen[3] were serious people. Konrad used to visit us often and our conversations were serious. He read a lot, mostly about travel. He wished to get to know the world. His favourite magazine was *Wędrowiec*, a weekly publication. We also used to attend lectures given by university professors at the Town Hall. Konrad was particularly interested in lectures dealing with natural science and literature. Whenever he was unable to attend a lecture he would ask me for a summary. I never questioned him about his line of studies but I knew he was very diligent ... He refrained from speaking about his acquaintances. He mentioned only a Miss Cezaryna, an unusual name for a woman that stuck in my memory; she was engaged to one of the university professors and used to visit the Syroczyńskis.'

4

Conrad apparently displayed an English-style reserve, not only in

[1] Antoni Syroczyński (1831–88) indeed spent a few years in Paris as a political *émigré* after the 1863 uprising.
[2] That is, after the disastrous end of the 1863 insurrection.
[3] Conrad was less than sixteen when he went to Lwów in 1873.

matters relating to his love affairs, possibly linked in some way with the name of Cezaryna, but also in other personal matters. He did not tell everything to his childhood friend. Admittedly, we learn from her of his desire to see the wide world; but from Konrad himself, from his autobiographical reminiscences *A Personal Record*, we gather that precisely at that time, at the age of fifteen or sixteen, his dreams took shape in the form of a decision to become a sailor; that the Cracow circle of relatives and friends reacted to this news with scandalized astonishment as if he had intended to enter a Cameldolite[1] monastery; that his most honoured uncle Bobrowski, who had wanted to make a respectable landowner of him, viewed this idea as well-nigh a betrayal of patriotic duties; that he came all the way from the Ukraine to Cracow expressly to talk the boy out of it, and finally dispatched his nephew for a holiday in Switzerland, with a tutor, a student from Cracow university, to cure him of that dream; and that all the way there the said tutor dinned into Conrad's ears various arguments; that during a hiking tour through the Furca pass the tutor finally capitulated before his charge's obstinacy; that there had been plans to send Konrad to the Austrian naval academy in Pula, but the young man's dream was not of a naval career but of 'the sea'; and that at last one Mr Baptistin Solary in Marseilles undertook to place the young desperado on a French vessel as a deck hand so that he should get to know 'ce métier de chien'.[2] And thus on the Mediterranean, under the French flag, the sailing career of the later master in the British Merchant Service began.

Apparently this entire family drama occurred off stage. We might assume that the boy was placed at the Syroczyńskis in Lwów to improve his French and that those mysterious studies mentioned by Mrs Kałuska were connected with the chosen profession, and that the trip to Marseilles was attributed to health reasons so as not to raise a scandal. Mrs Kałuska goes on to say that soon after Konrad's return from Lwów to Cracow, Mr Bobrowski came to see his nephew, 'and, anxious about his pale looks, took the child to a doctor, who pronounced him in danger of a chest ailment' – the cause of his father's death – 'saying that the only way to keep him alive was to let him live by the sea. Thus Mr Bobrowski, complying with Konrad's wish, placed him at a naval college in Marseilles.'

The above memories end with a melancholy epilogue:

'We only had one letter from Konrad, from Marseilles, but being (as usual) absent-minded, he forgot to give his address ... Later when I

---

[1] An order of contemplative hermits.
[2] Fr.: 'this miserable way of life'.

wanted to write to him I thought that perhaps he had forgotten about us; I did not want to be over-presumptuous towards a famous writer...'

Simple, yet lively, beautiful and melancholy, images evoked by Mrs Kałuska from Conrad's youth bring the great writer closer to his mother country and people. Reading, in his wife's book* and in the recently published comprehensive biography,* the unanimous accounts of the heart-felt nostalgia for Poland experienced by Conrad towards the end of his life, and of his repeated plans to return to Poland for good, we are certain to understand better the words of Conrad's lifelong friend and an equally great writer, John Galsworthy, who tried to throw light on those impulses: 'the cradle called him to the grave'.[1] And from our own Polish point of view we might feel more self-assured repeating the beautiful comment of Żeromski, who himself is now talking Polish to Conrad when they meet in the Elysian Fields: 'He was bound to direct his gaze towards us, because Poland is so rich in emotions that no one noble can escape from her embrace.'[2]

'Conrad in Cracow', by George Palmer Putnam[3]
Outlook (New York), 3 April 1920

'That is where Korzeniowski lived.' Konstantin Buszczyński,[4] then Consul-General of Poland to the United States, pointed out a drab building, none too interesting in outward appearance. We were driving through the streets of Cracow, in reborn Poland, last November, my host exhibiting the highlights of his extraordinarily fascinating native city.

'Indeed!' I breathed. I supposed he referred to one of the old Polish kings, or perhaps a lesser patriot–martyr, with whose memories Poland is proudly replete.

His interest, at least, was more lively than my own. At a word the driver pulled the pair of fine black mares to a halt beside the narrow sidewalk.

'There,' said he, pointing to upper windows of the building at No. 9 Ulica Szpitalna, which is by way of saying Hospital Street, 'is where we had great fun as youngsters; Josef and I used to throw toy torpedoes

---

* Jessie Conrad, *Joseph Conrad as I Knew Him* (Heinemann, London, 1926).
* G. Jean-Aubry, *Joseph Conrad: Life and Letters* (Heinemann, London, 1927), vols I–II.
[1] 'L'Appel de la naissance à la mort', J. Galsworthy, 'Souvenirs sur Conrad', *Nouvelle Revue française*, 12 (1 December 1924).
[2] *Elegie i inne pisma literackie i społeczne* (Warszaw, 1928), p. 148.
[3] Original in English.
[4] Konstanty Buszczyński (1856–1921), founded a renowned seed firm in Cracow.

down on the black caftans of passing Jews, enjoying ourselves hugely when they exploded ... A pogrom, I suppose,' he laughed. Poles today don't relish that word, or the way it has been misused over here.

'And in there, in a corner of the courtyard,' he continued, pointing through the archway, 'that strange boy told us – his play-mates – the most extraordinary stories. They were always of the sea and ships and far-away countries. Somehow, the scent of salt water was in the very blood of Conrad.'

And at that a great light broke upon me. Joseph Conrad! Of course; Teodor Josef Konrad Korzeniowski and the best-beloved creator of *Lord Jim*, *The Nigger of the 'Narcissus'*, and the rest of them, one and the same being!

I did know that Joseph Conrad was not his real name – not all of it, anyway. Afterward I remembered, too, that I had known he was a Pole. But at the time all that was quite outside of my mind.

So I was at the boyhood home of Joseph Conrad, with a boyhood chum of his! At once we left the *fiacre* and entered that historic court-yard. And there, as we strolled about, even climbing the outside stairway to the balcony on the third floor whence a door opened into the old apartment once occupied by Conrad, Buszczyński reminisced.

'My host's father, Stephan, and Conrad's father, Apollo Korze-niowski, were intimate friends. Conrad's mother died in Siberia, and his father followed her shortly after he had been returned to his home from Siberian exile, his health ruined and his spirit all but broken.

'He was suspected of complicity in the anti-Russian uprising of 1863,' Buszczyński told me. 'Only suspected, though. If anything had been proved, he would have been shot.'

On the grave of the elder Conrad this inscription was placed by his friend Stephan Buszczyński:

> I will rise, Lord, when you call me;
> But let me rest, for I am very weary.

At the time of his father's death, 1870, Conrad was about thirteen years old. My informer's memory placed his birth in the year 1859, but in Richard Curle's biography, doubtless more accurate, the date is given as 1857.

'What tales that boy told us!' my companion went on. 'Over on those steps we often sat, a group of us, while Conrad spun yarns, as you Yankees say. They were weird and fantastic almost beyond belief, but in the way he told them they seemed to us actual happenings. The power of weaving tales – tales that literally seemed to live before one's eyes – was born in him. And always they were about the sea. Curious, that, for outside of Asia there probably is not a single other city so far from salt water as Cracow, and Conrad had never seen it.'

The youthful story-teller was a flat failure in his study, with the notable exception of geography. In that he excelled, and small wonder, as he loved it. Even with a private tutor he could not keep up with his classes. He was sickly, too, and very nervous, and given at times to epileptic seizures. And always he talked of the sea, and yearned for it, declaring that only as a sailor could he be well and happy. Which prediction, it happens, worked out exactly. I'm told that during his twenty seafaring years the Polish mariner was practically an embodiment of perfect health.

An uncle, then in Russia, supplied the funds for Conrad's upbringing. Finally the boy's condition grew so serious that Stephan Buszczyński wrote to him urging that his charge be permitted to have his way.

'While that letter made its slow way toward Central Russia,' Stephan's son told me, 'Conrad disappeared. He had done what many a lad has done before and since, run away to sea. A long run, too. Finally the tutor, who was sent in pursuit, located him at Trieste on the Adriatic just as he returned from his first cruise, a short one on a small steamer to Venice and back. But even that brief experience had worked wonders. Apparently the psychological effect of winning his wish had conquered the physical disabilities. The epilepsy had gone never to return.'[1]

A few months later, after another enforced try at landlubber life in Cracow, Conrad was sent to sea; this time in style and with the approval of his uncle. His 'official' maritime career commenced at Marseilles when he was seventeen years old.

Three years after that, for the first time he set foot in England. And then, too for the first time he learned to speak English, and later to write the language. It is common knowledge now that he does the latter rather well. Indeed, there is no exaggeration in saying that the prose English of this Polish sailor, who spoke English first when he was twenty and wrote his first book when he was nearly forty, is unsurpassed – which is a literary phenomenon in itself unmatched.

Conrad went to sea in 1875. Thirty-nine years later, in 1914, Buszczyński and his boyhood friend met again in Cracow for the first time since that parting. It was just before the Great War broke over Europe, Conrad having brought his wife and children to see his boyhood home. And what a happy reunion it must have been for the two Poles, both practically raised by the same father!

[1] The story is entirely apocryphal.

'It was in June, 1875, that I last saw your father,'[1] said Conrad to Buszczyński at that time, his words exactly remembered by the friend to whom he spoke them. 'In my mind now I can see him as clearly as in life and hear his words as he bade me God-speed and pressed my hand: "Conrad, you have your wish. You shall be a sailor. But wherever ships carry you, remember always you are a Pole and that you shall come back to Poland" . . . I never forgot.'

Adam Pulman[2] to Konrad Korzeniowski
Beinecke Library, Yale University, New Haven, Conn.

14 March [1874], Cracow
You are wrong, dear Konradek, in assuming that I have already passed the examination. Not yet, and this event, pleasant because it is associated with the possibility of respite, will take place towards the end of next week. This is why I have not written to you and why I shall write little now.

I have recently had a reply from Granny allowing you to visit me. But Granny cannot decide on her own without your uncle. We shall ask him then, and I do not expect him to refuse.

I am leaving sometime around 21–22 March. I do not know yet where I am going. Anyway, I shall inform you about my itinerary and everything a few days before my departure, so that on the 24th (as you are free then) we shall probably meet at my new place. I have to warn you though that – barring some unpleasant surprise at the doctoral examination – I shall be in a jovial mood as these last months have tired me terribly. So you will have to comply with my disposition, abandon illness and sadness in Lwów, and, apart from a small supply of books, you must bring a considerable amount of willingness to jump, run around, go for strenuous walks, show good appetite, etc., etc.

But, seriously, I am very upset by the news you have sent me.[3] I know it is not your fault and you must be even more upset to see the days wasting away when time is precious to you, as in one or one and a half years from now you are to start your chosen profession. I know all that and it would never enter my mind to blame you, a mature boy, as if you were a child.

Only do not lose heart, and God forbid you should abandon yourself to despair or apathy. The misfortune, as it came no one knows whence, will likewise disappear. When you cannot do anything, wait patiently

---

[1] Conrad never met Stefan Buszczyński after leaving Poland in September 1874.
[2] Adam Marek Pulman (b. 1846), son of Herakliusz, studied medicine in Cracow 1868–75. Conrad's tutor in Cracow 1870–3.
[3] News of an illness which had prevented him from returning to school.

and when the headache is gone set yourself to work. This way, whatever was, is, or will be, I expect my pupil not to put me to shame and, eventually, to grow up to be a splendid man. So although your head may ache, hold it high.

Carry on writing to me and in my next letter I shall let you know about everything, and after that, I expect, we shall not have to communicate by letter.

Yours

Adam Pulman

N.B. You did not tell me whether you received 5 zl. sent to you before Christmas.

Adam Pulman to Stefan Buszczyński

Biblioteka PAN, Cracow, MS 2064

Czerniowce,[1] Carolinengasse,
The House of Badian
10 March 1879

Dear Mr Buszczyński,

On my return from the country, where I spent a couple of weeks, I found your letter among my correspondence. I need not say what pleasure it gave me.

Yes, indeed, I am the same Pulman who had the honour of experiencing your kindness in Cracow. After I had left the university and obtained a doctoral degree, I worked for a time in the provinces. Having, however, retained some unfavourable recollections of the old days, I have temporarily broken off most of my past connections and it is therefore not surprising that you have not heard anything about me. Now, having had enough of the provinces, I have begun to feel the need for new life and people, and so I have settled down to live and work in Czerniowce.

I used to correspond with Konradek for a time and would be still doing so, for I love him dearly; but our correspondence ceased suddenly when several of my letters addressed to Martinique remained unanswered – that is where I lost trace of him.

Not till last year, while visiting Lwów, did I hear accidentally about his duel, his dangerous weakness,[2] Mr Bobrowski's trip to Marseilles[3]

---

[1] Now in the USSR; Cernauti in Rumanian, Chernivtsy in Ukrainian.

[2] Pulman must have heard rumours about Conrad's wound, which was presented by his family as received in a duel.

[3] Called by a wire from Conrad's friend Richard Fecht, Tadeusz Bobrowski went to Marseilles on 8 March 1878. He learned there that his nephew had tried to commit suicide. See *Conrad's Polish Background*, pp. 173–80.

and Konradek's transfer to the British Merchant Marine. At the same time I learned also of another, even sadder event – of the death of Mrs Bobrowska, my good, second mother. I heard nothing about Mr Bobrowski. Your letter brought fresh and awful news. But I try not to believe it, as I would rather assume it to be only ill-founded rumour.[1] I have long been thinking about getting Konradek's address but it seems difficult. Perhaps for you, with your many connections, it would be easier: through Chodźko,[2] the Paris *émigrés*, the British Merchant Marine shipping office, etc. It would be a great joy to me to get news of my dear Konradek.

If I happen to learn something new I shall let you know without fail; and for my part I take the liberty to ask you for a similar favour.

With all respect.

Yours sincerely,

Pulman

Warm regards to Kostuś (Pan Konstanty).

Kazimierz Bobrowski to Konrad Korzeniowski

Biblioteka Narodowa, Warsaw, MS 2889

Leopoldów,
18/30 April 1882

My dear Konrad,

Your wandering way of life, my dear Nephew, allows only casual correspondence and in that too we do not seem to over-indulge; it gave me, therefore, all the greater pleasure to get direct news from you and I hasten to send off my reply so that it reaches you in Falmouth[3] and sets your mind at rest about Tadeusz. I had recently a letter from my brother with the allowance he sends us every quarter; he writes that the pain in his fingers has diminished; his health has improved, but he is still planning to go abroad for treatment, particularly in order to meet you there.

The fact that you received no reply from Tadeusz may be attributed only to your letter having been lost. I shall let him know about your stay in Falmouth, as from what he told me about you, I see that he had not expected your return until late autumn, and wondered how to arrange it so that your return from the sea should coincide with his expedition to a health resort.

---

[1] Buszczyński must have heard something about the real cause of Conrad's wound.
[2] Wiktor Chodźko, Conrad's friend in France, also a seaman.
[3] Conrad, second mate on board the *Palestine*, remained in Falmouth from December 1881 till September 1882 while the barque was undergoing repairs.

Together with this letter I am sending one to Tadeusz enclosing your missive and hoping that Tadeusz's reply will find you still there.

I thank you very much, dear Konrad, for the warm sentiments you expressed in your letter towards my little flock; you are a frequent subject of our conversation, so although you are personally unknown to my brood they are by no means indifferent to you. They often ask after you, not only in their letters to us, but in those to their uncle as well. The four elder children are at school and this year the fifth is to go too, but my eldest daughter is finishing at the high school and as she is not returning home we shall be left just the two of us and our two-year-old son.

My wife, who cherishes the most friendly feelings towards you and has an affectionate memory of your kindness during her stay in Cracow, has asked me to send you her warm compliments. And my son Tadeusz joins me in sending you our most affectionate regards and best wishes for the success of your forthcoming journey. Commending my entire little brood to your kind thoughts, I remain

Always your loving uncle

K.Bobrowski

Stefan Buszczyński to Konrad Korzeniowski

Biblioteka Narodowa, Warsaw, MS 2889

Venezia, Riva degli Schiavoni
Casa Kirsch
28 October 1883

My dear and beloved Konrad,

I cannot tell you what great joy your letter[1] has afforded me: truly it was the nicest surprise. But it took a long time to reach me. They sought for me at various addresses I had left while I travelled from place to place for the benefit of my health. Thus it followed me to Cracow, Teplice, Reichenhall [in the Bavarian Mountains] etc., finally to Venice; this is the route it had to cover, having been detained several times at post offices. In short, judging by the date on your letter (14 August) it took two months to reach me.

This is why I am so late in replying.

You gave me your address, but unfortunately I do not know how long you intend to stay in London. Perhaps you have already left on some long voyage. Perhaps one should look for you in America or Australia? Probably when you wrote you did not know where your

---

[1] Of 14 August 1883; see *Conrad's Polish Background*, pp. 205–6.

duties would take you. Meanwhile I venture to dispatch these few words. When I get your new address I shall write in greater detail on many things that will no doubt be of interest to you.

Now and then I get news about you from your esteemed uncle. I grieve at not having seen him for such a long time. We were so near each other and yet unaware of it! You, dear Konrad, as it now transpires, were in Marienbad at the same time as I was taking a cure in Teplice. I left Teplice on 6 August and your letter dated 14 August was posted there. Had I known it, either I would have stopped in Teplice to greet you most warmly and to meet the esteemed Mr Tadeusz, or I would have paid you both a visit. But too late now ... It grieves my heart to think that cruel fate willed it thus.

Thanks to your uncle I am acquainted with the many sad and terrifying adventures that befell you on your journeys. It would be a real pleasure for me to hear from you. Having loved and admired your father more than most people I have known, I have bestowed upon you my most affectionate feelings. Believe me that they have not changed and never will change, but may increase on account of your personal qualities and virtues.

Likewise my son cherishes the memory of your great friendship.

After almost six years in Dresden, Riga, Lwów and again Riga, studying first chemistry then agronomy, with difficulties because of the Turkish War, conscription etc., Kostuś has now successfully completed his agronomy studies. Now he runs his estate in *Niemiercze* near *Mohylów-Podolski*, which you probably vaguely remember.

As for myself, after my long wanderings I have settled again in Cracow. But owing to my enfeebled health (chronic catarrh with a bad cough) I must spend this winter in Italy. Should the weather here become too chilly, I shall go further south in search of a warmer climate. If you are good enough to write to me, pray use the above address and my letters will be forwarded according to my instructions.

My daughter (Świderska, by her second marriage) and her husband have spent a whole month with me here. They left recently. Next month I am expecting a visit from Kostuś.

Your portrait has touched me deeply. I thank you most warmly for having sent it. From my heart I commend you to God. Your true friend,

S. Buszczyński

'On Conrad and Kipling', by Jan Perłowski[1]

Prezegląd Współczesny (Warsaw), 1937, no. 4

Professor Józef Ujejski's work *O Konradzie Korzeniowskim*,[2] published last year, is the type of book which one likes to read more than once. As a result, the author is bound to hear for a considerable time various opinions provoked by his monograph. *O Konradzie Korzeniowskim* gives a thorough analysis of Conrad's attitude towards art, the real world and his own fantasy life; also a very frank and yet extremely cautious appraisal of everything that concerns the national feelings of 'that queer fellow', as Kipling used to call him. This moderation of approach was due not only to the precise scholarly methods customary to Ujejski. It was produced by a sense of propriety towards people recently dead: whatever our reservations, we may not judge them as severely as those who, together with their whole epoch, belong entirely to the past. While our contemporaries enter the 'silent eternity' we are still in the ephemera which until yesterday was theirs too; we are a party to a suit in which they have for ever renounced their right to speak. In time we shall be followed by more impartial judges.

I fully share this point of view, particularly with respect to myself. Conrad's generation was well-nigh my own; his Ukrainian world was also my world, rich in memories and traces of the sixties. By reconstructing this environment of my youth, as well as my and other people's later thoughts, I want only to record the misty course – from the tragic days of the post-1863 insurrection to the vacuum of foreign lands – along which, I venture to suppose, the writer's soul progressed. I shall set down the evidence and make some speculations upon it.

I met Konrad Korzeniowski only once, for a brief moment; but for many years fate connected us in a special way. Mr Tadeusz Bobrowski, his uncle and guardian, author of the well-known memoirs, was a colleague and friend of my father. After my father's death he became my guardian as well. I am in possession of a daguerreotype, from the time of Tzar Nicholas I, when both young men studied law at the University of St Petersburg and when Tadeusz, obviously a born leader, acted as mentor to a circle of his contemporaries. From the valley of the river Dniest where my family home was, I travelled across the 'blue Ukrainian steppes' beyond Oratów, to Kazimierówka. There, in a small country house, among miniature-sized furniture, lived that

---

[1] Jan Perłowski (1872–1941), professional diplomat, author of political and literary essays.

[2] 'On Konrad Korzeniowski' (Warsaw, 1936). French translation *Joseph Conrad* (Paris, 1939). The first extensive study of Conrad's thought.

short in stature but outstanding man to whom several generations are considerably indebted for the preservation of our Ukrainian world and its noble traditions. Bobrowski appears in all Conrad's biographies but always conforming to an established pattern: either as a *deus ex machina*, a decisive factor at times of crisis, or as the object of some distant and obscure cult of his nephew. Even Conrad when mentioning his uncle confines himself to generalities. 'For a quarter of a century the wisest, the firmest, the most indulgent of guardians, extending over me a paternal care and affection, a moral support which I seemed to feel always near me in the most distant parts of the earth.' Even here, in spite of the laconic style reminiscent of a tombstone inscription, Conrad makes clear that he knew and loved him from afar. But that is not enough to get an insight into their real relationship. Moral support? Could Bobrowski have played a part in the moral aspect of Conrad's life? We ought to try to get better acquainted with the squire from Kazimierówka.

Włodzimierz Spasowicz, in his obituary, described Bobrowski as a typical product of French eighteenth-century *esprit*.[1] It would be difficult to find a more apt characteristic. In our province French influence has survived until my generation and Bobrowski could have indeed been affected by it, if only via the traditions of Krzemieniec[2] and of the stately homes of the Ukraine which the young gentry used to visit occasionally. Bobrowski possessed all the characteristics of a man of the Enlightenment. Lively by temperament, with a brilliant rationalistic intellect, he was absorbed solely in worldly affairs; even in the face of the greatest adversity he showed unabashed optimism, which was admirable but sometimes seemed like indifference. His sense of humour was sharp and laconic, typical of that sarcastic epoch. He had a tendency towards epicurean tastes. He was a gourmet. His interest in social affairs ranged from current social events in the Kiev, Podolia and Volhynia provinces (to which he gave a perhaps too forcible expression in his memoirs) to the public affairs of those provinces, analysed by him with the thoroughness of a professional lawyer. He was a jurist not only by education but also thanks to his characteristic cool-headedness. He had a sharp understanding of the complexities of local affairs and was quick to form judgements, invariably mature in substance and for the most part light, almost epigrammatic, in form. He was ambitious but endowed with a great civic sense and perfect integrity. He acted as guardian to many orphans of landowning families. Whenever legal or

[1] Published in *Kraj* (St Petersburg), 1894, no. 6.
[2] The seat of a famous Lycée (1804–33); the main centre of learning and culture in Volhynia, which produced many eminent Polish scholars and men of letters.

social problems arose he was ready to advise, persuade or arbitrate. His judgements were valued by public opinion. He was surrounded by general respect. In the marketing rooms at the Kiev agricultural fair, contentions would break off, loungers would sit up as soon as he appeared: short, with a bald head, Roman features, clean-shaven face, always with an apt remark and a ready wit. In view of this general feeling it was not surprising that our leader had a high opinion of himself. This only further enhanced his authority among the gentry. Even the most spirited of them dared only smile surreptitiously when he had hundreds of copies of his lithographic portrait signed 'Tadeusz Bobrowski', modelled on the then popular pictures of notable men, made and distributed among his followers. His attention was centred primarily on himself.

He used to speak of the distant Conrad often and at great length, although, in fact, the uncle and the nephew had known each other only very slightly having spent barely a few months together in their whole life. Bobrowski in spite of his ethical conservatism was an advocate of everything called 'progress' in those days. His ward's initiative afforded him pleasure and was, to some extent, a source of personal pride. He was all the more ready to show it as many critical comments had been reaching him from all sides. It was regarded a mistake on his part to have allowed a fifteen-year-old orphan to go to the end of the world as it were 'to meet his doom'. Now facts decided in the uncle's favour. 'I've let him go,' he once said, 'on condition that he applies himself to his nautical studies.' We know from elsewhere that at the beginning Conrad fulfilled that obligation only partially.

As I was listening to Mr Bobrowski I thought of another conversation with him shortly before. It so happened that I too had found myself at a cross-roads leading to different schools and professions. My family had decided that it would be best and most proper for me to go and seek advice at Kazimierówka. Thus I stood before Mr Bobrowski and presented him with my dilemma. I had hardly finished when my guardian remarked without a moment's hesitation: 'I assume that everyone ought to choose the way he likes best.' Today I still regard those words as extremely wise. Conrad, I think, must have heard approximately the same. In *A Personal Record* he writes explicitly that his uncle did not want to bear the blame for having spoiled his life and therefore did not stand in his way.[1] And Bobrowski made it quite clear that he had arrived at this decision as quickly as he always did, and without getting involved in superfluous detail. The speculations of some of Conrad's biographers about his uncle's entreaties and threats seem to be completely unfounded.

[1] *A Personal Record*, p. 42.

And could the uncle's letters reaching him abroad dispel the impression of benevolent indifference which this kind of approach was bound to leave upon the young man? I, too, used to get letters from Bobrowski. Having come of age, I sent him a sincere appreciation of his wise and kind protection. To this he replied extensively, recalling my father's memory: 'I am now transferring that old and long-lasting friendship to his son.' A phrase both simple and sympathetic. However, years later when his letters to Conrad appeared in print I found a similar sentence in a letter written at the time when, following his father's death, the twelve-year-old boy found himself bereft of both parents. 'The whole affection we felt for your parents we now bestow upon you,' wrote Bobrowski. This kind of stereotype in matters of sentiment was quite in keeping with Bobrowski's disposition. 'A charming letter,' says an English commentator unaware of the situation. Let us compare, however, the date of Apollo Korzeniowski's death with the date on the letter. The death occurred on 23 May 1869 and the letter was written on 20 September. Bobrowski delayed his affectionate message for a full four months. This disclosure does not entitle us to any new conclusions but confirms our previous ones. Bobrowski was one of the worthiest men born in the Ukraine, but he was not a man of tender heart and feelings. Conrad could not but sense this as everyone else did. The remark about 'moral support' in distant parts of the world could be an expression of resignation of a homeless wanderer, unable to find support anywhere else. Bobrowski, a man of unwavering patriotism, bears no responsibility for his nephew's national feelings. However, if I am right in assuming that one of the reasons for Conrad's inward tragedy was the feeling of estrangement from his home country, then, we might conclude, the highly respectable but cold personality of his uncle did nothing to improve the situation.

From what Bobrowski used to say about Conrad's maritime career I remember one or two details which correct the misconception that Conrad's transfer from a French to an English ship, at the time of very strained relations between England and Russia, was caused, albeit partly, by his hatred of Poland's traditional enemy. Bobrowski stated clearly that Conrad joined the British Merchant Navy because it led to a more interesting and advantageous career.[1] Apropos of this he related an incident justly regarded as an example of his ward's presence of mind.

---

[1] The immediate cause of Conrad's joining the British Merchant Marine was that he could no longer serve in the French, and failed in his attempt to enlist into the US Navy.

There were several other candidates when Conrad was first examined by the English officials. All were nervous because the examining officer was known for being not only strict but also quick-tempered. When it was Conrad's turn, the officer looked at his papers, eyed the candidate coldly from head to foot and asked sarcastically:

'So you served in the French merchant service?'

'Yes, Sir.'

'I'd better warn you that I have the worst possible opinion of their marine.'

To which Conrad replied: 'I entirely share your opinion, Sir, and let me add that that is precisely the reason why I want to join the British Mercantile Marine.'

I remember one occasion when Bobrowski explained the real reasons why his nephew could not at first contemplate returning home. Some people have maintained that 'Apollo Korzeniowski's son' could not pay even a short visit to the Ukraine. That is not quite accurate. In this particular case the father's revolutionary past would not have had any bearing upon his son's fate. At the time when Conrad reached military age the Russo-Turkish War was on.[1] For obvious reasons he did not comply with the recruiting formalities, and in the event of his returning to Russia, he might have had to face accusations of desertion.[2] Moreover, Conrad's return for good was never included in Bobrowski's plans. Contrary to some speculations, his uncle had never seriously considered the possibility of getting him to settle down at Kazimierówka in order to 'teach him the management of the estate'. Just think: he would have to change his way of life, his perfect, highly egocentric system. No, Bobrowski had nothing in him of the benevolent Judge Soplica[3] who intended to offer the other Tadeusz 'a small village to begin with'. And anyway Bobrowski's estate was quite modest in size.

Bobrowski spoke little about Conrad's father and generally in quite a different tone from the public one used in his memoirs, which were intended for publication. Bobrowski was not a man of literary persuasion and if from a distance he kept track of new publications, it was in the role of a censor rather than of an admirer. Most certainly he never read the poems and translations of his brother-in-law. Endowed with a highly rationalistic mind, he tended to belittle Apollo, whom he regarded as a man incapable of managing his own affairs, who in the time of

---

[1] Lasted from 1877 to 1878; ended with a peace congress in Berlin.

[2] The Russian consul in Marseilles refused Konrad Korzeniowski permission to remain abroad (see *Conrad's Polish Background*, p. 176).

[3] One of the main characters in Mickiewicz's *Pan Tadeusz*.

the insurrection 'over-acted as a Red' in order to convince himself and others that he was not a mediocrity. Possibly Bobrowski's words were tinged by a grudge towards his brother-in-law for all the suffering inflicted upon his sister; anyway, he always emphasized that after the insurrection 'Korzeniowski used to cast gloom all round, posturing as a broken-hearted bard'. My father, who encountered him frequently at different stages of his life, used to speak of him in similar terms. He said that Korzeniowski had a gift for getting along with ladies but men found him an irritating mixture of Romanticism, Messianism and socialism, not uncommon among his contemporaries. Apart from that he was regarded as a man of honour but exceptionally high-strung and weak. When he returned from his Russian exile he seemed the very image of the deepest despair and misery. On his departure for Galicia, when a group of friends came to say goodbye, he prophesied the complete annihilation of our country in the jaws of the Muscovite Leviathan. Describing the prevailing mood of the time, an eye-witness, himself a former exile to the depths of Russia, repeated Korzeniowski's words and added his own exasperated comment: 'And what was the use of such talk when everyone knew that!' Reconstructing the spiritual and mental development of Conrad, who was at that time entering his formative years, one cannot leave out the details connected with his closest environment.

At last, just a few years before Bobrowski's death, I met Conrad at Kazimierówka. I had heard that he came to his uncle to obtain money for some enterprise, as far as I remember, in Africa. I do not know whether he got it. It was winter and the snow had levelled out the slight undulations of the countryside near Oratów. With some difficulty I drove up to the manor-house concealed in a not very large park and there I found a small all-male group. Some came expressly to look at the exotic arrival. I saw him standing in the middle of the room surrounded by a friendly circle of men; emigration in search of livelihood was regarded as normal in the Ukraine and, contrary to some beliefs, the idea of blaming Conrad never entered anybody's mind. All the gentlemen were obviously ready to make friends with Conrad but his manner cast a chill. He answered all questions with a strained politeness, he spoke with concentration and listened carefully but one could not fail to notice his extreme boredom. Left alone for a moment, he would raise his head and stare into a corner of the living-room as if his thoughts were miles away. He spoke with a hint of a foreign accent and occasional bursts of our characteristic borderland intonation. Finally, when the guests stopped pestering him, he stood politely beside a chattering group, looking conspicuous by not asking anyone any questions. And yet those people, or at least their sons, had been the closest friends of his father and mother. He spoke only once, to ask about a new railway line which was to link Humań, hitherto cut off from the world, with the port of Odessa. This started a long conversation about sea tariffs and freights and about the effect of transport on the price of grain. At last there was a subject of common interest. I listened attentively, with a growing antipathy towards the stranger, and therefore, as soon as there was a lull in the conversation I asked, perhaps not too tactfully, how long ago he had left the country. His eyes glinted. He understood in an instant and answered as if reading my thoughts: 'Ah, well, half a lifetime ago.' It was a way of refuting a charge which had begun to take shape in me.

Then I started telling him about a lady who bore the same name as he did and who years ago had been known all over the Ukraine. I reminded him of Miss Regina Korzeniowska, an outstanding personality combining patriotic feelings, a scholarly mind and eccentricity. No less a man than Julian Bartoszewicz[1] had praised her merits, and humorous anecdotes about her life have entertained even the following generation... I imagined that those reminiscences would interest Conrad and help him cast aside his reserve. The result was quite the opposite. He looked perplexed, made a wry face and began to speak quickly, avoiding my subject. Meanwhile we were joined by somebody else. On the mantelpiece stood an old clock with a pendulum; according to Bobrowski it dated from the eighteenth century. There followed an inspection of the antique piece and a conversation about English chronometers, supposed to be the most accurate in the world. As I started to get bored I went out on the balcony where a strong south wind was blowing, bringing thaw. Conrad slipped out after me. Earlier, when he had been searching for a Polish translation of some English expression, I had suggested the correct word. Now he approached me, both hands deep in his pockets in the English way, exclaiming with that characteristic merry tone of voice used by the English under similar circumstances: 'A breezy day! Very fine! Isn't it?'

I was much younger than Conrad but did not feel impressed by him in any way. None of us knew yet of his talent. Only once had Bobrowski made the passing remark that his nephew wrote something in English. Laughing, I replied not too politely: 'Why not say it in Polish?'

He lifted his head and turned away with a frown. Several people came out on the balcony and a young puppy with muddy paws rushed towards us, jumping. Conrad leaned forward, turned the puppy on its

[1] Julian Bartoszewicz (1821–70), historian and editor.

back, and, petting it for a long while with obvious pleasure, kept on repeating over and over again, partly for the benefit of the dog, partly for me: 'Doggy, doggy, doggy ... you dirty dog!...'

I left Kazimierówka the same evening. This was my only encounter with Conrad. I was unaware of his inner conflict. Nor did I know that while he was grating upon my feelings, I was wounding his.

Years passed, Bobrowski was no more and a deathly silence descended upon Kazimierówka. There followed a time when most probably no one in the Ukraine ever thought of Conrad. Then his first novels began to come out, but in Poland few people noticed them. No chance reader, however, was likely to forget those books readily; he would return to them again and again, each time with a strange feeling. Those were not the English love stories one commonly read. I remember having once lent one of those slim volumes in the Tauchnitz edition to a girl who returned it several days later with the passing remark 'This is the Słowacki[1] of the tropical islands.' Through the lips of that ingenuous girl the Ukraine was reclaiming the English writer. There was something in that remark. While some of Conrad's books failed to appeal to our mentality, others reached deep down into our hearts, as deeply as only our great Ukrainian poetry could reach. Is it possible that Conrad carried away with him something from his homeland? His great feeling for nature, earth, sky and sea takes us sometimes to the shores of pantheism, as does Beniowski.[2] He had a deep insight into those unknown worlds, into the souls of men from different races and continents; he looked at them as if through the eyes of an exile, through the atmosphere of his own nostalgia. He seemed close to us because he never ceased to be a wanderer among strangers. And in our collective impressions of those visions, reaching deep and far into infinity, we shared his cosmic terror, his awareness of the fathomless void where human life flickers briefly in a small circle over the abyss. This world did not offer him shelter. The world of fantasy and reality, colourful and dismal, throbbing with life and utterly deserted; this world would not have existed for us if Joseph Conrad had not been born in the land of poets, at a time of great enthusiasm and black despair; if he had not left that land with the thought that it was for ever. His language and the subject-matter of his writings made him a stranger to us; but through

---

[1] Juliusz Słowacki (1809–49), beside Mickiewicz the greatest poet of Polish Romanticism. Conrad thought highly of him; see his interview with Marian Dąbrowski in the present volume, p. 199.
[2] Słowacki's long digressive epic, left incomplete.

his emotions he inadvertently belonged to us: he was one of us in a specific way.

I do not know if Mrs Orzeszkowa read all his books and if perhaps the surly tone of the article on 'The Emigration of Talent' was dictated by a regret that such a great Polish talent did not reveal itself in Poland. But I do know that although other similar opinions have been voiced, the general public has not shared the unfriendly sentiments about 'that gentleman who writes novels in English'. It was accepted that any Pole might seek his livelihood elsewhere, that he might write in a foreign language and even become famous as a result. Yes, the better known he was abroad, the more effectively he could serve the Polish cause. It has been proved many a time during our national disasters. But years went by and Conrad did not fulfil our expectations. His later works, which accounted for his fame in England, seemed to us different and more remote. His thoughts and feelings were more English. Our disappointment grew as this writer, forgetting his home country, merged more and more with his English environment, to such a degree that he even began delivering in real earnest inspired speeches on its behalf. In all his works there was no mention of Poland. We were baffled. But none of us suspected that things would get even worse when he finally remembered Poland.

Approximately ten years after Conrad's first book, there appeared a collection of his short stories, the first of them again a masterpiece: 'Typhoon'. Then followed a story about an English country girl, 'Amy Foster'. It did not take long, however, to notice that the title was misleading and the real protagonist was in fact Yanko Goorall, shipwrecked on the shores of England, originally from 'the eastern range of the Carpathian mountains, from the remote provinces of Austria'. Is he Polish? No. He is 'a Sclavonian peasant'.[1] That much for the English public to which Conrad apparently did not want to admit his interest in Poland. But for us, in spite of the Eastern Carpathians, Yanko Goorall is obviously a young shepherd from around Poronin or Zakopane. Why this strange deception? The author seems to be saying to his former compatriots: 'There you are: I've tried to tell the English about you, but it didn't work out.' The gist of the story is in fact the inability of the arrival from the East Carpathian mountains to communicate with the people among whom he found refuge. Even the woman who loved him, the mother of his child, grabbed the infant and ran away terrified, leaving the dying Yanko alone raving in his unintelligible language.

[1] Not a quotation from *Amy Foster*, but Perłowski's own interpretation. He misses the fact that the way Yanko Gooral's origin is identified in the story reflects the consciousness of the narrator (very vague on this point), not of Conrad himself.

Did the author intend it as an explanation of his own actions? A Polish reader puts the book aside feeling resentful.[1] What is the meaning of that story? Obviously an inner struggle is taking place in the soul of the author: something pulls him to his homeland and something draws him back. He would like to forget his past but its phantoms keep haunting him. In front of his eyes float images of Poland, where he spent barely four years of his life, following his exile in the East and before his wanderings in the West; faded visions of his motherland preserved in his memory, and in his troubled heart a distant muffled cry. And so the time goes by, years pass.

Then, shortly before the war, in 'Prince Roman', Conrad speaks about Poland openly and with deep affection, although slightly reminiscent of the kind bestowed upon a dear but departed person. Love without duties. Evidently Conrad does not believe in Poland's future but still nurtures a deep hatred for her oppressors. In *A Personal Record*, which appeared almost simultaneously, he avows at the beginning 'having broken away from my origins under a storm of blame' and entreats that 'no charge of faithlessness ought to be lightly uttered'. 'Love itself wears at times the desperate shape of betrayal.'[2] And so once again he was at war with himself, even after so many years. Is he then, in spite of appearances, still faithful to his old love? If so, it is difficult to understand a paragraph at the end of the book. 'English –the speech of my deepest affections, of hours of toil and hours of ease ... of thoughts pursued, of remembered emotions – of my very dreams! And if (after being thus fashioned by it in that part of me which cannot decay) I dare not claim it aloud as my own, then, at any rate, the speech of my children.'[3] Thus all he has carried away from Poland is that which 'decays':[4] his bodily shell and nothing beside. And although he does not yet feel worthy of the name of a true Englishman he consoles himself with the thought that his children will embody this ideal. He writes those words at the time of Września,[5] during the strikes in Polish schools, in the most tragic moments of our fight for the souls of our children. And in the same book he records with reverence that an old relative of his prophesied at his cradle, 'He will see better times';[6] he recalls Russia with hatred, the insurrection with pain; confesses that the year 1863 'coloured my earliest impressions'.[7] Impossible to understand this chaos.

Time passed, the war broke out and I found myself in Switzerland,

---

[1] This was not at all the common reaction of Polish critics to *Amy Foster*.
[2] Pp. xiv, 35, 36.   [3] P. 136.   [4] Not a quotation from Conrad.
[5] In 1901 schoolchildren in Września near Poznań were flogged for their refusal to obey the order abolishing Polish as teaching language.
[6] P. 47.   [7] P. 56.

where a group of Poles set about doing something. A committee, headed by Sienkiewicz and Paderewski, was formed in Vevey, for the purpose of helping war victims in Poland. In effect the committee's aims were far greater – it was to be concerned not only with financial help but with propaganda. We wanted to remind the world that Poles exist and that Poland wants, and still has, a right to exist. Conrad declined to collaborate with us under the pretext that the 'Ambassador of Tzarist Russia' played some part in the work of our committee. Thus Conrad was giving a lesson in patriotism to Sienkiewicz and Paderewski.[1] I recall the moment when the lawyer Osuchowski,[2] vice-chairman of the committee, a withered old man, his eyes aflame with the most noble zeal, informed us, shaking his bony arms in the air and stammering with emotion, that 'Mr Konrad Korzeniowski, an outstanding English writer, has failed us.' We lapsed into silence. Although Conrad's past was familiar to us all, we couldn't get over the surprise. Why, even foreigners kindly disposed towards Poland worked on the committee! Whence came his reluctance? Sienkiewicz, with his wonted calm, gave a simple answer: 'It's normal. Man is often vindictive when he has done wrong.'

Years went by and with the passing of time passed Joseph Conrad's life.

On a certain morning in 1928, in Madrid, I was called to the telephone. A familiar female voice spoke to me:

'My father arrived yesterday. Please come tonight. You'll find just the two of us and my father.' This invitation was made by the charming Mrs Bambridge, wife of a member of the British Embassy, daughter of Rudyard Kipling.

Naturally, the author of *Kim* was in my mind all day. Waiting for the evening I recalled those old times when Kipling and Pierre Loti opened to us distant exotic worlds, which made us strangely unsettled in our grey, European, Polish reality. But while the French author unfolded a colourful panorama before your eyes reflecting only his own, monotonously melancholy soul, Kipling aroused our deeper and more vital emotions. His world of the jungle, the snow-covered Himalayas, back streets in tropical towns, Brahmin temples – it was all just the décor for a great drama, where the part of the protagonist was played not by an Indian or a Malay, but by a white man, with light eyes, clear mind and will-power, by a servant and representative of the powerful Empire.

---

[1] A tendentiously hostile interpretation; see Conrad's telegram of 27 March 1915 in this volume, p. 227.

[2] Antoni Osuchowski (1849–1928).

The English poet gave us fragments of a rhapsody about a state which, two thousand years after Rome, followed its example, 'creating one family out of different nations'. In a Pole of the end of the nineteenth century, images of such a power did something more than just stir up a longing for exoticism. The great writer was not only a great artist. He was an English statesman. He taught his countrymen the meaning of the 'hereditary instinct of continuity' which, according to his own words, forms the essence of national feelings. He was an avowed 'apostle of English literary imperialism', as some contemptuous critics have called him, unmindful that every great idea is word before it becomes flesh. And so, walking that evening along the Avenida Castellana, I repeated in my mind the first lines of the poem, representative of the deepest meaning of Kipling's thoughts. As always when convictions are strong, even when concerned with terrestrial matters, they rise towards religion:

> God of our fathers, known of old –
> Lord of our far-flung battle-line –
> Beneath whose awful Hand we hold
> Dominion over palm and pine –
> Lord God of Hosts, be with us yet,
> Lest we forget, lest we forget![1]

Those words, in which the great Englishman summed up the history and the spirit of contemporary, post-Cromwellian England, brought to my mind another inspired masterpiece about the greatness of Britain. It was a piece of prose, but such prose that it sunk into one's memory like poetry. An English sailor returns home after a long absence. It is night-time. 'The lights of the earth mingled with the lights of heaven; and above the tossing lanterns of a trawling fleet a great lighthouse shone steadily, like an enormous riding light burning above a vessel of fabulous dimensions.' In the mind of the homesick sailor the real picture of his country blends with the ideal vision, such as he dreamed of during his long meditations about his country's destiny. 'The dark land lay alone in the midst of waters – like a mighty ship bestarred with vigilant lights – a ship carrying the burden of millions of lives – a ship freighted with dross and with jewels, with gold and with steel.' And here from the writer's heart bursts out a hymn in praise of England, a hymn of all-embracing love which accepts his country such as it is, whole, and without reservations:

She towered up immense and strong, guarding priceless traditions and untold suffering, sheltering glorious memories and base forgetfulness, ignoble virtues

---

[1] *Recessional* (1897).

and splendid transgressions. A great ship! For ages had the ocean battered in vain her enduring sides; she was there when the world was vaster and darker, when the sea was great and mysterious, and ready to surrender the prize of fame to audacious men. A ship mother of fleets and nations! The great flagship of the race; stronger than the storms! and anchored in the open sea.[1]

This text you may find even in English anthologies for schools and the author of this masterpiece is Konrad Korzeniowski.

And this is why, ascending the stairs of the hospitable house, I was filled with solemn admiration for Kipling and with a sense of my own painful humiliation. The English patriot Joseph Conrad was my countryman. At a time when Poland did not have her own state he announced to the world that Poles did not even have their own motherland.

My hostess introduced me to her father as a particular admirer of his and I openly admitted regarding his works as of great importance, and not only of a literary kind. Soon the conversation turned to the subject of Conrad. Kipling spoke with quiet animation and I was struck by the magnanimity with which he praised and discussed Conrad's outstanding talent that was overshadowing his own writings of recent years.

He began with some commonplace remarks about Conrad's language and style. 'His spoken English was sometimes difficult to understand but with a pen in his hand he was first amongst us.'[2] Reading Conrad's novels he often wondered how this foreigner had come to use some expression, or juxtaposition of words, never encountered before but which rendered perfectly and in a thoroughly English way a new thought. Kipling assumed it to be an outright case of 'a substitution of his former personality'.[3] But this applied only to the language. There was nothing English, according to Kipling, in Conrad's mentality. 'When I am reading him,' he continued, 'I always have the impression that I am reading an excellent translation of a foreign author.'

And Kipling proceeded to explain his idea, which corresponded so remarkably with the impressions of some Polish readers.

According to him, apart from a great talent and unique technique, Conrad attracted English readers by his exotic mentality. In every average Englishman there lurks an emotional complex suppressed by his puritanical culture. Conrad released those forces. His characters, drawn with extreme mastery and acceptable to the English reader, have the temperature of their feelings a degree or so above the English norm. As a rule, Conrad's characters eventually reach 'to the pitch of their emotion',[4] but as the whole process takes place gradually, the

---

[1] *The Nigger of the 'Narcissus'*, pp. 162–3.   [2] English in the original.
[3] English in the original.   [4] English in the original.

reader experiences an intensification of his own feelings and, 'getting red in the face',[1] goes through emotions hitherto unknown. 'Have you noticed,' continued Kipling, 'how many of Conrad's characters are consumed by one idea or one emotion? Have you noticed the intensity of fear and terror? That man must have gone through nightmares himself. And love in his books is of the most romantic kind imaginable. An English reader, seemingly cold, adores sincere exaltation, just as every Englishman adores the Romantic music of Chopin.'

I was struck by the comparison. Kipling did not know the Polish poetry of words but knew the greatest Polish poet of sound.

Moreover, in Kipling's opinion, Conrad's moral world is equally un-English.

'Of course you can find everything in English literature,' he said, 'especially nowadays when writers seek originality. But Conrad was sincere. In the novel which he valued most among his works and which indeed is a masterpiece, *The Nigger of the "Narcissus"*, we find emotions alien to our society. Although Conrad hated Moscow and loathed Russian writers, in this book he is more Russian than English. His "purely human" attitude to the Negro does not fit in with the English mentality, which may be Christian but not "humanitarian". That book could have been written by Maxim Gorki, if he had had Conrad's talent. Conrad's spiritual alienation is even more marked in another novel of his, equally great from the artistic point of view, *Lord Jim*. The very foundations of this novel are extremely un-English. First of all it should be noted that the basic idea, countrary to some opinions, is not the inner drama of a man guilty of an offence and plagued by remorse. The basic issue of the novel centres on the question whether a man is responsible for his actions. Conrad expresses the opinion that under certain circumstances the responsibility may be reduced to such an extent that it almost ceases to exist. Conrad is undoubtedly right; it is indeed so in certain cases. However,' continued Kipling, 'I would not encourage Conrad to expound his theory before any English jury which, until now, has maintained our old Anglo-Saxon view that every man is responsible for his actions.'

At this point the conversation changed to the subject of the autobiographical character of *Lord Jim*. I recounted in detail Conrad's past. Kipling made some reservations.

According to him, if the sinking ship, deserted by Lord Jim, a member of the crew, in a moment of some mental blackout, is meant to be Poland, then why, having realized his mistake, did Conrad not return aboard the *Patna*? In the novel it was impossible. The ship

[1] English in the original.

managed to reach the shore and Jim's return would have been of no consequence. But *Patna* – Poland was in danger for many years following the publication of the book. Conrad could rectify his mistake at any moment but did not do so. The misunderstanding is obvious: Conrad's novel cannot be regarded as autobiographical.

Then we went back to the subject of the first stage of Conrad's life, particularly the years overshadowed by the panic of insurrection. We spoke of his hatred for Poland's oppressors, which, although acquired in Vologda and the Ukraine, lasted all his life, whereas many other feelings lost their intensity. 'I always thought him a queer fellow,'[1] concluded Kipling. There is obviously something in it. 'He hated Russia with frenzy.'[2] I recall situations which were, perhaps, not unlike some events in Conrad's life.

And Kipling mentioned one of his own earlier stories which I, too, remembered after a couple of sentences. The story was based on life. Somewhere in the uplands of Central Asia, where English and Russian forces were in dangerous proximity, the representatives of both sides came together to discuss some border incident. Russia was represented by military men, heavy, tall, bearded, dressed in uniforms 'like over-elaborate night-shirts', and their chests covered with 'small crosses'. On the English side we saw typical gentlemen, colder than usual, because in that desolate spot 'Muscovy's soul' discarded its European mask and uncovered its true character: false, brutal and cruel. An old man in rags wandered round the camp. He was a dumb, mentally deranged creature who, in spite of manifest discouragement, clung to the English and revealed a hatred and terror of the Russians. The Russian officers' behaviour was correct; after several conferences the signing of the document took place, farewells were exchanged and the Cossack unit disappeared down a mountain gorge. It was a day of festivity. In the evening a celebratory dinner was held in the English camp and while the commander was proposing the health of Her Majesty, something inconceivable happened. The old vagabond, unable to speak any human tongue, stood up immediately at the words 'the Queen'. His whole behaviour, in a way obvious to any Englishman, betrayed not only his Englishness but his gentlemanly upbringing. The incident created a general stir.

Trying to unravel the mystery, a group of English officers concluded that this miserable creature, stripped of all human attributes, was a former member of the Civil Service on the northern border of India. As a young man engaged on a secret mission, he had disappeared and was never heard of again. He fell into Muscovite hands and spent many

[1] English in the original.   [2] English in the original.

long years in Muscovite dungeons. It was not known how he got out. He returned a wreck of his former self. He had forgotten his own past, he had forgotten everything except some vague memories of his former countrymen and an unabated hatred of his tormentors: a stigma as permanent as the marks left by irons on his withered limbs.[1]

'Could something similar have happened to Conrad's soul when he was still a child?,' asked Kipling.

It was getting late, our conversation had run its course and I walked out into the murky Madrid streets.

In the following years, as I was re-reading Conrad's novels, Kipling's question came often to my mind. Could 'something similar' have indeed happened in his life?

Many among us tended to explain Conrad's mystery in the simplest terms: 'Home is where I prosper.' However, it is enough to glance at any book of his to realize the jarring superficiality of this interpretation. Although there is no direct relationship between the natural talent and the moral worth of a writer, there are limits to the cynicism of talented people. This uncommon spirit could not create for himself so common a reality. It is necessary to look somewhere else for an explanation; obviously, on a higher level.

In the course of time, books started coming out on Conrad's early years and the hitherto scattered details could be fitted into a cohesive whole. I was becoming convinced that the clue to the riddle could be found in his childhood years. This past is well known now. Drawing from the historical sources on contemporary Ukraine and supplementing these with my own memories I have tried to reconstruct Conrad's life.

How did this world, extinct now, look through Conrad's childish eyes at the time of his awakening consciousness? Children's memory seldom extends back beyond their fifth year but it usually retains later events. Conrad, we take it, did not forget the year of the insurrection. By then he and his parents are in exile and the little boy's first impressions are not those of home. They are more like scenes out of Orłowski's album:[2] troikas with wooden bow harnesses, blockhouses, onion-shaped domes, a bearded mob. Occasionally the tinny clang of bells from Orthodox churches and deep sounds of foreign, incomprehensible speech reach his ears. But he begins to grasp the meaning of words in his own language, catching fragments of phrases and finishing them in his own mind, pondering over their gloomy tone and the sullen faces. Fear is creeping into the child's soul.

[1] A garbled reference to 'The Man Who Was', from *Life's Handicap* (1891).
[2] Aleksander Orłowski (1777–1834), Polish painter and draftsman, spent many years in Russia.

This feeling of fear, bordering occasionally on terror, is never to leave him. It is not just his imagination: he knows and sees it confirmed every day, with growing certainty that some evil and relentless force threatening complete annihilation hangs over him, his parents and their closest circle of friends. This evil and omnipotent force can reach him everywhere. In the course of several years, which to a child drag like decades, news of fresh misfortunes keeps coming in from his country. He watches his father bidding farewell to his uncle, who is departing to Siberia certain that he will never return.[1] At the end of his short visit to the Ukraine, wide-eyed, he sees the gendarmes leading his mother with himself in her arms into a coach which is to take them back into exile. Later, when a bit older, he understands everything. Fear mounts in him but hatred is being aroused simultaneously. The lives of people whom he loves and who are similar to his family represent one long chain of suffering and anguish. Somewhere far away there exists a country wholly inhabited by Poles, all equally oppressed, and their misery will never end. His omniscient father, broken down but calm, says so. His mother, who is soon to die of worry, says the same. Conrad is eight years old. Fear, a feeling of hopelessness and of hatred, are deeply ingrained in his personality. He will never be able to get over the trauma. The ghost of national annihilation will always be with him. Russia and the Russians will remain objects of hate throughout his life. But does he simultaneously learn to love Poland?

For almost three years following his mother's death he stays in exile, in the same atmosphere of stoic resignation, but deep down one can sense despair. His father, a man of strong patriotic feelings but weak and lacking in will-power, suffers – for the first time in his life, not on account of his own ineptitude. As a result his deep pessimism, acquired in the days of adversity, centres on the national cause. For him that cause seems lost: only someone completely blinded can claim otherwise.[2] Was not the insurrection sufficient proof? It is time to recognize once and for all that the situation is absolutely hopeless and, holding one's head high, to wait for the end to come. This is what his father says, coughing and sick, disguising his weak character with the strength of reason. And should anyone rebel against this theory of total despair he would be cowed by the erudite bard and intimidated by the mood prevailing among other exiles.[3] For Apollo was by no means an

---

[1] Apollo did not see his brother Hilary Korzeniowski before the latter's exile.

[2] The author is evidently ignorant of Apollo Korzeniowski's publications of 1868 and 1869, and also of his letters from that time, which flatly contradict his statement.

[3] This reconstruction is contradicted by Korzeniowski's extant manuscripts of that period, and does not find corroboration in any other documentary source.

exception. Let elderly people recall the atmosphere of the post-insurrection years in the borderland provinces, even ten years later. And so,
little Conrad learns to love Poland as someone dear but already dying.
He loves Poland as a memory of the past but her present frightens him
and her future looks to him like a black abyss.

Finally Conrad with his father find themselves outside the Russian
cordon, in Galicia. The surroundings are different but the atmosphere
remains the same. The ageing exile declines more and more, in body
and spirit. He suffers privation. In spite of a gradual change in Austrian policy, there is a feeling of gloom.[1] This part of the country
shared with Russian-occupied Poland the great moral suffering of the
cataclysm of the insurrection, and now it is full of exiles who spread
their mood of despair. Moreover, there is the old stagnation and
poverty. Heated discussions are taking place and the former insurgents,
instead of being comforted, listen to words of reproof. In those circumstances the twelve-year-old boy looks around, listens, observes and
comes to the conclusion that his father, wise and prophetic, is right as
usual. Less than a year after leaving the Ukraine, his father dies.
Recalling his death almost half a century later, Conrad writes: 'I looked
forward to what was coming with an incredulous terror, I turned my
eyes from it sometimes with success, and yet all the time I had an awful
sensation of the inevitable.'[2] That 'awful sensation' of imminent
disaster, implanted during his Russian exile and intensified later by
tragic experiences during his adolescence, will stay with him throughout life. Like Pascal, he had visions of a gaping abyss. In this permanent state of anxiety, confirmed by witnesses in later years, the annihilation of the Polish nation was to remain a kind of dogma for him.

The three years[3] spent in Poland after his father's death did
nothing to change his mood. His bitterness was augmented by bereavement. In Cracow Conrad was surrounded by patriotic phraseology, a
defiant attitude towards the 'Stańczyks'[4] who condemned the insurrection, 'open letters to Prince Bismarck', as well as incompetence,
impotence,[5] and general hardship which made everyone think primarily about himself. The lively boy with a critical mind found no
encouragement in his surroundings. From the moment he was left
alone in the world, his situation became unbearable. Słowacki com-

---

[1] In fact the late sixties and early seventies were in Galicia a time of fairly lively
activity, both political and cultural.
[2] 'Poland Revisited', *Notes on Life and Letters*, p. 168.   [3] In fact, more than five.
[4] Popular name given to the Cracow conservatives, from the title of a political satire
published by them in 1869, *Teka Stańczyka*.
[5] Again a biased opinion: the years 1869–74 were in Cracow a period of rapid change,
both in politics and in urban development.

plained of 'hardly knowing his family home',[1] but Conrad could have said this with more justification. After his father's death he did not even have a family. We have already seen how little his distant uncle did to replace it; now that he had become his guardian he sent him, from time to time, instructive letters and small sums of money for his maintenance, from the meagre inheritance of the orphan himself. Conrad made casual boyhood friendships but throughout Poland there was not one person whose heart warmed to him. Thus, when he set off as a fifteen-year-old boy to Marseilles, the moral balance-sheet of his young life looked hopeless. A lack of faith in his country's future was deeply ingrained in his soul, and he was never given a chance to love anyone there sincerely. Besides he knew that he was not loved by anyone either. And so he was alone in the world. He had no ties with Poland. Many years later he was to admit not having felt a stranger when he found himself abroad for the first time and we understand why.[2] In his own country he felt just as much a stranger as anywhere else. He had ceased being a child now. He was roused by adolescent emotions. He broke away from the world which was presented to him as dying and hurled himself into a whirl of life such as is conceived by a teenager. Hence ideas, seemingly unusual but in fact the most obvious for a child: the sea, far-away lands, sun, colour, adventures – everything straight out of books by Marryat and Cooper. And thus Conrad cut himself off from his motherland.

From this point his thoughts and emotions developed in later life along a straight line. Years pass, he became assimilated and absorbed into his new environment. He hardly met any Poles and when recalling Poland his thoughts continued from where he left off at the time of his father's death, or dwelt upon the stagnation of Cracow, the crushed Ukraine, the prison-like Vologda. The underlying theme was always the curse of Muscovy and the hopeless state of his motherland, to which he never felt closely bound, having only passed through it fleetingly. But those childhood years, when in various temporary homes Poland was personified by the permanently mournful circle of exiles, gave him a deep hidden attachment, which, like qualms of conscience, was to stay with him for the rest of his life. 'I never, in mind or heart, separated myself from my native country,'[3] he wrote once to a Polish friend; 'Will you forgive me,' he asked a relative, 'that my sons don't speak Polish?'[4] To

---

[1] From the poem 'Hymn' (1836).
[2] I am unable to identify the source of this statement.
[3] To Kazimierz Waliszewski, 15 November 1903; *Conrad's Polish Background*, p. 258.
[4] See Karola Zagórska's 'Under the Roof of Konrad Korzeniowski' in the present volume, pp. 230–46.

an invitation issued by a Polish emigrant living in England, he answered: 'We shall talk about this far-away country which we both love.'[1] This state of mental distress is clearly seen in the story 'Prince Roman'. He has this to say about Poland: 'That country which demands to be loved, with the mournful affection one bears to the unforgotten dead and with the unextinguishable fire of a hopeless passion...'[2]

This feeling of hopelessness was never to leave him, even when Poland was being resurrected from her grave. He looked, he saw but he did not believe. When war broke out his doubts got even more profound. All hopes were but illusions, all promises were but cunning devices. The brutal force which governed this corner of the world would destroy all our dreams, as it had so many times before. 'I am glad,' he wrote in 1915, 'I have not so many years left me to remember that appalling feeling of inexorable fate, tangible, palpable, come after so many cruel years, a figure of dread, murmuring with iron lips the final words: Ruin – and Extinction.'[3] It was an echo of the catastrophic visions which were already terrifying him at the bedside of his dying father. 'Whatever may be the changes in the fortunes of living nations, for the dead there is no hope and no salvation.'[4] The Polish nation was 'deprived of all hope and even of its last illusions, and unable, in the trouble of minds and the unrest of consciences, to take refuge in stoical acceptance.'[5] Here again we hear the echo of the desperate sermons of his father, dead fifty years earlier. And what did predominate in his soul troubled by confused thoughts and emotions? Was it not a sense of guilt which no reasoning could abate? After the death of his cousin he wrote to the widow: 'the thought that a day would come when I would be able to confess to him my whole life and to be understood – this thought was for me the greatest consolation.'[6]

So would it be true that Conrad indeed never departed 'in mind and heart' from his native country?

The fact that he kept returning to it, with a heavy heart, is sufficiently borne out by his own words quoted above. He did not leave his homeland in his thoughts either, although 'he could not think of Poland often

[1] 'A fragment of Conrad's letter, communicated to me by Mr Hubert Spiridion Kliszczewski, descendant of a family settled in England since 1831. My acquaintance with Mr K., who preserves Polish traditions in the fourth generation, I owe to Mr Chwalewik, an eminent Conrad scholar, who persuaded me to write this essay.' (J. Perłowski's note) The quoted letter is otherwise unknown.

[2] *Tales of Hearsay*, p. 51.   [3] 'Poland Revisited', *Notes on Life and Letters*, p. 171.

[4] Letter to Spiridion Kliszczewski, 13 October 1885; Jean-Aubry, *Joseph Conrad: Life and Letters*, vol. 1, p. 81.

[5] *Notes on Life and Letters*, p. 171.

[6] To Mrs Aniela Zagórska, 6 February 1898; *Conrad's Polish Background*, p. 224. The original sentence is in French.

because it felt bad, bitter, painful'.[1] But this is not where the clue to Conrad's problem may be found. There is something in the human soul which rises above thoughts and feelings and which constitutes its greatest force. The theologians regard it as a virtue: it is faith. Conrad, through no fault of his own, lost his faith in Poland when he was a child, at the age when every one of us acquires it, through no merit of ours. This has to be remembered when passing judgement on him. His problem is but a small part of a great problem, which, until now, no one has been able to solve. Faith is a state of grace. But we all feel that the lack of faith may become a grave sin.

Stanisław Zaleski to Konrad Korzeniowski

Biblioteka Narodowa, Warsaw, MS 2889

[printed address]
Śnieżna, Kiev Province
District of Skwira
25 February 1894

My dear Konrad,

I am writing to you first, in deep sorrow, bereaved of your much regretted Uncle Tadeusz, whose death is a great loss, an enormous loss, to all of us. And to you primarily, dear Konrad, I wish to offer my condolences because you were closest to his heart and he was the only one you had in the world. Believe me that on having learned this painful news all my thoughts went towards you, augmenting my sadness and grief.

I am not going to describe the details of our beloved uncle's death, as Tadeusz Florkowski claims to have done so already,[2] but if you should wish to know more please write and I shall send you all the information.

Now I must comply with Uncle Tadeusz's wish to advise you of the following: several years ago your Uncle lent 15,000 roubles to my mother and asked me to write the promissory note to your name and left it in my safe keeping.

Eight per cent interest was always paid in advance. To the above-mentioned note he has attached a letter in which he asked me to inform you about it in the event of his death and to pay the stated sum of 15,000 roubles at the specified date. The appointed time for the payment is 15 February 1895, old style. Would you therefore instruct me,

---

[1] See Conrad's interview with Marian Dąbrowski in the present volume, p. 201.
[2] Tadeusz Florkowski wrote to Conrad on 9/21 February 1894.

dear Konrad, by what means you wish me to pay you 15,000 roubles on 15 February 1895.

As Uncle Tadeusz used to collect 8% interest from those 15,000 roubles, payable in advance, and amounting to 1,200 roubles, this sum is due to you for the year from 15 February 1894 to 15 February 1895. I wish to send you this money right away but again I have to ask you to inform me where is it to be dispatched.

If Tadeusz Florkowski is correct and you intend to come to Odessa this year perhaps you would consider paying us a visit; it would afford us the greatest pleasure, we would talk about our much regretted uncle, also about the payment of your legacy which on 15 February 1895, old style, will be at your disposal, while 1,200 roubles interest could be paid at Śnieżna.

So if it is at all possible, dear Konrad, do not deny us this visit and rest assured that it would give us the greatest pleasure; and from the business point of view a meeting would be most beneficial.

In any case please answer this letter so that I know what to do.

Please accept, dear Konrad, my most cordial avowal of friendship. I remain, as always, at your service.

Stanisław Zaleski

Stanisław Zaleski to Konrad Korzeniowski
Biblioteka Narodowa, Warsaw, MS 2889

[printed address]
Śnieżna, Kiev Province
District of Skwira
10/23 April 1894[1]

Dear Konrad,

On my return yesterday from Warsaw, where I stayed a considerable time with my mother, I found your letter and thus hastily dispatch your interest amounting to 1,200 roubles, for the period from 15 February 1894 to 15 February 1895, to the given address, asking you to acknowledge its receipt with a word. As to the capital, after making enquiries at next February's Agricultural Fair in Kiev as to the cheapest means of sending money to London, I shall dispatch 15,000 roubles to the given address, to the name of Mr A. Krieger.[2]

Wherever you are fated to go, west or south, keep your promise and write to me from time to time with your news. It will give me the

---

[1] Zaleski made an error in dating his letter: it should be either 11/23 or 10/22 April.
[2] Conrad's friend and business partner in London, Adolf Krieger.

greatest pleasure and in my reply I am always sure to find something to tell you from here that might interest you.

Presuming that the fate of Kazimierówka, nowadays a cheerless place for us, may be of concern to you, I wish to communicate that Mrs [Zuzanna] Bobrowska[1] went there with her son Tadeusz and, following a deliberation and brief consultations with the executors, Syroczyński and Florkowski,[2] it has been decided that until Michał comes of age the *status quo* will be maintained, that is no one will live at Kazimierówka and the leaseholder will continue to administer the estate.

Mrs Bobrowska and Michał will leave for a six-month stay at Nizhny Novogorod on the Volga, where she will live with her son Stanisław who is to return from St Petersburg in half a year and settle there for five years.[3] Then, probably, when Michał is of age and Stanisław entitled to go home, they will all return to Kazimierówka to divide the property. Until then it remains undivided under the administration of the executors Syroczyński and Florkowski, who are now also Michał's guardians.

My mother is sorely grieved by the death of our beloved uncle and her health not being too good, she asked me to send you her best regards and assurances of her most affectionate feelings.

May God allow us to meet again and meanwhile I trust you to keep your promise that I should hear from you now and again. I embrace you warmly with your image forever present in my heart and memory.

Your devoted

St. Zaleski

'Joseph Conrad in Cardiff', by Witold Chwalewik

'Józef Conrad w Kardyfie', *Ruch literacki*, 1932, no. 8

Conrad did not travel much in England and he stopped in Cardiff only a couple of times. Those casual visits nevertheless contribute to a succession of episodes which form a comprehensive whole. They also throw some rather unexpected light on Conrad's attitude towards Poland. This fact will help to provide additional breadth to the seemingly narrow, 'regional' ground covered by this essay. Thanks to Conrad's posthumous biography by G. Jean-Aubry we know the exact date of Conrad's first visit to Cardiff. It occurred in 1885, one year prior

[1] Widow of Tadeusz Bobrowski's brother Kazimierz.

[2] Tadeusz Florkowski and Stanisław Syroczyński, both Bobrowski's former pupils.

[3] Stanisław Bobrowski had been arrested on 15 January 1892 for unauthorized teaching of artisans, and sentenced to eighteen months in prison (in St Petersburg) and five years of exile.

to Conrad's receiving British nationality. He was twenty-eight years old. Seven years earlier he got his first job on a British ship and ten years later he was to become known as the author of *Almayer's Folly*. In the spring of 1885, he sailed aboard the *Tilkhurst* from Hull to Penarth, that is to Cardiff. After he boarded the ship, the *Tilkhurst* set out on her voyage to the Indian Ocean and to Singapore.

During his few days' stay Conrad met the Spiridions, whose family name was Kliszczewski. He got their address from a Polish sailor, met accidentally, one Andrzej Komorowski, originally a peasant from the Congress Kingdom of Poland, who, in order to escape military service, had left home in 1880 or 1881. Young Komorowski at first wandered across Germany, then found his way on to a boat bound for Cardiff where he landed in the streets without money or knowledge of the language. He was rescued from misery by a fellow-countryman, an inhabitant of Cardiff, Mr Spiridion Kliszczewski, who had left Poland after 1831 and after long peregrinations settled finally in the Welsh capital as owner of a watchmaker's shop. When the police brought him a boy who on account of his foreign looks and aimless wanderings had aroused their suspicions (no other charges were made), Mr Kliszczewski gave the youth some clothes and a pound note, and found him a job on a ship. Komorowski served on several American boats but did not make sailing his profession: in time he settled down in Chicago and became a businessman. Conrad remembered Komorowski as the only countryman he met among sailors in the course of many years! When Komorowski had come into contact with Conrad in 1885 and learned of his intended trip to Cardiff, he asked him to visit the Kliszczewskis and to repay a debt incurred some years ago.

The *émigré* Kliszczewski at that time was a sick man well advanced in age. His son, Spiridion Kliszczewski, ran the family business; later, like Conrad, he used his Christian name as his surname. Conrad went to Kliszczewski's home (at 29 Duke Street; the house was later demolished) on a Sunday morning. The host's grandson, young Hubert Kliszczewski, was also there at the time: he had come to visit his sick grandfather, and at his bedside the young boy met the unknown visitor, a foreigner with a dark complexion. On learning that the stranger was Captain Conrad, a Pole who had recently returned from some distant islands in the Indian Ocean, the boy was amazed that anyone with such bad English pronunciation could command a British ship. He was also struck by the captain's distinguished manners – by the politeness shown even towards a youngster who had hitherto assumed that crudeness of manner was more typical of the profession. Another thing which the boy found intriguing was the guest's wearing a soft felt hat instead of the shining top hats worn in those days by the officers of the merchant navy. Strangely enough, when on leaving the house the visitor put on his soft hat, he looked not unlike an Anglican priest. The conversation between the stranger and the grandfather was in Polish, so the boy did not understand it. The captain and the boy left the house together, the first to go home, the second to get medicine for the patient. The two of them got into a hansom cab, a vehicle unknown nowadays in towns and confined to museums, and for a while drove together. Before the boy got out Conrad had questioned him about his school; the youngster never got over his amazement that a foreigner with such a strong accent could be an English officer.

His impression changed when several years later Conrad paid another visit to the Spiridions in Cardiff. On that occasion he stayed for a few days at their home. Hubert thought that Conrad's English had improved considerably and that his appearance was more in keeping with that of a properly dressed English gentleman: he wore a tweed suit and a bowler hat. His courteous manner remained unchanged. To a child brought up in the English way it seemed strange to see the guest kiss his mother's hand. It was obvious that close friendship had sprung up between Hubert's father and the guest. They were approximately of the same age. As Józef Spiridion Kliszczewski's Polish was not fluent they conversed in English, mainly about Poland and international politics.

This friendship was reflected in correspondence. Conrad's letters from distant ports were a source of joy to the recipient who liked to read them aloud to his sons.

The third and longest visit of the traveller–author to the Spiridions in Cardiff took place many years later, in December 1896. Conrad had by then severed his links with the sea, and he had already two novels to his credit: *Almayer's Folly* and *An Outcast of the Islands*. Józef Spiridion Kliszczewski had even helped Conrad to get the second novel published. Fisher Unwin, the publisher, had asked the author to put down a deposit of £60 as a guarantee.[1] As Conrad was short of £10 to make up the required sum, Kliszczewski lent him the money, which Conrad paid back a few months later.

When he came to Cardiff before Christmas 1896 Conrad was working on a new book, a sea novel which, in fact, helped him to 'find himself' as an author. Hitherto he had been unable to direct his imagination away from the land and on to the open sea. 'The Rescuer',

---

[1] Not confirmed by the extant correspondence between Conrad, Unwin, Garnett, and Marguerite Poradowska. Conrad needed money and apparently used the alleged 'guarantee' as an excuse.

later renamed *The Rescue*, would have been the exception, but the author struggled over that book in vain and did not finish it till twenty years later. In his first novels his imagination hovered over Borneo. In 'The Sisters', an unfinished work, his memories took him back to the Ukrainian steppes. Suddenly he was carried away on the *'Narcissus'* over the Indian Ocean, aboard 'the lonely ship on the blue sea'. It was a vision incomparably more substantial than the vague shapes of his earlier books: he was better at finding the right word and lyrical inspiration took the place of rhetorical pathos.

He brought his manuscript to Cardiff. Jean-Aubry errs in maintaining (*Joseph Conrad: Life and Letters*, I, p. 79) that the only occasion at that time when Conrad interrupted his work was during his Christmas visit to Cardiff. On the contrary, the host prepared a special room where the author could concentrate on his work. And concentration was essential to Conrad when his imagination was busy creating the last and certainly the most beautiful chapters of the novel. He worked and lived at 78 Cathedral Road. Leaning out of the window he could see the long street with trees and rows of identical pseudo-Gothic houses. With that stereotyped architecture before his eyes, his mind was engaged on creative day-dreaming.

It absorbed him completely. Talking to his host's sons he would summarize the plot of the novel and relate separate episodes. Other subjects were of little interest to him. He was not any more the pleasant *causeur* he used to be. He became rather quarrelsome and in conversation tried to impose his own, firmly established views upon others. It was clear that the bad illness of several years before had affected his health. His dignified manner remained unchanged but (at least so it seemed to Klemens, Hubert's brother) he had lost his distinguished appearance. He walked little; his head was usually nestling between his slightly raised shoulders; his expression was severe. His impulsive voice and gestures made him look French rather than British; the effect was enhanced by his beard.

It was Christmas time. Everybody gathered at table on Christmas Eve and the conversation turned to Polish matters. The host addressed the guest (in English, for he was not fluent in Polish), expressing his dearest wish, to see Conrad use his talent to glorify Poland's name and to depict in his novels the unhappiness of his native land. Conrad seemed quite annoyed. Throwing up his arms he exploded, at first in French: 'Ah, mon ami, que voulez-vous? I would lose my public...' He could not make a living by his writing if he were to use it as a tool of propaganda. It would be impossible for him to write about Poland.

This strange outburst is well remembered by the host's sons, Hubert and Klemens, who were present on that occasion. Possibly this incident, in spite of its violence, did not register permanently in Conrad's memory. But Józef Kliszczewski remembered it till the end of his life. From that time he bore a grudge against Conrad. He came to the conclusion that there was a strange contrariness in Conrad's character, that he was 'perverse'[1] – the more one asked him to write about Poland, the less he was inclined to do so. Kliszczewski, the son of an *émigré*, grew up in a foreign country without losing his strong attachment to Poland. He was one of those patriots who cannot bear a single word of criticism about their home country. He neither liked nor was interested in literature. But, it seemed only natural to him that Conrad, as a writer of fiction, ought to serve his country with his pen, writing in the style of informative propaganda.

After Christmas Conrad stayed on a few more days in Cardiff. In the visitors' book of the town's Public Library the signature 'Jph Conrad (Korzeniowski)' can be found under the date 30 December 1896. Possibly Conrad left on this or the following day.

It is certain, however, that Conrad did not see in Cardiff the New Year's Day edition of the local paper *Western Mail*. When the news of the writer's visit to Wales reached the newspaper, Arthur Mee (now dead and not to be confused with someone of the same name who was at one time a well-known political commentator) interviewed Conrad. As a result there appeared on 1 January 1897 a short article, worth noting because it is the first printed mention of Conrad's Polish connections. Here is the full text of the article:

A NEW NOVELLIST [sic] ON DICKENS
MR JOSEPH CONRAD'S OPINION ON DICKENS

A rising novelist has been staying at Cardiff for the last few days in the person of Mr. Joseph Conrad. Mr. Conrad was the guest of Mr Spiridon [sic], at whose residence in Cathedral-road [sic] he was seen by one of our representatives. Mr. Conrad is the author of "Aylmer's [sic] Folly" and other works, and his novels have appeared both in serial and book form. He is tall, dark, and of decidedly Celtic appearance; and questioned as to the affinity between the Celts and the Poles – Mr. Conrad is himself a child of that downtrodden and unhappy nation – he replied that they have much in common, the temperament of both being dreamy, poetic, and romantic.

Mr. Conrad himself has undergone many vicissitudes and strange experiences, which he doubtless finds of value in his present walk of life. His father took part in some political agitation, and (like many more of his countrymen) was consigned to Siberia, together with his family, the latter including little Joseph, a child of three or four years old. Mr. Conrad's earliest recollections, therefore, are of the most dreaded of all the wide dominions of the Czar, and it is not

---

[1] English word in the original.

surprising that he should entertain a hearty admiration for our own land of liberty. In this view, by the way, his host smilingly concurs.

"My father ought to have known," is his observation, "for he tried nine countries!"

Our representative gathered that Mr. Conrad, like many another of his countrymen, had dropped his surname, the latter being not altogether pronounceable by English lips.

After a few years the Conrad's were released from Siberia, and young Joseph then got into the English Navy, and subsequently into the mercantile service, varying his career with a lengthy sojourn in the interior of Africa. He was yet a seaman when the passion for writing took possession of him, and he found himself the wielder of a facile and fluent pen. The encouragement of friends determined him on his new career, and, though he is now by no means a young writer, he speaks of it with an enthusiasm that is contagious.

In the course of conversation, Mr. Conrad took occasion to refer to an expression in "Westminster's" notes of Monday, where Dickens is spoken of as looked down upon by certain fashionable critics of the day. He does not think this view of Dickens is at all widespread.

"Dickens," he said, "still keeps up his popularity. I fancy he has left his mark, not because he is a caricaturist (as many people say), but because of his extreme simplicity, and his vividness of expression. His is not high art, but it conveys an exceedingly fine sense of humanity. I fancy that Dickens will never cease to be one of the masters: he is inimitable, and much more accessible to the general mind than Thackeray. He did not give a new form to English, but he used it as it had never been used before, and his very defects help to make up his greatness."

As our representative left Mr. Conrad took occasion to express his high opinion of the "Western Mail" as a bright and original paper, and this (he added) was the general estimate in the circles in which he moved.

It is obvious that the biographical data at the beginning of the above article lack precision. The facts were not supplied by Conrad himself, for during the interview he never referred to his Polish background. The journalist when leaving the house gleaned additional information from the host. Conrad was most indignant at the amplified version of the interview and his relations with the Kliszczewski family were almost broken off.[1] The motive was the same as before. In Conrad's view the spreading of information about his background would be highly detrimental to the popularity of his books and might even undermine his very means of subsistence. He was an incorrigible pessimist, but he misjudged the psychology of the contemporary English reading public.

It soon became widely known that the author of *Nigger of the 'Narcissus'*, *Tomorrow*, *Heart of Darkness*, *Lord Jim* and many excellent books highly praised by the critics was not English but Polish. Obviously the informa-

---

[1] Conrad's letter to Joseph Spiridion Kliszczewski of 5 April 1897 – with the request of a loan of £20 – does not confirm this version. See F.R. Karl and L. Davies (ed.), *The Collected Letters of Joseph Conrad*, vol. 1 (Cambridge, 1983), pp. 349–51.

tion published by a provincial Welsh newspaperman did not play a major part in the enlightenment of the general public. It was soon accomplished by other persons. But although the 'worst' became known, Conrad's success did not suffer by it. He was not damaged in public opinion. It would be interesting to know what he thought at that time of the exaggerated caution he had displayed in Cardiff. His relations with József Kliszczewski, in spite of an occasional exchange of letters, were never again as close as before. Highly reserved about matters relating to national conscience, Conrad may have seen things from a more distant perspective. He weighed those problems in his mind and worried about them all his life trying, more than once, to prove that he did not abandon his national duties. However, he never succeeded in convincing himself about it. The Cardiff memory of conflicts might have appeared to him as an irony of fate since his foreign origin helped him to gain a good reputation among the critics and to increase his popularity with the public.

'The Emigration of Talent', by Wincenty Lutosławski[1]

'Emigracja zdolności', *Kraj*, 1899, no. 12

Whenever anyone endowed with exceptional ability chooses to make his home in a foreign country, we universally deplore his loss, his pursuit of material gain or his disregard of national duties. That is why Warsaw overflows with gifted men who perform ordinary office jobs on the railway, who copy documents or deal with simple account-sheets, instead of taking part in the progress of humanity and working for their country in a wider field.

This being so, it might be worth considering whether in fact our country suffers such a great loss through the emigration of its most talented citizens, incapable of finding suitable work at home and seeking a wider arena for their activities. Recently a position of distinction in English literature was gained by a compatriot of ours, Mr Konrad Korzeniowski, known under the pen-name of Joseph Conrad, an *émigré* from 1863.[2] His novels are marked by a Polish nobleman's panache, intensified by many years of sailing round the islands of the Pacific. During my visit to his country place near London,[3] I put a simple question to him: 'Why don't you write in Polish?'

---

[1] Wincenty Lutosławski (1863–1954), philosopher, an international authority on Plato. For many years he lectured abroad.

[2] That would have made Conrad much older, and his decision to remain abroad based on a conscious choice of an adult.

[3] The visit took place in summer 1897. Lutosławski received Conrad's address from Henry James. See Karl and Davies, *Letters*, vol. II, pp. 357–60.

'I value our beautiful Polish literature too much to bring into it my clumsy efforts, but for the English my gifts are sufficient and secure me my daily bread.'

This reply may sound paradoxical but none the less it conveys a deep truth little understood at home. Our works of literature, written predominantly by the *szlachta*, have seldom been stimulated by material needs. We are true artists and we sing for ourselves. Consequently, in art we occupy one of the first places in the world, although we seldom have the courage to admit to ourselves that the author of the 'Improvisation'[1] was, in fact, a greater poet than Goethe or Victor Hugo.

But literary activity has a right to manifest itself elsewhere, not only in true works of art. Its aim is to popularize ideas and feelings, to stir the masses. In that respect we are outdistanced by such a small nation as the Danes, who publish some of their works in scores of thousands; we may be even behind Finland where it is quite usual to publish a novel in several thousand copies.

Consequently, those who remain at home out of duty and have to write for their living must lower the level of their work and instead of cultivating their talents allow them to wither away. The same authors should follow Konrad Korzeniowski's example and master the English language, which is universally known, and write for their living in English instead of Polish. Thus, they would have enough time left to communicate their best thoughts to their compatriots, in their mother tongue and couched in the best possible form.

The same situation as in literature obtains in other fields. Whenever there is a truly gifted man, he cannot find an outlet for his talents and his mind is doomed to shrink gradually until it withers away completely. Our greatest poets had to leave their native land before they developed their talents. Our singers and musicians sing and play for the Americans because we cannot afford to pay for their music and songs. In industry and trade the situation is the same: existing conditions are not conducive to the development of outstanding abilities and a genius who would amass millions in America is hardly able here to pay his ancestors' debts and leave his children reasonably provided for.

Somebody may say that I advocate stuffing one's pocket. But money is indispensable for realizing the most idealistic aims and it is more sensible to get it from wealthy neighbours than to tear it away from each other at home. Let us consider, for example, a scientist who through false patriotism insists on educating our youth in Warsaw, Cracow, or Lwów. In return for hundreds of humiliations, he would eke out a bare living just sufficient to protect his family from hunger – but

---

[1] A fragment of Mickiewicz's *Dziady*, part III.

insufficient to afford scientific expeditions or to buy books necessary for academic research, etc. As it is, any scientist wishing to contribute to international scientific work must publish his papers in a foreign language.

Let us assume now that this scientist abandons his narrow prejudice and accepts a chair in one of the big American universities where his lectures and publications bring him ten thousand roubles a year. He can then acquire the necessary means to widen the range of his research and each year he will be in a position to invite several able students from home, who will successfully accomplish their work under his guidance and return to their country influenced by American energy and productivity – those characteristics we so badly lack.

And are books written by Poles abroad lost to their countrymen? Far from it: the books are Polish even if published in a foreign language because they are the fruit of the Polish spirit, different from the spirit of other nations. The more books published, the greater will be the respect bestowed on Poles abroad and the quicker will the bad reputation fade away that has been created by our political *émigrés* – by men forced to leave their country under the pressure of events and therefore unprepared to compete with foreigners.

There can be no worse error than to equate our political *émigrés* with those seeking material advancement: it leads to false analogies. The political *émigrés* have lost their national character because they were weak and few in number. The economic emigrants have no need to lose their national identity because they are the most courageous individuals and they form a large group. Our emigrants in America are far from having lost their identity; I have even met Jews there who as soon as they arrived in America became Polonized. As to the more extensive rural emigration to America, the phenomenon is too recent to foretell its fate. But one thing may be said for certain: if our intelligentsia, consciously striving to make use of its own potential in the New World, helps and protects the peasants, there will be a far greater probability of sustaining national feeling and even of exercising a beneficial effect upon those left behind by lending them material and moral support. Irish emigration is a good illustration of the point. The Irish were a poor nation as long as they persistently refused to leave their land. As soon as they grew wings and began to settle in America, their home country gained considerably in strength.

We have abhorred emigration since the olden days when the concept of nationality was closely linked with the concept of country and each nationality was practically speaking confined to one country. Today almost all nationalities compete with each other for command of the globe and wherever we go we meet Englishmen, Italians and Germans. Are we to leave all the wealth and benefits available to those who, undaunted by distance, travel to the farthest confines of this small planet in search of what they need? Our peasants have already solved this question. Those who have settled in the United States do not wish to return and instead send home vast sums of money; occasionally, bringing all their savings, they return to die on their native soil. Such cases are still few and far between, as large-scale emigration is only a phenomenon of the recent past. Nevertheless, they exist. And in countries where large-scale emigration has been going on for a long time, such as the Swiss canton Graubünden, it happens much more frequently. There a traveller beholds charming small houses inhabited by people who, having gained financial independence elsewhere, have returned home with money accumulated abroad.

If our most gifted citizens go overseas, they will bring new national strength to their compatriots there and we shall not lose by it because what we need at home is not so much the most gifted, but the most patient and most enduring. At home the most gifted are doomed to a miserable existence: they want to move forward too fast along a road where it is only possible to crawl on all fours and where more often than not great ability is wasted. It is out of place, therefore, to accuse those unable to stand the stifling atmosphere of disloyalty to the country; those who are brave enough to set out into the world in order to participate in the international struggle for material and moral wealth, a large portion of which will eventually be brought back home. And as to the problem of loss of national identity it might be remembered that those who lose their sense of nationality are useless to us anyway, even if outwardly they belong to our nation. The existence and strength of a nation depend not so much on the number of bodies but on the worth of souls. One great soul may do more, even if confined to lifelong exile, than a million faint-hearted cowards clinging to ancestral cottages and scared of the ocean. We must not, therefore, accuse those who seek an outlet for their energy by disregarding national frontiers. If they are strong and of noble character they will be constant and faithful in their love; they will not forget the mother who fed them and will lay at her feet their fame, and the rich fruits of their labours in far-away lands.

'The Emigration of Talent', by Eliza Orzeszkowa[1]

'Emigracja zdolności', *Kraj*, 1899, no. 16 (23 April)

When two people are engaged in a highly interesting discussion, conducted in a most interesting manner, a third person, particularly if much concerned with the subject, feels overcome by a desire to beg pardon and break in on the conversation. Thus I wish to ask leave to join in the conversation between Messrs Lutosławski and Żuk-Skarszewski[2] on the emigration of our talent to various countries of the world. Although the conversation appears to have reached its end, the exchange of the last sentences has somehow left in mid-air the sound of unfinished or hesitant words, some of them twisted, as it were, into question marks, and I am asking, therefore, to be allowed to add a number of sentences.

First and foremost I wish to convey to Professor Lutosławski my best regards, awakening in his memory a certain day in July, very agreeable for me, when in the depths of Białowieża Forest we sat together on a huge moss-grown log as if it were a plush-covered settee and talked about our intelligent youth leaving the homeland. No black print-marks flickered in front of our eyes as we looked at primeval oaks and spruce that shook their crowns, reaching to the sky with a soft and continuous sough. It seemed to me then that those giants of the huge forest, close to the sky, addressed the multitude of trees which had not yet risen much above the ground with words like these: 'Grow where nature has sown you, throw fresh and salutary shadows around you, let your falling leaves fertilize the common soil, let your spreading boughs fill the empty air and give shelter from icy blasts and sweltering heat. For if you failed in this, if you vanished, what would happen? What would happen? The forest would wither and run to waste!' This is what I heard in the soughing of the Białowieża oaks and spruce-trees when I was sitting on a felled giant with the esteemed professor, arguing with him on the very same subject as later prompted Mr. Żuk-Skarszewski to oppose him in *Kraj*. Notwithstanding the pleasure and honour afforded me by the visit of the illustrious guest, I kept on arguing ...

[1] Eliza Orzeszkowa (1841–1910), novelist and publicist, eminent liberal thinker and moral authority, Polish patriot greatly concerned with the emancipation of Jews and friend of several Bielo-Russian and Ukrainian writers. Spurning the idea of emigration, she spent most of her life in provincial Grodno.

[2] Tadeusz Żuk-Skarszewski (1858–1933), well-known journalist and minor novelist. He opposed Lutosławski, writing in conclusion: 'I prefer a village schoolteacher in Przyszowa or Poniemoń [little villages in Poland] not only to a brilliant commentator of Plato, but to Plato himself – in Boston.'

And so now again I wish to join in the argument, but first of all I hasten to say that I am doing it with the highest respect for the enormous knowledge, academic merit, unquestionable and proven integrity and personal courage of my adversary. But – *errare humanum est*. Even the most excellent minds and purest hearts may err. And it befalls sometimes that we have to oppose the nicest people, for as Mr Żuk-Skarszewski rightly says: 'Plato's famous commentator is a friend to us, but an even greater friend is a sense of duty.'

We are all well aware of the basic reason for the emigration of our talent: the difficulty of finding professional, remunerative work in many fields of activity. Who knows, however, if this state of affairs would have such widespread and lasting consequences if it were not for the specific atmosphere characteristic of our time? Following the confusion and impoverishment which the historic disaster brought upon our society, the call for organic work rose and gained in popularity. The watchword was 'Work and get rich!' The advice was sound; the nation had to build up its physical strength right from its very foundations. At the same time academic and philosophic trends propagated the motto: 'Knowledge is power!' Again it was right. Knowledge acts as a powerful lever in a society striving for higher levels of life. The slogans were sound but the trouble is that even pure, white snow mixed with soil becomes grey. Banners of stout proportion exhibited appropriate devices originated in the most noble minds: 'Work and get wealthy', 'Knowledge is power'; but on the lower levels, on small paper flags of the masses, those catch phrases became somewhat different: 'Work to get wealthy', 'Knowledge is the only power.' Ostensibly the changes are trifling: one little word added here or there, but the meaning is distorted.

As a matter of fact neither work nor knowledge can be regarded as ends in themselves. Someone has wittily remarked that work is worth as much as a knife and fork for cutting up nourishing and wholesome food. There is no particular reason for admiring the work of a man who sweats away at an unnecessary job of carrying stones from one spot to another; and only a minority of men extol the work involved in the production of Krupp cannon or of some other kind of more recent and improved weapon – for I do not claim to be acquainted with the latest developments in this field. As to knowledge, it is an immensely precious lantern when it illuminates the sanctuary of good and pure hearts, but try to set its glow as bright as you may amidst egoism and evil passions and you will see what magnificent and holy sights it uncovers! Work is worth as much as the aim it wishes to attain: knowledge brings humanity much good in so far as it acts in conjunction with moral values to which it should always remain subordinate. Obviously, one of the purposes of work nowadays must be earning money, but it should never be its sole or main purpose, and this important fact has to be borne in mind. No one denies that knowledge is power in itself, but beside it there exist in mankind still more powerful factors, without whose support knowledge cannot achieve any good – this too is undeniable. Having distorted and degraded the slogans on organic work and knowledge, few people ever remembered this and the majority bowed down to two idols: financial gain and knowledge, with the latter being subjected to the former. Knowledge for the sake of gain; through knowledge to wealth! On the other hand, growing needs and more refined tastes have increased the very notion of gain, causing it to be expressed in ever larger figures; and coupled with our characteristic lack of enterprise and a liking for easy success common to all men, it gave rise to a new method of educating children for the sole purpose of earning good money, earning it fast and then having a good time. 'Learn, sonny, learn; you'll be King!' goes a peasant saying. Scores of fathers and mothers whose level of culture equals that of the peasants, told their sons: 'Learn, sonny, learn; you'll be an engineer!' And why precisely an engineer? Again, the answer may be found in a peasant parable: 'What would you do, sonny, if they made you King?' 'Well, Mum, I'd eat fat by the spoonful.' Where would he eat? With what spoon? Would it be to the advantage or disadvantage of someone else? Would it be to the detriment of something more important than food? Little is heard of the matter at home, and at school, obviously, the subject is never mentioned ...

That a generation brought up on such morality has not been downright corrupt and that it has produced a certain number of noble and pure hearts has to be attributed to an interplay of causes, to inherited instincts and to various qualities latent in the great soul of the nation. A number of our Argonauts has dispersed over lands and waters with one, or at least one predominant, idea of 'eating fat by the spoonful' and we never hear of that delicacy being sent home to grease the wheels of our social machinery. Of course, there have been some few exceptions, but they are nowhere near offsetting the losses.

And the losses are very important. When there is work to be done with a great objective in view, even a slight loss of manpower is detrimental and when that loss is on a major scale the serious danger arises that the work will not be carried out and the object will not be attained. Where in the world could you find a physical or moral law to the effect that the more difficult and the greater the work, the more diffused must be the energy? Notwithstanding that, we even get another piece of advice: let the weakest and least gifted carry on with their work while the strongest and most talented give it up! Let them go away so that some time in the future they may bring home millions amassed elsewhere! I pray your forgiveness, excellent professor, but those millions sound to me like a stray echo of the distorted and degraded watchword 'Work to get rich!' Moreover, those fortunes are extremely doubtful. With very rare exceptions the sums have been quite modest, and seldom exceeded tens of thousands brought from distant lands and from beyond the seas by our Argonauts' ships, which by now could make up a huge fleet. And let me ask a question: even if those millions were not fiction, but reality, could they fill the gap left behind by the builders of a new and improved social order, when they desert their job? I doubt it; material wealth benefits society on condition that it is morally healthy, and that it cannot be when the most gifted and energetic individuals neither live nor work here. In such a case millions might increase, but common sense and virtue would decline and the fortune would serve no purpose except ... for the top people to squander it at Monte Carlo and for lower classes to eat 'fat by the spoonful'.

The idea of absolving talented individuals from bearing their share of the work and suffering common to all society seems to me highly unjust. Since when is it fair for him who is most richly endowed by nature to be expected to give least to others? Just because his greater gifts offer him better possibilities of escape from 'unpleasant circumstances' – he escapes, leaving his less gifted and weaker brothers to their fate. 'You manage as best you can while I, most fit to cope, will fly off to where things are better, and in due course will send you some money and fame, having had my share of them first, naturally.' His brethren scowl with regret, but cannot fly off. If they could, they would also fly away: since the most gifted ones do it, obviously it is worth following their example. Moreover, the others will be working for something immensely attractive because immensely great: namely for the good of the whole humanity! How absolutely different it is from being stuck in one parish all one's life, devoting one's energies to humble endeavours!

Services rendered to humanity deserve the greatest respect and admiration whenever encountered. But such services are very rare, particularly among the exiles who in flesh and blood belong to a section of the human race which they have deserted. Rare, because they are deficient in that particular quality of stamina, that *nervus rerum*[1] of all

[1] Lat.: 'Vital element'.

great deeds, which gives the ability to love and endure. In the majority
of cases *qui embrasse trop, n'étreint rien*[1] and he who strives to embrace
the entire globe will fail even to protect the smallest tree from being
broken by a gale. Serving humanity in general reminds me always of a
heroine in a novel by Dickens. With a sweating brow and ink-stained
hands she buried herself in correspondence supposed to alleviate the
fate of negro children in Africa and meanwhile her own hungry children fed on raw turnip and bruised their noses falling down the
stairs.[2] The wide-ranging aspirations of our great men on how to
serve humanity sooner or later boil down to the strikingly concise *ego
sum*,[3] even if at first the goodwill was truly genuine. At best they may
have constructed somewhere far away a beautiful bridge; they may
have raised the standard of forestry, written a good book, discovered a
new element in the composition of the air; but will all this pay off their
entire debt to the world for the dowry from Nature, greater than others
have received? Will this atone for their guilt at not having contributed a
single brick to the bridge which trembles under the feet of those who
are near and dear to them, of their not having contributed to the
expansion of the mind of someone close, of not having introduced a
healing and invigorating atmosphere to the family to which they are
indebted for not having been brought up as savages and fools? I doubt
it.

For it should not be assumed that the only *raison d'être* on this earth
for talented individuals is the construction of bridges, improvement of
forest cultivation, writing of books, invention of new machines, and the
like. All these are necessary, even highly necessary, but represent only a
part of the responsibility, usefulness and social value of gifted men.
There remains a great deal more to be done in the spiritual sphere
where things cannot be measured, weighed or counted; in the sphere
which nonetheless exists, with a considerable bearing upon measure,
weights and numbers. It may be expressed as follows: a good man –
improves, a wise man – educates, a brave man – comforts, an inspired
man – elevates others. It is neither possible to list nor to calculate the
various ways in which one individual may influence another, particularly the influence exerted by talented individuals upon those less
privileged. The effects may be visible or invisible, intentional or unintentional. Those visible and intentional lie on the surface. All you have
to do is to pick up the Catechism and read about the seven acts of
charity for the body and the seven acts of charity for the soul, in order
to learn what – apart from building bridges, raising the standards of

[1] Fr. equivalent of 'to bite off more than one can chew'.
[2] Mrs Jellaby in *Bleak House* (1853).   [3] Lat.: 'I am.'

forest cultivation, treating the sick, bringing legal suits, in short, apart from all professional work – what the talented and the 'most talented' may do for their society. But the matter has a still deeper and a more subtle aspect: the unintentional emanations diffused by strong and good spirits; that moral atmosphere which hovers over the country, begotten and brought about by the virtues and talents of its citizens; those instinctive impulses transmitted between individuals, describing ever-growing circles and ending up by encompassing the entire community. Physiologists maintain that certain nervous states are infectious; the same may be said of certain spiritual states – and, in fact, both may amount to the same thing. No one knows how much good or bad he or she has caused unintentionally through some unconscious gesture, look, movement, exclamation, smile, handshake, expression of the face, way of living. No one can determine what exactly would be missing if he or she were not present in a particular place. No one will ever know to what extent his moral stance is indebted to the atoms inhaled unawares from the spiritual atmosphere which surrounds him and which is the product of men both known and unknown to him. An act, an idea that appear to be my own are never that. I am but a retort where particles thrown in by the common will, the common mind, no one knows by whom, how and when, are clarified and find their shape. It may be that a man, who did not do anything particular and lived an ordinary life, had a beneficial effect on the general atmosphere by the very fact of having been where he was. Hence our Argonauts who sail away take with them all those intentional and unintentional benefits that could have accrued had they stayed. But, as it is, their own greater talents and energy will not bring about any charitable acts, will not contribute towards the creation of such an atmosphere which would promote the development of lesser talents and energies. Instead, at some future date they might bring back millions or write a good book in some far-away place.

Speaking of books, I must say that this gentleman, who writes popular and very lucrative novels in English,[1] has almost caused me a nervous breakdown. My gorge rises when I read about him. Why, are creative artists to join the exodus? Until now we have heard only of engineers, attorneys and opera singers. It begins to look as if writers are to be given absolution. I do not know much about books on chemistry or even philosophy, and occasionally I can even perceive reasons justifying their publication in foreign languages; but when it comes to fiction writing, which is part of literary creation, and since I belong to

---

[1] This was Orzeszkowa's interpretation of Lutosławski's article, misleading also on that point.

this particular guild and am familiar with its duties, *forts comme la mort*[1] – I object most emphatically. Creative talent forms the very crown of the tree, the pinnacle of the tower, the life-blood of the nation. And to take away that flower, to remove that pinnacle, to drain away that life-blood from the nation in order to pass it on to the Anglo-Saxons (who anyway lie on a bed of roses) just because they pay better... It is even hard to think about it without shame. And to make matters worse, that gentleman bears the same name and may even be a very close descendant of Józef Korzeniowski, whose books brought tears to my eyes when I was a teenager, the first tears of compassion, and imbued me with my first noble enthusiasm and good resolutions. But no Polish teenager will ever shed a single altruistic tear or make a noble resolution over Mr Konrad Korzeniowski's novels.

However, upon due consideration, I do not feel particularly saddened by that fact; believing in the superiority of the elements which make up creative power, I do not expect that ours would ever fall under the influence of a street vendor or pedlar. Anyway, we are not starved at home to such an extent as to have to feed on crumbs from the high table. In this respect, we are as great as lords...

Let me consider now the promise, dear to our hearts, that the Argonauts will eventually return. Who knows if and how that promise will come true? I think Mr Żuk-Skarszewski's doubts are well founded and the reasons that render their return rather improbable are most relevant. But apart from that, even if a certain percentage of those men did return – what would they bring? As to the millions, I have already expressed my general scepticism, and as to other gains, my imagination conjures up the following images: balding heads, lips mispronouncing their native language, hearts embittered by life's thorny path, limbs weakened by years of drudgery, in short, the entire human mechanism ravaged by time. Such relics of former gifts and talents will be no compensation to local enterprise and business for their healthy and buoyant youth spent elsewhere; moreover, I doubt whether the contribution made by those human relics to the family atmosphere will bring about an expansion of chests and improvement of minds in their brethren. The following image persistently comes to my mind: some huge rubbish dump where clumsy simpletons crawling on all fours rummage among old rags, while tall and muscular men depart far away to return later and, as tokens of love, confer upon the dump the benefits of bald heads, rheumatism, shrunken hearts, enfeebled arms, tongues saturated with alien speech, so that only a vague notion of their native language is preserved!

[1] Fr.: 'as strong as death'.

Moreover, all privileges are dangerous, particularly those granted to talented people; for as Mr Żuk-Skarszewski rightly enquires – how is one to judge? by what criteria? And in our society the danger of committing an error is increased by widespread megalomania. Here is not the place to discuss the causes of that mania, but it is general knowledge that we have always an abundance of leaders and no one willing to join the ranks, and that those forced to do so attribute their misfortune to unfair people or fate, but never to their own short-comings. We regard ourselves as extremely talented and made for the highest offices; if we fail to attain them it is only because the world is imperfect or because we are unlucky. Our country abounds in 'geniuses without portfolio', such as Mr Płoszowski.[1] And Słowacki had dedi-cated several stanzas to parlour-maids suffering from aristocratic spleen.[2] Anyone who wants can become an artisan, small farmer or tradesman, but not our son who is gifted, extremely gifted; he must be and ought to be a writer or a famous musician or at least somebody with a large income and a good position in the world. Our son, having grown a bit, thinks of himself the way his parents have thought and uses all his power, however feeble, to rush for the summit. If you point out the summits of Patagonia, saying that they are reserved only for the most capable men – he will tear down to Patagonia with a clear awareness that, being most capable, he will reach them. Meanwhile, the Patagonian summits turn out for the most part to be inaccessible, while here, on various heights, walls are crumbling and there is no one to repair them. I believe that one moral rule ought to prevail on all the levels of human capabilities, from the lowest to the highest. Honesty is one thing and dishonesty another, both for those who are clever and for those who are not; moreover, those who have brains ought to be more responsible for their acts – as being more qualified to give and to receive, and also to understand the meaning and importance of their actions. *Noblesse oblige!* This is a wise proverb when applied to all kinds of nobility.

Indeed, I quite agree with our esteemed professor that the more capable the individual, the richer his intellect and the stronger his character, the keener and more varied his mental suffering under 'the unpleasant circumstances' and in 'the stifling atmosphere'. That is how it is in this world: everything has to be paid for. Greater ability coupled with greater inner needs and a keener sensitivity to pressures from the outside mean wider horizons and a thinner skin more susceptible to

---

[1] The hero of Henryk Sienkiewicz's *Bez dogmatu* ('Without a Dogma'), 1891.

[2] Allusion to *Beniowski*, canto 1, 193–7; however, Słowacki writes there not about parlour-maids but 'simple *szlachta*'.

suffering. Well, so what? Perhaps on some other planet there exists such a paradise where it is possible to think and feel deeply – and not to suffer; but that is not possible on our earth. Consequently, should one stop thinking and feeling? 'Thinking causes headaches and particularly heartaches', says Renan who, nevertheless, did nothing else all his life but meditate, and – how right he was! 'The road to fame leads through palaces, to wealth – through the market-place and to virtue – through the desert' claims an oriental proverb. One should add that this desert is full of thorny and sometimes bloody cactuses. Nevertheless, some adventurers are prepared to brave the desert and more's the pity that there are always too few of them. Someone once said: 'The lonely eagle looking down at the earth from his mountain nest thinks from time to time about the happiness of a flock of sparrows twittering merrily.' The eagle is sad because he is lonely; but would anyone urge eagles to change into sparrows? Everybody knows that pearls lie on the bottom of the treacherous sea; does it mean that divers should not explore the sea depths in search of them? He who claimed that reaching high with one's thoughts and heart is like imbibing intoxicating nectar would be a deceiver; on the contrary: it means transforming bitterness into sweetness for the good of others. Art is not the only domain where man may create masterpieces: frequently, serving a cause he loves, he cannot fail to create masterpieces of patience in himself. In the domain of suffering there is only one way, one basic command: what is necessary must be endured. Of course, the first thing is to decide if something is necessary. But when you have weighed the problem in your conscience and the answer is in the affirmative – suffer you must! In ancient Roman history a Stoic by the name of Musonius[1] was threatened with exile to savage Illyria unless of his own free will he stopped propagating his own principles. Musonius wrapped himself up in his tattered toga and said, '*princeps obstui!*'[2] and left for Illyria. That's just it: *princeps obstui!* Let us stand by our principles. The most able and the least able; in joy and in suffering; in pleasant and in unpleasant circumstances; we must always stand by our principles, for otherwise all of us, every single one of us, on account of singular gifts or unusual suffering will obtain leave from his conscience and off he will go. Towards heathen summits which, anyway, only one in every hundred thousand of us will succeed in conquering.

All this talk about suffering sets aside the need to talk about the cowardice of those who are stuck in the 'stifling atmosphere', and about the heroism of those who leave behind there only their near and dear

---

[1] Caius Musonius Rufus, teacher of Epictetus, expelled from Rome in 65 AD.

[2] The expression does not make sense in Latin, which was not one of Mrs Orzeszkowa's strong points.

relatives and friends. It is not the first time that I have come across such a strange classification. In a review of one of my novels I once read that my Australian who had renounced the post of public prosecutor in a very distant town and settled down in his home village as a lawyer showed himself guilty of cowardice and faint-heartedness.[1] The most earnest admirer of the judicial office would probably never hit on the idea that prosecutors are heroes; nor would the most fervent enemy of Christianity go as far as to claim that 'to teach the ignorant, to cheer the sad, to advise the irresolute, etc.', and, in addition, to be doing all this in the 'stifling atmosphere' and under 'unpleasant circumstances', is equivalent to being a faint-hearted coward. But occasionally one sees things in print which make one doubt one's own eyesight. The honourable Professor Lutosławski withdrew the accusation of cowardice from those who cannot pluck up enough courage to go to the other end of the world for the sake of the chief prosecutor's office or such like. It is understandable: in a mind as enlightened and in a spirit as noble as that of the honourable professor, such a verdict could be nothing but momentary *lapsus calami*.[2] And as to the Warsaw critics, they may be pleased to hear that most probably the measure they apply to judging heroes and cowards might have lessened the number of cowards and increased the number of heroes ...

I do not know if it is true but apparently the sword that threatened Damocles' head was hanging by a thin string consisting of just a few threads. Sometimes the fate of nations hangs on such threads and one of them has seemed to me for a long time to be the emigration of talent. I have always experienced the greatest surprise that until now nobody has paid any attention to this fact and no one thought of setting out some principles or theory on the subject.

Economic causes are not sufficient reason because economic causes are not acts of Providence but man-made situations, which in human hands may undergo various changes, modifications, applications and adaptations. Anyhow, some attempts ought to be made in order to clarify the matter, to smooth out the humps and to check excess. It must be acknowledged that it is extremely difficult to analyse and solve this problem. A great many complex issues, doubts and aspects are involved. The elementary question of daily bread always comes to the forefront; if you tell someone, 'don't take your food from here', you must add where he is to take it from, or else when hungry he will refuse to obey. Next comes the problem whether, if some professions are non-

[1] Roman Darnowski, hero of Orzeszkowa's novel *Australczyk* ('An Australian'), 1895.
[2] Lat.: 'slip of the pen'.

existent at home, one should discourage young people from undertaking studies in that particular field? And if so, how to prevent the decline in importance of certain branches of knowledge in the public mind? And what lines of study and professions should one advocate as substitutes for those we are dissuading young people from? And as one should always bear in mind economic growth and development, would it not be possible to replace those questionable millions which lure our Argonauts over the mountains and beyond the seas by a guaranteed sum of (let us say) only tens of thousands which could be obtained on our soil? Perhaps we have here our own still untilled and yet fertile fields? And if we do, where and what are they? What is needed to till them? What capital? What skill? What training and what qualities of mind and character? The atmosphere is stifling and the human spirit must be strong not to disintegrate. Is it therefore not possible to find means of refreshing that atmosphere on the one hand, and of strengthening the human spirit on the other? What are those means? Perhaps something could be done in the spheres of family and social life, in art, humanitarian and public spirit, pedagogy, mental hygiene, goodwill and mutual assistance? And so on and so forth. Investigation and research on a great scale are required. I have already written somewhere else and I shall repeat here again that nothing can be done by one man, however competent. What is needed to solve the problem is collective will and versatile intelligence. The problem is difficult and who knows: perhaps this difficulty accounts for the neglect that surrounds it. Because as people we are weak and we like to turn away from difficult tasks for as long as possible by shutting our eyes to the problem, and occasionally we try to convince ourselves that nothing can change because of economic causes. This is how, once upon a time, an ostrich was shot while hiding its head in the sand.

'*Lord Jim*', by Maria Komornicka[1]

Chimera, 1905, 333–4

Lord Jim by Conrad (Korzeniowski). A curious book of unusual content and artistry, a delight for any, even slightly, discriminating reader. It is a drama of the 'heroic imagination', of a 'greed for power too heavy to bear', of a half-conscious megalomania, 'exalted egoism'; in other words, it is the operation within an individual of the imperative of perfection, which at the height of human exaltation becomes the imperative to face death... of a fearless, voluntary *salto mortale*[2]...

---

[1] Maria Komornicka (1874–1949), literary critic, poet and writer of short stories; she studied for a few months in Cambridge. In 1910 she became insane.
[2] Italian: 'leap into death'.

The author possesses a mind cultivated to a degree almost unattainable in our country; he is a consummate and exacting artist in complete control of himself; he is wise, vigilant, intellectual; he is on a level with the greatest masters of the English novel (such as Meredith); he pursues truth in the refractions of light and shade, perceptible only to the 'everlastingly alert', vigilant in noble individuation, alien to coarse truisms; he pursues it in flashes, in glimmers, in 'psychological impressions' decoded instantaneously by the brain which overlooks, as it were, their sensory externality... He revels in the paradoxicality of phenomena, ennobles commonplace words by unusual juxtapositions necessitated by his super-subtle celebration of the art of writing; he divides things seemingly indivisible, subjects them to complicated experiments and reconstructs them a hundred times amazingly, unexpectedly enriched. Let us add the boundless perspective of complete awareness, of the whole range of human nature, and the beautifully wise smile of maturity in the face of the strangest simplicity of things already experienced... Let us add the unceasing attention given to the reader: the author is not an improviser 'singing to himself' but a strategist of impressions, a conscious manipulator of words, a Machiavelli constantly considerate of our point of view, our degree of concentration; he is the artful and refined Amphitryon of an intellectual feast who enjoys an apparent, but scrupulously composed, disorder, a magician able to dazzle the spectator by speedy revolutions of the one and the same constantly changing mass of phenomena, a master of the pointed phrase. Not the least charm of the novel consists in its 'colonial' character. Here the homeland extends over the entire globe – and in the current of clear thoughts, in the unfolding of images, in the noble calm and all-embracing goodwill you feel poignantly the bold, convex-breasted swift flight of a bird, of the extensive and dauntless freedom of a citizen of the world, of a liberated man.

'A Pole or an Englishman?', by Wiktor Gomulicki[1]

'Polak czy Anglik?', *Życie i Sztuka*, 1905, no. 1 (supplement to *Kraj*, St Petersburg)

For some years now the English literary world has been rejoicing in the acquisition of a new author, Conrad, who represents a truly masculine, solid talent that combines the vigour, if not of an old sea-dog, then at least of a 'sea-puppy', with great sensitivity, psychological insight and genuine gentlemanlike notions about honour and upright behaviour.

---

[1] Wiktor Gomulicki (1851–1919), poet, journalist, novelist.

For some months now, thanks to an interesting article by K. Wali-szewski,[1] the readers of *Kraj* have been aware that this new English writer, on a par with the much praised Kipling, is Polish through and through and a Polish poet's son, and that his name is Konrad Korze-niowski.

His works are therefore bound to arouse keen interest among Polish readers. An interest that is even extended to Conrad's physical appear-ance. Looking closely at his chiselled features, as if hardened by the salty sea air, we try hard to find in them some 'Polishness'. Having found it – we feel gratified.

How much happier we would be to find Polish traits in Conrad's works! But this is more difficult; in fact, well-nigh impossible.

Lord Jim has appeared just now in a Polish translation,[2] one of the best, or at least most significant novels by our... how shall I say it? compatriot or ex-compatriot. Spurred by the above-mentioned curio-sity I read it in one evening – although it seems to me that I would have done the same without this additional incentive.

The novel is of the kind that grips the attention and holds the reader spellbound throughout. To be precise it is not a novel but a long short story. And to be still more precise it is not even a short story but a psychological study. And yet it has none of the characteristics of a scholarly dissertation: it is neither colourless nor lifeless. On the con-trary, it bubbles with animation, exotic scenes, wondrous images of nature and cosmic turmoil. The rich contents make the framework of this modest-size volume almost burst at the seams.

In order to write such a book one has to have a wealth of knowledge and experience, to think things over a great deal and feel a lot... *Lord Jim* is not a work of a young, but of a mature man. Of a man who, having discarded many springtime illusions, has not lost any of his springtime sensitiveness or ability to react to the most subtle stimuli.

The central theme is unusual, although decidedly coherent. A ship glides along the sea in the dead of night, full of travellers fast asleep in their cabins and on the deck. The ship is time-worn and dilapidated and she ought to have been withdrawn from service long ago, but the owner, a dishonest profiteer, in collusion with an equally dishonest captain, continues to take passengers hoping for the best. But one night the ship comes into collision with some underwater object, possibly a

---

[1] Kazimierz Waliszewski, 'Polski powieściopisarz w angielskiej literaturze' ('A Polish Novelist in English Literature'), *Kraj* (St Petersburg), 1904, nos 3–5, 7. Before writing the article Waliszewski corresponded with Conrad; see *Conrad's Polish Background*, pp. 235–43.

[2] By Emilia Węsławska, Warsaw, 1904.

reef, leaving a hole in the old hull. It is the final death-blow to the ship. The captain and his three most trusted mates, having looked at the damage, conclude that the ship is doomed to sink in a matter not even of hours but of minutes.

The captain and two of his mates behave like downright scoundrels. Without any attempt to avert the disaster and without any warning to anyone they hurriedly lower a lifeboat, get inside it and escape. But at the last moment, just before getting into the boat, one of them dies from excessive emotional stress. The scene is being watched from nearby by a young, noble-minded 'ship chandler'[1] – Jim. One sweeping glance is enough for him to take in the situation; his instinct for self-preservation momentarily overcomes his sense of honour – and he blindly jumps into the boat and sails away with the rascals...

Then Jim, who because of his gentlemanly qualities is nicknamed 'lord', feels a pang of conscience. Tormented by remorse (although, as it later appeared, the wretched ship has not sunk), divested by the court of the certificates of his previous service, he retires into obscurity, earns his living in the most remote Malay ports and, finally, unable to live any longer with a blot on his conscience, ends it all with a death near suicide: allowing himself to be killed.

As we see, the plot of the novel is thoroughly English, marine, exotic – not in the least 'ours'.

And form?

A Polish reader cannot describe the form used by Conrad otherwise than as 'eccentric'. This term, taken from a foreign language, implies everything. Once and for all we have dubbed 'eccentric' whatever in the behaviour of the English grates upon our peculiar Slavonic sensibility.

An Englishman never writes straightforwardly – in our meaning of the word. The line of the story in his novels must always turn and twist in convoluted meanders like the intricate paths of a maze. It is only with the greatest difficulty that the Polish mind can find the right direction in that labyrinth, hold course and avoid getting lost.

It seems that the English are unable to swallow anything without a pinch of 'eccentricity'. It is a fact taken into account by all their writers. Even Dickens, the real genius of a simple and unaffected approach, gave in occasionally to eccentricity out of consideration for the demands of his compatriots...

Conrad, like all religious, political or literary converts, carried the 'Englishness' of form to the extreme. I have seen Polish readers picking up his book time and again, and putting it down protesting their inability

---

[1] Gomulicki got confused: it is only after the *Patna* catastrophe that Jim works for ship chandlers.

to 'get the hang' of it. Indeed, reading it one sometimes gets the impression that the printer mixed up the pages of the manuscript and that what was supposed to be at the end, he placed in the middle, and moved the middle to the beginning.

It is not my intention to blame the author by stressing these peculiarities of form. I am quite willing to recognize their peculiar flavour which stimulates well-trained minds to a more lively activity.

Be that as it may, the Polish reader unable to find Polishness in the contents of the book would be even less successful in looking for it in the form: everything about it is essentially and typically English.

Such a discovery causes painful disappointment. We should like so much to reclaim our compatriot, to 'restore' him to our native literature. But it is difficult to part with faith, even when it is based on illusion. And still more difficult to part with hope...

I was on the point of closing Conrad's book, saying to myself quite dispiritedly: 'No, this writer did not break away from Poland – he was never part of her.' But suddenly some voice inside me seemed to call out: 'And perhaps all this is just symbolic?' That ship doomed to sink... those travellers overcome with sleep and exhausted by religious ecstasy ... those selfish men, who driven by greed for life escape from the ship they are responsible for ... and particularly that basically noble-minded young man, a stray among scoundrels, who for the rest of his life suffers pangs of conscience that prey on his heart like the Promethean vulture ... that *szlachcic* who had found prosperity, love and trust in a foreign land and yet looked for ultimate relief in voluntary death ... Is it possible that the hidden meaning of it all is only such as it appears to English readers?

Sometimes we are woken up at night by a loud moan. We rub our eyes and look around: there is no one else in the room. The moan came from our own breast.

We had gone to sleep peacefully making plans for future amusements; our dreams had even been pleasant.

Then our soul artificially put to sleep regained momentary consciousness and revealed its presence by means of a moan.

In Conrad's novel I detect a moan – perhaps unconscious...

Well, is it symbolic?

Only Konrad Korzeniowski could answer that question.

'An Interview with J. Conrad', by Marian Dąbrowski

'Rozmowa z J. Conradem', *Tygodnik Ilustrowany*, 1917, no. 16

I had to wait a long time for an interview with the greatest writer in England today, and I owe it probably only to my nationality that I was at all able to see our compatriot whose name is on the lips of all literary England.

On a beautiful London afternoon, when golden shafts of sunlight pierced the grimy layer of cloud enveloping the City buildings, I went to one of the busiest parts of the Strand, close to the Thames, to meet a friend of Conrad's, the only Pole in England who knows the writer intimately.[1] He began by saying: 'You're lucky. It will be the first interview ever granted by Conrad. American and French journalists have written and are still writing about Conrad but they have never seen him in person, let alone interviewed him.'

'I'm extremely happy that you have made it possible. Am I right in thinking that the fact that I am Polish induced Conrad to agree to your suggestion?'

'Undoubtedly, yes.'

The door opened. There stood a well-proportioned man in an old-fashioned overcoat, which in England represents the attribute of a non-Philistine exterior just as a cape does in Poland. His features modelled by the winds and waves looked exceptionally masculine. He had some striking physical characteristics, typical of the 'borderland'[2] people. He had the eyes of an old sea-dog; they seemed to look into the soul of the earth, into the depth of the sea.

For the sea is the soul of the earth. And if man rose from dust and will return to dust, then the earth could have risen only from the sea and will one day vanish into the sea. Conrad wrote that Maupassant was one of those about whom it is said: 'Nous autres que séduit la terre'.[3] There are but few of whom one may say, as of Conrad: 'Ceux que séduit la mer'.[4]

A short, wedge-shaped grizzled beard, the left arm already contorted by illness, but his physique as a whole reminiscent, as Continental people would say, of a stout oak battered by storms.

A short introduction followed.

'I'm a bit late, am I not? It was difficult to get away. They are starting a new weekly – some friends of mine – we got talking...'

Perfect Polish. No trace of an accent.

'So you would like to know something about my life. Humph. I've nothing to hide. I'm always telling and will tell everything. Apart from various follies and personal pranks that journalists are so keen to seize

---

[1] Józef Hieronim Retinger (1888–1960), literary scholar from Cracow, internationally active in politics. At that time he directed a Polish Bureau in Arundel St.

[2] General name given to the eastern provinces of old Poland: Ruthenia, Bielo-Russia and Lithuania.

[3] Fr.: 'we who are fascinated by the earth'.

[4] 'Those who are fascinated by the sea'.

on. So everything – except murder and imprisonment, as Baudelaire says,' Conrad laughed.

'I left Poland at the age of seventeen. My secret wish was to go to sea, to join the English merchant marine. Just like that: straight from the fifth form at St Anne's High School. When my father died I had lessons with a tutor. Finally my uncle–guardian yielded to my pleas and let me go. But only to France, to Marseilles. I dreamt of England, but could not speak a word of English. My uncle would have made me study English for at least a year. And that I didn't want. My soul yearned after the sea. I travelled through Vienna and Zürich. In Pfäffikon I stayed for a day with Oksza-Orzechowski.[1] You probably know that he was the representative of the National Government in Constantinople. After 1863 he lived in Switzerland. It was there that I said my last farewell for many, many years to my native language. They laughed at me at Oksza's house: "You want to become a sailor, but have you got a knife in your pocket?" I had not, I knew nothing about it. Later, vous savez, c'est vrai, à chaque matelot son couteau![2] Ha! Ha! Well, next day I was off to Marseilles through Lyons. There I met Chodźko, the son of Ignacy Chodźko.[3] He, a sailor himself, introduced me to other sailors. I joined the French merchant marine. It all went very well.

'I had a good time, an interesting life. Oh, yes, several times I even carried war contraband, arms for the Carlists to the shores of Spain. "Voilà un Polonais qui sait faire son métier,"[4] the French used to say. Life was exciting and happy.

'But it was time to get a profession. Only an Englishman can be a real sailor. I came to London. "You'll have to pay for your training," my friends in Marseilles warned me. Well, so I paid. And before long I left London for the Sea of Azov in a grain ship.[5] As we passed through Constantinople I saw the tents of the Russian army at San Stefano.[6] A strange feeling. Yes, my father... Ah, I was young, interested in everything, the sea beckoned me...' Conrad paused.

It struck me that I was spoken to by Józef Konrad Korzeniowski,

[1] Tadeusz Orzechowski-Oksza (1837–1902).

[2] Fr.: 'to every sailor his own knife'.

[3] Wiktor Chodźko, Conrad's friend in Marseilles, was son not of Ignacy, a well-known writer of tales, but of Aleksander (1804–91), a noted orientalist and professor of Slavonic literatures at the Sorbonne.

[4] Fr.: 'There's a Pole who knows his job!'

[5] The steamer *Mavis* was, in fact, Conrad's first British ship. He boarded her in Marseilles on 24 April 1878, not as a regular crew member but probably as an unofficial apprentice. He disembarked in Lowestoft on 10 June.

[6] The *Mavis* entered Constantinople on 2 May. The Russian army, stationed at nearby San Stefano, was waiting for the conclusion of the Berlin peace conference.

whose father... I understood that secret forces were at work in the soul of this *expatrié* Pole, and that his soul was ours, ours. *Impatrié*.

A grave silence lasted for several minutes. I had the impression that following a storm the sea depths were settling down; the towering waves grew smaller and from some distant shore, perhaps even from the steppes of the borderland, the lighthouse was throwing powerful beams of light into space.

'Please, ask questions,' Conrad broke the silence sharply.

Ask questions! Just try asking questions at such a time.

'I can't. I wouldn't like to ask you meaningless questions like a young journalist. I would like to talk with you like one Pole to another; I would like to hear from you many beautiful, firm words, commandments; I would like to find in the English writer the immortality of Poland.'

'The immortality of Poland? You – we. No one doubts it. English critics – and after all I am an English writer – whenever they speak of me they add that there is in me something incomprehensible, inconceivable, elusive. Only you can grasp this elusiveness, and comprehend what is incomprehensible. *That is Polishness*. Polishness which I took from Mickiewicz and Słowacki. My father read *Pan Tadeusz* aloud to me and made me read it aloud. Not just once or twice. I used to prefer *Konrad Wallenrod, Grażyna*.[1] Later I liked Słowacki better. You know why Słowacki? Il est l'âme de toute la Pologne, lui.[2]

'As to others, oh, yes. Old, grey-haired Pol[3] with his white, drooping, bushy moustache, who used to visit father. I remember him well...

'I am not familiar with more recent literature. It is a shame but I must confess in all humility that I don't know it. I had to work hard as a sailor. Now illness hampers my writing. Two months in a year are wasted. Seventy thousand words. It is no joke. And I write slowly, very slowly. And now again three quarters of a novel are written and I still have not found a title for it. So, there you are.'

Again a pause. Conrad's ever-changing expression altered and a shiver ran through him. His cigarette went out.

'What the devil's the matter with this cigarette? Because, you see, strictly speaking I'm a sailor. C'est mon métier.[4] I look at the sea as my place of work. Here, on land, I can't go into raptures over the sea. Only aboard a ship does a man get the feel of an expanse of water. He can't see the land. I can't look at the sea from the shore and admire it

---

[1] Historical patriotic poems by Adam Mickiewicz (1827, 1823).
[2] '*He* is the soul of all Poland.'
[3] Wincenty Pol (1807–72), poet and geographer, popular for his stirring patriotic verse.
[4] 'It's my profession.'

d'une manière littéraire.[1] It is mine, after all. I belong to the last romantics, don't I?'

'Excuse me, Sir, but do you know Mickiewicz's *Sonety Krymskie?*[2] Did you find there some elements of your own creativity?'

'No, none at all. Mickiewicz had before him a stormy lake. You find the real sea only on the way to Singapore, to Australia. Oh, but you're probably surprised that I, a Pole, became a sailor, a captain. That's it. Some insignificant boy, from the borderlands, from an out-of-the-way province, from some place called Poland, became a master in the British Merchant Marine without any backing. Do you understand? I should like to live once more through that moment in Singapore, when I was addressed for the first time as captain.[3] A German boat. Ha! Ha! Ha! They had to recognize me as a captain. You understand: the Prussians recognizing us, saluting us...

'I have a reasoned hatred of the Prussians for their policy of extermination and for the way they despise us. I find Austria least objectionable. It is strange but I have quite a liking for the dynasty. Indeed, it is interesting. As a child I was even supposed to go to the naval college at Pula.

'One vice-admiral of the Austrian navy is Polish,' my friend added. Conrad's eyes smiled.

'Well, that's about all. Now you must ask questions. Why don't you go ahead?'

'All right. I am going to. Do you like the Polish translations of your books?'

'Oh, not at all! To begin with I was never even asked for permission to translate my books and besides, the translations are extremely poor. It is real agony for me to read things that were written in English in my native language. After all, I know Polish and French quite well. And the Polish translations are so careless, so unfaithful to the original. The French are faultless, but the Polish always irritate me. For example this fragment in a Lwów daily paper. Awful, absolutely awful.[4] Even 'Malay' has been translated as 'little Negro'...'

'Are you not thinking, Sir, of visiting Poland? There is a new tendency at home, just now, towards direct contacts with Western men of talent. Recently Émile Verhaeren delivered a lecture in Warsaw...'

---

[1] 'In a literary way'.

[2] 'Crimean Sonnets' (1826), a cycle in which a few poems have as their subject the sea.

[3] As master of the barque *Otago* Conrad spent three days (1–4 March 1888) in Singapore; according to Norman Sherry (*Conrad's Eastern World*, Cambridge, 1966, p. 246) there was at that time a German ship in port.

[4] *An Outcast of the Islands*, serialized as *Banita* in *Kurier Lwowski*, 1913, translated by Wila Zyndram-Kościałkowska.

'I've been to Poland twice. If it weren't for my illness – gout – I would go willingly. It's my motherland. Although one never meets quite the same person twice on this earth, something pulls me to Poland. Only once during my wanderings did I meet a Polish sailor, a native of Warsaw, in the Sailor's Home, in the port of London. He came to me one evening; the following morning, at dawn, he was to sail. We shook hands. They complained about him that he was slow-witted and indolent at sea. I never saw him again.'

A melancholy silence followed.

'I'd like to ask you to say a few words, for us, over there, at home. I know that men of great talent can say a lot in one word, in one sentence. I don't know if I am expressing myself clearly...'

'Oh, yes, I got your meaning. Great words, great words to you, to you over there ... it's difficult, very difficult. I'm neither a great man nor a prophet. But there burns inside me your immortal fire: small, insignificant, just a lueur,[1] but it is there. When I ponder the present political situation, c'est affreux![2] I can't think of Poland often. It feels bad, bitter, painful. It would make life unbearable. The English say "good luck" when they part. I cannot say this to you. But in spite of everything, in spite of impending annihilation, we live. Two personal things fill me with pride: that I, a Pole, am a master in the British merchant marine, and that I can write, not too badly, in English.'

'*A Son of Two Countries – Some Reminiscences of Joseph Conrad Korzeniowski*', by Tola Zubrzycka[3] [=Otolia Retinger]
'Syn dwu ojczyzn', *Iskry*, 1931, nos 8–10

Last December seventy-three years had passed since the birth of that great compatriot of ours, Joseph Conrad Korzeniowski, who has been in his grave for almost seven years now.

In the whole civilized world he is known as Joseph Conrad. His books, translated into many languages, have made his name famous. He wrote in English, for it so happened that since adolescence he had been living abroad. Both his life and his books were uncommon. And as such they ought to be discussed in an uncommon way.

The subject is enormous – and difficult. All I intend to do in this essay is to tell of the days when I used to meet Conrad; to relive in detached images the moments spent in the atmosphere of Conrad's home.

[1] A 'glow'.   [2] 'It's awful!'
[3] Otolia Retinger's maiden name. She was by that time divorced.

Żeromski's[1] description is so beautiful and apt that I wish to quote his words before I begin to speak for myself.

Conrad's life and works bear witness to his great will-power, truly unparallelled. As a boy of seventeen he ran away from his homeland, from a town steeped in the past, and gave himself up to working in foreign ships and exploring foreign seas. He served as a seaman, officer and finally captain. Only as an adult did he begin writing. In a long sequence of excellent books he told settled inhabitants the world over why he ran away from his homeland; what he experienced on the rough waters of the great oceans, what he had seen on distant shores. Those are stories told by a man who in his wild youth had seen our earth from many points, lit up differently by the sun and moon, by the heat of the tropics and the cool light of the north; by a man who for dozens of years had to cut his way through nature's deepest wildernesses, and who had seen all human misery. The sea was the dream of his childhood and the sea is the content of his most essential epos. He has no peers in the mastery of recreating the splendour and terror of the ocean by means of the word. In all of his most celebrated works the sea constitutes the stage with the moving shadows of tragic, comic or miserable actors...

It has been said that this foreigner was the first to tell the English – sailors for centuries – what the sea is like ...

Conrad was a lover and celebrator of the ship. For him a ship was a living being, beloved and esteemed; his familiar home, his master and friend, benefactor and defender ...

The community of seamen scattered over the waters of our globe was in fact his country. On his long journeys to immensely distant destinations, he, the interested observer, the lover of the sea and of all its affairs, learned, penetrated, understood the souls of the sailors, and remembered all their words and actions.[2]

When I met Conrad he was already a respected English writer; international fame was soon to follow. It was about a year and a half before the First World War.

At that time he was living with his family at Capel House in Kent.[3] His small, very modest house stood some distance from the village. The gate was covered with a creeper. I do not recall what kind.

All round were meadows, woods, a gentle, peaceful landscape, serene and natural.

It took a couple of hours from London to the medium-sized town of Ashford.

It was then, at the station, that I saw Conrad for the first time.

At once I was struck by his Polish looks, eyes, voice, borderland accent.

---

[1] Stefan Żeromski (1864–1925), the leading Polish prose writer of the time, a moral authority of the progressive intelligentsia.

[2] 'Joseph Conrad', *Wiadomości Literackie*, 1924, no. 33 (17 August 1924).

[3] Conrad lived in Capel House, Orlestone, near Ashford, from June 1910 till March 1919.

Medium height, broad-shouldered, slightly stooping, with a character-istic outline of eyebrows, lively, nervous movements and a special, as if shy, charm, almost youthful in spite of greying hair and furrows on his brow.

I was immediately taken by his great simplicity of manner, dignity and natural elegance, although he wore that day an outmoded grey coat and a large hat.

He was moved by meetings with his compatriots. Hyper-sensitive, nervous and often ailing, he shunned strangers and made new friends with difficulty.

It was only later that I appreciated my luck in being able to get to know this exceptional man.

Approaching someone of great renown one is usually either pre-judiced or filled with uncritical admiration: it is difficult to forget about the greatness of the man and that sometimes creates an artificial atmosphere of constraint.

With Conrad it was different. Right from the beginning, without any preamble, everything was straightforward. He took care to make us comfortable in his small, old-fashioned car as we left for the week-end at his home.

It was the first, unforgettable week-end which was to be followed by many more in the course of the next year.

At the house we were greeted by Jessie, Conrad's wife, the doe-eyed little John, and the teenager Borys.

My English was poor at that time and I could hardly understand Jessie's soft and indistinct pronunciation. But very soon I gained confidence. She was calm, invariably cheerful and extremely kind. She could not move without a cane owing to constant pain in her leg. In spite of that she was always active, full of initiative, the practical soul of the house and above all Conrad's guardian angel.

Of course I mean Conrad as I knew him! Not the wanderer in the wildest corners of the world, nor the sailor enamoured of the elements, ships and adventure.

This present Conrad, worn out by fever, with a declining health, devoted to his work and family, was strangely 'unreal' in his everyday existence on land.

Jessie was in charge of the modest family budget and did the cook-ing herself. Otherwise, he used to say, he would probably stop eating.

Jessie typed his manuscripts, read the proofs and also, unfortunately, was continually unwell because of all her operations which, neverthe-less, did not ruffle her serenity.

The rooms in Capel House were not large. Comfortable, old-fashioned furniture made them look very cosy. On the ground floor were the dining-room, living-room, the boys' room, what was called the den, full of tools, stones, in short: treasures. The first floor consisted of bedrooms and a guest-room – a large room with a low ceiling and wide windows facing the garden. What a marvellous rest it was after the hubbub of London: to fall asleep with absolute silence ringing in one's ears and to wake up to the whistling of blackbirds!

Nelly, the maid, knocked at seven o'clock bringing a cup of fragrant tea and toast. After that one could still sleep before breakfast was served downstairs at about nine.

Jessie in her blue dressing-gown presided over the important ritual: making toast, pouring out coffee, offering various kinds of marmalade.

Conrad may have been still a bit out of sorts. No one knew how he slept or how he felt because his hospitality and politeness were always unfailing. It was hard for the eight-year-old Janek[1] to remain at table, so the two of us conspired and disappeared. We rushed of course to the garden, to the meadows. The little boy told me all sorts of extremely important things and let me into his secrets. We were followed by Hadji, John's black dog, who had a passion for retrieving bits of wood thrown into the pond.

My young companion was charming, lively and bright. We made a compact of everlasting friendship.

It was still winter when I first visited Capel House. But English winters are mostly without snow, grey-green, pastel-shaded, with flocks of sheep grazing on the fields, often blurred by mist, at times smiling discreetly with a pale gold sun.

Then Borys took me for a drive in the same funny, small car along smooth asphalt roads among the still leafless woods.

He was shy, blushing, wore large spectacles and went to school at Ashford.

At noon we had a formal lunch on account of the chicken in mayonnaise, Jessie's traditional masterpiece. Later I was to assist Jessie many times in her cooking and housekeeping activities; we became friends quite easily, although she was much older and wiser.

The living-room, also used by Conrad as his study, was the nicest room in the house.

There stood his desk, a kind of davenport, a few exotic knick-knacks on the walls, several faded photographs and family souvenirs from Poland.

And the fireplace! The delightful English fireplace encircled with deep arm-chairs and a sofa formed the snuggest and cosiest corner.

[1] Diminutive of 'Jan' (John).

We spent long evenings sitting near the fire. Conrad would liven up. Sometimes he talked about distant seas and ports but most likely about his early youth and family.

He was also fond of talking about literature; his favourite authors were the French masters of the word whom he admired. On those occasions he liked to speak French. In English he always had a marked foreign accent. He spoke Polish clearly with a charming Ukrainian accent. Sometimes, unable to find some word, he would switch into French.

We tended to forget about the time as the evening hours slipped by unnoticed. In the glowing circle of the fire Conrad would evoke a new, strange world. He never told fantastic stories about unusual adventures; he hated showiness, easy effects and all posing.

And yet he knew how to create a unique atmosphere, full of subtle charm. His dark eyes with drooping lids radiated a powerful spirit and individuality. Images of peculiar suggestiveness and colour emerged through his nervous manner and broken sentences.

It was quite uncanny how strongly his distinct personality made itself felt at times.

He was subtle in the extreme, a sensitive observer, an aesthete, thinker and above all a poet. Sometimes he was tragic, difficult and complex in his moodiness; sometimes he was simple, warm-hearted, intimate. But he always looked at the world through his own heroic eyes; he always approached life from its romantic side.

At that time I was unfortunately unable either to appreciate many things or to profit fully by those conversations.

But even so I benefited quite a lot by them and in later years it became easier to understand Conrad's works and his great soul.

Later, when we became closer, he spoke about his tragic childhood.

Born in the village of Debreczynka[1] in the Ukraine, deprived of a family home as a small child, he accompanied his parents into exile. A staunch patriot, his father was sent into the depths of Russia for having taken part in a liberation movement preparing an insurrection.

After a few sad years he lost his beloved mother and when finally his sick father was given permission to travel to Cracow, long and difficult months followed, which he described later and I quote elsewhere.

As a twelve-year-old boy he followed his father's coffin. The orphan was taken care of by his uncle Tadeusz Bobrowski, the only close relative left (others perished fighting for the liberation of Poland).

---

[1] A double error. The name of the hamlet and estate which Apollo Korzeniowski administered was Derebczynka; and Conrad was born not there, but in Berdyczów.

In the spring the woods round Capel House became blue with a profusion of bluebells.

We used to gather them by the armful, bantering with the cuckoos.

Once at the beginning of the summer we went to Sandgate for a picnic to meet Borys who was there at the naval college.

A picnic in the English sense consists of lunch or tea eaten in the open air, with the provisions packed into most practical containers, special baskets fitted out with all the necessary accessories.

Sandgate lies at the mouth of the Thames. We went there by motor-boat; and we were barely able to discern the banks of that huge river.

The brilliantly shiny scales of water, the sun and speed intermingled with the inseparable noise and stench.

Conrad was happy and cheerful, obviously enjoying being on the river; he was looking forward to seeing his son and felt relaxed and carefree.

Janek played about, leaning over the side of the boat; his father would scold him, while at the same time gazing lovingly at him.

We were all cheerful; Conrad joked about Jessie's famous chicken with asparagus which we had solemnly prepared for the occasion. He was telling us about some strange Malay dishes.

We returned at dusk. Conrad asked all sorts of questions about Poland and my family home in the country; he seemed overcome by feeling about his country which he had not seen for so long. Perhaps it was nostalgia?

It was a great day when the Conrads and their sons came to stay with us in London.

Both my Irish housekeeper and I were full of apprehension about making our special guests really happy.

The flat, although small, was rearranged quite comfortably for the occasion. The guests were put up in the two rooms on the upper floor, unaware that their hosts had to squeeze on two sofas downstairs.

We lived at that time in one of those comfortable modern furnished apartments. Ours was exceptionally nice, having been decorated by an artist.

I received our long-awaited guests in the living-room, feeling nervous like any young and inexperienced hostess. I was thrilled to realize that Conrad Korzeniowski in the flesh was sitting by our fireside.

I had pondered at length over the menu with Kathleen, our plump housekeeper. We produced a Polish-style meal: beetroot soup, *pieroźki* (a kind of ravioli), lamb chasseur, poppy-seed cake. Conrad was delighted; Jessie and the boys professed their liking for the dishes, so strange to the English palate.

Suffice it to say that it was a success, and both cooks could rest on their laurels.

Our guest had to see his publisher in London. Otherwise I doubt whether he would have repaid my visit quite so soon. He had a strong dislike of going up to town and for Jessie it was a complicated expedition. And so their friends would stay with them without expecting to be repaid a visit (anyhow, customs over there are different in that respect). At the Conrads' I met a number of notable writers and men famous today. But as the Conrads did not like commotion and the house was not big enough to invite more people at once, we were alone most of the time.

At the beginning of 1914 Conrad finished *Chance*.[1]

The recollection of this excellent book, which was read by us immediately on its completion, is linked in my mind with a new epoch.

One Saturday in the spring, sitting beside the fire, I had an idea. An idea which at first took Conrad aback: he should go to Poland, visit the places he had known in his youth, show them to his wife and children and they could all be our guests at our country estate.

At first the idea seemed difficult to carry out. Jessie's health presented the major obstacle. But in fact it was she who was not frightened by the project; on the contrary, she approved of it, and shared our view that the boys, as well as she, ought to see Poland.

She might have been frightened for Conrad though, as such a return could be a great shock for him.

Meanwhile Conrad, in great excitement, hardly believing his own words, was making plans for the journey.

The idea was to take the long sea route and go through Hamburg on account of Jessie, for whom a train journey was too exhausting.

In June the final decision was made. On my last visit to Capel House we spoke of nothing else but the journey. Conrad was excited and cheerful. Sometimes he became lost in thought and nervous.

Even I thought sometimes with apprehension about the whole plan. How would poor Jessie stand the travel? How would our friends feel in Poland?

Conrad, like us, did not suspect what was to happen and that, alas, only a part of our plans could be realized.

We left London on 25 July.

The first evening of the journey was extremely cheerful, we all felt in a truly holiday mood. Conrad beamed.

We boarded the boat at Harwich and the night and the next day

---

[1] The author confuses *Chance*, completed in March 1912, with *Victory*, finished in June 1914.

were spent at sea. It was rather rough. The reason for the strong and unpleasant rocking was a double movement of the waves, causing rolling and pitching according to Conrad. The deck became deserted, the passengers dispersed into their cabins; poor Janek felt a bit seedy and stayed in the cabin with his mother.

Conrad walked up and down the deck alone. He was strangely irritable and developed a grievance against the captain. There was almost a scene between the two of them.

I spent this entire beautiful windy Sunday lying on my back in the cabin. I preferred looking at the waves from afar, through the skylight, rather than risk being sea-sick.

I am sorry to have missed that day with Conrad; I had looked forward very much to spending it in the company of that excellent seaman.

In the evening we approached the estuary of the Elbe river; the tossing subsided and the travellers emerged again into the open. In spite of the unusual hour we all crowded into the dining-room to make up for enforced fasting.

Our mood improved greatly and the night brought us much-desired sleep and rest.

Entering the port of Hamburg at dawn delighted us all. The sight was magnificent.

The boys were amazed by the great activity of the huge port, Conrad took photographs and looked attentively at his old world. Żeromski, speaking of him as of a famous sailor, said that after long years of enforced stay on land, at the sight of a port filled with funnels and masts, Conrad would cry out one word which contained his whole life: 'Ships!'

Then we visited the famous Hagenbeck zoo, at that time the biggest in Europe. The next stage of the journey was to Berlin.

A strange atmosphere prevailed there: agitated people stood in groups in front of the latest news-sheets pinned to the walls, and snatched the latest editions of newspapers from each other...

And we were heading towards the middle of that volcano which was about to erupt. Half-consciously we sensed something evil but we failed to realize – at least some of us – what was going on.

The last stretch of the journey seemed interminable. Conrad controlled his nervousness with difficulty, the boys were tired by the heat, Jessie, smiling peacefully, patiently bore the inconveniences of the stuffy carriage and the uncomfortable position of her leg.

The uncanny atmosphere, as if before a storm, became intensified after we had crossed the Austrian frontier. The bridges were guarded, the train officials looked very uncertain.

Our arrival at the station in Cracow in the evening of 28 July was quite a shock. What a terrible turmoil and confusion: trains full of men in uniform; soldiers everywhere – farewells, women weeping. War![1]

Late at night I accompanied Conrad and Borys to town. We walked slowly up St Anne's Street, Conrad recalled his school years, gazed with affection at the aged walls of the Jagiellonian Library outlined against the starry sky. The market square was already quiet by then.

Suddenly the hourly bugle-call sounded from the tower of the Church of Saint Mary. Conrad strengthened his grip on my arm and stopped short.

The faithful city of his youth was welcoming the sailor from distant seas.

We stood engrossed in thought and silence, for there was no need for words.

This solemn moment of concentration linked us with a new tie of joint experience. The memory of that occasion became deeply engraved in my mind as an inseparable part of the onset of the war.

While Jessie rested for a couple of days, Conrad visited his old colleagues and acquaintances. People began calling to see their famous countryman.

The atmosphere was charged, the German ultimatum seemed imminent.

It was quite impossible even to think about our guest going to the country, at least for the time being.

I went there alone, still on my Austrian passport.

The hateful barrier at the Russian checkpoint was lifted for the last time to let me in. A day later there was not a single Russian left...

How sorry I felt looking at the rooms prepared for our dear guests. Hornbeams and lime-trees would have soughed for them in the park; how much more comfortably I could have received them here than in the small London flat which was not even our own!

I was still hoping that their visit only needed to be postponed.

Meanwhile they all went to Zakopane, where Conrad had relatives. I joined him there for a few weeks.

The boys and I used to go for walks in the mountains, and I helped Jessie in her shopping, as part of their luggage had been lost on the journey.

Conrad immersed himself in reading. He devoured books, new to him, admired Wyspiański,[2] delighted in his beloved Prus.[3]

[1] Between Austria–Hungary and Serbia.
[2] Stanisław Wyspiański (1869–1907), eminent painter and the leading Polish dramatist of his time.
[3] Bolesław Prus, pen-name of Aleksander Głowacki (1847–1912), a leading Polish novelist and liberal publicist.

He spent long hours in lively discussion with Stefan Żeromski.
Meanwhile history was in the making.

One used to see soldiers go off to the front, one eagerly waited for
news, anxiously expecting to hear about the activities of the Legionaries.[1]

In this unique atmosphere of anxiety and hope, of trust and fear,
starting nursing courses and sewing workshops became a part of the
down-to-earth problems of everyday existence.

It was impossible to press for the Conrads to be allowed to go to our
country house. It had been occupied by the Austrians, although, as it
turned out, all was quiet there till November. But who could have
foretold that? Anyhow the problem was settled by bad transport.
(Later, when returning from Zakopane to Cracow, I spent three whole
days travelling.)

'A Few Reminiscences of Conrad', by Aniela Zagórska[2]

'Kilka wspomnień o Conradzie', *Wiadomości Literackie*, 1929, no. 51

To Maria Dąbrowska

The year 1914, 3 or 4 August, Zakopane, a beautiful morning. I return
home and catch unknown voices in the living-room – Mother is talking
with some visitors.[3] I go in; a greying elderly man with a stern face
and distinguished appearance rises from an arm-chair. Conrad! He
smiles; his face changes completely. I immediately get the impression of
having known him for years. I never saw a face which a smile would
change quite so much. At first stern and as it were intent, it literally
turned radiant and bright with a strangely artless and almost childlike
warmth. Conrad's smile revealed all his goodwill towards men. His
great kindness and simplicity coupled with a powerful personality, of
which one was always aware – there were perhaps the main source of
the attraction that never failed to captivate his friends. Moreover he
had a special charm of his own, which I now find impossible to define.
During the two months the Conrads stayed with us, scores of people
passed through our house; all of them – young, old, children – adored
Conrad and vied for his attention. Indeed it was all due solely to his
personality; Conrad's fame did not matter here because at that time
only few people in Poland had read his books.

---

[1] A voluntary Polish formation, organized by Józef Piłsudski (1867–1935), the future
national leader, fighting on the Austrian side.

[2] Aniela Zagórska (1881–1943), daughter of Karol and Aniela, née Unrug; a distant
relative and distinguished translator of Conrad into Polish.

[3] Mrs Zagórska ran a pension, 'Konstantynówka', at Jagiellońska Street in Zakopane.

I must point out, however, that Conrad was in a particularly equable and serene frame of mind throughout his visit. His wife commented on it with amazement more than once. Apparently, at home he was prone to fitful and capricious moods; visitors coming to meet him could never predict in what temper they would find him. At our house, however, he used to chat with practically everybody in a relaxed and lively manner.

Soon after his arrival at Zakopane, Conrad announced his determination to meet Żeromski. I was fully aware of Żeromski's high regard for Conrad's talent and I was delighted at the prospect of their meeting. On the other hand, however, I was slightly apprehensive: it was impossible to foretell how such an encounter would end. With people as hyper-sensitive and impulsive, and therefore unpredictable, as Conrad and Żeromski, a lot depends on some minor detail or other – a word or a glance.

Conrad was a great admirer of Żeromski's works. He valued *Popioły* and *Syzyfowe prace*[1] most highly; he said more than once that the latter book ought to be translated into English. We often spoke about *Popioły*; the mastery with which Żeromski had managed to portray Napoleon was a source of constant wonder to Conrad, who was always fascinated by the emperor. And as to Żeromski, the first book of Conrad's he read was *Lord Jim*. It left a lasting impression on him and next to *The Mirror of the Sea* it remained his favourite.

At the time, however, Żeromski was not at Zakopane. He arrived a few days later. Conrad went over to pay him a visit but did not find him at home. A couple of days afterwards, as I was approaching the house, I saw Żeromski sitting on the terrace with both Conrads and my mother. I was struck by the immense vivacity with which Conrad was engaged in conversation. Żeromski did not speak much but listened to Conrad smilingly. It was obvious that both men were at ease in other's company. I cannot remember what the conversation was about, but I recall Conrad suddenly addressing Żeromski: 'Do you know, that I am not only famous now but I am even beginning to be popular.'

Those words made me feel a bit uneasy; what if Żeromski thought Conrad conceited? I glanced quickly at Żeromski: nodding his head slowly he smiled in his own unforgettable, kind manner. He understood what Conrad meant – he could feel the well-nigh childish joy that lay behind those words, the directness and trust conveyed by that confession. I must emphasize here that nothing was more alien to Conrad

---

[1] *Popioły* ('Ashes', 1904) is a long historical novel of Napoleonic time; Conrad's opinion of it, none too high, is expressed in his letter to Edward Garnett of 2 September 1921. *Syzyfowe prace* ('Sisyphean Toils', 1898) is a contemporary novel about the enforced Russification of Polish youth.

than conceit and boasting; neither before nor after did I ever hear him make a similar remark. And although basically Conrad had – and had to have – a sense of his own worth, he went through periods of gnawing doubts. Perhaps no real greatness is free from them.

That was the only meeting between those two men. Żeromski left Zakopane the following day and Conrad departed several weeks later, never to return to Poland.

Żeromski's personality made a strong impression upon Conrad. He spoke about him with immense warmth, glad to have had the opportunity of at least that one meeting and a chance to talk. And if only he could have foreseen the service Żeromski was going to render him less than ten years later, by introducing him into Polish literature! Conrad was simply delighted with Żeromski's foreword to the Polish translation of his books. I am using the word 'delighted' without the slightest fear of overstating my point. In his foreword Żeromski professed that Poland needs and desires the spiritual nourishment contained in Conrad's works.

Conrad felt very indebted to Żeromski, as we can see in the letter in which he thanks Żeromski for 'the great favour' he had done him: 'I confess that I cannot find words to describe my profound emotion when I read this appreciation coming from my country, voiced by you, dear Sir – the greatest master of its literature.'[1]

On one occasion, however, things worked out differently. I was very keen to arrange a meeting between Conrad and Jan Rembowski,[2] who, at that time, was already a sick man and increasingly disliked meeting new people. I succeeded in persuading him to come and visit us; he admired *Lord Jim* greatly and was most interested in its author. I was certain they would like each other.

Rembowski came by one evening. As soon as he arrived Conrad became silent, and as Rembowski was by nature a man of few words – the conversation faltered. At last we moved to the dining-room. In spite of my efforts the atmosphere was getting more and more exasperating. Rembowski hardly said a word and Conrad seemed quite different from his usual self. Normally he would be very lively and talkative in the evenings but this time he sat silent and looked gloomy. I was confused and could not make out what was on his mind. I felt sorry for Rembowski and was annoyed with Conrad, who knew that the guest had come specially to meet him. I brought up all possible subjects, addressing each man in turn and trying to draw them into conversation. All in vain. Conrad did not speak even once to Rembowski.

[1] Letter of 25 March 1923; full text in *Conrad's Polish Background*, p. 289.
[2] Jan Rembowski (1877–1923), draftsman and painter.

Finally our guest got up to say good-bye. I accompanied him to the hall, thinking how to explain Conrad's behaviour to him, when he suddenly spoke: 'Thank you for having invited me. I found Conrad very charming.'

I sighed with relief.

'I am so glad you liked him. But as a rule he is more talkative and I don't know what was the matter with him tonight.'

'Never mind,' Rembowski interrupted, 'his company is most congenial indeed.'

I had hardly entered the living-room when Conrad called out:

'My dear, what a charming man! I am quite impressed by him.'

'Do you mean to say you liked him?' I exclaimed in surprise. 'Then why didn't you say a word to him? How could you...'

'Well, somehow I wasn't in the mood.'

Only later did I come to understand Conrad's silence. I noticed that whenever he cared about somebody or was anxious to make a good impression on a person he particularly liked, he would lose his habitual ease and simplicity; either he would become unnaturally talkative (as during his meeting with Żeromski) or else he would sink into gloom. I dare say I knew how he felt on that occasion. He was intimidated by apprehension, 'What does this man think of me? Does he also take me for a deserter?'

Conrad could never shake off the bitter memory of a letter he had once received from Orzeszkowa.[1] This letter must have been worded rather sharply and inconsiderately; or else perhaps it touched on his deepest and most painful emotions and thoughts. There is no doubt that Conrad's dual loyalty to Poland and England – with the evident supremacy of the latter – constituted a constant source of distress for him. My conviction is based not only on observation but also on his own words. He broached the subject only once in the course of the countless conversations we had together. It was no more than just a hint. I could see how difficult it was for him.

Let me recall an excerpt from Conrad's *Some Reminiscences*, from the chapter where he talks about his paternal uncle Mikołaj Bobrowski, a Napoleonic soldier who while retreating from Moscow got lost in a Lithuanian forest with two friends. Eventually they reached a village held by the Russians. There they managed to catch a dog, which they killed and ate to keep off starvation. Referring to that story (as a child he always listened to it with horror and disgust), Conrad wrote:

[1] No trace of such a letter has ever been found and it is improbable that Mrs Orzeszkowa would have written it. Possibly Zagórska confused Orzeszkowa's article 'The Emigration of Talent' with a letter.

Pro patria!

Looked at in that light it appears a sweet and decorous meal.

And looked at in the same light, my own diet of *la vache enragée*[1] appears a fatuous and extravagant form of self-indulgence; for why should I, the son of a land which such men as these have turned up with their ploughshares and bedewed with their blood, undertake the pursuit of fantastic meals of salt junk and hard tack upon the wide seas? On the kindest view it seems an unanswerable question. Alas! I have the conviction that there are men of unstained rectitude who are ready to murmur scornfully the word desertion. Thus the taste of innocent adventure may be made bitter to the palate. The part of the inexplicable should be allowed for in appraising the conduct of men in a world where no explanation is final. No charge of faithlessness ought to be lightly uttered. The appearances of this perishable life are deceptive like everything that falls under the judgment of our imperfect senses. The inner voice may remain true enough in its secret counsel. The fidelity to a special tradition may last through the events of an unrelated existence, following faithfully, too, the traced way of an inexplicable impulse.

It would take too long to explain the intimate alliance of contradictions in human nature which makes love itself wear at times the desperate shape of betrayal. And perhaps there is no possible explanation. Indulgence – as somebody said – is the most intelligent of all the virtues. I venture to think that it is one of the least common, if not the most uncommon of all.[2]

But let me return again to Orzeszkowa. I offered once to give Conrad a copy of *Nad Niemnem*[3] so that he could read it.

'Don't you dare!' he shouted.

'But Konrad, please...'

'I don't want anything of hers,'[4] he interrupted furiously, 'you don't know what a letter she once wrote to me...'

On his arrival in Poland Conrad knew from our contemporary literature only *Popioły* and *Panna Mery*.[5] During his two-month stay he devoured almost all that was worth reading in fiction and drama. 'Devoured' is the right word, for he read with unusual, unbelievable speed. I was constantly bringing him new books; he used to get impatient when on his finishing one, there was not another at hand. In every case his judgement was correct – in respect both of the book as a whole and of the particular style of each author. Wyspiański and Żeromski made the greatest impression on him. 'Oh, how I would like to trans-

---

[1] Fr.: 'manger de la vache enragée', to endure privations.

[2] *A Personal Record*, pp. 35–6.

[3] 'On the Niemen' (1887), Orzeszkowa's best-known novel, centred around the idea of fidelity.

[4] To Józef Ujejski Zagórska quoted Conrad as saying: 'Don't bring me anything by that hag!': Ujejski, *O Konradzie Korzeniowskim*, p. 17.

[5] 'Miss Mary' (1902), by Kazimierz Przerwa-Tetmajer (1865–1940), poet and fiction writer; a scandalous novel about a beautiful Polish–Jewish heiress.

late it!' he said once about *Warszawianka*.[1] The poem 'Gdy przyjdzie mi ten świat porzucić'[2] enchanted him. His favourite books by Żeromski were *Popioły* and *Syzyfowe prace*.

I should also mention Prus, whom he valued as highly as the other two writers. The first work by Prus that I gave Conrad was *Emancypantki*,[3] one of my favourite books. I was anxious that he should like it and I warned him: 'Perhaps the first volume will not be up to your expectations, but don't give up, carry on reading.' (In the case of *Chłopi*[4] I could not persuade him to read further volumes; 'I know already what's coming,' he said.) Having finished the first volume of *Emancypantki*, he said, 'There is nothing the matter with it. It is quite beautiful.' When he finished the entire novel he remarked with amazement, 'Ma chère, mais c'est mieux que Dickens!'[5]

In order to appreciate this comment fully one must know that Dickens was one of Conrad's favourite writers.

First I gave him *Lalka*[6] to read, then *Faraon*;[7] once I asked if the Egyptian landscape as described by Prus corresponded to reality.

'Not in the least,' he replied, 'but it does not matter; that isn't what the book is about.'

Conrad kept asking for more books by Prus and at last I had to say: 'That's the lot. The rest isn't worth reading; they are his early works – not very interesting.'

'What do you mean?' he bridled, 'I want to read the entire Prus, down to the last line. Please get me all there is.'

He read with passion *Pałac i rudera*[8] and *Powracająca fala*,[9] books which, I must confess, left me thoroughly bored.

There was, however, one book that I could not persuade Conrad to read. It was *Skalne Podhale*.[10] I fought a long battle, but to no avail. He read a few stories and that was the end. I tried to translate for him, to explain the dialect of the mountain people – all in vain. There was a

---

[1] *Varsovienne* (1898), poetic drama about the 1830 insurrection. The title is taken from Casimir Delavigne's poem, which has become one of the most popular Polish patriotic songs.

[2] 'When I shall have to leave this world', Wyspiański's short poem.

[3] Long novel about the emancipation of women (1893).

[4] 'The Peasants' (1904–9), the main work of Władysław Stanisław Reymont (1867–1925), which brought its author the Nobel prize in 1924.

[5] 'But, my dear, it is better than Dickens!'

[6] 'The Doll' (1889), Prus's main work, a novel of contemporary Poland.

[7] 'The Pharaoh' (1896), Prus's novel about the power struggle between the state and the clergy in ancient Egypt.

[8] 'The Palace and the Hovel' (1876).   [9] 'The Returning Wave' (1880).

[10] K. Przerwa-Tetmajer's long cycle of tales about the Carpathian highlanders (1903–12).

stumbling-block he could not overcome. Once I read to him about Sablik's hunting expedition from *Janosik*[1] and that too failed to arouse any response.

One day Conrad returned from town carrying a volume of short stories by Sieroszewski (whom he greatly respected), *Z fali na falę*.[2]

'Konrad,' I cried out, 'why did you buy it?' (I knew the Conrads were short of money being cut off from England), 'I could have borrowed it from the library!'

Conrad, slightly offended, replied: 'My dear Aniela, you are obviously under the impression that I never buy books.'

During my stay at Oswalds (three weeks after Conrad's death) I found, among several books that were in the room where Conrad had been ill and died, Strug's *Dzieje jednego pocisku*.[3] I had sent it to him a few years earlier. He did not often write to me about the books he used to receive. Let me quote from his letter posted on 24 November 1922 after he had received a copy of *Pożoga*[4] by Kossak Szczucka:

Thank you for *Pożoga*. C'est très, très bien. It seizes hold of and interests one both by its subject and by the way it is written. And also as a documentary it has a great value – for the author knows how to observe and has a soul which is grandement humaine.[5] To say nothing of the style, which reflects so fully her sincerity and her courage – toute la tonalité du récit me charme par la note de simple dignité qui est admirablement soutenue.[6]

Having read *Trzy po trzy*[7] by Fredro, he wrote: 'thank you ... for all the books you have presented me with, in particular for Fredro, qui m'a donné un plaisir extrême à lire et à regarder les images' (27 January 1922).[8]

The evenings were the pleasantest time of the day. The house became quiet; we used to gather in the living-room – my mother, Conrad and I – we often talked till late at night. Conrad was an

---

[1] *Janosik Nędza Litmanowski* (1912), part II of Tetmajer's historical novel *Legenda Tatr*.

[2] 'From Wave to Wave' (1910), Wacław Sieroszewski (1858–1945), author of short stories and novels, a socialist, spent many years in exile in Siberia.

[3] 'A Story of One Bullet' (1910), a novel about the 1905 revolution in Poland; Andrzej Strug was the pen-name of Tadeusz Gałecki (1873–1937), well-known novelist and active member of the Polish Socialist Party (PPS).

[4] *Pożoga: wspomnienia z Wołynia 1917–19* ('The Blaze: Reminiscences of Volhynia 1917–19, 1922), by Zofia Kossak-Szczucka (1890–1968), later a well-known Catholic writer.

[5] 'Human in the grandest way.'

[6] 'The whole tone of the story enchants me by the note of simple dignity which is admirably maintained.' Full text in *Conrad's Polish Background*, p. 284.

[7] 'Tattle Prattle' (written 1844–6), an autobiographical book by Aleksander Fredro (1793–1876), the best Polish comedy writer.

[8] 'Which gave me very great pleasure, in reading and in looking at the pictures.' Full text in *Conrad's Polish Background*, pp. 277–8.

unsurpassed *causeur*. Once he told us of an adventure from his youth; it took place on some island in the Pacific, inhabited by cannibals. Conrad went ashore with several sailors to look for a colleague who had disappeared and failed to return on board. After many difficulties they managed to find the lost man – he had been captured by the cannibals and held prisoner. The rescue party got him back to the safety of the ship. From the whole story I remember best the retreat, which took place under most threatening circumstances;[1] but I remember not so much Conrad's words as the play of his features, so unbelievably and constantly changing as he talked.

Once I planned that we should spend the evening reading Słowacki, and all day I kept looking forward to it. After supper we sat, as usual, in the living-room. I began with *Grób Agamemnona*.[2] I read it aloud, without interruption and not lifting my eyes from the book; finally, having reached the end, I looked up at Conrad and felt frightened. He sat immobile, looking angry and pained; suddenly he jumped to his feet and rushed out of the room, without saying a word or even looking at either my mother or myself, like a man deeply hurt. He did not reappear that evening. It was such a shattering experience to see him, as it were, escaping from the poem, that I never dared raise the subject and the reading of Słowacki came to an end. It had probably been a long time since Conrad had read that poem and he was overcome by a sudden and unexpected emotion which he could neither control nor conceal.

Once we were looking over some book together. Conrad was seated; I stood next to him and noticed a large scar on the crown of his head.

'What's that scar you've got there?'

'Oh, that's nothing much,' he replied reluctantly, 'I got it in some scuffle in a port.'

'And I thought you'd got it in a duel. Did you ever fight one?'

Conrad looked thoughtful and smiled faintly.

'Oh, yes. I really got it then; I was shot right through,' he touched his breast fleetingly. Suddenly he started up; 'Mais moi, je lui ai fracassé la patte,'[3] he added with a vindictive twinkle in his eye.

Several years later I read the description of this duel in *The Arrow of Gold*. It is one of Conrad's most autobiographical novels.

---

[1] Apparently an episode from Conrad's *The Rescue* (Part II, ch.2) and certainly not an authentic reminiscence.

[2] *Agamemnon's Tomb*, song VIII of a longer poem *Podróż do Ziemi Świętej z Neapolu* ('The Journey from Naples to the Holy Land', 1839). Contrasting their behaviour with that of the Spartans at Thermopylae, Słowacki castigates Poles for their lack of faith and shirking of national duties.

[3] 'But I broke his arm for him!'

We did not speak much about his own books; at that time the only one I knew was *Lord Jim* in Polish translation. Once he spoke about *Heart of Darkness* – I do not remember exactly what started it. He said: 'The Polish title should be "Jądro ciemności".'[1]

I have one more recollection about that novel. I once asked Conrad a direct and, I must admit, very childish question. 'Please tell me what of all the things you've seen in life has made the greatest impression on you.'

Before I had even finished, I wanted to bite my tongue out. However, to my surprise, Conrad became very thoughtful and after a while answered me:

'A certain woman. A Negress. It was in Africa. She was pacing up and down in front of the station building and was covered with beads, bracelets...' Conrad turned to my mother: 'C'était la maîtresse du chef de la station.'[2]

It struck me as very strange. In my mind I saw a small station like (for instance) Wołomin, transported into the depths of Africa; the railway line cut through the jungle; a paved platform and the Negro woman, hung with trinkets, parading provocatively back and forth before a stationary train...

Not until seven years later, when I read *Heart of Darkness* for the first time, did I appreciate fully the absurdity of that picture. Only then did I understand that the whole strange magic of Africa became embodied for Conrad in that savage and impressive woman who stood on the bank of the Congo, stretching her bare arms in despair after the steamer which took away her idol, her lover.

On another occasion I asked Conrad which of the women in his novels he liked best. He answered almost without hesitation, 'Freya. She is the heroine of the short story "Freya of the Seven Isles".'

It did not mean much to me at that time, since I had not yet read that particular story. Later, however, I was often surprised by Conrad's liking for Freya; his works abound in characters just as charming and yet more interesting.

Many books and articles mention Conrad's dislike of the Russians. It is a puzzling characteristic for a man who was such a lover of humanity and who had such a deep understanding of human nature. One of Conrad's essential qualities was a combination of great strength with great kindness; natures of that kind are not given to hatred. And yet it is true that Conrad hated the Russians. It shows, more than anything else, the depth of the psychological shock experienced by him in childhood as the result of suffering imposed on his parents and himself

[1] 'The core of darkness'.   [2] 'She was the station-master's mistress.'

before he even understood the violence done to his country. The Russians were the source of all misery: they were the direct cause of his mother's death and of his father's prolonged illness, which also ended in death. One can easily understand the effect it had on an over sensitive child. But that feeling of hatred and abhorrence towards anything Russian did not diminish with the years. It remained alive and powerful, and on occasions showed up with almost childish vehemence. I am thinking here about a memoir on Conrad written by an English captain who had spent several months travelling with him. A few weeks after Conrad's death, when I was at Oswalds, I found the relevant piece in a heap of cuttings which had been sent to Mrs Conrad. The story was banal and uninteresting but contained one curious detail. The captain mentioned with obvious amazement that whenever anyone pronounced the word 'tzar', Conrad would spit.[1] No one who has met Conrad can doubt the authenticity of that story.

Let me describe another incident from first-hand experience. During Conrad's stay at Zakopane a certain Russian lady, very charming and intelligent, called on me. When Conrad entered the room I introduced him and the conversation was resumed. After the guest had left, Conrad asked who the lady was. So with much feeling I began telling him about this charming and kind person and about all the interesting adventures she had gone through during the Russian Revolution...[2] Conrad interrupted suddenly: 'Do you mean to say she is Russian? Is it possible that I shook hands with a Russian woman?'

He was terribly vexed and I stood aghast, unable to grasp what had gone wrong.

'I'd like you to know,' he continued excitedly, 'that I used to break off friendships and even more than friendships, in order to avoid shaking hands with Russians. And now it has happened ... here, in Poland of all places.'

I am certain that his hatred towards Russians was kept alive by the constant torment that stemmed from his sense – right or wrong – of guilt in respect of Poland. The love for his country, which never found an outlet in any action, did not allow him to forgive and forget. But his personal feelings ended where his work began. To prove his objectivity I have only to mention some of his characters like Nathalie Haldin, Tomassov, or the young Russian from *Heart of Darkness*.

Those who knew Conrad maintain that he was quite indifferent to nature and that he never felt any need for it; sometimes he would not

---

[1] Seemingly the reference is to J.G. Sutherland, *At Sea with Joseph Conrad* (London, 1922), but no such account appears in that book; the story is probably apocryphal.

[2] Of 1905.

leave the house for several weeks on end. I imagine that he must have been simply saturated with the beauty of nature and that his recollections were ever ready to spring up in his uncommonly accurate memory. Let me recall a minor detail which for some reason I keep remembering, although many other important events from that period have become blurred. One evening, when the full moon was rising, green against a purple sky, I called out: 'Konrad, come and look at the moon!'

'Leave me alone,' he snapped, 'do you think I've never seen a moon?'

His gallantry, full of unique charm towards women, had to be seen, as it defies description. He had a high respect for women, as I noticed all really strong men have. I remember once a young man speaking with contempt about the courage of women. Conrad interrupted him: 'The colonization of America showed that women are at least as brave as men,' he said dryly.

Soon after their arrival Jessie asked me to teach her Polish. We were both very enthusiastic about it but as our life was extremely eventful then, and every day brought countless excitements, we only had a few lessons. I remember Jessie having said to me: 'My main reason for wanting to learn Polish is that Conrad always speaks Polish when he is unconscious during illness.'

At first Conrad addressed my mother and myself in French; we always answered in Polish and after a week or so he became quite confident in his native tongue. Undoubtedly his constant reading also played an important part. His Polish was not only fluent, but exceptionally beautiful; in all fairness I ought to add, however, that occasionally his use of some words was incorrect. But that happened very rarely.

Conrad's attitude towards his wife was most considerate and affectionate. They were a very happy couple. In contrast to his impetuous nature and occasionally capricious moods, Mrs Conrad put up a front of unruffled peace and great tact. Conrad appreciated it fully. Once when we talked late into the night he spoke about his wife.

'Tell me, Konrad,' I finally asked, 'what would you have done if you and Jessie had not met?'

'Well, my dear, you might give me at least some credit,' he said with mock resentment, 'after all it was I who sensed that Jessie was for me.'

He had a particularly pleasant attitude towards his sons – his elder boy was sixteen at the time and his younger seven. I remember how once Conrad came into the room laughing: 'Imagine what a little scene I saw just now. Janek bends over the table, completely absorbed in drawing a picture. Borys leans over his shoulder, asking: "What's that? Is it raining?"'

'"No. That's the man's hair."'

And here Conrad chuckled again. I would like to explain how it happened that Conrad called his elder boy Borys, as this name has given rise to occasional misunderstandings: some accuse Conrad of being a Russophile. But the simple truth is that Conrad had not been aware of the specifically Russian character of that name. It is ironic in a way that Conrad, who loathed everything Russian, gave his son a Russian name. The following letter to my mother, Aniela Zagórska (née Unrug), explains the situation:

> Stanford-le-Hope,
> Essex.
> 21 January 1898

Chère Cousine,

I have received the wafer – accompanied by a bitter complaint that was not quite deserved. Les apparences mentent quelquefois.[1] But that does not altogether excuse me.

The baby was born on the 17th of this month and I particularly waited these three days in order to be able to inform you definitely that tout va bien.[2] The doctor reports that it is a magnificent boy. He has dark hair, enormous eyes – and looks like a monkey. What upsets me is that my wife maintains that he is also very much like me. Enfin! Please do not draw hasty conclusions from this surprising coincidence. My wife must be wrong.

He will be christened in the Chapel of the Cloister of the Carmelites in Southwark (London).[3] The principle on which his name was chosen is the following: that the rights of the two nations must be respected. Thus, my wife, representing the Anglo-Saxons, chose the Saxon name Alfred. I found myself in an embarrassing situation. I wanted to have a purely Slavonic name, but one which could not be distorted either in speech or in writing – and at the same time one which was not too difficult for foreigners (non-Slavonic). I had, therefore, to reject names such as Władysław, Bogusław, Wienczysław etc., I do not like Bohdan: so I decided on Borys, remembering that my friend Stanisław Zaleski gave this name to his eldest son, so that apparently a Pole may use it. Unless, Aniela dear, you care to suggest a nicer name (and there is still time) please remember that there is a certain Alfred Borys Konrad Korzeniowski, whom I commend to your heart in the name of God and of those who, after a life full of trouble and suffering, remain in your and my memory.

I kiss your hands. A warm embrace for Karol.

> Your loving,
> Konrad Korzeniowski

Conrad never received a reply to that letter because on 19 January 1898 my father had died.

---

[1] 'Appearances can sometimes be deceptive.'   [2] 'All is well.'

[3] There has never been a Cloister of Carmelites in the borough of Southwark, and Borys was baptized only on 29 January 1899 in Hythe.

I would like to add one more detail that concerns Conrad's attitude towards the events that took place in Poland during his stay in Zakopane. He had great respect and enthusiasm for the then commander-in-chief.[1] But he did not believe that the efforts of the Polish Legions would bring about positive results; he feared that more blood would be spilled unnecessarily. He came to Poland after more than twenty years to find himself amidst preparations for an armed attempt to regain independence and the circumstances could not but remind him of some childhood experiences (in 1863 Conrad was six years old) of defeat, mourning, hopelessness. Conrad's youth coincided with the post-insurrection atmosphere. His beloved guardian, Tadeusz Bobrowski, his mother's brother, was on the side of the Whites in 1863. He was a man of great kindness and intellect but a staunch opponent of the insurrection. It must have had an effect on Conrad: he did not believe it was possible to regain independence. All his childhood memories revived in that memorable summer of 1914. I shall never forget his expression when he looked at marching Legionaries or listened to their songs.

A year later he was to write in 'Poland Revisited':

It was a wonderful, a poignant two months. This is not the time, and, perhaps, not the place, to enlarge upon the tragic character of the situation; a whole people seeing the culmination of its misfortunes in a final catastrophe, unable to trust any one, to appeal to any one, to look for help from any quarter; deprived of all hope and even of its last illusions, and unable, in the trouble of minds and the unrest of consciences, to take refuge in stoical acceptance. I have seen all this. And I am glad I have not so many years left me to remember that appalling feeling of inexorable fate, tangible, palpable, come after so many cruel years, a figure of dread, murmuring with iron lips the final words: Ruin – and Extinction.[2]

There is one more thing I should like to state: Conrad came to Poland as soon as it became possible, that is when he had reached a certain degree of financial independence. Until 1913 he was beset with money problems; he was not a popular author, although his first book won him great acclaim among the critics and intellectuals of England. It was not until *Chance* appeared in 1913 that the general indifference of the public was broken through. And then followed a period of reasonable financial independence – although by no means of wealth. Records to that effect can easily be found in old and new books on Conrad (and this is why I am not going to dwell on the subject), but in spite of it the myth about his wealth still lingers on in our country.

---

[1] Piłsudski, commanding the First Brigade of the Legions.
[2] *Notes on Life and Letters*, p. 171.

The position of the Conrads in Zakopane was most precarious, because they were cut off from England. After many attempts of various well-meaning and influential people the Conrads were finally given a permit to travel. At that time we were all convinced that the war would not last more than three months. On their last evening – 8 October – we all gathered round the dining-room table, waiting for the carriage to come and take the Conrads to Chabówka, as beyond that point the railway line was closed. The highlander who drove the cart was late; instead of coming at nine o'clock, he arrived about eleven. And so we waited without undue impatience, chatting for the last time. The Conrads intended to come by car to Zakopane the following spring. We planned various excursions for them round Zakopane and further afield. Everybody made an effort to remain calm and merry; after all we were to see each other in a few months' time.

Finally the coachman arrived. We gathered in front of the house. A thin film of snow covered the drive. The coach moved off as we were calling 'Goodbye, see you soon.'

That was Conrad's last visit to Poland.

'My Meeting with Joseph Conrad', by Kazimierz Górski[1]

'Moje spotkanie z Josephem Conradem', *Przegląd Wołyński*, 17 January 1932

I met Conrad in Zakopane at the beginning of August 1914.

A few days earlier I had arrived there with my family for the holidays. The war caught us unawares like many other Poles, Russian subjects, but I was in no hurry to return home; it was tempting to live through great historic events among people who represented the most diverse shades of Polish political thought.

My intentions were gratified by my meeting with Conrad, which took place through Mr and Mrs Gielgud. Mr Gielgud,[2] a strikingly handsome octogenarian, physically lively and mentally alert, was the retired head of a section in the Ministry of War in London and former secretary to Lord Palmerston, well versed in European politics. He had known Conrad in London and lost no time in asking the writer to come and see him.

---

[1] Kazimierz Górski (1863–1943), physician and amateur painter.
[2] Adam Jerzy Konstanty Gielgud (1834–1920), son of political *émigrés*, had been living in England since 1840. He was a British civil servant, head of the Warrant Department in the War Ministry. He wrote extensively about Polish affairs (*Observer*, *Westminster Gazette*). In 1899 he retired and settled in Cracow; in 1914, compelled to leave Austria, he emigrated to Switzerland.

Conrad was staying with his cousin, Mrs Zagórska; the Gielguds and ourselves in the Stamary Hotel. We used to meet almost every day after breakfast on the sunny side of the terrace where, stretched out comfortably in wicker arm-chairs, we passed the time pleasantly, discussing various subjects, mainly connected with the war, and possible horoscopes for Poland.

The conversation was mostly in Polish. Both Mr Gielgud and Conrad had an excellent command of their native tongue. Gielgud wove in English expressions more often than Conrad, who rarely used English, although of course he spoke the language very well, though with a strong Slavonic accent.

Contrary to the prevailing opinion both Gielgud and Conrad believed that the war would last a long time, because – in spite of the certainty of Germany's defeat – England was unprepared for it and would not be able to mobilize all her resources at short notice. The fate of France filled them with apprehension in view of what they believed to be France's inadequate military preparations and the suddenness of the German onslaught. But they put their trust in French patriotism. They estimated that the war would last about three years, which at the time seemed quite improbable to me. Both Gielgud and Conrad thought that a favourable solution to the Polish problem could be achieved only if Russia were defeated by Germany, and Germany by England and France.[1] Were the war to end differently, Polish prospects for independence would, according to them, be doubtful. France, bound to Russia by a treaty, and England, even more so, failed to appreciate the significance of the Polish question in European affairs. Poland's one hundred and thirty years' captivity had made the West European nations lose the habit of reckoning with Poland and with the need to restore her independence.

I was struck by the phlegmatic composure with which Conrad would utter opinions so unpleasant for us all to hear... He watched with great scepticism the Poles preparing to play an independent military role in the war; he knew nothing about Polish politics or politicians.

The more we saw of each other, the closer we became. Conrad noticed that I did some painting, making the most of good weather. He became interested in my work. I suggested he should sit for a portrait and he agreed on condition that it would not be in oils: he was afraid of too many sittings. And so I began to work on a crayon drawing. Conrad would come to me and while I sketched we chatted informally on various subjects of common interest. Conrad was obsessed by the thought that he would run out of money to keep his family and himself

[1] Such, precisely, were the calculations of Piłsudski.

in Zakopane; he was afraid that he would have to remain in Austria, for a long time, unable to communicate with any of his friends outside her borders. He complained about the none-too-good state of his finances. Although he was at the time a writer of world renown, his publishers skinned him without mercy. The cost of living in England was high and the government pension he received as a Royal Poet[1] amounted to £100 a year, the same amount as when it was first established in the sixteenth century. Conrad was familiar with contemporary Polish literature, but betrayed no particular interest in it. He was unable to write in Polish and felt indignant with people who pressed him to do it. He said he had lost the habit of thinking in Polish and in order to write in that language he would have to transform the entire nature of his talent. I suspect he was also afraid that writing in Polish would damage his relations with English publishers.

On several occasions Conrad's whole family attended the sittings. Mrs Conrad, a portly lady with pleasant features and glowing with good health, would take a seat next to my wife and, crocheting warm socks for her husband who suffered from gout, would join in the conversation. On one occasion she told us how Conrad created his novels. He would apparently begin writing quite unexpectedly in whatever room he happened to find himself, as if in a trance, oblivious of the world around him, and continue to work until he brought it to the desired point. During such a fit of creativity he felt no need of sleep or food and no one was allowed to disturb his solitude. Only his wife was permitted to enter the room where he was working; she would place here and there a dish of food, which he would discover and consume with shouts of surprise and joy. Sometimes periods like that used to last several weeks and they were a real torture for the household.

Conrad was accompanied in Zakopane by both his sons, one aged sixteen and the other eight. The elder of the two was called Borys. When my wife heard this name she asked Conrad: 'And is the younger one called Gleb?' 'Why?' Conrad enquired. 'Because the names of Borys and Gleb, Russia's patron saints, were often given there.' 'I don't know,' answered Conrad, 'Borys is a beautiful Slavonic name.'[2] It was not pleasant for us to hear, from the son of an insurgent, words that betrayed his ignorance of the many subtleties concerning our oppressors.

---

[1] Since 1910 Conrad had been receiving a yearly stipend from the Civil List Pension, but he was not, of course, a Royal Poet.

[2] The gibe misses its target, because both Borys and Gleb, sons of Vladimir the Great, prince of Kiev (d. 1015) were venerated as (orthodox) saints mainly in the Ukraine.

Conrad's portrait was a success and I presented it to him to comme-morate our meeting. He seemed pleased and said he would have it reproduced in the collected English edition of his works.

In mid-September the weather in Zakopane deteriorated; after ground frost and sunshine came rain. Conrad experienced every change of weather acutely; his attacks of gout became so painful that he had to spend whole days in bed. Moreover, he worried about not being able to get out of Zakopane while his reserves were running low. After some hesitation Conrad wrote a letter to the United States Ambassador in Vienna, Mr Page[1] – I believe he was a man of letters – and described his difficult position to him. He soon received a very kind reply together with some money and with a written permit to leave Austrian territory for Italy. One rainy and misty October evening I bade Conrad farewell. It was difficult to get him seated in the carriage as he could barely walk. He was driven to the nearest railway station on the Hungarian side whence he could get a main-line connection to Vienna.

I received two very nice and friendly letters from Conrad: one from Vienna, the other one from Leghorn[2] written before boarding the boat for England. In the spring of 1916, when I was already in Odessa, a post-card arrived from Mrs Conrad with a picture of the Conrad house. Mrs Conrad told me of their safe return home and of Conrad's contin-uous grave illness. This post-card took over two years to reach me by way of Sweden. Had Conrad remained a Pole? I do not think I shall be far off the truth in saying that towards the close of his life he was Polish only by origin. His adventurous life, spent under circumstances so unlike any-thing he could have found in his native country, and his phenomenal gift for languages outshone the images from his Polish past. His profound feeling for the atmosphere of the foreign country where he lived for such a long time, together with his great capacity to assimilate the spirit of his environment, had tied him emotionally to foreign culture. At the time I met Conrad he was no longer a Pole.

Permit to leave Poland in 1914
Biblioteka Jagiellońska, Cracow, MS 6391

Permit
Mr Józef Konrad Korzeniowski and his family, all together four per-sons, are hereby authorized to occupy seats for a single journey on the

[1] Walter Hines Page (1855–1918), journalist and publisher, in 1899 launched the publishing firm of Doubleday, Page; after 1913 he was US ambassador to the Court of St James. The US Ambassador in Vienna to whom Conrad wrote was Frederick C. Penfield.

[2] Conrad did not go to Leghorn, but sailed for Genoa.

train, running according to the war time-table, from Zakopane station
to Vienna, via . . . or via Cracow – or, if need be, to travel by motor-car.

Nowy Targ, 6 October 1914

(signed) Grodzicki

Instructions:

Telegram to Paderewski

Archiwum polityczne Ignacego Paderewskiego (Wrocław, 1973), vol. i, p. 67

27 March 1915

Paderewski[1] Claridge's Hotel London
With every deference to Your illustrious personality I cannot join a
committee[2] where I understand Russian names will appear.[3]

Conrad

Conrad to the Secretary of the Polish Association in London[4]

Polish Library, London

Capel House,
Orlestone
nr Ashford,
1st June 1915

I beg of you, dear Sir, to express to the Chairman and members of the
Polish Association in London my gratitude for the honour they have
bestowed upon me by their kind appreciation of my literary work and
particularly for their brotherly recognition of my Polishness from which
I have never parted in the depth of my heart.

I remain, dear Sir, respectfully
yours
Józef Konrad Korzeniowski

The Right Hon. Secretary of the Polish Association in London.

---

[1] Ignacy Paderewski (1860–1941), famous pianist, internationally active for the Polish
cause.
[2] Polish War Relief Committee, formed 9 January 1915 in Vevey.
[3] The Committee was ostentatiously supported by Russian ambassadors to Paris and
London, who wanted to stress that its field of action was within the Russian bailiwick.
Conrad was strongly opposed to such 'internalization' of Polish affairs by Russia.
[4] Towarzystwo Polskie w Londynie. At that time its secretary was probably Władysław
Hiller.

Conrad to the Secretary of the Polish Association in London
Polish Library, London

> Capel House,
> Orlestone
> nr Ashford
> 27 Sept. 15

Dear Sir,

I apologize for the delay in replying. Your letter had not found me at home.

I am sorry not to be able to comply with your request. I am incapable of speaking in public, having, as the result of an illness four years ago, entirely lost my voice; even during ordinary conversation I am sometimes obliged to whisper.

> I remain your respectful servant
> Joseph Conrad

Conrad to J. H. Retinger[1]
Biblioteka PAN, Cracow

> Thursday
> [31? August 1916]

Très cher,

B[orys] reported to me his conversation with you as to the thing nearest his heart just now.

In this connection pray let me know if you had time to mention that matter to Northcliffe?[2] Pour gouverner ma conduite.[3]

Also what is it I hear from B[orys] about Mr Belloc?[4] Would he really take up the matter in L[and] & W[ater]? If so pray send him my memo[5] if you think it may be done.

Jessie's story of your political success has heartened me very much. May all possible luck attend your diplomatic genius in the hard fight.[6] All send their love.

> Yours ever
> Joseph Conrad

[1] In English in the original.
[2] Lord Alfred Charles William Northcliffe (1865–1922), a big newspaper proprietor, exerted considerable influence on public opinion and the government.
[3] 'To guide my conduct.'   [4] Hilaire Belloc (1870–1953), writer.
[5] Apparently Conrad's 'Note on the Polish Problem' (*Notes on Life and Letters*), which he presented as a memorandum at the Foreign Office in August 1916.
[6] Retinger was trying, unsuccessfully, to open negotiations with Austria–Hungary about a separate peace with the Allied Powers.

Conrad to J. H. Retinger[1]
Biblioteka PAN, Cracow

Capel House,
Orlestone,
Nr Ashford
19 March 1917

My dear Joseph,

Thanks for the *Paris-Midi* which has just arrived. We thought you were in Switzerland. For mercy's sake send us news of Tola,[2] because Jessie never stops worrying.

I am not going to talk about our business. I find recent events depressing. There is gaiety here, which is absolutely foolish in view of the situation.[3]

My health has been rather poor since you left. Jessie grows anxious as time goes on. News from B[orys] is good. He is somewhere near St Quentin. He seems happy with everything and everybody. So much the better.

We wait for word from you on the Great Event. Jessie and John send their love to you all.

Yours as ever

J. Conrad

PS. Neither seen nor heard from anyone since you left. Sand[eman][4] wrote one or two letters about available actresses.[5] I signed a contract with Irving[6] for *Victory*. As to work – nothing!!! The ghost of Ruin prowls round Capel House. The door should be slammed in its face but I am not strong enough.

Conrad to J. H. Retinger[7]
Polish Library, London

22 June [19]17

Tres chèr Ami,

This moment we receive a pc from dear Tola which has relieved our very great anxiety. Our warmest congratulations and most affectionate

---

[1] In French in the original.   [2] Otolia Retinger, who was expecting a child.

[3] This refers to the reception given in the UK to the news about a revolution in Russia.

[4] Christopher Sandeman (1882–1951), journalist, traveller and wealthy businessman.

[5] Actresses who were to act in the stage adaptation of *Victory*.

[6] Henry Brodribb Irving (1870–1919), actor and leading theatre manager.

[7] In English in the original.

welcome to Miss Retinger.[1] May her shadow grow bigger and bigger
for the proper number of years – and thereafter 'never grow less'.

You have been very dear and good to our big child in Paris.[2] We
had a long letter from him. We are very grateful to you.

Jessie is writing to your wife and sends her love to you. We both long
to see you both. But when will that be?!

Ever yours

J. C.

'Under the Roof of Konrad Korzeniowski', by Karola Zagórska[3]

'Pod dachem Konrada Korzeniowskiego', *Kultura* (Warsaw), 1932, nos 2–3

Some day I should like to write down everything I remember about the
time I spent with Konrad Korzeniowski. For those before whom
Konrad unfolded his vision of the world, every bit of information about
him is important and relevant, and every detail of his life interesting.

I shall begin with the recollections of my first stay in England.
During the war, in 1916, I met Konrad in London. As he did not let me
know when he planned to come and meet me, I was expecting to hear
from him any day.

I was sitting in the hotel lobby reading a newspaper, when, lifting my
eyes, I saw and recognized Konrad although he stood with his back to
me. I jumped to my feet, walked towards him and took him by the hand
the very moment he was pronouncing my name. He beamed at me with
pleasure.

'I didn't write because I was ill,' he said quickly, 'I was in bed but I
wanted to come for you personally. You'll stay with us till the end of the
war, won't you?'

No, I could not stay till the end of the war, but I was very much
looking forward to spending several days with Konrad and his wife. I
was ready to start straight away, so having checked on the trains we left
immediately for the station. On the way there we did not speak to each
other, we were too much moved.

'We've still got time,' said Konrad at the station, 'and I'd very much
like you to eat something.'

We sat down at a table. All around us were men in uniform. Konrad
informed me that now, during the war, the atmosphere in London had
changed. I asked him the obvious and yet natural question: was he
certain the Allies would win?

---

[1] The Retingers' daughter.   [2] Borys Conrad.
[3] Karola Zagórska (1884–1955), a singer.

'As to that I never had any doubts. But this whole affair seems to drag on a bit longer than people expected. Borys is still at the front. Till now he has not been wounded; of course no one knows what may happen any minute. Jessie and I are well aware of it whenever a letter arrives. C'est la guerre, ma chère, une guerre terrible.'[1]

We spoke Polish, of course, but Konrad was wont to throw in French sentences now and again. Strangely enough he never mixed English into his Polish. That struck me more than once several years later when I was staying longer with him; and whenever in the course of general conversation I addressed him personally in English he would answer me in Polish.

People kept crowding past us as the place was rather full. Near by sat a woman with her face hidden in her hands, crying bitterly.

'The English have great self-control,' Konrad observed, 'but you do see people crying nowadays.'

'Obviously war is a terrible thing,' I answered, 'but we Poles may rejoice that it finally came. We shall be free.'

Konrad looked at me closely through his monocle.

'Do you believe it, my child? Completely free?'

'I not only believe it but I know for sure. There can't be the slightest doubt,' I exclaimed impulsively.

It was time to leave and go to the train. We took two window seats in an empty compartment. It was a beautiful September day and a gentle breeze blew in through the window. We sat silent and then all at once we started talking simultaneously – about our relatives and about things in general.

It was my first visit to England. A few years later I went there for a longer time, but my first impressions overshadowed all subsequent ones.

Konrad and his wife were then living at Capel House, Kent. It was a small, grey house, old, like most English houses in the country, and extremely charming. Lawns, a small orchard and meadows beyond –no fencing to cut one off from the green stretch of space in the distance. In front of the house a medium-sized tree, beautifully shaped, looked very decorative from the distance against the grey front wall.

The garden was misty, green and smelled of grass. A low front door led to a smallish hall, through which one entered the rooms – also with low, wooden ceilings. Fireplaces everywhere, of course, and that day bouquets of roses on the table and mantelpieces. We were welcomed at the door by Konrad's wife. John, Konrad's younger son, ran towards

[1] 'That's war, my dear, a terrible war.'

us. I was struck by his likeness to his grandmother (Ewelina Korzeniowska, née Bobrowska), whose photograph was hanging on the wall;
I could remember her myself from my childhood at my grandparents,
the Zagórskis.

'I also think that Janek resembles my mother,' said Konrad. 'But
maybe I am only imagining it because it gives me pleasure,' he added
jokingly. 'One of my friends always calls him "the Polish boy" '
(Konrad had Cunninghame Graham in mind).

When I spoke about Janek, I called him 'Johnik' because this was
the name my sister and I always used when referring to him.

'Please, call him Janek,' Konrad asked, 'I like it best... That is
what your mother used to call him. "Come here, Janek," she would
say, I can almost hear her – over in Zakopane, in the living-room...
She played patience and Janek stood beside her looking at the cards,
with his arm affectionately round her neck. I liked to see them like
that.'

Konrad showed me round his house, which – as I said – was not
very large. The first thing that caught my eye on entering Konrad's
bedroom was a photograph of my father. It stood on the mantelpiece
in a time-worn frame. Konrad led me towards it ceremoniously.

'And this is Karolek Zagórski, relative and dear friend,' he said,
pointing to the picture. 'This photograph kept me company faithfully
on all my wanderings; I always had it with me,' he said emotionally
and stopped short. 'It is terrible for me that he is gone,' he added
softly. 'All my life I kept hoping we would meet some day.' After my
father's death Konrad wrote to my mother: 'During the painful
moments the thought that a day would come when I would be able to
confess to him my whole life and to be understood – this thought was
for me the greatest consolation. And now this hope – the most precious of all – has vanished for ever.'[1]

Konrad's face reflected genuine grief. Looking at him one got the
impression that he had not got over the recent loss of a friend. And
yet a dozen or so years had passed since my father's death.

In the evening, as we were sitting by the fire, Konrad again spoke
of my father.

'Uncle Bobrowski was closest to me. And Karol came right after
him. Large-hearted and intelligent – and socially the nicest man.
Witty, gay et d'une élégance qui lui était particulière ... et quel
charme![2] Uncle Tadeusz respected him greatly. All sorts of things
come back to me from those rare moments spent with the family. I am

---

[1] French in the original; full text in *Conrad's Polish Background*, p. 224.
[2] 'With an elegance that was all his own – and what charm!'

happy to have you both – and your mother – most happy.' (In saying 'you both' Konrad meant my sister and myself.)

'Do you realize, my dear, that you are our first visitor from my family? Years ago Aunt Marguerite[1] came to stay here. I am very attached to our dear Marguerite, but blood ties are quite a different matter.'

Musing about the old times we sat long into the night, and so next morning I was late waking up. One of my favourite memories of England is that particular morning. The chirping of birds came in through the open windows. I was surprised by the great variety of sounds. 'There must be more birds in England than anywhere else in the world,' I thought to myself. Colourful gaiety, polyphonic rejoicings, flutter of wings, and the very air-space – everything felt as close as if it were inside oneself. The view from the window had a distinct charm. Despite the noise of birds, gentle serenity and lasting peace seemed to emanate from it.

Janek called out good morning from downstairs and I began to hurry so as not to lose a single moment of the day.

In the early evening Konrad and I took a stroll in the garden. Konrad seemed sad.

'Time goes by so quickly,' he said, 'you've only just arrived and soon you'll be leaving... I'd like to talk more of the old days. But the people who knew most about them were your grandparents and your father. Everything seems to be receding more and more into the past...'

'It's for the best, Konradek.' (The first evening at Capel House Konrad showed me a photograph from his childhood saying 'and here is Konradek Korzeniowski'. After that I usually addressed him as 'Konradek'.) 'The present and the future are better. The time is coming which earlier generations could only hope for.'

He nodded thoughtfully, but I, taken up with new impressions, again started to extol England.

Konrad slackened his pace till he stopped. He took me gently by the arm, and tilting his head looked straight into my eyes. His lips twitched. A few seconds passed before he asked, slowly in a voice charged with emotion:

'Will you forgive me that my sons don't speak Polish?'

Instinctively, as quickly as possible, not to leave those words hanging in suspense, I began saying that after all it happened in a most natural way as their mother was English and they all lived in England and that

[1] Marguerite Poradowska, née Gachet (1848–1937), French writer, widow of Aleksander Poradowski.

it was not too late as Janek was still a child and that both boys had plenty of time ahead to learn Polish. We resumed our stroll till we were called to dinner.

'I'm grateful to you for not holding it against me,' he added. There was something in his voice that was hard to describe. It was as if it came straight from the heart.

I am certain that I could never inadvertently distort Konrad's words. They lie in my memory, untouched, as they were first uttered with their full and precious weight.

Then came the year 1920. The end of the winter, the early spring, the long summer and the beginning of autumn – throughout all those months I saw Konrad constantly. Even if we did not talk I could always look at him and feel his presence. Today I find it difficult to believe: what happened to all the things I was going to hear from him, to the things I wanted to ask him about or learn?

At the beginning of February 1920 I arrived at the Conrads' for a longer visit. At that time they were living at Oswalds, near the old and beautiful city of Canterbury (in Kent).[1] I was saddened by the thought of not seeing the delightful Capel House again. Borys, who had safely returned from the war, met me at Folkestone. Konrad came out of the house as we drove up towards it. He had aged since I had last seen him and looked haggard. As we entered the hall a big dog with brown and white spots jumped at me in an unceremonious greeting. Pots of hyacinths and lilies of the valley stood on windowsills. A corridor ran straight across the house from the front door to the back door that led to the garden, and it was kept open for light and fresh air.

What a lot of things had happened and changed since my first stay in England! I looked around with excitement and curiosity. The house at Oswalds was large and arranged according to all modern require-ments. There were old trees in the garden, which was beautifully kept.

One huge tree, a kind of hornbeam, grew outside Konrad's window. He was very fond of it and sitting in his arm-chair, at the far end of the room, he could see all of it, as it stood at some distance from the house. When we were strolling in the garden he would sometimes turn round and remark, looking at it: 'This is my tree.'

The lawn, which came almost to the very walls of the sitting-room, was green although it was still winter. Later it was strewn with tulips. A bower overgrown with a climbing rose-tree stood opposite the door leading to the garden. When it was in bloom it looked like a huge nosegay made up of small bouquets. A box hedge grew close to the

[1] Conrad moved to Oswalds in Bishopsbourne, his last home, in October 1919.

house and gave a pleasant fragrance when warmed by the sun. I was particularly fond of a bench that stood nearby, and of the sitting-room itself, where I spent the nicest moments.

It was a lovely room. Every single piece of furniture in the house was picked by Konrad. There was beautifully proportioned blue and white Chippendale furniture, a few white and gold Empire pieces covered with yellow satin and a piano which had a pleasant tone. A painting of the Dutch school was hanging over the mantelpiece, oval mirrors in carved gilt frames hung on the far wall, there was a beautiful Aubusson on the floor – that would probably be everything, apart from white crystal vases with daffodils (masses of which grew in the garden) in the spring. Later came tulips and then roses.

Several books and albums lay on a mahogany table in the corner of the sitting-room. The same photographs that I had looked at, one after the other, with Konrad at Capel House, all of them yellowed by time.

'And this is my "little corner",' said Konrad as he led me towards that table soon after my arrival. There were several books by Prus, a time-worn volume of Słowacki, *Kazimierz Wielki*[1] by Wyspiański, bound in a folk-style woollen cover – and the album.

Now Konrad added two more volumes to the collection: *Wszystko i nic*[2] and *Wisła*[3] by Żeromski; the other books I had brought remained in his study. And again he took the album and again we sat down on the yellow sofa, leaning over the faded photographs as we had done several years earlier, and then we returned to the little table.

'This is my beloved Prus,' Konrad pointed at a volume of *Emancypantki*. 'I can read it over and over again.' When I laid my hand on *Kazimierz Wielki*, he said, 'Not this one, though.'

'Why not?'

'It weighs me down. It's hard to pick oneself up afterwards,' he added.

How I wish I could render the intonation, the atmosphere of all he said... The words are fixed for ever in my mind but I doubt if it is possible to pass them on as they really were.

My mother's photograph fell out from between the pages of Wyspiański's book. 'Whenever I am in my little corner I always look at this photograph,' said Konrad. 'It has caught a lot of your mother's expression. I often think of dear Aniela. Her enquiring mind and imagination were quite amazing. She was interested in everything. You could talk to her about the whole world. I felt quite at ease, for instance, discussing England with her: unbelievable how well informed

---

[1] A long poem (1900).   [2] 'Everything and Nothing' (1919), a sequel to *Popioły*.
[3] 'The Vistula' (1918), a long historical essay.

she was about social conditions, how much she knew about the culture
and mentality of people here. Where did she find the time to read so
much? An uncommonly cultivated mind. Grande dame et artiste, une
combinaison bien rare.[1] At the same time she had the ability to adapt
to the circumstances. Times were hard in Zakopane during the war. And
the general feeling of insecurity. Your mother took everything in her
stride with youthful spirit and hope. Une femme tout à fait extraordi-
naire.'[2]

I was moved by Konrad's words and I told him how happy his love
and respect for my parents made me.

'Si ça vous rend heureuse,'[3] he replied, 'I shall say once again how I
loved and respected them.'

'But you are even happier than I am,' I cried, 'because the lives of your
parents were truly great and beautiful. They gave all they could to their
country. As long as Poland exists every generation will cherish their
memory. Just think of it. . . '

Konrad glanced at me abruptly. A magnificent glow lit up his face.
But suddenly it was gone and before I realized Konrad had left the room.

It is strange to say but whenever his face, as I saw it that day, comes to
my mind, I hardly dare to think of it. There must have remained in me a
shade of obedience to Konrad's will made apparent by his turning round
and leaving me alone.

On one occasion we looked through reproductions of contemporary
painters: Mehoffer,[4] Wyspiański, Fałat,[5] Malczewski,[6] Chełmoński[7]
and others. Konrad gazed intently at each picture in turn, putting it
aside and picking it up several times. This lasted so long that I was quite
surprised. It occurred to me that perhaps he was looking at them
automatically while his thoughts were taken up with something else. He
was just contemplating Malczewski's *Chimera* – the one that leans over
the pensive boy lying in a meadow, against the background of a stormy
sky. 'It has everything,' he whispered to himself.

'What are you talking about?' I asked.

'I'm saying that it has everything,' he repeated with his eyes still fixed
on the picture.

'Tell me, please, tell me what you think of it. It's my favourite and I
should very much like to know.'

[1] 'A great lady and an artist – a very rare combination.'
[2] 'A quite extraordinary woman.'   [3] 'If that makes you happy.'
[4] Józef Mehoffer (1868–1946), specialized in stained glass.
[5] Julian Fałat (1853–1929), a leading water-colour painter.
[6] Jacek Malczewski (1854–1929), distinguished symbolist.
[7] Józef Chełmoński (1849–1914), landscape painter.

'This picture awakens longing and, by the same token, alleviates it,' Konrad said with his typical smile. 'Drôle de génie,'[1] he added, and resumed looking at the reproductions. Then he laid them out neatly on the table and sunk into his armchair. 'I'd like to be able to afford to buy every Polish painting,' he said, 'I find Polish paintings so attractive that I'd enjoy having them around me.'

In Konrad's 'little corner' in the living-room one more book appeared on his table: Witkiewicz's *Matejko*.[2] It had been sent by my sister for Janek and Konrad had put it there. One evening he took it to his room and began looking through it. I was sitting quietly in the corner of the sofa. For a long time he was turning over the pages. Suddenly he spoke up: 'What an amazing unity of expression there is in his works. Et quelle grandeur!'[3] Even when depicting tragic moments, he primarily sees their majesty.'

He got up and rang for the maid to call his younger son. Janek came in and perched on the arm of his father's chair. I stood behind them. Konrad kept turning the pages anxiously. Every now and then he would cast a glance at the boy and his eyes seemed unusually big and shining. I was amazed by that look. There was something impetuous in it. Obviously he kept choosing pictures he wanted to talk about. But over-long and rather obscure descriptions of historic events could not evoke any interest in the boy; I doubt if Janek understood anything. Words of apparent praise for the artist were mixed with some strange and fantastic interpretations of the paintings. But the sentences lacked coherence and were like bits of disconnected impressions.

Some confused and involuntary force of emotion seemed to be behind them, something that carried you away, riveted your attention and left you breathless. He paused at 'Zygmunt's Bell'.[4] He began to say something about the cathedral, about Wawel Castle,[5] and suddenly he lapsed into silence as if he could not say anything in spite of wanting and trying to. I could hardly understand his last words: they were like disjointed sounds. There was silence – something seemed to hover over us. Janek did not utter a word, he just looked at his father. Suddenly Konrad stood up.

'It is late. Time for bed,' he said briefly.

---

[1] 'An odd kind of genius.'
[2] Lwów, 1908. Stanisław Witkiewicz (1851–1915) was an influential art critic. Jan Matejko (1838–1893) was the most important Polish historical painter with a great influence on national imagination.
[3] 'And what grandeur!'
[4] *Zawieszenie Dzwonu Zygmunta* (1874). Zygmunt's Bell, which weighs eight tons, is the biggest and most famous of Wawel's bells, dating from 1520.
[5] A Royal castle in Cracow, built in the fourteenth to sixteenth century.

He moved towards the living-room. I thought he was taking back the book. But he turned round in the corridor and returned to his seat. In his usual way he laid his elbows on the arms of the chair and clasped his hands before him. He was calm again. I said goodnight. He gazed without seeing me. I left the room. I was straining my ears for his steps on the stairs but did not hear them, although it was late when I fell asleep. That night he must have remained a very long time in his study.

Once, talking about Żeromski, I asked Konrad whether he had read *Róża*.[1] He had not. So I ran to my room and brought down a copy. I laid it on the table so that he could read it when he pleased. He picked up the book, which opened by itself at the page where two photographs were stuck in: 'Schoolchildren plant the tree of freedom on the slopes of the Citadel, 3 May 1919.'[2] All one could see in the first photograph was a crowd of human heads surrounded by rows of soldiers; in the second, one could distinctly make out the small tree, thin and leafless, put into freshly dug earth. Marshal Piłsudski stood bare-headed in the foreground. When I went for the first time to Warsaw after it was liberated I got those photographs in a bookshop and later I stuck them into *Róża*, to face page 23 where the Deity tells Anzelm how on some great day, chosen by the people, on a day 'between spring and summer', a crowd will stream to the Citadel to worship the red rose that blossomed out on the graves of the insurgents and fighters as the symbol of their martyrdom and heroism.

Konrad moved towards the light, and having opened the book on the table, leaned over it on his elbows. He did not ask me any questions and without a word remained a long time in that position. And I was feeling so eager to talk to him and to listen to anything he might have to say! I had to keep silent. I waited a while, then went out. The door to the garden was open, so I decided to take a stroll. A mist was rising and soon it became difficult to see anything. I turned slowly towards the house. The blinds in Konrad's study were down; I knocked on the windowpane and straight away felt frightened by this impulse. I peered inside: Konrad was sitting just as I had left him, over the opened book. He lifted his eyes and looked calmly in my direction. Having noticed me he continued looking, lost in thought. Then he smiled – not at me but at something in the distance.

We often talked of the war that had just ended and occasionally of the new Poland. I was surprised how well Konrad was informed on the

[1] 'A Rose' (1909), poetic drama about the 1905 revolution in Poland.
[2] On the anniversary of the Polish 1791 Constitution.

Polish situation. From time to time he used to get from Poland news-papers representing various outlooks but I did not get the impression that he read them at all thoroughly.

'It seems to me that it would be too much to expect things at home to run smoothly,' he said once. 'The most important thing is to have at last some peace on the frontiers. That is what I am anxious about.'

News began coming in of a quick retreat of the Polish army from Kiev.[1] Some newspapers published lengthy articles criticizing the commander-in-chief. I had just finished reading one of them in Konrad's study when he started looking through it carefully.

'Please, leave it here. I want to read it once again,' he asked as I was leaving the room with the newspaper.

We never had any discussion specifically about Józef Piłsudski or the part played by the Legions in the rebirth of the Polish state. Konrad was in Zakopane when the war broke out and saw everything himself; but then he did not sense the approaching liberation, he was full of doubts and misgivings.

Not a word passed between us about the news from Poland. I was not inclined to talk about it and Konrad must have felt the same way. Once, as we were leaving the dining-room, he stopped in the hall and looked at a coloured woodcut by Jastrzębowski,[2] representing Piłsudski on horseback. As we sat down in the study Konrad said, turning over the pages of some paper or other. 'He was the only great man to emerge on the scene during the war.' After a while he added, 'In some aspects he is not unlike Napoleon, but as a type of man he is superior. Because Napoleon, his genius apart, was like all other people and Piłsudski is different.'

This was just a passing remark, but it sounded like a statement closing, as it were, a question that had been thought over and settled in his mind a long time before. I have often regretted not having asked him there and then what his conception of Piłsudski was; not having asked him to specify in what, according to him, lay this 'difference' between the marshal and all other people.

One day it was exceptionally cold and after breakfast Konrad announced, 'I am so cold that even my brain feels frozen. I am afraid I shall not be able to work at all today.'

I asked if in that case I could read in his study; having received his consent I settled down on a cushion on the floor – facing Konrad, who

[1] Polish troops and their Ukrainian allies captured Kiev from Bolshevik forces on 8 May 1920, but had to leave the city on 10 June.
[2] Wojciech Jastrzębowski (1885–1960), painter and designer.

occupied his usual arm-chair near the fire. He asked me about various things from the past, so instead of reading I chattered away about our childhood, school years, hobbies, friendships, music, books. My sister and I were tutored at home and, ever since I remember, we played the piano; Anielusia was a voracious reader and she knew a great deal –but not I. I started getting interested in books much later and liked only a few. 'All in all I was not at all bright,' I ended my story.

Konrad was greatly amused and laughed aloud.

'Could you tell me what particular book attracted you at such an advanced age?' he asked and then a long and delightful conversation ensued which one day I might try to describe in detail.

After this gay and lively conversation, Konrad relaxed, listening to the crackling of the fire. And then from time to time he asked questions which I answered with pleasure, glad to see him interested in what was close to me. Affected by the memories of the past I drew nearer to Konrad and, leaning against his knees, I told him something I had often thought about and that suddenly came to my mind – the atmosphere I was brought up in.

'You see, Konradek, it may seem strange to you but I did not grow up in the gloom of captivity. People who were close to me would always give me a feeling of freedom. And in spite of everything that was happening I felt free. I understood this fully when we got independence. When one has an inner feeling of freedom and a strong conviction that in the end justice will prevail then one can bear things that seem unbearable. After all everything depends only on our inner attitude towards life.'

And then I added, 'But a great many did not want to wait. Their belief in freedom was a creative force – so they fought and perished. And about the majority of them no one will ever hear anything.'

Suddenly I became frightened. Konrad pushed me aside, stood up, moved the chair away noisely, walked to his desk and began looking through a pile of papers. Then he turned round and glared straight at my face, looking positively forbidding. His lips twitched as I had seen only once before. It seemed he was about to flare up but gradually his face became calm and serious. He turned away completely composed.

'Pardonnez-moi,' he said abruptly.

That year the late spring was quite warm and in the early evenings we often sat in the garden, on the lawn, in comfortable chairs, chatting or in silence.

One afternoon Konrad asked me again about the Ukraine, about the destroyed manor houses I used to know. Then we spoke about Poland.

'Tell me a little about life in the Polish countryside,' he asked.

'With pleasure. Do you remember Ukrainian homes from your childhood days?'

'I think not. But I can remember certain moments perfectly. I see them like pictures but on the whole rather hazily. And all this is lost to us for ever. But in Poland, thank God, something has remained and maybe some day I shall see it.'

'Of course you will see it, more than once. We might go there together... But meanwhile what shall I tell you? About the typical Polish countryside or about some particular place I know well?'

'Just as you like.'

'Then I shall tell you about Sulmów[1] where I spent most of my childhood; it is the corner of Poland I know best.'

So I told him about the landscape, the village, the local people and then about the house; it was not an ordinary country house but a kind of one-storeyed manor with a red tiled roof. The walls were covered with climbing pear-trees that reached as far as the first floor windows of the large living-room with gilt mirrors (one of them later mysteriously cracked). Next door was a small living-room with large doors and a balcony; further along was a room with green checked walls and a cheerful-looking portrait of a fair-haired great-grandmother; then a blue room with pastel portraits of lovely young people with fresh complexions. The windows in the downstairs hall had coloured panes, there was a stone floor and a wide flight of stairs – once I tumbled down from the very top. Flat stone steps led down from the porch; the drive in front of the house was big enough for a coach and four to turn round. Close by was the pond – the largest, for there were as many as three in the Sulmów park. Golden willows grew on the side banks and two sumac-trees in front.

'And do you know what a sumac-tree looks like when covered with dew or rain-drops?' I interrupted my story.

'Unfortunately no, and now I regret not having ever seen it,' he smiled playfully. 'Well, go on...'

'Lilies and roses were planted at intervals round the pond. We used to call the park beyond the pond *zawoda* [beyond the water]; peacocks liked to spend the night on the big willow-tree.'

I was overcome by the desire to go on recalling my life at Sulmów and I asked Konrad whether he had not heard enough about it.

'If you want to give me pleasure, please, go on,' he said. 'Weren't you afraid of getting lost in that park with three ponds? Or of drowning?' – he was pulling my leg again.

[1] Hamlet and estate of the Unrugs, near Kalisz, in central Poland.

'I was not at all afraid and I ran everywhere alone.'

'So peacocks slept in the old willow...,' Konrad picked up the thread of the story.

'Ah yes, that reminds me of something I must tell you; but listen carefully because it is going to be something very important, something about real happiness in childhood. It was like this: as many as six peacocks wandered about the garden, occasionally losing their feathers. Stasia, the blacksmith's daughter, found one in the very centre of the gateway. I too was possessed by the desire to find a lost feather. Day after day I would spend long hours looking for one, but in vain. And my desire was growing steadily. I used to walk with my head bent down, staring at the ground. I used to fall asleep and wake up dreaming about it – and still nothing happened. No sign of a feather. One day I ventured for pleasure into the high grass. It was in the apiary and the grass had not been cut for a long time. I was not even afraid of the bees, for the feeling of being able to hide in the grass made me happy. I had not gone far before I saw, right in front of me, an enormous peacock feather sticking upright as if it were growing out of the ground. I was quite stunned for a while and then I began shouting "I've got it, I've got it!" I was so happy...'

'And so you found it at last,' said Konrad tenderly. 'I shall call this "The Story of Karoleczka's Happiness" – do you mind?'

'Of course I don't. But now you must admit that if one patiently looks for something and wants it badly, one can occasionally find it, even if one is not actually searching for it at the time. Don't you agree?'

'Maybe. But few people look patiently and with unfading hope, even for their own happiness. That requires a small girl, the Sulmów park, the charm of a peacock feather, unknown grass where things easily get lost and are difficult to find. When you've got it – you've got a fairy-tale.'

'Yes. And this one is a happy tale,' I said after a while, 'but not all are like that. Some are sad and unhappy. I remember two such tales because I liked them most of all.'

'A fairy-tale about unhappiness,' repeated Konrad with an enigmatic smile, 'obviously the charm of sadness may sometimes be greater than the charm of happiness. But perhaps it is so only in fairy-tales and not in life? Sensitive children cry over them and yet are always willing to return to them. Don't you agree, my little girl? Mais qui sait ... le charme d'une fable triste est peut-être plus poignant et ne s'envole pas aussi vite.[1] And I hope you will be telling me about Sulmów from

---

[1] 'But who knows? ... the charm of a sad story is perhaps more piercing and doesn't fade so quickly.'

time to time. Now that I know what it was like there, I shall be glad to
visit it in your company.'

But there was no further chance to talk about Sulmów. Alarming news
kept coming from Poland. The Russian offensive was gaining strength.
I was filled with anxiety – waiting for the newspapers to be delivered.
There was no one to share my worries with, for I could not speak to
Konrad. Suddenly we stopped talking of Poland and in general we
spoke very little to each other. In that atmosphere of silence something
began to weigh heavily upon us. Being left alone became quite unbearable. And yet it was a time when I wanted so much to talk and talk to
him. But there was nothing I could do. And Konrad withdrew into
himself completely. It seemed as if he knew nothing of what was going
on in Poland. If in the course of general conversation someone
broached that subject, Konrad ignored it completely. Each day was
harder for me. I wondered whether he read any newspapers at all. And
once again I was under the impression that he did not even open them.
I used to find them in the room, in their usual place, apparently
untouched.

One day, during lunch, I said casually that I wanted to leave 'so as
not to be cut off from Poland in case something happens'. I did not
believe in the possibility of being cut off but said it on purpose. Konrad
did not react. I was not even sure if he had heard what I had said.

I spent the afternoon in the garden as usual. Konrad came and sat
down near me. He looked at me in silence with deep concentration and
enormous kindness. Finally he spoke as if with difficulty.

'I should like to keep you here for ever. But you will be better off over
there whatever happens.'

'Nothing is going to happen,' I cried out, 'only I would rather be
home now. Nothing is going to happen,' I repeated.

'Quite a lot has happened already,' he said sadly in a soft voice. 'And
where will people over there get the strength to bear it all, je me
demande...[1] You are not afraid; I am, though... But I cannot speak
about it. I cannot and do not want even to think about it. You feel like a
fish out of the water here. I too sometimes get the impression of not
being able to breathe. Let us not talk about it.'

And so we did not talk. But I stopped feeling lonely. Only the
sadness remained. Just as Konrad wished, we never returned to the
subject. Occasionally our eyes met and then we looked aside. I wanted
to get away from England and yet it was hard for me to leave; I wanted
to stay longer with Konrad.

[1] 'I wonder.'

A few days before my departure, in the early evening, I was sitting in my usual place in the garden when Konrad approached. He took the other chair and we just sat there for a long while. Looking at the sky, the trees, the countryside, I wondered if and when I should return there. For some reason I felt less worried that day than usual, but the thought of leaving made me unhappy and I did not know how to tell Konrad about it. I made some remark about the lilac hue in the air. Konrad did not react. He stroked my hair and his touch was as light as if I had some ingenious hair-style that he was afraid to disturb. I felt a surge of warm happiness and wanted to laugh. But then some strong emotion overcame me and I clasped his hand between mine.

A gentle dusk was falling. The air, really lilac, began to thicken and change into mist, which in turn darkened into violet. In that heavy colourful dusk that surrounded us, the dreamy words spoken to me next seemed to come from a great distance, they sounded so unreal. 'In Sulmów lilies and roses grow round the pond...'

I was to leave soon and I had not yet accomplished a task which I ought to have fulfilled on arrival. I had brought with me an old book, *Domowa zagroda*,[1] an outline of Polish history, by Aleksander Starża, published in Warsaw in the sixties. The first page carried a yellowed inscription: 'To Karolek Zagórski from Ewelina and Apollo Korzeniowski. May God let him love nothing but what is his own and his native land's.'

My parents' library, deposited with our relative in the country, was destroyed during the Bolshevik invasion. A dozen or so books which I had happened to take away earlier were saved. Among them was this book from my father's childhood years; I had brought it over for Konrad, but until now had not given it to him.

When I was first unpacking my trunk full of books I held this volume in my hand, but I put it aside; I wanted to give it to Konrad on some special occasion – not together with other books. More than once I had gone upstairs for it and returned without it. And so it lay in my room, day after day, until my departure. I picked it up, thinking, 'I am going to show it to him today... it is the last chance...' I entered the living-room. Konrad used to go in there sometimes when I sat there reading. I thought to myself: 'If he comes in I shall give it to him.' The afternoon went by but he did not appear; I was disappointed. 'I had better choose the simplest way,' I was telling myself, 'I shall go into his study and leave it there on the table where he is bound to find it.' The idea of

---

[1] Warsaw, 1847. Aleksander Starża was the pseudonym of Józef Aleksander Miniszewski (1823–63), journalist and novelist.

going up to him and announcing in a casual way, 'Look what I've got for you' did not appeal to me. So I went to the study as I could hear Konrad talking with Borys there. I sat down and waited, turning over the pages of the book. I could just leave it on the table but no . . . better do it a bit later so as not to attract too much attention. I did not want him to pick up and open it immediately. I sat there feeling strangely nervous. Borys had left the room and I was still holding the book. He is sure to ask me in a minute what I am looking at, and then. . .

Konrad asked, 'What book have you got there, Karolka?'

A few seconds passed before I answered.

'Oh, it is some old book, nothing special. . . I am trying to read but I can't. All my thoughts are preoccupied with departure. I am so sorry to be leaving.'

I quickly managed to divert Konrad's thoughts towards my departure and how sad it was making me. We went on talking. Then lunch was served; we stood up, I hesitated. . . I was standing next to Konrad, pressing the book to my side with one hand, and taking him by the arm with the other.

'Have you something to tell me?' he asked.

'No,' I answered with an effort.

At night, before going to bed, I decided to leave the book in his 'little corner'. I went to the living-room and put it there. But before I fell asleep I jumped out of bed, ran softly downstairs and took it back. Then I knew that I was not going to show it to him. I tried, but could not do it.

On the day I left Oswalds the morning newspapers brought news slightly different from the day before. Obviously it was before the press agencies received information as to the day and hour when Warsaw was going to be taken by the Russian hordes. A delay of a couple of days was expected. No one at that time knew anything about what was going on there. Nevertheless, during our last breakfast together Konrad and I greeted each other almost merrily. Obviously we must have had some good premonitions. Konrad, for the first time in my presence, glanced at the first page of the newspaper and observed, as if casually, 'So they have decided to postpone the taking of Warsaw for the time being.'

His words were slightly tinged with scorn.

A few days later, in Piccadilly Circus in London, I happened to see with my own eyes huge, coloured posters moving slowly and with dignity along the middle of the street. The red letters on those paper banners automatically caught everyone's eye.

'Piłsudski crushes the enemy.'[1]

Looking very serious, brightly dressed boys carried those huge signs in front of them along the main streets, announcing the important news to the civilized world.

I got hold of one such announcement and managed to send it off to Konrad on the day of my departure. I could visualize how he would open the package, spread the poster all over the table, and how the large letters would jump out at him: 'Piłsudski crushes the enemy.'

'Recollections of Conrad', by Karola Zagórska

'Ze wspomnień o Conradzie', *Twórczość* (Warsaw) 1969, no. 8

The room I liked best at Oswalds was Konrad's study. You entered it from the hall to the right. It was a spacious room with light walls and two large windows. One of them faced the drive. 'From here I can watch out for nice guests,' Konrad said; the other one looked out on the prettiest part of the garden, where Konrad could see 'his' tree. The largest wall in the room was covered with bookshelves – from floor to ceiling – and in addition flat bookcases full of books stood here and there. Between the windows, Konrad's secretary sat at the desk and took dictation from him. Konrad had given up writing himself many years ago and begun to dictate when gout impaired the use of his right hand. He told me once that even if he had no pain in his arm he would find it difficult to resume writing because 'it stops the flow of thought'.

In the middle of the room, closer to the fireplace, there was a large round table and next to it an arm-chair with a loose light-coloured cretonne cover. It was Konrad's usual place for dictating, correcting manuscripts, sitting with his family or friends. That arm-chair was a name-day gift from his elder son while a small boy. 'It was Borys's own idea to buy me a comfortable arm-chair – and he chose it himself,' Konrad repeated several times, always obviously moved. Opposite the arm-chair stood a small, cosy couch also covered with light cretonne. I used to spend hours sitting on it and talking with Konrad and it is with great affection that I think of it now.

On top of a bookcase behind the armchair there were various photographs. There was Borys in uniform, and several friends of Konrad's, among them Cunninghame Graham, Galsworthy and Edward Garnett. When I was in Konrad's study I often used to look at the photograph of Graham on horseback, taken in South America. It had

---

[1] English in the original. The Polish offensive, begun on 15 August, decisively repelled the Bolshevik advance.

a certain charm: it brought visions of unending open spaces of pampas; the rider and his horse stood immersed in grass as if in green water. My admiration for the person of Don Roberto – obviously not just for his photograph – was a source of pleasure to Konrad. 'Don Roberto' was the name by which he referred to Graham at home and among friends. He valued Graham's gift for writing highly and regarded him as a true friend. In addition he appreciated the beauty of this uncommon and colourful personality.

'Doesn't he look wonderful in that chair!' I exclaimed once to Konrad, pointing at Graham; 'all he needs is a ruff à la Velasquez.'

'My dear,' Konrad answered, 'Don Roberto is a descendant of the Stuarts.'[1]

Photographs of Konrad's wife and his uncle–guardian Tadeusz Bobrowski stood on the mantelpiece. And above it hung a valuable print of the port of Marseilles in the seventeenth century. On the wall opposite the door a coloured woodcut by Jastrzębowski depicted Marshal Piłsudski on horseback.

A cane – a gift from Jean-Aubry – stood beside the fireplace. Konrad always kept it near him and used it whenever he suffered from gout.

The fire was always lit even during summer. Konrad used to like to take coal out of a pretty brass scuttle and throw it on to the fire himself. I have a particularly clear recollection of it. One evening we talked till late at night. It became quite cold. Konrad did not let me help him: with his characteristic sudden and quick movement he took the bucket from me, saying, 'I am very fond of keeping the fire going. But it happens sometimes when I am sitting here all alone at night that I forget all about it. Feeling stiff and angry, I quickly add some coal, convinced that it is too late anyway – and I go on sitting here and feeling as if there was no warmth left in the entire world. And then suddenly and unexpectedly a flame erupts. Some tiny spark has stayed for my benefit... I like it when my fireplace takes me by surprise.'

In Konrad's room, cosy, light and warm, there were no superfluous objects and hardly any ornaments. The drawing-room, on the other hand, looked quite impressive.

It was a lovely room. White-and-blue Chippendale furniture, white-and-gold Empire-style pieces covered with yellow satin. Near the door leading to the garden a piano stood as if waiting to be played. Above the fireplace an old painting of the Dutch school; on each side of the large window oval mirrors in carved, gilt frames

[1] Graham was a direct descendant of Robert II (1316–90), king of Scotland after 1371.

reflected the ceiling, furniture and an Aubusson carpet on the floor. There was an old desk and crystal vases full of narcissus in the spring, then tulips and later roses.

One of Konrad's friends announced the arrival of a well-known American pianist and composer (John Powell), who had expressed a wish to play Chopin for Konrad. The idea appealed very much to Konrad and to all the members of his household and so we looked forward to the arrival of the guests one Saturday.[1] They came to lunch. Right from the beginning the atmosphere was pleasant and relaxed, as the American pianist had an easy manner and the conversation at table was lively. After coffee in the living-room, we went for a walk – and when we returned the concert began.

Tea was served in Jessie's room. Konrad's wife was extremely fond of music, so at first the conversation revolved around this subject; later we spoke about everything, including politics. The visitor mentioned the problem of the independence of Ireland and showed a great interest in the affair of Casement, who had been sentenced to death. Konrad listened for a considerable time to what the artist had to say, but I could see that his hands began to twitch – an obvious sign of irritation. Suddenly he moved restlessly in his chair and glanced sharply at the visitor.

'Well, Sir,' he said emphatically, 'Casement did not hesitate to accept honours, decorations and distinctions from the English Government while surreptitiously arranging various affairs that he was embroiled in. In short: he was plotting against those who trusted him.[2] Some people may call such a person a hero. It would not be so in our country – and Poles have a greater right to pass judgement in these matters. In our country people who plotted against the oppressors would have nothing to do with the tzarist court, nor would they seek any advantage through Russian privileges. Their lives ran along one line. Was it not so?' He turned abruptly towards me.

In spite of Konrad's tone and words I had the impression that the visitor did not understand Konrad's point and felt confused. Jessie with her customary tact quickly switched the conversation to a different subject and everything went off smoothly, only Konrad remained silent. The visitor had to leave for the station immediately after tea, so we all went downstairs to see him off. Konrad was exceedingly polite, saying farewell to the artist and thanking him for the concert, but

---

[1] On 3 July 1920.

[2] Cunninghame Graham expressed a similar opinion. See his letter to H. W. Nevinson of 27 November 1928, in Eloise Knapp Hay and Cedric Watts, 'To Conrad from Cunninghame Graham', *Conradiana* 5 (1973), no. 2, pp. 16–17.

anyone who knew him at all well could see that he was not quite himself.

I spent the evening with Jessie. It was late when Konrad looked in on us. He walked to the fireplace, took down his mother's photograph from the mantelpiece and contemplated it intently.

'Have you noticed how this photograph gets more and more faded?' he asked his wife. 'I am afraid it will soon fade away completely.'

'This room is very bright and old photographs dislike light. We'll have to have a copy made,' answered Jessie.

'Yes. But it will never be the same photograph. This one used to belong to my father,' said Konrad. He walked about the room turning the lights off one by one; then he went out of the dark room and returned with a burning candle. He approached the fireplace, bringing the light close to the photograph where the delicate oval of the face was barely outlined. Only from under her dark eyebrows the unextinguished eyes of Konrad's younger son looked at us.

'What a lovely face,' I said, standing right behind Konrad. He moved the candle and a gentle, warm glow slid over the picture, making it seem more charming and almost alive.

'I should like it to last with me till the end, till my end,' Konrad said slowly in Polish and blew out the candle.

Jessie turned on the bed-side lamp. I slipped out of the room and turning round at the door said 'Good-night'.[1] '*Dobranoc*,' replied Konrad.

Conrad to the Polish Minister, 20 February 1920

Archiwum Akt Nowych, Warsaw, sygn. 1041

His Excellency
The Polish Minister,[2]
London

Oswalds, Bishopsbourne,
Kent.
Feb. 20th, 1920

Sir,

I have long been aware of the state of ignorance of Western Europe as to the character, history, ideals and the very nature of the Polish Nation. I recognise fully the importance of the Association[3] proposed

---

[1] English in the original.

[2] Eustachy Kajetan Sapieha (1881–1963), the first Polish envoy to the United Kingdom, later (1920–1) minister for foreign affairs. The original letter is in English.

[3] Towarzystwo Anglo-Polskie (Anglo-Polish Society), formed in Warsaw in November 1919.

in your Excellency's letter. It is with the greatest regret then that I feel myself compelled to state plainly that I am not the right sort of person to take the initiative in that matter. To set going and bring to a successful issue the organisation of such a Society is a task for a man of social connections, acquainted with influential people, and known personally to the wider world.

This is not the case with me. I have led a retired life. I have formed no social relations. My circle of intimates contains not a single influential personality either in the literary world or any other; and even with those my intercourse is made difficult and irregular by the unsatisfactory state of my health. The question of physical fitness has its importance. I am ill now. It is the reason why I am dictating this letter in English. I have been ill for nearly two months and it is impossible to say how long it will be before I am fit to come up to town. This sort of thing happens to me every year and often more than once a year.

There is another consideration which I must submit to your Excellency. I left Poland in the year 1874. My last visit (to the most distant part of Ukraine) was in 1892.[1] Since that time owing to the death of my uncle I have not even had any letters that would have kept me in touch with the inner life of Poland, its problems and its perplexities. My accidental presence with my family in Cracow and Zakopane during the months of August and September, 1914, gave me really no further insight. In the general trouble of minds and consciences caused by the events which made the future of all mankind dark, it was impossible for me to learn much, and even to think connectedly, of the special problem of Poland.[2] As to the actual events of the last three years I am absolutely in the dark, not so much perhaps as to facts themselves but as to their profounder significance. The plain truth is that I am not qualified to take the part your Excellency suggests, in an important undertaking which *must not* be exposed to the slightest chance of failure.

It remains for me only to apologise for the length of this letter. If I have enlarged to this extent in answer to your Excellency's communication it is only out of my deferential regard for the Representative of the Polish State.

I am, Sir, your most obedient servant

Joseph Conrad

[1] Actually August and September 1893, and to the centre of the Ukraine.
[2] But compare his political memorandum of 1914, in *Conrad's Polish Background*, pp. 303–4.

Conrad to the Polish Legation in London[1]
Archiwum Akt Nowych, Warsaw, sygn. 1041

Oswalds, Bishopsbourne, Kent
July 28th, 1920

Mr Joseph Conrad presents his compliments and hopes this communication will be passed on to the Legal Councillor of the Polish Legation, or the favour may be done to him of advising him how to proceed in the matter in which he seeks advice, on the ground that the act he contemplates would benefit two ladies of Polish nationality at present domiciled in Warsaw. Mr Joseph Conrad is desirous of conveying the complete ownership of the copyright of all his works for translation and publication in the territories of the Republic of Poland (and eventually in all the territories which composed the late Empire of Russia) to Miss Angela Zagórska, for the joint benefit of herself and her sister, Carola Zagórska, absolutely, and for as long as his rights of copyrights endure under the laws of the Republic of Poland; the above gift being made in consideration of his affection for the aforesaid ladies and of the bond of relationship existing between them and himself.

Mr Joseph Conrad wishes to execute this deed in the strictest form of legal conveyance so as to make it absolutely valid in the courts of the Polish Republic and establish the right of the above persons beyond any question.

Mr Joseph Conrad offers his apologies and begs to offer his thanks in anticipation for the Legation's assistance in this matter.

Conrad to the Polish Legation in London[2]
Archiwum Akt Nowych, Warsaw, sygn. 1041

Oswalds, Bishopsbourne, Kent
1 Aug[ust] 1920

Mr Joseph Conrad begs to present his warm thanks to the Polish Chargé d'Affaires for his ready response to Mr Conrad's request.

---

[1] The original letter is in English.   [2] The original letter is in English.

Conrad to the Polish Legation in London[1]

Archiwum Akt Nowych, Warsaw, sygn. 1041

Oswalds, Bishopsbourne, Kent
22 Sept[ember] 1920

Mr Joseph Conrad presents his compliments and thanks to the Chargé d'Affaires of Poland.

Mr Conrad while awaiting the reply from Poland has instructed his solicitor to prepare a formal Deed of Gift according to English procedure. This document together with a translation into Polish language, which perhaps the Legation will consent to certify as in all points correct, he intends to send to Miss Angela Zagórska.[2] With this legal expression of Mr Conrad's will and act Miss Zagórska could address herself to an advocate who would know what steps to take to make the instrument valid in Polish Courts – or should that be legally impossible, would prepare a corresponding deed in accordance with Polish procedure which he could send over here for Mr Conrad's signature to be witnessed and legalised at the Polish Legation in London.

This course will have the advantage of making Miss Zagórska's rights secure as before any English Court. This may be of some importance as Mr Conrad's testamentary dispositions direct the sale of his copyrights outright on the best condition obtainable 20 years after his death.

Mr Joseph Conrad wishes to convey his deep sense of the attention given by the Legation of the Republic to his request and begs the Polish Chargé d'Affaires to accept the assurance of his highest regard.

---

[1] The original letter is in English.
[2] Conrad sent it to Zagórska with his letter of 19 January 1921; see *Conrad's Polish Background*, p. 265.

Conrad to Karola Zagórska
Biblioteka Narodowa, Warsaw, MS 2889

Oswalds
Bishopsbourne,
Kent
[March 1923]

My dear Karolka,
  Ci-inclus[1] chéque for 952,50 lire for April.
  I am unbelievably tired. I have had a lot of work this month and
there is still some to be done before I go to the United States. I am
sailing there with my old friend, Captain Bone, on the *Tuscania*, returning probably by the same boat about 10 June.[2]
  To tell the truth the journey does not appeal to me. But it has to be.
Everybody tells me that it will be very advantageous for my business
affairs. So it is a kind of duty envers ma petite famille.[3]
  Poor Jessie is again troubled by her knee. How long her cheerfulness
will stand up to it, I really do not know. She asks me to give you her
love. So does Jan. He has just gone outside and I can see him through
the window running in the garden with our little dog. It is the son of the
old Hadji and rather like his daddy. Hadji has aged a lot and can only
walk in a dignified manner. So do I, as a matter of fact. My health is
fair. America will put it to the test. There is one thing I like the
Americans for: they are friendly towards Poland. I have friends over
there whom I have never even seen. I wonder how they look. I know in
advance what they will be saying.
  We have not seen Borys since Christmas. He is working, is in good
form and doing quite well as far as I can make out.
  We shall be here until September.[4] Then – all depends on God's
will. Probably 3–4 months in London and in the winter somewhere in
southern France. After that I do not know and it is not really worth
thinking about.
  You will hear once again from me, from England – in April. Then
Jessie will be writing.
  I embrace you a hundredfold

Always yours

Konrad

---

[1] 'Herewith.' Conrad was sending Karola Zagórska, at that time in Italy, a monthly
  allowance.
[2] Conrad sailed on the *Tuscania* from Liverpool on 21 April and returned on the *Majestic*
  to Southampton on 9 June.
[3] 'Towards my little family.'   [4] In the end, the Conrads did not leave Oswalds.

Have you seen Żeromski's marvellous preface to *Almayer*?[1] Only why does he insist on talking about my 'steamers?' The whole world knows that I served in sailing ships. I am even the last one to have done it. Le dernier des Mohicans.[2]

From 'Back to Conrad', by Hanna Peretiatkowicz

'Powrót do Conrada', *Wiadomości* (London), 1949, no. 11

I am trying to recall, sentence by sentence, the atmosphere and all the nuances of that fascinating conversation; I am trying to call up a mental image of Conrad's profile as he leaned forward, as if listening intently, and the expression of his swarthy, nervous face. I am trying to reconstruct all the circumstances of my visit to Oswalds many years ago.

Was I fully aware at the time of the true meaning of this visit? I remember feeling overwhelmed by Conrad's 'borderland' type of hospitality. It was a beautiful July day, full of sunshine and the scent of flowers, as we strolled on the lawns at Oswalds; I remember the intoxicating smell of hay drying in the sun, arranged in cone-shaped stooks just like at home; I eagerly answered all the questions my host asked me in his old and somewhat muffled voice.

We spoke Polish. It never occurred to me that it could have been otherwise, although I remember Conrad frequently using French words. What was his Polish like? I do not know. It seemed good. It never even crossed my mind to analyse his spoken Polish.

All his questions concerned Poland, but his interest was not confined solely to literature, art, politics or the economic problems of the country.

He wondered also about the prosaic aspects of our everyday life. For example: what was the price of flats in Warsaw? Was it easy to find a good maid? Was life in the suburbs cheaper than in the centre of the town? What was life in Cracow like? And what about life in the country?
. . .

I was not in the least surprised at the things that interested the English writer. After all he was my countryman. Not until much later did I come to realize that at the time I had not taken into account the pomp of the English standard of life, nor the different character of the environment. He lived there, because he had to.

Did he want to? – only he could have known the answer.

---

[1] More precisely to the first volume of Conrad's selected works in Polish, *Fantazja Almayera* (Warsaw, 1923).
[2] 'The last of the Mohicans.'

I must admit that in my state of acute alertness I was surprised repeatedly by strange and sudden pauses in our conversation. It seemed to move swiftly without a shade of constraint or awkwardness. I felt encouraged by the frequent smiles that brightened Conrad's swarthy face, like flashes of sunlight. Then a sudden pause; the silence dragged; Conrad seemed to fade, to sink into himself.

My confidence began to vanish. Perhaps I was talking too much, perhaps I was being too forthright?

But Conrad quickly came to my rescue. Again he smiled. His hospitality towards his guest, an uninvited guest at that, became more pronounced. He repeated the same or similar questions which I thought I had already answered.

Perhaps he did not hear me the first time?

Now and then I got the impression that he was far away from our time and place.

. . .

Did I know at the time of my visit to Oswalds that in the last years of his life Conrad was contemplating 'leaving everything' and returning to Poland?

No, I did not know anything about it. He never spoke of it to me. It was only after his death that his closest friends (like John Galsworthy) mentioned the project, and his wife wrote about it in her memoirs.[1]

I was familiar with the atmosphere in the homes of the 'borderland' people, most of them tucked away in the suburbs of Warsaw, and their inhabitants perpetuated the tradition of lordly largesse and generous hospitality that by far exceeded the meagre clerical incomes of the former bigwigs from Bielo-Russia or the Kiev district. Old habits were discarded unwillingly.

For example, visitors, even if coming from another part of the city, would not leave after a mere few hours – they would stay overnight, chatting and eating almost until dawn. I have just read in Jessie Conrad's memoirs how her foreign husband refused to reconcile himself to short conversations with his friends and how he liked to keep them by the fire well into the night, when the entire household was fast asleep. Conrad must have felt in his element then. And as to Jessie, she had to have a large tray of cold snacks ready beforehand.

The only difference with us was that instead of cold snacks we would serve hot borscht and meat pies straight out of the oven.

[1] In *Joseph Conrad and his Circle* (Jarrolds, London, 1935), p. 263.

... Conrad was silent.

Perhaps he was not listening.

But then I happened to mention such names as Berdyczów, Włodzimierz Wołyński, Żytomierz, and the names of some villages well known
to me from our holiday expeditions from Kiev – names probably rarely
recalled by Conrad himself and quite unknown to his immediate circle.
Conrad suddenly livened up and asked one question after another. He
seemed moved.

Our pace quickened as we strolled from one path to another.

And all of a sudden it seemed to me that I had aged and Conrad had
become younger; that the gap between the famous English writer and
an unknown Polish girl from the distant borderland country had nar-
rowed, as if filled up by those brief moments of shared emotion. We
recalled places and times that had passed for ever.

...

I went to England for the first time in the summer of 1923. I was the
only Polish passenger on an English boat and my favourite 'companions' on the journey were *The Nigger of the 'Narcissus'* and Almayer
absorbed by his 'folly'.

Soon I found myself in Kent, in the idyllic Garden of England.

My relatives lived in Hythe, an old fishing village perched on a steep
cliff overlooking the Channel. And suddenly a revelation: Bishopsbourne and 'Oswalds' were barely thirty miles from Hythe! The idea of
my visiting Conrad in England seemed far-fetched when conceived in
Warsaw, but now it began to look feasible.

A fairly large parcel which I had brought from Poland kept getting in
my way: it contained a selection of the most recent volumes of poetry
and a dozen or so copies of a monthly literary magazine, *Skamander*.[1]

But what about all the stories told of Conrad's 'splendid isolation'
and of his dislike of intruders ... and what if the intruder was from
Poland? Yes, Poland was the key word. In it lay my entire hope of
success as well as the possibility of failure.

Finally I summoned up my courage and wrote to Oswalds a short letter
in Polish. Next day brought a reply in English.

'Dear Madam, Mr Conrad thanks you for your letter, and suggests
that you should come to Bishopsbourne...'; then followed a time-table
of trains and detailed instructions of how to get to the house. The
invitation to tea was signed by Lillian Hallowes, Conrad's secretary.

The die was cast.

[1] Published in Warsaw, 1920–39.

However, instead of going by train I decided to travel by car. I launched an attack on my English brother-in-law, a perfect gentleman, to persuade him to take me there, but he could not understand why I should want to see an English writer and why I should force myself to pay this awkward visit. But as I insisted, he was prepared to drive me there, on condition that he went only as a chauffeur. Anyway, he was not invited. While I was being bored stiff on my formal visit, he could take a walk by the stream, where apparently there were trout at this time of the year. So he could relax for a couple of hours in the open, with a fishing rod. All right – it was a deal.

Already on my way to Oswalds, I became anxious and beset by doubts.

Was the expedition not just a foolish caprice which would get me in an awkward fix? For it would certainly be a bitter disappointment (for an ambitious and enthusiastic Polish girl) to meet with a cool, casual reception on the part of the giant of English prose, and my compatriot. And it was not until I was on my way there that I became fully aware of the fact that I was taking upon myself, quite spontaneously and incompetently, the job of representing, at least to a certain extent, the young people of Poland, who dabbled in writing and who cherished Conrad's works.

Perhaps it was still not too late to turn back?

The peaceful village of Bishopsbourne with its fifteenth-century church[1] lay in a valley of lush, emerald-green pastures, with flocks of grazing sheep. Barely a thousand steps from the church, at the back of a garden, I found an impressive modern house. A brass gate was left open to welcome visitors.

A gravel drive led to the porch. Peace, luxuriant foliage and silence – such was the atmosphere of this secluded spot.

The car stopped. The 'chauffeur's' back looked unnaturally stiff and straight.

Suddenly, as if from nowhere, a butler appeared who opened my door, and an elderly man with a monocle, in a light-coloured suit, slowly descended the steps of the house.

A quick, all-embracing glance, a moment of unbearable embarrassment, and a voice saying in Polish: 'Judging by the tone of your letter I expected to see a grey-haired matron...'

A smile brightened my host's swarthy face. My fears melted away in that warm smile. They vanished – and so did my 'chauffeur'.

---

[1] In fact it dates from the twelfth century, with later additions.

When after a few minutes we began strolling on the lawn, I instantly forgot about the vast expanse of land and water which separated me from home. The aroma of drying hay and the sky-high warble of larks made the surroundings even more familiar. My first impression of Conrad – 'an absolute stranger, a foreign gentleman with a monocle' – dissolved in a flash. Gradually, as I felt more at ease, and as my confidence increased, the conversation became more lively, touching upon various subjects which would not have been of any interest to English people.

As I have already mentioned, in spite of my thorough preparation, when the time came for me to recite a difficult lesson – the professor was not there. My excitement was subsiding and in its place came amazement of the fact that here I was, walking side by side with someone whom I had known for a long time and who was not intent on being a 'great man'.

I knew that Conrad had just returned from a very successful voyage to the United States, where he had had an enthusiastic reception.[1] The news was proclaimed from the roof tops. And it seemed to me that Joseph Conrad, the tamer of the high seas, the fearless sailor, the famous writer of the twentieth century, had remained behind on the steps of the house, and that now I was being accompanied by someone else: by an elderly man, world-weary and sick (I did not know that he used to suffer from bad attacks of malaria). It was amazing how close I felt to that man.

We were called to the house for tea.

I was scared. I would rather have skipped tea altogether. Conrad, as if sensing my hesitation, smiled and pointed out the shortest path to the house.

On a cosy verandah full of flowers I met Mrs Jessie Conrad; her face looked benign and smiling but her eyes were strangely penetrating, pale and cold. I also met Conrad's secretary, Miss Lillian – a slender, inconspicuous woman, also with a fixed smile – who failed to attract my attention.

The sons were absent.

I remember a large table spread with cakes and fruit. Conrad, full of nervous energy and with typically Polish hospitality, kept passing me all kinds of delicacies, pressing me to eat; the ladies behaved with equally typical reserve.

---

[1] See note 2 to p. 253.

After tea we had a quick look at the small drawing-room on the first-floor, where a wide open window looked out over the garden and meadows. Then we walked over to Conrad's study, which was overflowing with books: they stood on shelves, filled glass bookcases, lay in stacks on chairs, on the sofa and on the floor. A real deluge of books.

I did not dare approach Conrad's desk, so I took a seat at a large round table in the middle of the room; the table was also cluttered up with books. Conrad walked from one end of the room to the other, talking constantly; I listened, following him with my eyes. I felt at home.

All of a sudden, Conrad, as if he remembered something, quickly walked to his desk, picked up a large open book and coming towards me said with a smile: 'And now you'll have the pleasure of meeting a friend, certainly a good friend of yours.'

It was *The Blaze* by Mrs Szczucka.

I blushed.

What surprised me was that when I was telling him in the garden of the unpleasant adventures during our return journey to Poland from Russia, now Bolshevik, Conrad listened in silence, without showing by a word or the flicker of an eye that he already knew all about it from the accurate and deeply moving account in 'The Blaze'.

'An outstanding book,' he said, walking up and down the room and turning the pages. 'I think it ought to be translated into English. I've just written to the publishers. Do you know the author? I've translated entire chapters for my ladies. It's a gripping book!'

I shared his view and it made me happy to hear him speak on the subject like this; I remembered again what the book had meant to us all.

Suddenly it occurred to me that I had left the parcel from Poland on the porch. Conrad fetched it himself and unwrapped the collection of slender volumes. He took them out one by one and, standing beside him, I commented briefly on the authors. I remember that I tried to draw his attention to an insignificant-looking volume, *Droga do Emaus*, by Leonard Podhorski-Okcłów,[1] a nostalgic glorifier of Bielo-Russia, his native country, from which he was forced to flee.

And when we were so absorbed by the books that we forgot the world around us, we heard an impatient car horn outside.

A glance at the mantelpiece clock confirmed that two and a half hours had passed since my arrival. I sprang to my feet in a fluster,

[1] 'The Road to Emmaus' (Warsaw, 1923).

gathering all the English periodicals Conrad had given me. He protested unexpectedly. 'Look, I've got an idea: I shall send someone to see to the driver and you can stay to dinner with us. We eat quite early, just after seven.'

Those words were spoken to the accompaniment of another sounding of the horn. I was in a state of utter confusion, all the more as Conrad had already rung the bell on his desk.

'But this man is not my chauffeur, he is my brother-in-law,' I cried in despair, 'please don't do anything!'

Conrad looked at me with surprise.

'Please, forgive me, but I must be frank with you. He is my brother-in-law. He drove me here and went off to some stream nearby to catch trout. You do understand, don't you? Anyway he had to wait somewhere. I asked him to call for me not later than in two hours' time. So here he is...'

Conrad seemed rather amused.

The third protracted hooting increased his merriment. But I felt ill at ease, for I suddenly recalled the terms of my agreement with the 'chauffeur'. Meanwhile Conrad gave some instructions to the butler.

It soon turned out that the butler was asked to get a bouquet of sweet peas ready for me. In spite of feeling quite pleased with myself and (for the time being) safe beside Conrad, I walked towards the car with a trembling heart, carrying books and flowers.

Conrad welcomed the driver with a smile and a friendly gesture. My brother-in-law, quick to grasp the situation, got out of the car and the two men shook hands.

'What fish?' Conrad enquired.

'No fish,' confessed my brother-in-law.

'Bad luck,' commiserated Conrad, smiling cheerfully.

In spite of repeated invitations to dinner, my brother-in-law would not be persuaded to prolong this fabulous visit; and he made sure I saw the dirty look he gave me.

Conrad accompanied us to the end of the garden, walking beside the car. When we started on our way I looked round and saw him, alone, framed within the open gate. I kept waving until we turned the corner – he stood motionless in the same place.

I felt a strange pang. Not listening to what my companion was saying, I was thinking that in a few weeks I would be back at home, in Warsaw, and that all I had to do was decide on the day and hour of my departure.

But would Conrad ever return?

...

Soon after I had returned to Warsaw, I received three parcels from Conrad (sent by his secretary) with copies of *The London Mercury*, a monthly magazine chosen for me by the writer himself. The last parcel arrived in May 1924 and it contained an interesting analysis of Conrad's writings by Edward Shanks.[1]

...

What did the small house at Aldington look like at the time it was occupied by a little-known writer of modest means, with his wife and two sons, Borys (twelve years old) and John (six),[2] and with a faithful maid and a dog called Escamillo? The answer may be found in a simple letter from Mr Dryland.

I managed to establish contact with the owner of the small house, called Church Cottage, who in spite of being an octogenarian affectionately remembers his former tenant. Mr Dryland now lives in Hythe, but continues renting his cottage to people of limited means.

In the opening paragraph of his letter Mr Dryland says:[3] 'to begin, I must tell you, my school-days ended when I was twelve years old, therefore letter-writing is not one of my good points' – then he describes Conrad's arrival in the hamlet and his search for a place to live for his family and himself, for somewhere 'where he could do some writing'. Conrad began to chat to Mr Dryland and asked him whether he would consider doing the cottage up and then letting it. Mr Dryland agreed and set to work. 'I scraped and scrubbed the oak beams which were covered with whitewash for years and years...' Then he raised the ceilings in the rooms by two feet and made a study for Conrad out of a windowless tiny box-room on the first floor, by knocking down part of the wall and putting in a window. 'He was very pleased,' Mr Dryland assured me.

As we know, this was the house where Conrad wrote *Under Western Eyes*.

Unfortunately Conrad was very ill, continued his landlord: 'he had trouble with his hands. They became swollen to twice their natural size, he was almost as helpless and weak as a child. I used to go and help his nurse, when she wanted to put clean sheets on the bed. I remember him telling me about a voyage he had on a ship, when they had to get kettles of boiling water to thaw the blocks and pulleys before they could hoist the sails of their ship.'

Mr Dryland's daughter, Mrs Freda M., also wrote to me, recalling

---

[1] Edward Buxton Shanks, 'Mr Joseph Conrad', *London Mercury* 9 (March 1924), pp. 502–11.

[2] In fact Borys, born 1898, was eleven, and John, born 1906, three.

[3] All following quotations are in English in the original.

her childhood (she was ten at the time) when she was an inseparable playmate of Conrad's sons. She said: 'He certainly impressed the young generation, as his strong personality was so impressive. He looked as though he was deeply thinking... He must have had a message for the western people and an interest in youth.

'My father thinks he was exiled from his native Poland under Russian territory – he certainly served a hard task-master in his sailing days.' And further on: 'I think he was, at the time I remember him, rather financially embarrassed, as I seem to remember he had a grant from the king, whatever that may be, but it always puzzled my small brain.'

'My Encounter with Conrad', by Roman Dyboski[1]
'Spotkanie z Conradem', *Czas*, 1932, no. 71

I

After Conrad's death his two-volume biography by M. Jean-Aubry appeared, containing, as is customary in England, a selection from his correspondence. One English critic decried it as monotonous, arguing that in his letters to friends Conrad seldom wrote on any other subject but those of his books that happened to absorb him at the time, family members and their illnesses. Although later publications of letters to his closer friends (such as the volume of letters to Edward Garnett) presented a considerable amount of interesting material, some of a more general nature, thereby belying that critic's statement, nevertheless it contained a grain of truth. Conrad wrote with great difficulty, and as he set himself very high standards, concentration was essential for him; as a natural reaction after many years at sea he longed for a peaceful life at home: all that taken together accounts for the fact that although during the last years of his life he frequently moved house he nevertheless always preferred staying at home, at some country place amidst the rich greenery of the gardens of southern England – particularly those of Kent, called the 'garden of England' par excellence. He disliked going to London, shunned literary dinners, social gatherings and public appearances. His growing asthmatic troubles may have contributed to his fondness for home life.

Being to some extent aware of the situation I did not intrude upon the great writer during my post-war period of lecturing at London University in spite of my strong wish to meet him. All I did was to send

---

[1] Roman Dyboski (1883–1945), historian of English, American and comparative literatures, professor of the Jagiellonian University in Cracow.

him two volumes of my lectures on Polish literature published in Oxford[1] and a copy of an article of mine published in an American periodical about the significance of religion in Polish national life.[2] In reply I received a letter which I have kept as a precious souvenir. In Conrad's view people in England know very little of Poland and do not have much sympathy for our country. He expresses his appreciation of my endeavours to acquaint the English with facts from Polish history.

Oswalds, Bishopsbourne, Kent
22 Feb. '24

My dear Sir,

I am sorry I am so late in thanking you for the 2 vols. of *Polish Literature* which I have read with the highest appreciation – and for the brochure on "The Religious Element in Polish National Life" which told me many things I did not know before. I can hardly express my sense of the good and patriotic work you are doing by your publications in English, so attractive in matter and style. People here know very little of Poland – and I am afraid that there is not much general sympathy for the new State. But all this arises from sheer ignorance which only concise and perspicuous exposition of historical truth can gradually dispel. Pray accept my warm and most respectful regards and believe me most sincerely yours,

J. Conrad

2

It was not till several months after the receipt of the above letter and two months before the death of the great writer that I got the chance of meeting him in person. One day in June 1924 I received from our envoy (now ambassador), Mr Skirmunt,[3] an invitation to a luncheon at our legation, where Conrad was to be present. At that time Mr Skirmunt was trying to revive the Literary Association of Friends of Poland, a society (established by Thomas Campbell,[4] the poet) that had flourished for a number of years after the 1831 insurrection. In the present and happier era Conrad was to become its new chairman. The society did not have to resort to charity any more, as in the days of the Great Emigration: its only aim would be to promote a better knowledge and popularity of Poland in Britain. I may add that the idea of reviving the society proved premature and did not materialize till several years later in the form of the currently existing Anglo-Polish Club, attached to the university. To me personally, however, the initiative of 1924

---

[1] *Periods of Polish Literary History* (Oxford University Press: London, 1923) and *Modern Polish Literature* (Oxford University Press: London, 1924).
[2] 'The Religious Element in Polish National Life', *Sewanee Review*, 1923, no. 10.
[3] Konstanty Skirmunt (1866–1951), Polish diplomat, 1922–34 envoy to London.
[4] 1777–1844.

remains memorable, because it gave me my only chance to meet Conrad – for whom it proved to be the only occasion when he came into contact with a representative of the independent Polish state.

At the reception, apart from a few legation officials Miss Alma Tadema[1] was also present, the daughter of an outstanding painter, and herself a well-known friend of Poland during the war and in the pre-war years. Conrad came accompanied by his young French friend-cum-secretary and later biographer, M. Jean-Aubry (who has given his own account of the occasion in *Tygodnik Ilustrowany*).[2] Conrad's charming and courteous phrases, while greeting our representative, uttered with great fluency in faultless Polish, contrasted strangely with his grave countenance, typical of his last years and well known from his portraits. Further conversation was in French on account of those present who did not know Polish. Conrad had an excellent command of French and spoke it with native fluency, which obviously gave him great pleasure. By contrast, when I was sitting next to him at table and addressed him in English I realized that this great English writer spoke English with a very pronounced foreign accent.

3

I cannot recall now the exact conversation at table and later over coffee in Mr Skirmunt's study. Two typical fragments, however, have stuck in my memory: one throws light on Conrad as a sailor and writer of sea stories, and the other on Conrad as a Pole and descendant of noble ancestors.

The first was provoked by Mr Skirmunt's courteous manner, for which he is well known and justifiably admired in London. Knowing that Conrad at his rare public appearances must be pestered by questions about his and other people's literary activities, Mr Skirmunt switched the conversation to Conrad's sailing past and asked if he still liked going to sea occasionally. Conrad answered with a slight shudder: 'No, I've had enough of the sea.' In order to discover the deeper meaning of his brief reply I enquired politely: 'Perhaps you think the same of the sea as the retired Swedish captain in *Anna Christie* – the play by O'Neill that is having such a success in London just now.[3] He always said "that old devil, the sea".' Conrad bridled up again and answered: 'That's exactly how I feel but I wouldn't put it in quite the same words as Mr O'Neill; he has no sense of style.' Let us overlook the

[1] Laurence Alma Tadema (1862–1940), novelist and playwright, daughter of Lawrence Alma Tadema.

[2] 'Józef Conrad a Polska', *Tygodnik Ilustrowany* 1925, nos 41–4.

[3] Published in 1922.

critical remark aimed at the American playwright, whose rampant and deliberate brutality of language must have jarred on a stylist as precise as Conrad; instead let us consider a while how well his statement about the sea fits in with his entire literary output. Heroic struggles of a lonely individual against some unknown, mysterious and powerful element surrounding him form the well-nigh constant and unvarying subject of Conrad's novels; and the struggles of a seaman in a sailing ship – for this was the kind Conrad sailed in – against the demonic elements of the sea constitute the prototype of this situation. Descriptions of combats that Conrad had personally lived through may be found in *The Shadow-Line* and *Typhoon*. Another collection of sea stories, *The Mirror of the Sea*, shows even more clearly that Conrad's love of the sea was not what a sentimental landlubber might imagine; and above all he loved the ships – man's allies in his fight against the elements.

4

The second fragment that has stayed alive in my memory from that one conversation I had with Conrad occurred a bit later, when our host broached the main topic of our meeting and began to coax the author to accept some post, even if only the honorary chairmanship, in the Society of the Friends of Poland, to be re-established in England. Conrad was obviously embarrassed and tried hard to make excuses: he explained that he never went up to town and never made public appearances on account of his health and literary work. Finally he agreed to his name being placed on a list of sponsors of the organization, but refused categorically to take an active part in any functions. Later, when we spoke tête-à-tête, Conrad confessed to another cause of his reluctance towards the whole project. In this view the spreading of propaganda designed to attract the attention and sympathy of the great western nations was unbecoming to Poland's historic culture. 'It is all right,' he said, 'for other nations which until recently lived in obscurity under foreign domination: for Serbs who were for hundreds of years slaves of Turkey, for Czechs encrusted with German influence for such a long time, but for us, who withstood the hundred years of slavery and emerged the same as we had been for nearly a thousand years, for us such exertions are superfluous; those who want to may always find us at the same outpost where we have always fought for Europe's civilization.' I was deeply moved listening to these arguments in which the noble chivalric pride of an old-fashioned Pole blended with English gentleman-like dislike of notoriety and publicity. Unfortunately, it was my host's wish that I should point out that in the present situation, owing to the Americanization of the world, publicity is a powerful factor even in international relations and a country which neglects this aspect is doomed to lose in the international forum. Conrad, feeling that his words might have been understood by me as critical of my own propaganda activities in England, hastened to assure me that he found my method of informing the English about Polish matters beyond reproach in respect of content and form and that he strongly approved of it. Those precious words, confirming once more the sentiments expressed in his earlier letter, were unfortunately the last I was to hear from the great writer. Several days later, meeting a greatly grieved M. Jean-Aubry at the British Museum, I was told that Conrad was more troubled by asthma and rheumatism than ever; and shortly afterwards, in a tiny French village on that Channel by way of which Conrad travelled to and fro into the wide world on countless occasions, the news of his death reached me.

'A Meeting at the Polish Legation in London', by Edward Raczyński[1]

'Spotanie w poselstwie w Londynie', *Wiadomósci* (London), 1949, nos 176–7

I remember stories that were part of our family tradition – stories about a learned traveller and writer Jan Potocki,[2] about General Józef Chłopicki,[3] about Adam Mickiewicz's visit to Rogalin[4] during the November Insurrection and the poem he wrote about his night-time wanderings along the unlit corridors of that vast mansion,* about August Cieszkowski[5] and Zygmunt Krasiński. In the early days of his youth, on one of his travels, my father struck up a friendship in Chile with Ignacy Domeyko,[6] who had settled there, surrounded by the deep respect and reverence of the local population. My father used to tell me, harking back into the still more distant past, how he had escaped from school to join the Polish Cossacks in Turkey,[7] and

---

* The manuscript of this poem, then in possession of my father, has been subsequently lost (author's note).

[1] Born in 1891; Polish diplomat, after 1945 *émigré* politician.

[2] Jan Potocki (1761–1815), author of 'The Manuscript Found in Saragossa' (1805).

[3] Józef Chłopicki (1771–1854), for a time commander-in-chief of the Polish forces in the 1830 insurrection.

[4] The home seat of the Raczyńskis, near Poznań.

[5] August Cieszkowski (1814–1894), philosopher and liberal politician.

[6] Ignacy Domeyko (1802–1889), emigrated in 1831, settled in Chile in 1838 and became an eminent geologist and educator.

[7] Recruited from Polish *émigrés* to fight against Russia, he took part in the Crimean war (1854–6).

about a campaign in which he took part a few years later as a papal zouave, and of the bad wound he received in the Battle of Mentana.[1] In my mind all those stories revolved round the names of various outstanding people with whom my father had been briefly in contact – men like Sadyk Pasha[2] or General Charette.[3]

For my part, although I have lived in an epoch rich in remarkable personalities, I have not exploited this opportunity as well as I could. I have known Conrad but briefly. Our first meeting took place in London, where from the spring of 1922 I held the post of secretary in the Polish Legation. From December 1922 I worked under Konstanty Skirmunt, a distinguished diplomat, man of great experience, wisdom and culture. It was Skirmunt's wish to breathe new life into the old Literary Association of Friends of Poland, or else to re-establish it in a new form. This was the origin of the Anglo-Polish Society in London. It seemed that Conrad would make an ideal chairman: he held an important position in English literary circles, was a British subject and at the same time a propagator of the name of Poland in the British Isles. In past years Conrad had given proof of his attachment to his native country by submitting a memorandum about Poland's situation and her needs to the Foreign Office. Our Minister, Mr Skirmunt, invited Conrad to the legation for lunch. I was present at the occasion. The conversation was in Polish. Conrad spoke the language fluently, although now and again he was lost for a word. His manner was most courteous but reticent, as if intent on controlling his reactions so as not to give away his true state of mind. He declined to participate in the Anglo-Polish Society, justifying his decision by a lack of time and a dislike of 'social work'.

Those reasons, although true, were somewhat inadequate for a full explanation. Social work, particularly when pursued in cooperation with other people with whom one has little in common, calls for a natural vocation. And Conrad's vocation was totally different. His health must have been also rather poor at the time: he died a few months later. I went to his funeral, acting as a deputy for Minister Skirmunt, and I placed a wreath on Conrad's coffin, on behalf of his native country.

On the car journey from London I was accompanied by Mr Jean-Aubry, Conrad's old friend, translator and author of a book on him.

---

[1] On 3 November 1867, in which papal troops defeated Garibaldi's insurgents.
[2] Michał Czajkowski (1804–1886), Polish novelist; in 1850 he was converted to Islam; he commanded the Polish Cossacks in Turkey.
[3] Athanase Charette (1832–1911) distinguished himself in the 1870–1 war with Prussia.

Aubry told me a lot about his deceased friend. I recall that according to him Conrad could just as easily have become a famous French writer, as he had an amazing knowledge of the French language and a great sensitivity for the most subtle nuances of meaning and form. Mr Jean-Aubry had had the opportunity to discover Conrad's mastery while discussing the texts of his French translations with him. When Conrad spoke, however, whether in English or in French, his accent was undeniably native – Polish. For my part I remember it as almost jarring. I have been told by my English friends that as the years passed his accent became more and more pronounced. I have the impression that towards the end of his life Conrad's thoughts and feelings often turned towards Poland, which was then rising from long captivity to independence and had its own newly established legation in London.

Among Conrad's faithful readers was Neville Chamberlain, Britain's former Prime Minister, who died during the last war, having been unjustly belittled in the public opinion as a naive and meek 'umbrella carrier'. As a matter of fact Chamberlain had a great strength of character. Moreover he was an admirer of noble heroes and also, it appears, of beautifully chiselled English prose. He found them both in Conrad's books. Chamberlain told my wife that he always kept one of Conrad's novels on his bedside table and that he read every evening at least a few pages which gave him an escape from the difficult responsibilities of his official post.

'At the Home of Konrad Korzeniowski', by Irena Rakowska-Łuniewska

'U Konrada Korzeniowskiego', *Pion* (Warsaw), 1934, no. 50

On one of the first days of June 1924 my friend Miss Świeżawska and I travelled from London to Oswalds to pay a visit to my relative[1] Konrad Korzeniowski – Joseph Conrad.

A vast expanse of green meadows and pastures stretched alongside the railway track; here and there we saw large hop-fields, typical of Kent.

After a couple of hours we arrived in Canterbury, which is quite close to Oswalds. At the station we were met by Konrad's car. A chauffeur in a white coat and cap opened the car door for us and we were soon on our way, moving swiftly along a smooth country road.

Before long we entered a park and saw in the distance a one-storeyed house, overgrown with vines, with large windows, a sloping roof and tall chimneys. The car stopped in front of the porch supported by two white

---

[1] Miss Rakowska's mother, Maria (née Ołdakowska), was a niece of Aleksander Poradowski, a relative of the Bobrowskis.

columns. A lovely, big dog, Scally, was the first to greet us there. We passed through the hall into the drawing-room. It was arranged with great taste, nothing stiff or official about it: occasional tables with many pretty objects on them, crystals, books in ornamental binding, cushions on the sofa. I was delighted to see a red-brick fireplace and above it a painting in a white frame, and pretty knick-knacks of Sèvres porcelain on the mantelpiece.

While I was looking around the door opened and Konrad's wife, Jessie, entered slowly, leaning on two sticks. She was very stout and had a kind face. She greeted us warmly, saying: 'Conrad is not feeling too well today. His arthritis is still bothering him but he will be down soon to meet you.'

After a while, which seemed to us an interminable wait, Konrad appeared; he welcomed me with a kiss and simple words of greeting. 'I am so pleased to meet you, my little cousin.'

This simple greeting touched me to the heart. Not wishing to waste a single moment of my stay at Oswalds, I watched Konrad while he talked to us.

His face was marked by suffering and weariness, but there was a soft, almost joyous expression in his eyes. He drew his chair close to mine, asked questions about various trifling matters, about my impressions of England, about my mother and the rest of the family. He recalled that once, on his way to see his uncle in the Ukraine, he had travelled by way of Lublin, where he met my mother; he said that he had kept a letter from her.[1] I listened to him talking, happy to see him and to feel at ease in his house.

Before lunch Konrad took us to the garden; Jean-Aubry, Konrad's best friend, was also there. The two of them used to work together or spend long hours talking in the study.

We walked along the gravel paths, with Konrad lovingly showing us the delightful garden near the house: on a green, freshly cut lawn various shapes of flower-beds surrounded by a short-trimmed border and in the centre a large earthenware pot, simple in design, with beautifully arranged flowers overhanging the sides; further down there was a long hedge, separating the flower garden from a small orchard; through an opening in the hedge we could see a vast meadow.

After lunch we sat and talked on the large terrace. Konrad was lying on a low deck-chair, his arms folded behind his head. He regretted the absence of his sons, of Borys and particularly of John, and worried about us being deprived of young company; he asked Jean-Aubry to

[1] Apparently lost.

make our first stay at Oswalds more pleasant: 'Vous êtes jeune, Jean, amusez ces demoiselles.'[1]

At tea, which was served in the garden near the terrace, I took over from Jessie who, because of constant pain in her knee, had difficulty getting up from her arm-chair. Konrad watched me with a smile, pleased to see me at ease in their company.

I left after tea, greatly impressed with their charming home, of which Konrad was the soul. How differently I had imagined him! He turned out to be relaxed, simple and pleasant; he also had an irresistible charm; one felt his great inner strength so that it was difficult not to look at him; and his eyes, at times disconcerting, inspired trust and respect. They reflected his powerful personality and great kindness; they seemed to look at some unknown world – sometimes gentle and sad, sometimes inscrutable; his eyes were the kind one never forgets.

Before long Konrad invited us again to Oswalds for a weekend. It was raining and Konrad was in more pain that usual; he was silent and spent most of the time in his room. However, he joined us in the evening, worrying that we were bored and trying to think up ways of entertaining us. He himself arranged the dining-room for a game of table-tennis, and watching us play he became animated and cheerful, picking up the small, light-weight balls that kept running away all over the floor.

In the evening Konrad and I spent some time talking – up to then, because of Jessie's presence, I had not heard him speak Polish. His lack of foreign accent surprised me, but he kept complaining of having already forgotten how to speak Polish. He told me about his plan to return to Poland soon, together with his family; he recalled at length his boyhood days in the Ukraine, where I had been born and brought up.

'Tomorrow, my child,' he suddenly said, as if summarizing his hitherto vague thoughts, 'if the weather is good I shall drive you to a nearby hill. You will see a view which strongly reminds me of the Ukraine. I go there quite often; I am fond of that distant horizon.'

The following day was clear and sunny. I went down early for breakfast. Konrad was already in the dining-room, warming up delicious eggs and sausages on a silver spirit stove; an English breakfast speciality. I offered to help, but with a warm smile and a decided yet courteous gesture he made me sit down and did all the serving himself.

After breakfast we went to visit the place he had mentioned the previous day. From the hill-top we could see green meadows interspersed with varicoloured fields, clumps of old trees here and there and

[1] 'You are young, Jean; entertain these young ladies.'

a wide horizon merging with the sky. It reminded us of the Ukraine. Our eyes met briefly and I could feel a close bond between the two of us; it seemed to me that I knew his innermost secret thoughts. We looked a long time in silence at this view that we both cherished so much.

I had already noticed that Konrad, emerging from one of his frequent states of reverie, would suddenly return to reality as if awakening from a deep sleep. Now, too, he suddenly turned round, gave me a smile and energetically opened the car door with a brief: 'Let's go home.' We drove back in silence.

Later that day we went to see Lady Millais, the widow of a famous painter[1] and herself a great friend of Konrad's. In a charming cottage nestling among red roses of the Crimson Rambler variety, while we were having tea, Konrad spoke at length about his past experiences in the South Seas.

He talked in such a simple, clear and interesting way that no one noticed the hours pass. We listened without taking our eyes off him. His expression was constantly changing as he now relived with undiminished intensity his old experiences. Some were full of terror, others were cheerful, sunny and calm, or else sparkling with wit. Konrad's eyes reflected the comic aspect of the incidents recalled. He laughed heartily at his memories. He spoke English beautifully, displaying the entire wealth of the language. But in spite of his long stay in England, he never lost his foreign accent – typically Polish, which made his pronounciation even more attractive. Konrad used to pronounce the consonant 'W', almost entirely ignored by native English speakers, as in Polish. I particularly remember the word 'wrong' which he used often and which has since acquired a special charm for me.

Konrad stopped his tale as suddenly as he had begun. We left Lady Millais's house, carrying away armfuls of crimson roses and the memory of the wonderful hospitality and the charming personality of our hostess.

I remember a lovely July morning; the sun was already quite strong, and multicoloured plants in a wide border blossomed along the hedge; the warm air was full of the scent of flowers, and a mound of petunias was overflowing on to the gravel path. I was passing near the opened window of Konrad's study when I heard my name called out. Konrad came to the window and sat on the ledge while we chatted. Every sentence of his made me sense his nostalgia for Poland; all his plans revolved round the idea of going back home.

[1] Sir John Everett Millais (1829–96), pre-Raphaelite painter, later President of the Royal Academy.

'I should like to return for good!, he said. 'I should like John to marry a Polish girl; please teach John Polish; my sons are quite different from me: they are not interested in literature, only in practical things. They never read any of my books.' (Borys had a *de luxe* edition of Conrad's works carefully arranged in a separate bookcase. He was proud of these books, but admitted to not having read a single one of them.)

I do not know if this was a complaint; I think it was just a statement of fact. Konrad broke off, became thoughtful and silent. There was a telling look on his face, but his eyes seemed oblivious of the immediate surroundings, of time and place. I walked away quietly so as nor to distract him with my presence. He did not notice me go. Suddenly, I fully understood what he had told me before that he never became attached to the place where he lived, nor to the things he possessed, and that he therefore felt best at sea. 'Rien qu'avec un sac de blé sur mon dos...'[1]

The most pleasant time of the day was the afternoon spent together on the terrace, looking over the small, colourful flower garden framed by the hedge. Konrad almost always kept us company; sometimes he was in an excellent mood, joking, telling amusing stories, showing interest in what each of us was busy with at the time – playing patience or doing needlework – he urged John to provide some entertainment for us, and he himself suggested various amusements for the rest of the day.

Konrad's attitude towards Jessie and John was extremely pleasant and affectionate; with Borys I saw him but briefly. He looked fondly at Jessie, calling her, like his sons did, by her pet name, Mrs C; he tried to brighten up her years of suffering with her painful knee, which had been operated on several times. He was full of solicitude for her. Sometimes he teased her, saying: 'She too is a great writer; she wrote a cookery book.'[2]

Jessie was indeed interested in cooking, and as she could not move much on account of her disability, she used to spend a lot of time in the kitchen, inventing new dishes. The food at Oswalds was excellent, quite un-English, more like an amalgam of the best gastronomic tastes from various countries.

The one thing Jessie never prepared was the salad dressing. At table I always sat next to Konrad; the first day I was surprised to see the butler place a bowl of salad and – separately – various seasonings in front of Konrad: he was the one who always dressed the salad himself.

---

[1] Fr. saying: 'With nothing but what I stood up in.'
[2] *A Handbook of Cookery for a Small House* (Heinemann, London, 1923). With a Preface by Joseph Conrad.

During meals Konrad was often talkative but sometimes he became lost in thought or very nervous; then he would not say a word. The silence was hard to bear. Konrad's hands groped restlessly on the table, moving a plate, pushing forks and knives about. The tension would become unpleasant. If someone ventured to interrupt the silence, Konrad made a sudden return from his day-dream voyage and with a charming and courteous manner adjusted to the general mood.

This was my last stay at Oswalds, my last meeting with Konrad. A few days later I learned about his sudden death.

Telegrams

The Times, 8 August 1924, p. 15 (same texts in *Daily Telegraph*, 8 August 1924)

The Telegram from the Minister for Religious and Public Education in Poland to the President of the Board of Education upon Conrad's death:

Profoundly grieved loss suffered English literature by death eminent British author, Joseph Konrad Korzeniowski, English by activity, Pole by origin. I beg you to accept my deepest condolence. Miklaszewski, Minister for Religious and Public Education, Republic Poland.

Mr Trevelyan sent the following reply:

Miklaszewski, Minister for Religious and Public Education, Republic Poland, Warsaw. I have been touched by your most kind message of sympathy, and beg you to accept my warmest gratitude. All in Great Britain deplore the loss of Joseph Conrad, a great son of Poland, and a master of English literature and language. I hope that in the memory of his life's work our two nations may remain united. Charles Trevelyan, President, Board of Education.

'The Statue of Man upon the Statue of the World', by Witold Gombrowicz[1]

'Wielki Conrad i szary czytelnik. Posąg człowieka na posągu świata', *Kurier Poranny* (Warsaw), 1935, no. 333

'For this miracle or this wonder troubleth me right gretly.' The quotation from Boethius on the first page of *The Mirror of the Sea* could just as

---

[1] Witold Gombrowicz (1904–69), one of the most prominent contemporary Polish writers.

well serve as a motto for a critique of Conrad. But since it has already been said so many times why we are so deeply moved by this miracle and this wonder, now at last it is necessary to say why this miracle and this wonder actually moves us so little. Contrariness is not just a trifle. Contrariness brings out certain contents that lie outside our principal, capital truth – it is a *votum separatum*[1] of the minority, and occasionally it may turn out that in a given case the minority is in fact a majority which has somehow remained unnoticed hitherto. In our eagerness to pursue what ought to be, we often forget what is; we say that a writer is excellent and we are therefore moved and enchanted by him; but we are not sufficiently alerted to the fact that precisely because of his excessive perfection we, in our miserable humanity tortured by perfection, may grow indifferent or even hostile to him.

To begin with, we must state impartially that although no one questions Conrad's achievements, he is not a writer much liked in Poland. It is enough to chat to people instead of reading articles. Except for professionals displaying what is called deepest appreciation, I have not met a single man in this petty-bourgeois land of ours whose attitude to Conrad goes beyond a fairly cool cult and an uncommitted approval. Thomas Mann boasts a number of spiritual followers in our country; Wells, Chesterton, Bernard Shaw often have a shaping influence – but not Conrad. In spite of excellent translations by Aniela Zagórska, in spite of Conrad's Polishness, we cannot say that his austere thought penetrates our hearts. This is the plain truth which anyone may easily verify in his own little circle of friends – a truth too plain to be accepted by the sky-soaring minds of devotees. I would naturally wish to avoid cheap paradoxes, but my unprejudiced observation reveals that our English compatriot is one of the most alien authors translated into our language.

This is simply tragic. We have always accused our great prose writers of excessive lyricism, of a lack (in a more general sense) of construction, of philosophy, of the exclusion of Europe, of world-wide horizons, finding in those shortcomings a justification for the paucity of our enthusiasm. But hark: our fellow-countryman Korzeniowski, transformed like Gustaw of 'The Forefathers' Eve'[2] into Conrad, emerges

---

[1] Lat.: 'separate desire'.
[2] In Adam Mickiewicz's powerful poetic drama *Dziady* ('The Forefather's Eve', 1832), the protagonist, who at first bears the name 'Gustaw', is a typical young Romantic poet. Under the impact of political persecution, to which he and his friends are exposed, his personality and his poetry change, and he adopts the name 'Konrad'. Becoming aware of his national responsibilities, he turns into a romantic patriot, no longer isolated and self-centred: 'My name is Million, because I love and am tortured for millions.'

from the wide expanse of water and, as if at the instance of a good fairy, gains everything. A Pole elevated to Englishman, a Polish borderland provincial elevated to the greatest merchant marine in the world, the son of Apollo Korzeniowski raised to the rank of a most refined European artist; heroism, great creative philosophy, wide sweeps of all the seas of the world – what else may one wish for a Pole? Yet in spite of it all, it is only our national pride that is gratified while the rest of our soul remains silent. And although at present we hammer it in – in an amusing and even slightly undignified manner – that Conrad has 'returned' to his native fold, and although scholars doggedly look for a sign of Polishness in his every sneeze (I personally think that our motherland ought to be of greater value to those patriotic hounds than a most illustrious artist, and it is therefore unseemly to peddle our motherland on the strength of circumstantial evidence, details, petty incidents, all of which are contrary to the overall shape of an entire life; I do not think that our country ought to be confused with details, nor should Conrad and his native land be dragged by the hair towards one another) – in spite of it all, I repeat, no closer links with Conrad have existed up to now.

The unsuccessful experiment of the good fairy suggests that perhaps it has not been a lack of greatness in our writers but an excessive inherent tendency towards greatness that has made them so distant and so abstract. A radical pessimist may see in this the tragedy of a nation systematically betrayed by its best representatives – under whatever conditions they develop they turn into eagles or into statues, not to mention Britishers – as if only a complete rejection of littleness could ensure the achievement of greatness; as if some defect in the psychological make-up of every Pole prevents him, having once reached a state of elevation, from retaining full humanity. Conrad transmutes everything into greatness, grandiloquence, cosmos. No other leading contemporary writer displays this characteristic to the same extent. And no other book does it to the same extent as *The Mirror of the Sea*.

Is there anything more personal, human and petty than reminiscences? If intensive labour on the compositional structure of fiction has thwarted all normal humanity, in this book at least we expect to hear a more homely and warmer tune. But no. The statue of man upon the statue of the world speaks about himself in the same language he uses when speaking about his heroes. And as a consequence he does not say anything about himself. The book is again devoted to the elementary forces of sea and wind, to the heroism of sailors, to ships... But we get the impression that Conrad does not speak about himself not because he does not want to, but because he cannot: his style does not allow of it; and to us the book radiates not freedom but, on the contrary, a tragically enslaved spirit unable to shake off the fetters of its own style, a style which allows only a fraction of truth, a fraction of reality – nothing over and beyond what may be expressed in a circumscribed manner. These gorgeously rich pages breathe poverty. There is no jester here, as in Shakespeare, to mock the lofty truths of the monarchs; everything is regal and everything is imprisoned in its own stateliness.

Perhaps in no other book of Conrad's is his mastery of style so fully displayed – a style able to turn modest recollections into a great paean. And nowhere else can we perceive more clearly the entire poverty of the style. It is so full of elevated truths, of cosmic truths, that certainly not one of the characters or facts described is or can be genuine. They are not allowed to be. We gape at the monotony of luxuriance – here we have a life seemingly stormy but apparently consisting of two elements and four winds, and we admire the excellence of the craft which for the hundreth time seeks out new images and words to express a few basic emotions. We sense the helplessness of dignity when faced by innumerable spheres, nooks and crannies of existence, and the powerlessness of power dependent on every change of tone, however slight. We wonder how it all fits us, how it fits the dimensions of existence; and we see it does not fit at all. And dazzled but unconvinced – as if only brushed by the wing of some enormous bird (please excuse an unavoidable metaphor) we close the book in admiration. The King – the Spirit![1] Another one! Next to all our King–Spirits, Montaigne, Rabelais or Pascal seem insignificant manikins, run-of-the-mill Hamlets next to a lion. We Poles cannot do without a lion's skin; our own does not suffice.

If somebody therefore wishes to know the reasons why Conrad fails to move him, he will find them all set out here in a perfunctory manner and with a hasty pen. If he is moved by Conrad, then obviously the reasons will be of no use to him. I presume that the shade of the great master will not be angry with me for these few trivial but frank words. And frankness, verily, is the first duty of smallness towards greatness; and the word 'verily' in this sentence testifies that I am not corrupt to the core and that within my modest means I, too, pay tribute to style.

---

[1] Allusion to *Król Duch* (1847), J. Słowacki's long mystical poem.

'The Conrad of my Generation', by Jan Józef Szczepański[1]

'Conrad mojego pokolenia', Życie Literackie (Cracow), 1957, no. 49

I belong to a generation whose contact with Conrad was particularly intimate. I say 'was', for the intensity of this relationship arose from the specific times and conditions of our existence – which, let us hope, will not recur. I mean, of course, the years of occupation.

No doubt the author of *Lord Jim* would have been surprised to learn what precisely turned him into the standard-bearer of his young compatriots. For if he ever expressed patriotic sentiments in his books, it was an English patriotism – a patriotism of affluence and domination rather than of oppression and revolt.

Graham Greene, when talking two years ago with Cracow writers, said that Conrad's popularity in England clearly dropped during the war and that its revival began only after the guns had fallen silent. These contrasting reactions in Conrad's two homelands seem significant to me and I would like here to ponder the matter, not from a literary point of view but from the perspective of the practical consequences of Conrad's writings.

I have become familiar with these practical consequences over a number of years, and I believe it would not be easy to find an analogy in the history of literature. For many members of my generation Conrad's books have indeed been something more than just literature. They provided a code of behaviour. Analysing today the causes of this state of affairs, I see them primarily in the context of the moral situation that the occupation presented to those engaged in active resistance.

Conrad's heroes – captains of small sailing ships, or white colonizers lost in exotic surroundings – are lonely men. True, there was a great power and a great tradition behind them, but in solving their immediate conflicts they could only rely on themselves. This fact gave rise to the entire system of Conradian morality. A morality that functions like the air bubble in the glass tube of a spirit level. Cut off from the world and public opinion, every man is his own judge. And not only a judge. A Conradian man represents a closed, autonomous moral system. This system is a true copy of those ethics that bind merchants or sailors: honesty, fidelity to the given word, self-respect and professional honour, with a touch of a certain romantic exaltation that bestows upon such virtues a hallmark of chivalric austerity. But, as I have said,

[1] Born 1919; a leading Polish contemporary writer, known for his concern with moral and philosophical problems.

Conrad's man is utterly alone with that ethical equipment. He does not believe in supernatural sanctions and his stage is usually restricted to the open sea or some distant part of the globe rarely visited by white men. Under such conditions the hope of impunity represents a constant challenge. The inner drama of Conradian men consists in their effort to balance the air bubble in the right place on the level, and for no other reason than their almost instinctive conviction that this very balance is man's supreme good. To put it less metaphorically, self-respect is the chief criterion for Conrad's characters.

It is well known that of all the countries in the world public opinion has acquired its greatest importance in England. This fact has added a certain exotic charm to Conrad's psychological constructions. A quiet, well-disciplined citizen could find in the situations described in Conrad's works not only a thrill of excitement at the sinister strangeness, but also comfort that the virtues he had implicitly trusted do not abandon the daredevils venturing into regions outside the traditional control of social institutions; that the national spirit thus accompanied the lonely skirmishers who strove over the centuries for the expansion of the empire. To a certain extent this is, of course, a simplification and, above all, a narrowing of the perspective of Conradian humanism. I think, however, that facts like those played a considerable part in the rise in popularity of Conrad's prose as well as in its decline during the war, as mentioned by Greene. The last war reduced the importance of lone skirmishers to the minimum. A mass war, conducted openly, with a gigantic machinery of information, increased the importance of discipline and public opinion. Conradian situations became too risky to be glorified. Precision in team-work and *esprit de corps* rather than a lonely struggle with oneself came to absorb all attention. I suppose that for the British at war, Conradian morality simply became an unpracticable anachronism.

In our country the situation evolved in the opposite direction. Underground work increased our sense of loneliness and isolation, creating a need for restriction that Conrad could not have imagined. Individual acts by members of the resistance had a lesser impact than the exploits of Conradian captains, which echoed in various ports and counting-houses hidden in the jungle. During the occupation public opinion existed only in a residual form and the possibility of immediate reward was never taken into account. We were all sceptical because too many values crumbled before our very eyes. We mistrusted big words and referred to patriotism but unwillingly. At the same time, however, we fanatically believed that our struggle was both right and necessary. For us fighting was a question of personal dignity and self-respect. Was there anything we could count on? Nothing but ourselves, and our will to resist. The situation created the moral climate of a Conrad novel. For us Conrad was more topical than ever before. His books became a collection of practical recipes for men fighting lonely battles in the dark that was dense enough to hide personal defeats and therefore represented an additional challenge.

I used to know a boy whose death was the direct result of his reading of *Lord Jim* (of the first part, I should add). The motif of the bulkhead that was supposed to break away at any moment and yet proved more durable than the nerves and courage of the unfortunate mate in the *Patna* became the boy's obsession. He was an uncommonly sensitive and highly strung person, lacking self-confidence and permanently filled with apprehension that, like Jim, he might fail at the decisive moment, break down and 'jump' prematurely. He kept repeating Jim's famous sentence: 'It is all in being ready', like an incantation, like a lesson that has to be learned by heart. It was precisely that fear of his own weakness that drove my friend to commit an act of unnecessary bravado which he paid for with his life. I once wrote a story (rather a weak one, in fact) about it, for the *Tygodnik Powszechny*.[1] But it was entirely based on truth and I mention it because similar examples of Conrad's influence upon my contemporaries were not unusual in those days. Of course I do not wish to make Conrad responsible for the tragic consequences of that particular case; all I want is to point out the seriousness of our approach to his works – especially to *Lord Jim*, and particularly to the first part.

It seems essential to me to make the above distinction. A moral conflict is usually presented by Conrad in two characteristic forms: one of them is a *test* – the opportunity to put into motion all levers of the autonomous system of ethics in which man is his own yardstick and arbiter. The second form of conflict deals with the consequences of defeat. In the gallery of Conradian characters we encounter time and again castaways or delinquents weighed down throughout their lives with the burden of defeat or disgrace. We get to know Jim in both these stages. And although the drama begins with his defeat, it is only in the second part of the book that we encounter the motif of disgrace, which is so firmly established, as it were, that it stigmatizes his entire life. In the first part Jim becomes aware of the circumstances of his test, analyses them, and makes various discoveries of great practical value for people who may find themselves in a similar situation. But during a battle men do not think about expiation for mistakes committed in the frenzy of events. Hence the second part of *Lord Jim* was much less interesting to us than the first.

[1] 'Przypadek' ('Accident'), *Tygodnik Powszechny*, 1948, no. 4.

Finally the struggle came to an end. People all over the world began to revert to the habit of inconsequential reading. Conrad's books regained their literary status – both for those who for a time did not find them of any practical use, and for others for whom those books were so highly topical as to be decisive in matters of life and death.

We in Poland are not familiar with the nature of the revival of Conrad's popularity in England, but we cannot detect any visible signs of his influence on post-war English literature. In those countries, however, which had to go through a period of occupation, Conradian echoes may be heard now and again. Perhaps Vercors's[1] writings are the most telling example. The roots of his work are to be sought in the resistance movement during the last war and it has the familiar ring of responsibility towards oneself – the climate of autonomous ethics. But the Conradian background in Vercors's prose is not limited to the moral atmosphere created by the pressure of circumstances. Vercors is clearly under the influence of Conradian poetics – the style of some of his stories almost seems an imitation. It is interesting, however, that Conrad, who, unintentionally and merely on the basis of a general knowledge of human nature, touched the core of life under the occupation, shows a far keener perspicacity than Vercors, for whom the occupation represents a concrete literary subject. It is my personal impression that none of the works of the glorifier of the French Resistance comes as close to the reality of those days (with respect to a moral diagnosis, of course) as Joseph Conrad's books do, for all their seeming distance in time and place. There is another element that deserves to be noted. Vercors shows a particular propensity for developing the aspects of Conrad's second type of conflict – the conflict caused by personal defeat, by a life burdened by irreversible facts. This set of problems belongs to the second part of *Lord Jim*, which in the turmoil of battle we tended to shove aside. If Vercors was indeed so much under Conrad's influence that he regarded his sensibilities and language as best suited to depict the situations at hand, we may assume that when he looked at those situations in retrospect, he blindly followed the recipes pertaining not only to the 'test' itself, but also to its consequences. Why then, does the final effect seem so unconvincing? Why do Vercors's reflections contain so much artificial rhetoric, however noble? Is this just a matter of derivation?

The story 'Les Armes de la nuit'[2] comes to mind as an example. The protagonist, while in a concentration camp, has committed an act that under normal conditions would be regarded as a crime, although there,

[1] Pen-name of Jean Bruller (b. 1902), a French writer known for his stories about the Resistance.
[2] Published in 1946.

behind barbed wire, it was only the outcome of an inhuman situation. Vercors shows this man after the liberation, burdened with the painful awareness of his 'loss of humanity', plunged in a kind of desperate asceticism, unfit for normal life because he feels unworthy of it. All that takes place in the stratosphere of the most noble principles, surrounded by an aura of uncompromising Conradian rigidity. And yet one cannot help feeling a false note in it all; the essential problem, the contemporary problem, is quite different. Conrad's type of tragedy, with which Vercors impregnated his subject, gives the impression of a literary mannerism, an anachronistic mannerism to boot.

I believe that our contemporary tragedy, evidenced by the experiences of my generation, consists in our inability to feel our 'loss of humanity' with the same acute horror; that we have found out that we are able to bear its loss with comparative ease of mind; in short that our humanity is less imposing and heroic than we were inclined to assume at the time of the test. Here lies the real problem for present-day literature, if it pretends to moralize effectively and in accordance with reality.

Vercors trusted Conrad too much, and this may have affected his clear-sightedness. We cannot expect even a master of the calibre of *Lord Jim*'s author to encompass with his intuition all possible forms of man's fate. Conrad did not experience winds which were not tempered to the shorn lamb. Having created the ideal of fidelity to oneself, extremely useful under certain conditions, Conrad worked out a theory of moral decline based on a hypothetical premise. A reality he could not possibly have foreseen exposed in our nature qualities which do not conform to the static standards of Conradian ethics. This working hypothesis proved too theoretical and today its literary interpretation often rings with beautiful but empty rhetoric.

Experience has revealed this duality in Conrad to us, but for the generations that will regard his works as literature pure and simple, Conrad will perhaps forever remain a monolith.

INDEX